History of Letter Post Communication Between the United States and Europe 1845–1875

Second Edition

George E. Hargest

History of Letter Post Communication Between the United States and Europe 1845–1875

Second Edition

George E. Hargest

Quarterman Publications, Inc.
Lawrence, Massachusetts

Copyright © 1971 by George E. Hargest

First Edition published in 1971 by Smithsonian Institution
Press, Washington, D.C.

Copyright © 1975 by George E. Hargest

All rights reserved. This impression may not be reproduced
in any form without written permission.

This Second Edition contains all the material contained in the first edition. New material has been added and corrections made (both textual and photographic) to the original for this Quarterman edition. The added section on pages 84–84b was originally published in *The Chronicle* of the U.S. Philatelic Classics Society, Inc. and is included with their permission.

International Standard Book Number: 0-88000-062-7
Library of Congress Catalog Card Number: 75-1787

Printed in the United States of America

Quarterman Publications, Inc.
5 South Union Street
Lawrence, Massachusetts 01843

Dedicated to
My wife, Lois

Preface to Second Edition

Four years have now elapsed since the initial appearance of *The History of Letter Post Communication Between the United States and Europe, 1845–1875* as Smithsonian Studies in History and Technology, No. 6. As the original edition, produced by the Government Printing Office, was limited in number, many postal historians who wanted it were unable to procure it when ordered. As a result it now sells at a large premium in the auction and dealers' markets. It is hoped that this edition will make the book available to many who still want it, especially those in Europe where the original distribution was small.

When I first started to write the book, I decided that it would be objective, that preconceived notions held by others would be avoided, and that there would be a reliance upon original sources as they could be found. The history of the steamship lines would be drawn for the most part from secondary works, since these had been well researched by other students. I was in a unique position to do this, as I had available to me the vast resources of the Clark University Library, where I served for 29 years as Assistant and Associate Professor of Economics and Business Administration, the Library of the American Antiquarian Society, and the Worcester County Law Library. I shall not, however, forget the first day I tried to look up a treaty in the British and Foreign State Papers. I found their location, and was confronted with a mass of books that ran from floor to ceiling, row after row. I finally found the index volumes and in that way was able to find what I wanted. The Senate and House executive documents were serialized at the American Antiquarian Society and this proved a great help in locating the needed documents. But research in any field requires a great deal of reading, out of which is culled the portions to which reference is made. Much of this reading, although not used in references, is very important, because one develops from it a point of view, or thesis, that leads to the telling of the story in such a way that it is reflected in the finished work.

No one could write a book as detailed as this one without making some errors. Those that have been discovered have been corrected in this edition. In regard to covers illustrated, the chief objective was to use those which clearly reflected the usual markings for route, service and rate. Although a number of beautiful covers were borrowed and appear as illustrations, the emphasis was not on their beauty, but rather to present covers in the condition in which they would be found by the average collector. All of the covers presented, regardless of their condition, have markings that are thoroughly explained and are usually typical of the route, service and rate.

The original book has won many awards: The Carroll Chase Cup, awarded by the U.S. Philatelic Classics Society in 1970; the Sylvester Colby Trophy, awarded by the American Philatelic Society as the Grand Award for Handbooks in 1971; The Eugene Klein Award, presented by the American Philatelic Congress in 1972; the Gerard Gilbert Award, presented by the France and

Colonies Group in 1971; the Crawford Medal, despite the poor distribution of the book abroad, awarded by the Royal Philatelic Society, London, in 1972; and the Nugent Clougher Award for 1973, presented by the Postal History Society of Great Britain.

I wish to acknowledge with great appeciation the kind assistance of Mrs. Susan M. McDonald, editor of the *Chronicle of the U.S. Classics Issues,* and of Mr. Walter Hubbard of London, for calling to my attention certain errors appearing in the book.

George E. Hargest

Vero Beach, Florida
January 1975

Preface

It is the purpose of this book not only to describe the postal services between the United States and Europe, but also to explain their development. The period considered begins with the subsidization of United States steam mail-packets in 1845, and ends on 1 January 1876, when France, the last of nineteen European countries to do so, placed in force the provisions of the treaty of Berne and became an active member of the General Postal Union. In order to keep the size of this work within reasonable bounds, it was necessary that its scope be in some way limited. Rather than narrow the limits of the period covered, it was decided to consider only letter post communication. Interesting as are the arrangements for the exchange of newspapers, printed circulars, and registered mail, they are not included in this work.

A table of United States postal rates to foreign countries is presented in the appendix. While this book confines itself to letter post communication between the United States and Europe, the scope of the appendix is broadened to include rates to all parts of the world. Since information regarding the broadened scope was available, it was felt that it would be of value to collectors to include it.

An attempt has been made in the book to retain the language of the sources from which information has been drawn. This is particularly true in regard to the names of countries and places of which mention is made. Many of the names are subject to a variety of spellings, especially those of the Turkish towns. Places in the appendix follow the spellings given in the tables of postages to foreign countries presented in the *U.S. Mail and Post Office Assistant,* and the names are sometimes misspelled in that source. The difficulties the Americans had when dealing with foreign languages are occasionally brought to the fore. For example, the port of Rivière-du-Loup on the St. Lawrence River is spelled, in the English version of the United States-French postal convention of 1861, as the Americans pronounced it, "River du Loup."

While I have largely drawn from primary sources for information relating to mail arrangements, the history of the steam-packet lines has been authoritatively presented in seveal works, and I have, therefore, relied upon these secondary sources for this information. Individual ship sailing and arrival dates have been taken from original sources.

It must be recognized, however, that much original source material that should be available no longer exists. The letterbooks of the Post Office Department in the National Archives contain copies of outgoing letters only. Nine of these letterbooks were examined in 1963, and not one letter relating to the foreign-mail service was found. Fortunately, many matters were referred by the Post Office Department to the Department of State, and correspondence on these matters exists. Congress occasionally requested that correspondence relating to certain matters be published, and postmasters general sometimes published correspondence to Congress in support of their requests for legislation. These letters are found in the House and Senate *Executive Documents*. While many changes in the original postal conventions were made by signing additional articles, changes were also effected through correspondence between the post offices of the countries concerned. Postmasters general sometimes made reference to these changes in their annual reports, but some that are known to have taken place cannot be supported by documentary evidence. The cover is to the postal historian what the artifact is to the archeologist, and in the absence of other evidence, the cover has been relied upon to supply the missing information.

Postal markings are considered only in relation to the function they performed. No attempt is made to present various types of markings performing the same function. This subject has been definitively covered for Boston in *Boston Postal Markings to 1890,* by Maurice C. Blake and Wilbur W. Davis, and, for the United States in *United States Postal Markings, 1851–1861,* by Tracy W. Simpson. Some postal markings, however, domestic or foreign, that are unique to a particular mail service, are illustrated and described.

Without the assistance, support, and encouragement of others, this book could not have been written. While it would be impossible to mention everyone who has in some way participated in this endeavor, I hope that I will be forgiven for acknowledging my special thanks to a few of them. I am particularly indebted to Dr. Clifford K. Shipton, Director Emeritus, and to Mr. Marcus A. McCorison, Director of the American Antiquarian Society in Worcester, Massachusetts, for granting me privilege of the library stacks, and to Miss Mary E. Brown, staff librarian, for her invaluable assistance. I wish to express my gratitude to Mr. Tilton M. Barron, librarian of Clark University, not only for his ready assistance, but also for his willingness to secure certain works on library loan. I also wish to acknowledge the assistance of Miss Geneva Chancey, librarian of the Post Office Department library in Washington, D.C., and of Dr. Arthur Hecht of the National Archives.

I am deeply indebted to Mr. Carl H. Scheele, Associate Curator in Charge, Division of Postal History, and Chairman, Department of Applied Arts, at the Smithsonian Institution, for the privilege he granted me of examining the foreign-mail covers in the Smithsonian collection, and for the use of the Smithsonian's extensive philatelic library.

My sincere thanks are extended to Mr. Melvin W. Schuh of Worcester, Massachusetts, not only for his extensive loan of covers for illustration, but also for his kind and patient counsel. I also wish to express my gratitude to Mr. Lester L. Downing of Concord, Massachusetts, for his many generosities in loaning works from his private library and covers for illustration, and for his information in regard to the sailings of the Cunard line.

I am particularly indebted to Mr. C. J. Starnes of Midland, Michigan, for his translation of Piefke's *Geschichte der bremischen Landespost,* and for sharing with me information on postal rates.

I wish to extend my sincere thanks to Dr. Robert de Wasserman of Brussels, Belgium, for his loan of photographs for illustration and his exchange of information on Belgian mails. I wish, too, to thank Dr. Jacques Stibbe of Brussels, for his kind and informative letters about Belgian mails. My gratitude is also extended to M. Raymond Salles of Paris for information about French mails, and to Mr. Walter Hubbard of London for photographs of covers for illustration and for his kind counsel.

For the loan of photographs for illustration as well as for items from their private libraries, my sincere gratitude is extended to the late Hugh J. Baker, Jr., Mr. J. David Baker, Mr. Arthur E. Beane, Jr., Mr. William C. Coles, Jr., Mr. John A. Fox, Mr. Creighton C. Hart, Mr. Karl Jaeger, Mr. Millard H. Mack, Mr. Mortimer L. Neinken, Mr. James E. Schofield, Mr. Tracy W. Simpson, and Mr. George T. Turner.

For their advice and encouragement, as well as for their many kindnesses over the years, my thanks are extended to Mr. Richard B. Graham, Mr. Robson Lowe, Mr. Elliott Perry, Mr. Marcus W. White, and the late Maurice C. Blake.

I also wish to acknowledge with thanks the kindness of Dr. Robert L. D. Davidson, editor of the *Chronicle of the U.S. Classic Issues,* in granting me permission to use portions of my articles which appeared in that journal.

Contents

	Page
INTRODUCTION	1
1 Negotiation of the United States-Bremen Postal Arrangement of 1847	3
2 Negotiation of the United States-British Postal Treaty of 15 December 1848	23
3 Postal Relations with France	40
4 The United States-French Postal Convention of 2 March 1857	70
5 The Prussian Closed-Mail Convention	85
6 Postal Relations with Belgium, 1844–1868	99
7 Amendments, New Conventions, and the Operations of the Steamship Lines	109
8 Postal Conventions Effective After 1 January 1868	147
9 Postal Relations with France, 1870–1876	164
10 Depreciated Currency Covers	184
Bibliography	194
Appendix: Postal Rates to Foreign Countries, 1848–1875	196
Index	227

Introduction

In the winter of 1844 the citizens of Boston voluntarily cut a path through the ice of East Boston harbor to free the Cunard line's *Britannia* and allow her to sail to sea. While the people of Boston were so extravagantly demonstrating their high regard for the British steamship line, Congressmen in Washington were contemplating it with a growing concern. It was not that Cunard's performance had been unsatisfactory. It had, in fact, exceeded all expectations. Since 1840 its passage time between Liverpool and Boston, via Halifax, had averaged only fourteen days, and sailings were being maintained with great regularity. It was, rather, the success of the Cunard line that was forcing Congress to take a critical view of the whole situation involving postal communication with Europe.

The advent of the steam packet had blunted American prestige. For many years American sailing packets had dominated the "Atlantic shuttle." Although the sailing packets were still carrying the bulk of European emigrants and freight—including coal to America for use by the steam packets—most of the mail, cabin passengers, and *fine* freight were now carried by the British steamships. Their progress appeared inevitable, and the American flag would soon take second place on the "Atlantic ferry." American pride, inflated by a surge of new nationalism, was piqued. But Congress was concerned with far more than piqued pride. The United States was becoming increasingly dependent upon the British for its postal communication with Europe. Additionally, the Cunard line was under contract to the British Admiralty, subsidized at £81,000 sterling annually, to carry the mails, and each of its ships carried on board an off-duty officer of the British navy as an agent of the Admiralty. The close tie between the British Admiralty and the contract mail packets was noted by Congress.

During the 1840s there was a great expansion of American foreign trade. Total foreign trade averaged $197 million annually during the first five years of the decade and $259 million for the last five years.[1] The second half of the decade was characterized by a general tendency toward freer trade. In 1846 Great Britain repealed its Corn Laws, and in the same year the United States reduced its tariff. Increased industrialization in Great Britain, coupled with high prices for foodstuffs caused by crop failures, particularly in Ireland, were also important causes of the increased American foreign trade.

The representatives of American commercial interests, now prosperous, began to flex their political sinews. Interested as they were in the rapid transmission of business information, particularly in regard to prices, the cost of disseminating such information was also a matter of their continuing concern. The postal reform achieved in Great Britain stimulated them to press for lower and more uniform rates of postage in the United States. As early as 10 June 1840, Daniel Webster introduced a resolution in the Senate calling for lower rates of postage and the use of postage stamps.[2] A British General Post Office order of June 1840 announced the inauguration of the Cunard packet service, with "the Postage remaining as at present, viz. an Uniform Charge of 1s. the Single Letter. . . ."[3] A later General Post Office order of February 1841 applied the one-shilling-packet rate to a letter whose weight did not exceed half an ounce, instead of a single letter consisting of one sheet of paper.[4] Although this British packet rate represented a considerable reduc-

---

George E. Hargest is an associate professor emeritus in Economics and Business Administration, Clark University, Worcester, Massachusetts.

---

[1] George R. Taylor, *The Transportation Revolution*, p. 445. Semi-averages were constructed, from annual data presented. See bibliography (pp. 194–195) for complete citations.

[2] Van Dyk MacBride, "Barnabus Bates—The Rowland Hill of America," *The American Philatelist* 60, no. 8 (May 1947): 635.

[3] Frank Staff, *The Transatlantic Mail*, facsimile of original order reproduced, p. 144.

[4] Ibid., p. 173.

tion in postage in comparison with the rates of 1837, American postal rates remained high, and agitation for postal reform in the United States was beginning to attract the attention of the public.

Important as this reduction in postal rates was to American business, the Cunarders themselves were making additional savings possible. Their relatively rapid crossings, together with the regularity and certainty of their sailings, were obviating the necessity for sending many duplicate copies of the same letter by different ships in order to be certain that a copy would arrive as early as possible, or would arrive at all. This had resulted in a considerable saving in clerical cost as well as in postage.

There were, however, other aspects of the foreign-mail service that inconvenienced and annoyed merchants. Since the Cunarders ran to Liverpool, letters addressed to other parts of Europe were forwarded from England, often with great difficulty. American businesses usually employed a British banking, merchandising, or brokerage firm to act as their agent for forwarding mail. Agents on the continent were also employed. The agents paid the necessary postage and attended to the expeditious routing of letters. The act of 3 March 1845 authorized the postmaster general or the secretary of state to empower United States consuls to pay foreign postage and forward letters.[5] Certain consuls were so empowered, but the consular service in general was not used for this purpose. The cost and cumbersomeness of forwarding mail through agents was an annoyance to American merchants who exerted political pressure upon Congress to eliminate the necessity for the procedure.

Another source of annoyance was the impossibility of fully prepaying the postage to a European destination on letters sent from the United States. Nor could the full postage be collected from an American addressee on letters received from Europe. Some of the postage always had to be paid or collected in the United States and some in Europe. As it was a common practice of business to refuse to pay postage on and receive letters from persons unknown to them, American merchants were forced to rely upon agents, if new contacts were to be made. Most of these difficulties arose because the United States had no postal convention or treaty with any European country. When postal conventions existed, accounting between the post offices of the contracting countries was established, which made it possible to pay the whole postage on letters sent or received.

Great as was the stake of American commercial interests in postal reform, it was not they who carried the fight to the public, but rather, a small group of "reformers" who spearheaded a campaign for lower and more uniform postal rates for both domestic and foreign mail. Spawned in the seething cauldron of social change that was America in the 1840s, zealots such as Barnabus Bates, Joshua Leavitt, and Elihu Burritt,[6] among others, waged a propaganda campaign on the public platform and in the press, for cheap postage. In this struggle, their chief antagonist was the United States Post Office Department with its army of 14,000 postmasters, clerks, and other employees who feared that cheaper rates would lessen their emoluments.[7]

But neither the Post Office Department nor Congress could long resist the rising tide of public opinion and the political pressure being exerted by American commercial interests. Congress, caught up as it was in a surge of nationalistic feeling, also lent a sympathetic ear to those who demanded that the American flag be kept upon the high seas. In 1844, Congress, by a joint resolution, paved the way for the establishment of a United States postal service to Europe, and in 1845 passed an act providing for the subsidization of United States mail packets, as well as the reduction and simplification of postal rates. These acts of Congress initiated the development of the United States postal service to European countries, and it is to this development that the following chapters are directed.

---

[5] Act of 3 March 1845, sec. 6–5, U.S., *Statutes at Large* 748–750.

[6] Frank Staff, "Campaign for Cheap Postage Was Rife With Propaganda," *Postal History Journal* II, no. 1 (Jan. 1967): 15.

[7] MacBride, "Barnabus Bates", p. 636.

Chapter 1

Negotiation of the United States-Bremen Postal Arrangement of 1847

Organization of the Ocean Steam Navigation Company

The groundwork for the foreign mail provisions of the act of 3 March 1845 was laid by a joint resolution of Congress voted on 15 June 1844. While the act of 3 March 1825 [1] had given the postmaster general permission to make arrangements for the exchange of mail with foreign countries, it had not been incumbent on him to do so, and by 1844 no such arrangements had been made with any European country. The joint resolution authorized the postmaster general to make such arrangements with the proper authorities of France and Germany. He was also authorized to make arrangements with "the owners or agents of vessels plying regularly between those countries and the United States, whereby a safe and, as near as possible, a regular direct mail communication . . . shall be secured—so that the entire inland and foreign postage on letters and other mail matter . . . may be paid at the place where they are respectively mailed or received." [2] The joint resolution was specific on two points. Prepayment or collection of the entire postage required that international accounting be established by postal convention. Any such convention must include provision for optional prepayment if the entire postage was to be "paid at the place where they [letters] are respectively mailed or received."

Since larger measures were being debated, Postmaster General Wickliffe did not immediately act upon the authorization granted by the joint resolution. At the time it was voted, there was a Whig Senate, a Democratic House, and President John Tyler, who was neither Whig nor Democrat. Despite this unpropitious political situation, Congress passed the postal act, which President Tyler signed in the waning hours of his administration. On the following day, James K. Polk became president, and shortly thereafter Cave Johnson became postmaster general.

Although the act of 3 March 1845 was a product of the Tyler administration, it clearly reflects the nationalistic feeling that swept Polk into the White House. It authorized the postmaster general to make contracts for the transportation of the United States mail between any United States ports and those of any foreign power, such contracts to be made for a period of not less than four or more than ten years. All contracts were to be made with citizens of the United States, and the mail was to be transported in American vessels by American citizens. Preference was to be given to such bidder as proposed to carry the mail in steamships, and who stipulated that any of those steamships would be delivered to the United States Government, on demand, for the purpose of being converted into a vessel of war. Just compensation was to be paid the owner of any vessel so delivered.[3] The

---

[1] U.S., 4 *Statutes at Large* 102–114. See bibliography (pp. 194–195) for complete citations.

[2] U.S. 5 *Statutes at Large* 718–719.

[3] *Ibid.*, 748–750.

act also provided for the subsidization of a line of American mail packets to ply between New York and such port or ports of foreign countries as the postmaster general deemed appropriate. In addition, new and lowered rates of domestic postage as well as a packet rate to be used by the American packets when they came into operation were provided. These rates are outlined in Table 1.

In October 1845 Postmaster General Cave Johnson invited tenders for mail services from New York to Liverpool, Bristol, Southampton, Antwerp, Bremen, Hamburg, Havre, Brest, or Lisbon.[4] Immediately there was considerable lobbying, not only by shipping people, but also by foreign commercial interests who sought to have a particular foreign port selected as a European terminus of the American steamship line.[5]

The Belgian resident minister argued that Antwerp was the port of entry between Belgium and the countries of the Tariff Union, comprising twenty seven states and thirty million customers. Belgium offered remission of tonnage and ship duties and the sea postage charge. When bargaining got tight, Belgium offered to bear some of the expense of establishing the steamship line.

The movement for the selection of Bremen was spurred by Senator Arnold Duckwitz, postmaster of the Free Hanseatic City of Bremen. Through the American consul, Colonel A. Dudley Mann, Duckwitz let it be known that Bremen offered a free port, tax-free loading of coal at Bremerhaven, and liberal trade laws. From Bremen there would be 21,000 square miles of German trade territory, and beyond Bremen would be Austria, Italy, Switzerland, Denmark, Norway, Sweden, and Russia. A railroad, in its last stages of completion, would unite Hanover with all parts of Germany and Austria; railroads, already in the process of construction, would soon connect Bremen with most of the countries beyond.

Colonel Mann, ardent and articulate in his support of the selection of Bremen, was recalled to Washington. The Bremen senate, realizing the opportunity this fortuitous circumstance presented, sent with him C. Th. Gevekoht, a merchant who had spent a long time in Baltimore. Together they waged a campaign in behalf of Bremen. In this they were supported by the Prussian resident minister, Freiherr von Gerolt, and the efforts of the three were finally successful.[6]

Lobbying for the steamship contract had begun long before the passage of the act of 3 March 1845. As early as 1841, E. K. Collins, who ran the Dramatic line of Liverpool packets, headed a lobby that "argued for government aid to build mail steamers as potential cruisers."[7] After passage of the act the lobbies swung into high gear. Of the tenders received, that of Edward Mills was the most favorable. He asked for $300,000 a year for a steam service to Havre. As it was finally negotiated, Mills was awarded a five-year contract valued at $400,000 a year for a fortnightly service to Bremen with permission for alternate sailings to terminate at Havre.[8] Such a service would have required four steamships, and as it was finally arranged, $100,000 annually was allocated to each ship. Since Mills was a promoter with little experience in the shipping business, the award of the contract to him aroused a good deal of criticism. Mills organized the Ocean Steam Navigation Company in May 1846 and immediately set out to secure subscriptions to its $1 million of authorized stock.

While a good head of nationalistic steam had been generated for the subsidy of a steam packet line, Mills had trouble in raising capital. This may have been a vote of no-confidence in Mills. Albion states that "the *Herald* expressed the fear that the new company would become a Wall Street plaything like the Harlem and Erie railroads."[9] Some American merchants preferred the Cunard line and looked upon the line to Bremen as unwanted competition.[10] It is certain that American shipping interests did not share the public's enthusiasm for the Ocean line. With great difficulty Mills raised $200,000. Then the Germans chipped in. Bremen signed for $100,000; Prussia, $100,000; Hanover, $25,000; Saxony, $20,000; and lesser amounts from Oldenburg, Hesse-Nassau, Hesse-Darmstadt, Frankfort on the Main, and certain Thuringian states. The German states raised, in total, $289,000, which affected American investment so that $600,000 was finally subscribed. Mills, however, was able to build only two steamships and was forced to assign part of his contract to Messrs. Fox and Livingston who organized the New York and Havre Steam Navigation Company.

---

[4] N. R. P. Bonsor, *North Atlantic Seaway*, p. 50.

[5] Christian Piefke, *Geschichte der bremischen Landespost*, Chapter 22.

[6] Ibid.

[7] R. G. Albion, *The Rise of New York Port*, p. 323.

[8] Bonsor, *North Atlantic Seaway*, p. 51.

[9] Albion, *New York Port*, p. 323.

[10] Piefke, *Bremischen Landespost*, Chap. 22.

The Ocean Steam Navigation Company (Ocean line) placed orders for two steamships of about 1,700 tons each with Westervelt and McKay. The engines and boilers were produced by the Novelty Works. While this yard had built many sailing ships, they lacked experience in building steamships—a fact that later became evident. The first of these ships, the *Washington,* was launched in January 1847, and the *Hermann,* ten months later.

Mail Between Great Britain and the United States Under the 1845 Rates

Because much of the mail between the United States and Germany passed in transit through England, it is necessary to discuss the method by which mail was exchanged between the United States and Great Britain. The act of 3 March 1845 established new rates for domestic postage as well as a packet rate for mail to be conveyed by the proposed line of American steamers, whose subsidization was provided for by the act. In 1845 the steamers of the British-owned Great Western Steam Ship Company were still plying between New York and Liverpool, but the competition offered the Cunard line by the steamships *Great Western* and *Great Britain* of that company was on the wane, and in 1846 they left the Atlantic ferry. The 770-ton auxiliary-screw United States-owned steamship *Massachusetts* made two voyages between New York and Liverpool during 1845 [11] while the 1,400-ton auxiliary-screw British steamer *Sarah Sands* made nine round voyages on the same run during 1847.[12] As auxiliary steamers, they were primarily sailing ships that used steam when the wind failed, or to increase speed in a light breeze. They did not offer the Cunard line serious competition. After the *Great Western* and *Great Britain* left the scene, and before the Ocean line began to run in 1847 the Cunard line was operating the only full-fledged steamships plying the North Atlantic. They were also, during this period, the only steamers conveying mail at a *packet* rate.

It is, therefore, desirable at this point to understand the method of handling mail between the United States and Great Britain under the provisions of the act of 1845, as well as under the then existing British rates. As there was no accounting between the post offices of the two countries, each had to charge and retain its own postage. The British, for example, always had to collect their packet postage on letters received in Great Britain, as well as on letters posted there. Similarly, the Americans always had to prepay the domestic postage to the port (Boston) on letters posted in the United States, and to collect the domestic (inland) postage from Boston to destination. On these incoming letters a ship fee of 2¢ per letter was also charged and collected. The rates are best understood when presented in outline form, while the method of marking letters is best described by illustration. The rates are presented in Table 1.

Covers

Figure 1 illustrates a letter which was posted in Edinburgh, addressed to New York. The 1s. packet postage was prepaid by a strip of six 2d. stamps issued in 1841. The letter left Liverpool on board the R.M.S. (Royal Mail Steamer) *Acadia* of the Cunard line on 4 December and arrived in Boston on 19 December 1845,[13] whence it was forwarded to New York, a distance of less than 300 miles. It was, therefore, rated for a collection of 7¢, indicated by a manuscript 7. This represents 5¢ inland plus 2¢ ship postage.

Figure 2 presents a letter posted in Wilmington, Delaware, on 13 August 1847, addressed to Liverpool. It is prepaid 10¢ for a distance of more than 300 miles between Wilmington and Boston by a 10¢ stamp of the 1847 issue. Both the town mark and the grid canceling the stamp are in dark olive-green.[14] On the reverse is an AMERICA/LIVERPOOL marking bearing the date of 28 August 1847, and on that date the R.M.S. *Hibernia* of the Cunard line, which had sailed from Boston on 16 August, arrived in Liverpool. The Liverpool office applied in black ink a handstamp that imitates a manuscript marking intended to indicate a postage due of 1s. This peculiarly shaped marking is immediately to the left of the 10¢ stamp. The cover is in the collection of Mr. Creighton C. Hart and is presented here with his kind permission.

---

[11] Bonsor, *North Atlantic Seaway,* p. 49.
[12] Ibid., p. 50.
[13] All sailing data related to the Cunard line have been taken from incomplete records of the Cunard line by Lester L. Downing. These records have been completed by the author from Custom House reports in the *Shipping and Commercial List and New York Prices Current.*
[14] See Creighton C. Hart, "1847 Covers from Delaware," *Chronicle* 46 (Dec. 1963); see also "Early Transatlantic 1847 Covers," *Chronicle* 20, 1, Whole No. 57 (Feb. 1968).

FIGURE 1.—COVER, from Edinburgh to New York, 1845.

In 1847 Great Britain issued a 1s. stamp that was extensively used to prepay the packet rate. The stamp is hexagonal in shape, and most of these stamps have all margins meticulously cut away. Figure 3 presents a letter from a London merchant addressed to "Mess Abraham Bell & Son/New York." The clerk who applied the 1s. stamp to this letter carelessly neglected to cut away the margins. On the reverse of the letter is a double-lined Maltese-cross marking inscribed LS/ 15 JA 15/1848, applied in orange-red ink. This is a marking of the Lombard Street office at London, showing the letter was sent from there on 15 January 1848. The letter was sent to Liverpool, whence it was conveyed to Boston by the R.M.S. *Acadia* of the Cunard line. Arriving in Boston on 1 February 1848, the letter was sent to New York where it was rated for a collection of 5¢ inland plus 2¢ ship postage, a total of 7¢.

Mail Between Bremen and the United States Before the Postal Arrangement of 1847

Prior to 1841, all mail between Bremen and the United States was conveyed by private sailing ships. On 30 August 1841, the General Post Office at London and the Post Office of Bremen signed a postal convention which made service by the Cunard packets available at reduced rates.[15]

Article I set a sea rate of 6d. per half ounce for direct sea conveyance to or from London, via Cuxhaven, via Hamburg, or direct to Bremerhaven. "The British rate of transit postage to be taken on letters posted in or addressed to Bremen . . . passing through the United Kingdom to or from its colonies or foreign countries, shall be that which is now, or shall hereafter be, taken upon letters between the United Kingdom and such colonies or foreign countries."

Article II set a transit rate between Cuxhaven or Bremerhaven and Bremen at 4 grote (2d.). Thus, a total rate of 8d. (16 grote) was established for transit between London and Bremen. Since the British transatlantic packet rate was 1s. (24 grote), letters sent between Bremen and the United States frontier by this route required that 40 grote be prepaid in Bremen on letters sent, and collected there on letters received. The British share of this postage was 1s. 6d. (36 grote). The London office appears to have performed the accounting on all letters sent by this route. Distinctly British *1/6* markings appear on all single-rate letters,

---

[15] *British and Foreign State Papers,* vol. 30, pp. 338–340.

FIGURE 2.—COVER, from Wilmington, Delaware to Liverpool, 1847.
(*Creighton C. Hart collection*)

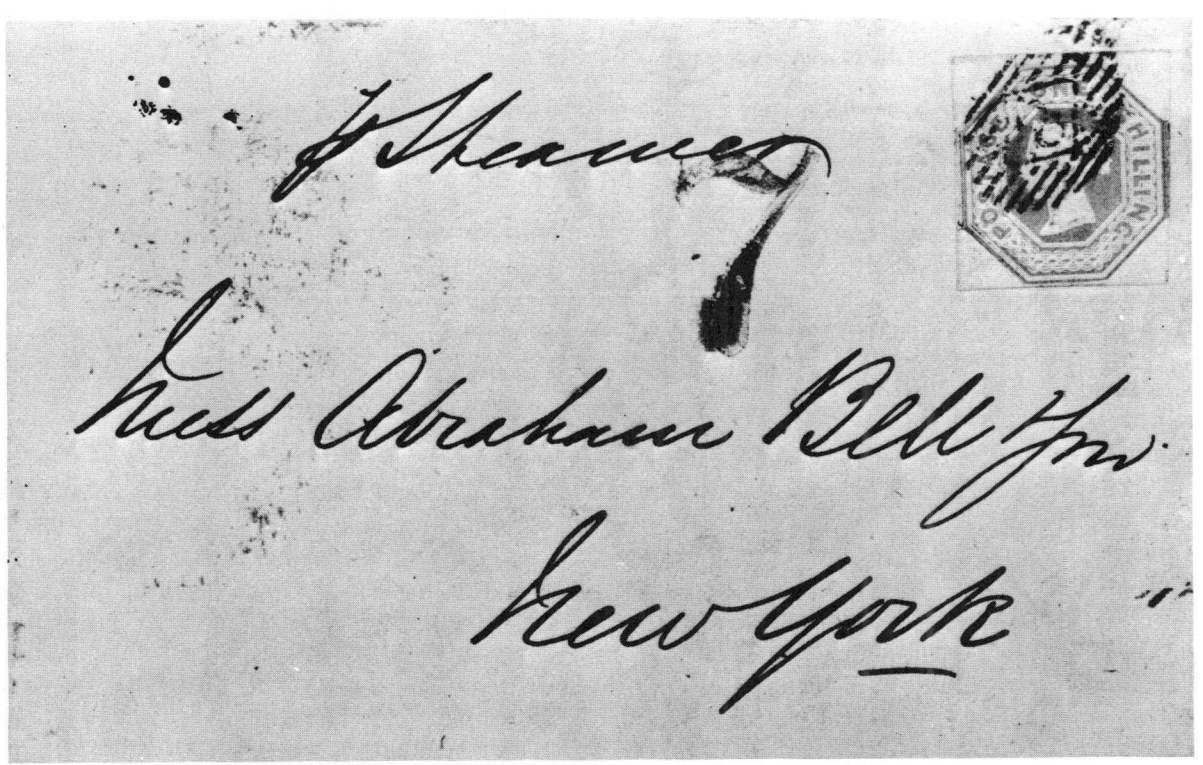

FIGURE 3.—COVER, from London to New York, 1848.

TABLE 1.—*United States and British Postal Rates (in Effect 1 July 1845)*

United States Rates [a]

Inland or domestic postage:	
Single rate for letters not exceeding one-half ounce:	
If conveyed under 300 miles	5¢
If conveyed over 300 miles	10
Rate progression:	
For every additional half ounce or fraction thereof, 1 additional rate	
Packet postage (to or from port of arrival or departure):	
Not exceeding one-half ounce	24
Exceeding one-half but not exceeding one ounce	48
For every additional half ounce or fraction thereof	15
Ship rates (for private ships, not under government contract):	
Addressed to the port of arrival	6
Addressed to a destination beyond port of arrival	
Inland postage from port to destination, plus 2¢ ship postage per letter	

British Rates [b]
(between any point in Great Britain and the U.S. frontier)

Packet postage (by Cunard contract packets):	
Not exceeding one-half ounce	1s. 0d.
Ship rates (for private ships, not under government contract):	
Not exceeding one-half ounce	8d.
Rate progression (applicable to both packet and ship rates)	
Not over one-half ounce	1 rate
Over one-half but not-over one ounce	2 rates
Over one but not over two ounces	4 rates
For every additional ounce or fraction thereof, 2 additional rates	

NOTE: No triple rate or further odd-numbered rates existed.

[a] Rates as stated in act of 3 March 1845; 5 Statutes at large 733, 737. See also *American Almanac*, 1850.

[b] Rates were prepaid in Great Britain on letters sent, and collected in Great Britain on letters received.

in red on those from Bremen and in black on those to Bremen.

It might be well, at this point, to define the basic mail services then in use. "Direct mail," as the name implies, referred to mail conveyed directly from a port of one country to a port of another without passing in transit over the territory of an intermediate country. "Open mail" referred to letters routed by an exchange office to a foreign exchange office with whom it corresponded, which in turn, routed it to another office, and so on, until the letter reached its destination. This necessitated sorting of letters at each office and increased the probability that they would be mis-sent or charged with erroneous postage. It was also expensive and increased the time required in transit. This was in contrast to "closed mail" which was forwarded by an exchange office of origin in closed bags to an exchange office of distribution abroad. Such mail would pass in unbroken state through the territory of one or more foreign countries to a distributing exchange office where it would be opened and sorted for the first time. It was usually provided that closed mail be accompanied by a courier of the dispatching country when passing over foreign territory.

Another avenue of mail between Bremen and the United States was opened by the Anglo-Prussian treaty of 1 October 1846.[16] Under provisions of this conven-

---

[16] Ibid., vol. 34, pp. 34–38.

TABLE 2.—*United States and Prussian Postal Rates* (*Under the 1846 Anglo-Prussian Treaty*)

Postage	Up to ¼ oz.	Up to ½ oz.	Exactly ½ oz.	Up to ¾ oz.	Up to 1 oz.	Up to 1¼ oz
British transit	0s.6d.	0s.6d.	0s.6d.	1s.0d.	1s.0d.	2s.0d.
Transatlantic packet	1 0	1 0	1 0	2 0	2 0	4 0
Direct rate	1 6	1 6	1 6	3 0	3 0	6 0
Belgian transit	0 2	0 4	0 6	0 6	0 8	0 10
Closed-mail rate	1 8	1 10	2 0	3 6	3 8	6 10

tion, direct mail was routed via Hamburg or the Netherlands, closed mail, through Belgium. For direct mail, the Prussian exchange offices were Hamburg and Emmerich, and the British used London, Hull, and Dover. On closed mail, London was the only British office, while Prussia used Aix-la-Chapelle [Aachen] and Cologne. Rates to or from the United States were specifically provided for and are set forth in Table 2.

The rates set forth in Table 2 indicate that the progression used for the British transit and transatlantic packet postages was the same as that then in force in Great Britain. It is included in Table 1 as applying to the British packet and ship rates. For letters exceeding one ounce in weight, this "British" progression prescribed that for each additional ounce or fraction thereof, two additional rates were charged. The Belgian transit postage, however, used a different progression. The lowest rate was for a letter weighing "up to, but not including one-fourth ounce." From this rate the progression increased in quarter-ounce increments, but a rate for a letter that weighed exactly half an ounce was allowed. The treaty provided that 1d. (British) was equal to 10 pfennige (Prussian). It should be noted that there were 12 pfennige to the silbergroschen, which, according to this formula, was worth 2.4¢. Prussia rated letters in multiples of 10 pfennige, that is, virtually in pence. On closed mail, London performed all the accounting necessary for the preparation of the monthly reports, which Prussia, after review, approved or rejected. The London office marked the cover to show the breakdown of the total British debit or credit to Prussia. To this postage was added German transit postage to destination or from point of origin.[17]

After the United States-British treaty became fully effective on 1 July 1849, the 1s. transatlantic packet postage included in Table 2 was reduced to 8d. for a single rate, the progression remaining the same. Eightpence, or its proper multiple, therefore, can be substituted for the one-shilling rate in Table 2 to arrive at the proper rates after 1 July 1849.

Covers

Figure 4 illustrates a letter posted at the Bremen City Post Office on 27 August 1847, addressed to Baltimore. It was forwarded to England under provisions of the Anglo-Bremen convention of 1841 and was accordingly prepaid 40 Bremen grote. The prepayment does not show on the cover, but the Bremen Post Office marked it FRANCO, indicating that the required postage to the United States frontier had been paid. The Bremen double-circle marking, ST. P.A./BREMEN/27/8 abbreviates *Stadt Post Abteilung/Bremen/27/August*, and literally means "State Post Department." The London office applied an orange-red PAID/30AU30/1847 marking and also marked it in red manuscript *1/6* to indicate the British share of the postage, that is, 1s. transatlantic packet and 6d. Bremen–Britain transit postages. The oval L/AU 30/H, applied in black at Liverpool, is a packet mark and shows the date the letter was included in the mail to be conveyed by the next packet sailing, which, in this case, was that of the R.M.S. *Britannia* from Liverpool on 5 September 1847. Arriving in Boston on 19 September (not shown), it was forwarded to Baltimore, a distance of over 300 miles. The blue handstamp *12* shows it was rated for a collection of 12¢, that is, 10¢ inland postage plus 2¢ ship fee.

Figure 5 presents a cover mailed at Düsseldorf, Prussia, on 14 June 1847, addressed to "Mr. Thomas Lamb/Boston" through his Philadelphia agents. This letter was forwarded to either the Aachen or the Cologne office, whence it was sent through Belgium to London in closed mail under provisions of the Anglo-Prussian convention of 1 October 1846. The Düssel-

---

[17] *See* George E. Hargest, "Analysis of Foreign Rate and Route for Problem Cover," *Chronicle* 46 (Dec. 1963):

FIGURE 4.—COVER, from Bremen to Baltimore, 1847.
(*Melvin W. Schuh collection*)

FIGURE 5.—COVER, from Düsseldorf, Prussia, to Philadelphia;
forwarded to Boston, 1847. (*Creighton C. Hart collection*)

dorf office had marked it in manuscript at upper right, 5/8, which indicated that it weighed five-eighths of a zoll loth. Since the zoll loth weighed about 14 grams, this letter weighed about 8 grams, over one-fourth but under one-half ounce. Prepayment of postage was compulsory, and the full rate to the United States frontier was prepaid. The amount of this prepayment is not shown, but the Düsseldorf office marked it with a large P in oval, indicating that the postage was paid. The Prussian exchange office credited Great Britain with 22d. (or 220 pfennige). This is indicated by a red-crayon 22 at lower left, which was placed beside a manuscript "franco/via England," probably written by the person who posted the letter. It was then sent in closed mail through Belgium to the London office. As the accounting was performed by the London office, it was marked 1–/10 in red ink, indicating the British postage of 1s. 10d. (equivalent to 22d.), as is indicated on Table 2 for a letter weighing under one-half ounce. London forwarded the letter to Liverpool, after applying an orange-red circular PAID/17 JULY/1847 marking. Upon receipt in Liverpool, it was marked with a black oval L/JU 17/H marking, and two days later, on 19 June, it was sent to Boston by R.M.S. *Caledonia* of the Cunard line, which arrived there on 3 July 1847.

The letter is addressed to a Philadelphia agent who paid 12¢ upon its receipt (10¢ postage for a letter conveyed over 300 miles plus 2¢ ship fee). The agents crossed out their name and address, leaving the name and address of their client, "Mr. Thomas Lamb/Boston." The agents prepaid the letter for forwarding to Boston by affixing a 5¢ stamp of the 1847 issue in the upper left corner and posting the letter. Since Boston is over 300 miles from Philadelphia, a prepayment of 10¢ should have been made. The Philadelphia post office recognized the 5¢ prepaid by the stamp, but marked the letter in manuscript *Due 5,* which was to be collected from Mr. Lamb in Boston.[18]

Figure 6 illustrates a cover (face only) posted in Baltimore, addressed to Bremen. It is endorsed "p America Str. of 31 July from N.YK," and is prepaid 5¢ for a distance under 300 miles by a 5¢ stamp of the 1847 issue. R.M.S. *America* of the Cunard line sailed from New York on 31 July 1850, thus determining the year of this cover. The letter evidently weighed over one-fourth ounce but less than one-half ounce and was sent from England in the Anglo-Prussian closed mail. Since this was posted after the United States-British treaty became effective, the packet rate was only 8d., which, if substituted in Table 2 for a letter of this weight, makes a total postage due to Great Britain of one 1s. 6d. This amount is debited to Prussia by a manuscript *1/6.* This was equal to 36 Bremen grote to which was added the Prussian-Bremen postage of 8 grote; a total collection of 44 grote is indicated by a *44* in red crayon.

---

[18] Ibid.

FIGURE 6.—COVER, from Baltimore to Bremen, 1850.
(*Creighton C. Hart collection*)

The 1847 Postal Arrangement With Bremen

After it was decided that the United States' subsidized Ocean line was to run between New York and Bremen with a call at Southampton each way, negotiations for a postal convention between Bremen and the United States were immediately undertaken. When Gevekoht left Bremen for the United States on 28 November 1845, he carried with him instructions and the necessary credentials of authority from the Bremen senate for the negotiation of a postal convention. His instructions included the following provisions: [19]

1. The City Post Office at Bremen was to become an American Agency for the receipt and delivery of all letters and other mail matter conveyed between the United States and the Weser by the American line of steamers.
2. The mail bags arriving with the steamer were to be turned over to the Bremen City Post Office; mail bags for the United States were to be sealed at the Bremen City Post Office and pass unbroken through the German Postal Administration, directed to America, via Bremen.
3. If the Weser is ice-free, one or more steamers are to be held ready to carry the mail and passengers in about 3½ hours from the American steamer to Bremen. If the Weser is iced over, the mails are to be forwarded by courier.
4. The Bremen City Post Office is to be in charge of mails dispatched and received from Hamburg as well as from Oldenburg and the Netherlands. Mail matter for other German states is to be turned over to the Hanover postal system, since it can be forwarded more rapidly by the Hanover railroad.
5. For performing these services as an *exclusive* American Agency, the Bremen Post Office is to receive a portion of the American sea postage as commission, the amount of which is to be determined by the American Postmaster General.

From these provisions, the desires of Bremen can be clearly seen. It wanted to be made the "depot" for United States mail to and from Central and Eastern Europe. It wanted the exclusive right to handle all mail conveyed by the American steamers. These instructions reflect the bitter commercial rivalry that existed between the several German states. For example, the closing of the mailbags prescribed in clause 2 of the provisions would avert possible diversion of letters from Prussia and the Thurn and Taxis posts by the Hanover postal administration. As clause 4 discloses, Bremen wanted to "be in charge" of the mails dispatched to and received from Hamburg so that this rival city state would not have the opportunity of routing and distributing it. By obtaining the establishment of Bremen as an exclusive American mail agency, a monopoly by Bremen over all German mail conveyed by the American steamship line was secured.

As soon as Senator Duckwitz learned that Bremen had been selected as the European terminus of the Ocean line, he planned some far-reaching changes that he felt must be realized before the first American steamer arrived. On 28 February 1846 [20] he concluded a postal convention with Hanover which set up a post office at Bremerhaven and separately defined the postal responsibilities of Bremen and Hanover. It was imperative, he felt, that harbor improvements be made and that the railroad line between Bremen and Hanover be completed. In these matters, Duckwitz secured the cooperation of the Hanover minister of foreign affairs, Privy Councilor von Falcke,[21] who won for him the support of the Hanover government.

On 26 May 1847, Major Selah R. Hobbie, first assistant postmaster general of the United States, was given his instructions and credentials as special agent of the Post Office Department with power to formulate postal arrangements with Bremen and other European states. Specifically, he was instructed to proceed to Bremen on the maiden voyage of the *Washington* and also to visit Havre, London, and Paris to arrange for the reception, transmission, and delivery of the United States mail.[22]

It is strange that the first Bremen postal arrangement is not published in the Statutes at Large. The omission probably resulted from the fact that Congress was not given the completed text with the regulations until 3 February 1849, and then only after a resolution of the Senate called for particulars of the arrangement.[23] The House of Representatives, however, had earlier made some inquiries about our foreign postal arrangements. On 17 January 1848, it had passed a resolution requesting a report "of such measures as are rendered necessary by the present state of our

---

[19] Piefke, *Bremischen Landespost,* Chap. 22.

[20] Ibid.

[21] Ibid.

[22] U.S., Congress, Senate, *Executive Document* 25, 30th Cong., 2nd sess., serial 531, p. 5.

[23] Ibid., p. 1.

foreign mail service." [24] Postmaster General Cave Johnson made reply by reporting a twelve-page letter from Major Hobbie, dated 15 January 1848. Hobbie explained his part in the negotiation of the agreement and set forth a schedule of rates upon which tentative accord had been secured. Pertinent portions of his letter follow: [25]

> When I arrived at Bremen, in June last, I found a ready and willing consideration extended at once to the subject of our international mail intercourse with Germany, and to all suggestions for its improvement. Besides the post office authorities at Bremen, I met there the representatives from the post offices of Prussia, Hanover, Brunswick, and Hamburg; and a communication from the Directeur General of the Thurn and Taxis posts at Frankfort-on-the-Main, was brought to me by Charles Graebe, Esq., an American consul, and a zealous and devoted friend of American interests. The postal systems of Germany are a very complicated organization. The Prince of Thurn and Taxis (resident at Ratisbon, in the Kingdom of Bavaria) holds by ancient feudatory grant, revived at the Congress of Vienna, the exclusive right of mail conveyance in seventeen states of the German confederation; and in most of the remaining states, a right concurrent with the separate right of local governments. This circumstance I found, after my first visit to Bremen, and after I had an interview at Frankfort with the Directeur General of the Thurn and Taxis posts, embarrassed my operations with difficulties somewhat peculiar. The General and the local authorities entertained conflicting views. Deeming it unwise to excite jealousies, and not having time to follow out the negotiations with each, I judged it best to rely upon the agency of the government of Bremen, to effect the desired results of uniform and reduced postages in Germany upon American mails. I then adjusted with the post office authority of that government, all needful arrangements. . . .
>
> The post office authority of the Hanseatic republic of Bremen is exercised by a committee of its Senate, the principal member of which is the Hon. Arnold Duckwitz. With him my business was transacted and arrangements made. Through him the applications were presented to the different governments to reduce the postages and establish uniform rates on American mails.

It is undoubtedly fortunate that Hobbie delegated his authority for negotiation with the German states to Duckwitz, for this gentleman worked unremittingly and accomplished surprising results. When Hobbie arrived in Bremen, it was his intention to conclude an agreement with all Germany which would establish reduced and uniform postages. Duckwitz pointed out that if this were to be done, he would have to make separate agreements with at least seventeen German states. Hobbie is said to have described the separation of the German states as "humbug," [26] but Duckwitz persuaded him that best results could be secured if negotiations were conducted by the Bremen agency.

It was finally agreed that the German postage for a single letter of one-half ounce, or one German loth, should be 12¢, equal to 12 Bremen grote, 5 Prussian silbergroschen, or 4 Hanoverian gute groschen.[27] Added to this postage was the packet postage of 24¢, and finally, the American inland postage of 5¢ or 10¢. It was also agreed that only those German postal systems that would reduce their postage to 12¢ would be allowed to exchange letters by direct steamship. In accordance with the principle established by the joint resolution of Congress of 15 June 1844, optional prepayment of the international rate was to be provided. At the end of the negotiations, Duckwitz and others suggested that it might be proper for Bremen to charge a postage of 2¢ on letters conveyed between Bremen and Bremerhaven. Since Hobbie had no instructions on this point, he noted the request, and Duckwitz left the matter to be considered at a later date.

Although all difficulties were not yet overcome, the arrangement was signed at Washington on 29 March and at Bremen on 26 June 1847. Excerpts of significant sections of the text follow: [28]

1. The Post Office Department at Washington appoints the postmaster at Bremen its sole and exclusive agent for the receipt and forwarding of mail conveyed by the American mail steamers between New York and Bremerhaven.
2. On arrival of the steamers on the Weser, the captain will deliver the mail bags to the Bremen postal agent at Bremerhaven.
3. During the season of the year that will admit it, a Weser steamboat will be held in readiness to take the mails to Bremen; when navigation in the Weser is interrupted, or when the steamer arrives at night, the mail bags will be dispatched to Bremen by courier, the time of such transit not to exceed five hours.
4. All mail to America will be forwarded exclusively by the Bremen City Post Office, "the mail bags to be closed at the post office at Bremen, and all letters for steamers are to be delivered there."
5. The Bremen Post Office agrees that a separate bag may be exchanged with the Hamburg Post Office, to contain only the Hamburg matter, and no mail for points beyond Hamburg. Such bag is to be under the control of the Bremen mail agent at Bremerhaven.
6. The Bremen postmaster "is to take charge of the receiving, forwarding, and despatching of the mails, accounting to

---

[24] U.S., Congress, House, *Executive Document* 35, 30th Cong., 1st sess., serial 516, p. 1.
[25] Ibid., pp. 8–9.

[26] Piefke, *Bremischen Landespost,* Chap. 22.
[27] Ibid.
[28] *Senate Executive Document* 25, 30 Cong., 2 sess., serial 531, pp. 7–9.

the Postmaster General of the United States for the United States postage received by the postmaster at Bremen." For this service he was to receive a commission of twenty percent, "to be cast upon the amount of postage collected and credited to the Postmaster General of the United States."

7. The Post Office Department "of the Hanseatic republic of Bremen declares itself responsible for the Bremen postmaster in behalf of all services to be performed under this agreement."

It should be noted that the above agreement closely parallels the instructions given Gevekoht by the Bremen senate in 1845. The rate structure was not included in the agreement itself, but was established by regulations, which were signed at Bremen on 13 September 1847.[29] Significant portions of the fourteen clauses of these regulations are excerpted below, as follows:

1. Provided that the sender of a letter should have the option of
    (a) leaving the whole postage to be paid by the receiver
    (b) prepaying the whole postage to the place of destination
    (c) when sent from the United States, of paying the United States postage to Bremen, leaving the European postage unpaid; when sent from Bremen, of paying the European postage from Bremen, leaving the United States postage unpaid.

4. Since the mail agent at Bremen would have difficulty in determining distances under or over 300 miles in the United States, it was provided that when he collected the United States postage, i.e., on prepaid letters sent from Bremen, or on unpaid letters from the United States, he was to collect it as follows:

    At 24¢ the single letter—from or to the City of New York

    At 29¢ the single letter—from or to any other part of the state of New York, or from or to the states of New Hampshire, Vermont, Massachusetts, Rhode Island, Connecticut, New Jersey, Pennsylvania, Delaware, Maryland, or the District of Columbia.

    At 34¢ the single letter—from or to the remainder of the United States or Canada.

NOTE: Since the preceding schedule for the collection of postage according to places or states has in some published works been applied to all mail under the United States-Bremen arrangement, it must be emphasized that it pertained only to postage collected by the mail agent in Bremen. United States postmasters collected inland postage according to distances under or over 300 miles. The above schedule was never published and issued to postmasters in the United States, and they, in general, had no knowledge of it.

[29] Ibid., pp. 9–13.

7. Established the progression at an additional rate for each additional unit of weight, or fraction thereof.

10. Provided that each letter is to be marked with the stamp of the office mailing it on the face, and if from Europe with the stamp of Bremen on the back, and in case it is addressed to any other office in the United States than New York, then with the stamp of New York also on the back, the better to identify it for the accounts, in case it should be returned as dead or mis-directed. And if the letter is from the United States, it is to be stamped on the back by New York and Bremen in like manner. If it is an unpaid letter it should be marked on the face with the postage accruing to the country in which mailed, and chargeable to the country in which to be delivered. This entry should be made in figures in black ink. If the postage is prepaid to destination, it is to be marked in red figures with that proportion of the postage received which is to be accounted for to the country in which the letter is to be delivered, and stamped in red *paid all*. When the United States postage only is paid on letters *going* to Europe, or the European postage only is paid on letters *going* to the United States, the letter is to be stamped in black *part paid* and the amount is not to be stated on the letter, as it does not enter into the international account. The postmasters of Bremen and of New York will see that the entries on the letters are correct, and will supply all omissions of the mailing offices so far as in their power.

12 and 13. Mails between Bremen (city) and New York (city), and between New York and Hamburg (city) were to be made up in separate bags.

After the regulations were agreed upon and signed, the question of the 2¢ charge for postage between Bremen and Bremerhaven was again raised. Senator Duckwitz finally settled the matter by sending the following memorandum to Postmaster General Cave Johnson:[30]

Memorandum.—A question having been raised and submitted to the Postmaster General of the United States respecting the postage in Bremen, and the compensation to that office, and the same to decide so as to have 'the regulations' unchanged, the charge of 2 cents postage in Bremen was formally relinquished by   GUILDMEISTER

Thus, no inland postage was charged either in Bremen or in New York City. While the omission of the United States inland postage "in the port" was by intent of Congress, the omission of the Bremen inland postage was originally an oversight. Breman could have insisted that the regulations be changed to include it.

After the agreement was signed, Postmaster General Cave Johnson faced a problem. Wholly prepaid and unpaid letters could be sent to or received from Europe

[30] Ibid., p. 13.

only under the rates of the United States-Bremen arrangement, and could be conveyed only by Ocean line steamer *Washington*. During 1847 there were only three sailings from New York by the *Washington*: on 1 June, 23 September, and 18 November. Her first sailing in 1848 was on 20 February. On 20 March 1848, *Hermann* cleared New York for Bremen on her maiden voyage.[31] It is suspected that Postmaster General Johnson did not wish to place the agreement in force until the proposed monthly service could be maintained. He therefore waited until the maiden voyage of *Hermann* was announced. Whatever the cause for delay might have been, notice to the public and instructions to postmasters were not published until 1 March 1848,[32] and did not actually become effective until *Hermann* sailed on 20 March 1848.

Postal Rates Under the Arrangement With Bremen

The foreign postages agreed upon were included in clause 3 of the regulations and were additionally presented in tabular form in Exhibit *D* appended to the regulations. Total rates were arrived at by adding together the United States and foreign postages. The United States inland and packet postages, as well as the foreign postages, are summarized in Table 3.

The act of 3 March 1851, effective on 1 July, established the United States postage at 20¢ per half ounce, to or from any point in the United States. Thus, the 24-, 29-, and 34-cent rates were superseded by a sole rate of 20¢, to which the foreign postage was added to arrive at wholly unpaid or fully prepaid rates. In the accounts, 5¢ of the 20¢ rate was allocated as inland, and 15¢ as sea postage.

Although it was reported that, effective 1 July 1850,[33] a new German-Austrian postal convention would reduce rates throughout most of the German states, such reductions were not reflected in rate tables presented in post office instructions issued to postmasters on 14 June 1851. With reference to mail by the Bremen line, however, the instructions stated: "It is supposed that these Foreign Rates have been reduced under a *late postal* treaty between the German States; but official information of it has not been received. By prepaying only the 20 cents United States postage, and leaving the balance unpaid, the advantage of such reduction (if any) may be secured." Reduced rates were presented in the Postal Laws and Regulations for 1852 (as of 3 April 1852), as follows:

Letters to the cities and countries in Germany here named, if sent by the *Bremen line,* can be pre-paid to destination, if desired, by pre-paying the amounts here stated in addition to the U.S. postage of 20¢ per single rate. . . . Prepayment of the whole postage to destination, the U.S. postage only, or to send the letter wholly unpaid, is optional. It is advised to pay the U.S. postage only. . . .

Single rate of one-quarter ounce:
Cassel, Coburgh, Frankfort-on-the-Main,
Darmstadt, and Wurtemberg   7¢
Single rate of one-half ounce:
Oldenburg   2
Hamburg   5
Altona and Hanover   6
Brunswick, Gotha, and Prussia   7
Kiel and Lubec   8
Thurn and Taxis posts, and Saxony   12

On letters to the cities and countries on the continent of Europe (and Africa) here named, if sent by the *Bremen line,* it is advised that the U.S. postage only be prepaid, if prepayment is desired, leaving the foreign postage to be collected from the receiver. But letters to these places can be sent wholly unpaid.

Single rate of one-quarter ounce:
Austria, Baden, and Bavaria   7¢
Italy, eastern towns of   18
Basle and other parts of Switzerland   21
Alexandria, Cairo, and Greece   37
Single rate of one-half ounce:
Denmark   22
St. Petersburg and Cronstadt   24
Norway, (Bergen, Christiania, and "furthest" parts)   28
Sweden, Stockholm, and "furthest" parts   39

Operations Under the Bremen Arrangement

Steamship *Washington* left New York on her maiden voyage on 1 June 1847, and on the same day *Britannia* of the Cunard line sailed from Boston. *Britannia* arrived at Liverpool two full days before the *Washington*

---

[31] Bonsor (*North Atlantic Seaway*, p. 52), gives the date as 21 Mar. 1848. *The Shipping and Commercial List,* 18 Mar. 1848, shows the *Hermann* "up" for sailing on 20 Mar. 1848, while the issue of 25 Mar. 1848 shows that it cleared New York 20 Mar. 1848.

[32] *Senate Executive Document 25,* 30 Cong., 2 sess., serial 531, p. 13.

[33] *Senate Executive Document 82,* 32 Cong., 2 sess., serial 660, p. 34 (Mr. Lawrence to Lord Palmerston).

TABLE 3.—*Postal Rates Under the United States-Bremen Arrangement (1847)*

United States Rates	
Inland postage (single rate of one-half ounce):	
If posted or received under 300 miles from New York City	5¢
If posted or received over 300 miles from New York City	10
If posted or received in New York City	0
Packet postage:	
For letters not exceeding one-half ounce	24
For letters over one-half but not over one ounce	48
For every additional half ounce or fraction thereof	15
Total United States postage (for a single rate):	
If posted or received in New York City	24
If posted or received under 300 miles from New York City	29
If posted or received over 300 miles from New York City	34

Foreign Rates

Single rate of one-half ounce on letters addressed to: [a]

Altona	6¢	Mecklenburg-Schwerin [c]	12¢
Bremen	0	Mecklenburg-Strelitz [c]	12
Brunswick	[b] 6	Nassau [c]	12
Cassel [c]	12	Oldenburg	[d] 5
Coburg [c]	12	Prussia (and provinces)	12
Darmstadt [c]	12	Reuss [c]	12
Frankfort-on-Main [c]	12	Saxe-Altenburg [c]	12
Gotha [c]	12	Saxe-Meiningen [c]	12
Hamburg	6	Saxe-Weimar [c]	12
Hanover	6	Saxony	[e] 12
Hesse-Homburg [c]	12	Schaumburg-Lippe [c]	12
Kiel	11	Schwartzburg-Rudolstadt [c]	12
Lippe-Detmold [c]	12	Schwartzburg-Sonderhausen [c]	12
Lubec	9	Wurtemberg [c]	12

Single rate of one-half ounce on letters addressed to: [f]

Denmark—Copenhagen and "furthest" parts	22¢
Norway—Bergen and "furthest" parts	30
St. Petersburg and Cronstadt	24
Sweden—Stockholm and "furthest" parts	39

Single rate of one-quarter ounce on letters addressed to: [g]

Alexandria	37	Bavaria	22
Austria	18	Cairo	37
Baden	18	Constantinople	37
Basle and other parts of Switzerland	21	Greece	37
		Italy, eastern towns	18

NOTE. Rates as set forth in *Senate Executive Document* 25, 30th Cong., 2nd sess., serial 531, pp. 18–19.

[a] Postage could be prepaid or left unpaid, or U.S. postage alone could be prepaid, at option of sender.

[b] Reduced from 8¢ by 20 March 1848.

[c] Served by Thurn and Taxis posts.

[d] Reduced to 2¢ by 1851.

[e] Reduced from 18¢ by 20 March 1848.

[f] U.S. postage only should be prepaid.

[g] U.S. postage only should be prepaid.

reached Southampton on 15 June.[34] Not only was the speed of *Washington* disappointing, but she rolled excessively, much to the discomfort of her passengers. Both *Washington* and *Hermann* were built with narrow bottoms that made them load deep, forcing adjustments to be made in *Washington's* paddle blades, which were originally too long.[35] In appearance, they were described as ugly-looking, like men-of-war with the top decks cut off. *Washington* had a white gun strake which extended across her paddle box with a row of gun ports painted on it.

Hermann sailed from New York on 20 March 1848 and carried the first mail under the postal arrangement with Bremen. There are several "firsts" connected with this maiden voyage of *Hermann*. It carried the first mail under the first postal convention between the United States and a European country. This mail contained the first wholly unpaid and wholly prepaid letters sent from the United States to Europe.

Figure 7 illustrates a cover which was included in this first mail to Bremen. The letter is dated "March 17th" and was posted in New York, addressed to Berlin, Prussia. On its face are the figures *24* and *12* in lead pencil, which set forth the United States and foreign postages separately, and indicated a prepayment of 36¢. As required by clause 10 of the regulations, it was marked PAID ALL in red ink on its face. The credit for the foreign (German) postage is shown by a manuscript *12* in red ink. The AMERICA/ÜBER BREMEN handstamp was applied in black ink by the United States mail agent in Bremen and is, therefore, a marking of the United States post office. The New York circular town marking, applied in red on the face, shows the date of 20 March, the date of sailing of *Hermann*. At lower left is the endorsement "Per Steamer/Hermann." During the nine years in which *Hermann* plied between New York and Bremen, it sailed from New York on 20 March only in 1848. On the reverse is a small circular marking in black, bearing at its sides an N at left and a *1* at right, the significance of which is not known. In its center are the figures *16/4*, which indicates the date of 16 April. This marking is believed to be Prussian, and shows the date the letter arrived in Berlin.

All of the early steamships consumed enormous quantities of coal. Until 1850, when American supplies became available, coal used for the eastward runs was brought from England by sailing ships. Until about 1860, salt water was used in boilers, which rapidly deteriorated, decreased their efficiency, and necessi-

[34] Bonsor, *North Atlantic Seaway*, p. 51.
[35] C. R. Vernon Gibbs, *Passenger Liners of the Western Ocean*, p. 96.

FIGURE 7.—COVER, from New York to Berlin, Prussia, 1848.

tated frequent pauses to "blow out" salt sediment. The original boilers of *Washington* and *Hermann* were gigantic affairs that proved to be inefficient, and they were replaced by smaller ones in 1851. Since engines, boilers, and bunkers took up so much space, there was little left for passengers and cargo. The Atlantic crossings wore out the paddle steamers at a rapid rate, necessitating high repair and maintenance costs. "General experience up to 1850 established that an ocean steamship company had to earn an annual sum equal to 25% of its capital before beginning to show a profit." [36]

None of the early steamship lines wanted to run their ships during the winter months, particularly in December and January. Because winter weather on the North Atlantic was usually stormy, passengers and cargo were scarce. Only in dire necessity was a person willing to undertake a winter voyage, because ships were cold, the quarters cramped, and shipboard diseases were reputed to be more prevalent in winter. Merchants were unwilling to ship certain kinds of freight during the winter months because of the possibility of its freezing. Faced with greatly curtailed revenues and increased costs, only the heavily subsidized lines ran regularly throughout the year.

The experiences of *Hermann* and *Washington* during the winter of 1848–49 may serve as an example of the conditions ships might expect to encounter on the North Atlantic in winter.

The *New York Tribune* of Friday morning, 5 January 1849, carried the following news item:

> Arrival of the steamship *Hermann* at Boston—Boston, January 4th
>
> The steamship *Hermann*, Capt. Crabtree, which left Southampton, 12 December, arrived here this morning having experienced a constant succession of heavy westerly gales; put in for coals. Has 300 tons of freight. Anchored in Nantasket Roads last night at 9 o'clock. The following is a list of her passengers: [24 names were listed].
>
> The *Hermann's* mails will be sent this afternoon via Stonington.

The Shipping and Commercial List shows that *Hermann* arrived in New York on 6–7 January, that is, late Saturday evening or on Sunday.

Washington, which arrived in New York on 8 January 1849, had suffered damage in the same storm. The 13 January 1849 issue of the *Shipping and Commercial List* carried the following item under "Gales and Disasters:"

> The Steam ship Washington, Johnson, at this port from Southampton, 27th ult. lat. 51.28 lon. 34.20 experienced a hurricane from S.W. which lasted twenty three hours, then shifted N.W. when she shipped a sea which carried away two forward scuttles, and booby hatches, stove bulwarks and forward sky light, filling the cabin with water three feet deep.

Examination of the sailing dates of the Ocean line discloses that there was no sailing from New York during any January until 1854, and there were only two December sailings by the line from its inception in 1847 until it ceased operations in 1857.[37] The return trip from the November sailing from New York usually brought the ships back to New York in late December or early January, and the next arrival was not until early April. The failure of these ships to sail in winter created difficult problems for the postmaster general.

Until the harbor facilities at Bremerhaven were completed in September 1851,[38] neither the United States nor Bremen could effectively protest the irregularity of sailings. Not only would the Ocean line ships have to face the gales and cold of the North Atlantic, but they also would find no adequate protection against ice and storm at Bremerhaven. The run between Bremerhaven and Southampton was subject to particularly severe weather in winter. Upon the return of *Hermann* to New York on 23 December 1851, it was found that she had "cracked" in the intense cold.[39] She underwent extensive repairs and was reported to be in the Navy Yard from 7 to 20 March 1852.[40] Although Bremen frequently protested the continued irregularity of sailings, these protests appear to have fallen on deaf ears. Only in the fiscal years of 1855–56 and 1856–57 did the line make the twelve annual round voyages required by its contract.

One reason for the omission of the winter sailings was the method adopted by the Post Office Department for paying the subsidies. The Ocean line contract called for a subsidy of $200,000 for twelve round voyages per year. Actually, this was calculated at $16,667 per round voyage, and the Company was paid for the number of round voyages made. Under the act of 27 June 1848, the postmaster general was authorized and required to levy fines upon the contractors

---

[36] Ibid., p. 52.

[37] Sailing and arrival information for the Ocean line was taken from the appropriate editions of the *Shipping and Commercial List*.

[38] Piefke, *Bremischen Landespost*, Chap. 22.

[39] Ibid.

[40] *Shipping and Commercial List*, 20 Dec. 1851–24 Mar. 1852.

for any unreasonable or unnecessary delay in performance of a trip, but such fine was not to *exceed* one half of the contract price paid for the trip.[41] It appears that maximum fines were seldom levied, and it was cheaper for the contractor to forego the subsidy for the voyage and pay whatever fine was assessed than it was to make the trip. In his annual report for the year 1853–54, Postmaster General James Campbell complained that "on the Bremen line one of the monthly voyages has been omitted. These irregularities materially detract from the efficiency of our mail service across the Atlantic."[42]

The Bremen Closed Mail

The Post Office Department was trying to build an American packet service to England that would approximate that of the Cunard line. After the Havre and Collins lines started to run in 1850, it was planned that there would be twenty-six voyages by the Collins line, and twelve each by the Bremen and Havre lines, making a total of fifty round voyages by American steamers against a total of fifty-two by the Cunard line. Sailing dates were set on Saturdays for all lines, the Bremen and Havre lines' monthly sailings to alternate with the fortnightly sailings of the Collins line, so that there was a scheduled sailing from New York every Saturday, with the exception of one Saturday in the months of December and January. An act of 31 August 1852 [43] authorized an added sailing by the Bremen and Havre lines, which brought the American packet scheduled sailings up to the fifty-two then being maintained by the Cunard line. The steamship companies, however, regarded the additional sailings as a privilege rather than an obligation, for only in the fiscal year of 1855–56 did the Havre line make its scheduled thirteen round voyages, while the Ocean line made no more than twelve round voyages in any fiscal year during the entire life of the line. With these irregularities in sailings, it was indeed difficult for the Post Office Department to realize its goal of having Americans patronize the American lines.

During the winter of 1848–49, the Ocean line made no sailing from New York between 20 November 1848 and 20 February 1849. During these months letters wholly unpaid, or wholly prepaid with Bremen rates, as well as letters prepaid with the United States postage of 24¢, 29¢, or 34¢ were appearing at the New York office. These letters could not be sent by the Cunard line without forcing the mailers to suffer excessive overpayments of postage. How or when the letters were sent is not known. The evidence of one cover posted during this period and marked with a debit for the 24¢ packet postage indicates it was sent by sailing ship. During the winter of 1849–50, the situation was even more acute. There was no sailing by the Ocean line between 20 October 1849 and 20 February 1850, the November sailing of *Washington* having been canceled.

Postmaster General Jacob Collamer, however, now had a new avenue available to him for sending mail to Bremen. On 1 July 1849, the United States-British treaty had become fully effective. By Article VIII, the United States had the privilege of sending closed mails through England; by Article IX, closed mail was paid for by the ounce at two single-letter rates plus 25 percent. Transatlantic packet postage was 16¢ per single-letter rate and, thus, would amount to 40¢ per ounce (2 x 16¢ plus 25%). By the Anglo-Bremen treaty of 1841, the single-letter rate between London and Cuxhaven or Bremerhaven was 6d. (12¢). Application of the Article IX formula to this rate resulted in a postage of 30¢ per ounce (2 x 12¢ plus 25%). These two rates added together resulted in a total postage to the Bremen frontier of 70¢ per ounce. This was high postage, but Postmaster General Collamer decided to make use of the route. After the agreement of Bremen was secured, Britain was notified that the United States would exchange closed mails via the London-Cuxhaven or Bremerhaven route.[44]

The mail, already marked with Bremen rates, was forwarded in closed bags by the Cunard line to Liverpool, thence through London to Bremerhaven. The United States mail agent at Bremen rated, marked, and forwarded the letters as if they had been conveyed by the Ocean line, direct from New York. Except for the date of mailing, it is impossible to determine from the markings which route was used to convey a letter. On incoming mail by this route, however, endorsements "By closed mail, via London" are sometimes seen.

In the following year, the Collins and Havre lines began to run, both subsidized by the United States.

---

[41] U.S., *Postal Laws and Regulations,* Chap. 8, sec. 176, 1866, p. 45.

[42] *Senate Executive Document* 1, 33 Cong., 2 sess., serial 747, p. 631.

[43] *House Executive Document,* 32 Cong., 2 sess., serial 674, p. 643.

[44] Piefke, *Bremischen Landespost,* Chap. 22

Shortly thereafter, the Bremen closed mail was sent by these lines, rather than by the Cunard Line, so that the 40¢-per-ounce packet postage could be levied against their subsidies. The Bremen closed mail made available a weekly service to Germany, by direct steamers once a month and via England in the remaining weeks. At the request of Dr. Bartsch,[45] director of Bremen Posts, the Bremen closed mail was used throughout the year, instead of only during the winter months. The service was continued until superseded by the Prussian closed mail on 16 October 1852.[46]

Schedules prepared by the auditor of the Treasury for the Post Office Department for the fiscal year ended 30 June 1853—the last year the Bremen closed mail service was used—disclosed that mail was dispatched by this route during the third and fourth quarters of 1852 and the first quarter of 1853, after which only Prussian closed mail is reported. During this last fiscal year, a total of 53,064 ounces of Bremen closed mail was exchanged, of which the Collins line conveyed 27,290 ounces, and the Havre line carried 25,774 ounces. Bremen sent 35,980 ounces to the United States by this route, while only 17,084 ounces were dispatched by the United States to Bremen.[47]

Figure 8 presents a cover that was sent in the Bremen closed mail. A folded letter posted in Bremen on 30 December 1851, addressed to Baltimore, it is endorsed "pr. closed Mail via London." Since no inland postage was charged in Bremen, only the United States postage was paid on a prepaid letter. At left is a red-crayon *20*, showing a prepayment of 20 Bremen grote (20¢). To the right of the *20* is a large manuscript *20* in red ink, indicating the Bremen credit of 20¢ to the United States. At lower left is a boxed PAID applied in red by Bremen. In red at lower right is a circular NEW-YORK/JAN/21 marking which shows the date the letter was received by the New York office. Since there was no arrival by an Ocean line ship between 23 December 1851 and 18 March 1852, the letter could not have been conveyed by a ship of that line. The Collins liner *Arctic,* however, arrived in New York on 21 January 1852, the date in the New York postmark, and it is, therefore, presumed that it arrived by that ship.

Figure 9 illustrates an unpaid letter that was posted in New York, addressed to Dresden, Saxony. The New

---

[45] Ibid.

[46] *House Executive Document* 1, 32 Cong., 2 sess., serial 674, p. 645.

[47] *House Executive Document* 1, 33rd Cong. 1 sess., serial 692, pp. 731, 739.

FIGURE 8.—COVER, from Bremen to Baltimore, 1851.

York office debited Bremen with the packet postage of 24¢ by stamping it with a *24* in black ink at upper right. It also marked the letter with a boxed NOT PAID in red. At lower left is the endorsement "pr Canada." The circular NEW-YORK/AUG/14 postmark is applied in red, and Cunard sailing records show that the *Canada* sailed from New York on 14 August 1850.[48] The cover is docketed in red *New York–Dresden/1850,* and this year date agrees with the endorsement to the *Canada* and the sailing date of this ship. The Bremen office marked the letter with a 9/AMERICA/ÜBER BREMEN in red. This *9* or a multiple of *9* has been seen on a number of covers rated by the Bremen office. It is suspected that it means 9 grote (9¢), and that it represents the Bremen share of the transit postage. Saxony marked the letter *16 3/10* in red crayon. This indicated a collection in Dresden of 16 neugroschen and 3 pfennige. This collection included a small delivery fee [49] which was added to the amount in neugroschen that Saxony held to be equal to the convention rate of 36¢.

Figure 10 illustrates a letter posted in Schenectady, New York, addressed to Baden. The letter weighed over half an ounce, or 14.18 grams, but not over 15 grams. Since it weighed over half an ounce, two rates were required in the United States. The person posting the letter paid two 5¢ inland rates from Schenectady to New York city by affixing a 10¢ stamp of the 1847 issue. The letter was, therefore, forwarded from New York as if it were a letter originating in that port. The New York office debited Bremen with double the single-rate packet postage of 24¢, or 48¢. Since the Schenectady postmark bears the date of 14 April (1851), it is assumed the letter was forwarded via the direct route by the *Washington* which sailed from New York on 19 April 1851.

The foreign markings are of particular interest. The cover illustrates the complicated nature of the German rates, which involved several currencies. It might be well first to state the value in United States cents of the currencies appearing on this cover. In 1850, the thaler of northern Germany was worth 69¢; there were 30 silbergroschen to the thaler, worth 2.3¢ each. In Prussia, there were 12 pfennige to the silbergroschen, but the groschen in other states was worth 10 pfennige. The rix-dollar of Bremen was worth 78.3¢ and there were 72 grote to the dollar, worth 1.09¢ each, but generally considered to be worth 1¢. The

---

[48] Sailings of the Cunard line were taken from records of the line by L. L. Downing and are presented here with his kind permission. [*See also* fn. 13.]

[49] A. D. Smith, *Development of Rates of Postage,* pp. 107, 257.

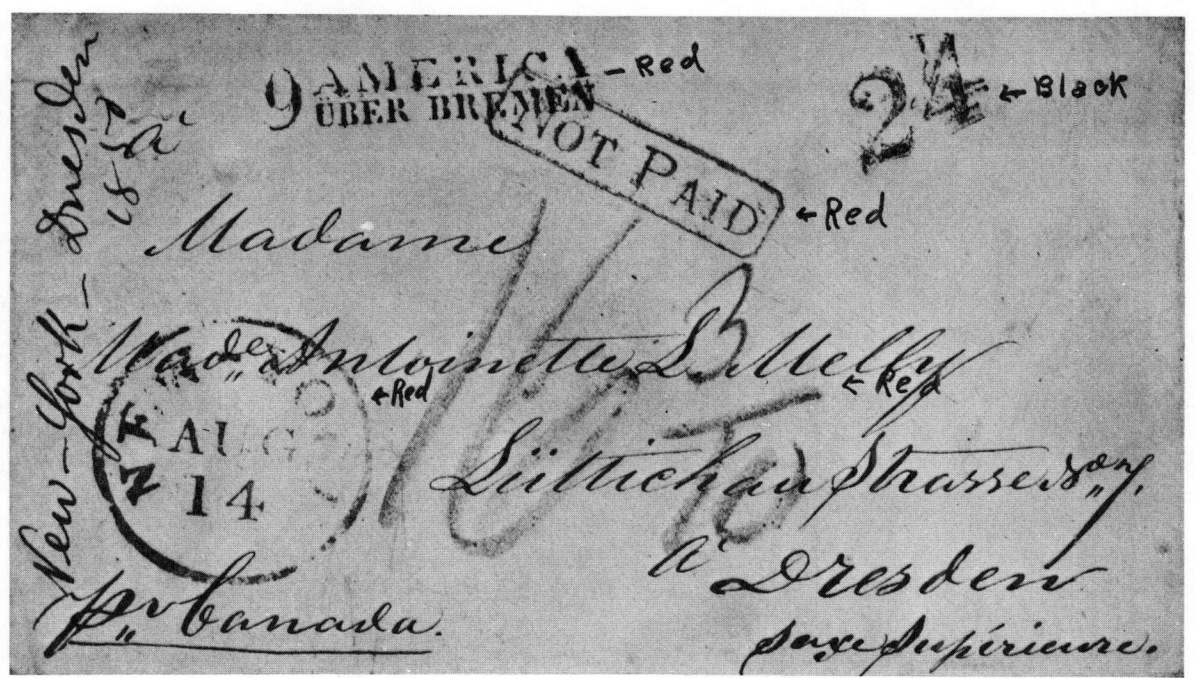

FIGURE 9.—COVER, from New York to Dresden, Saxony, 1850.

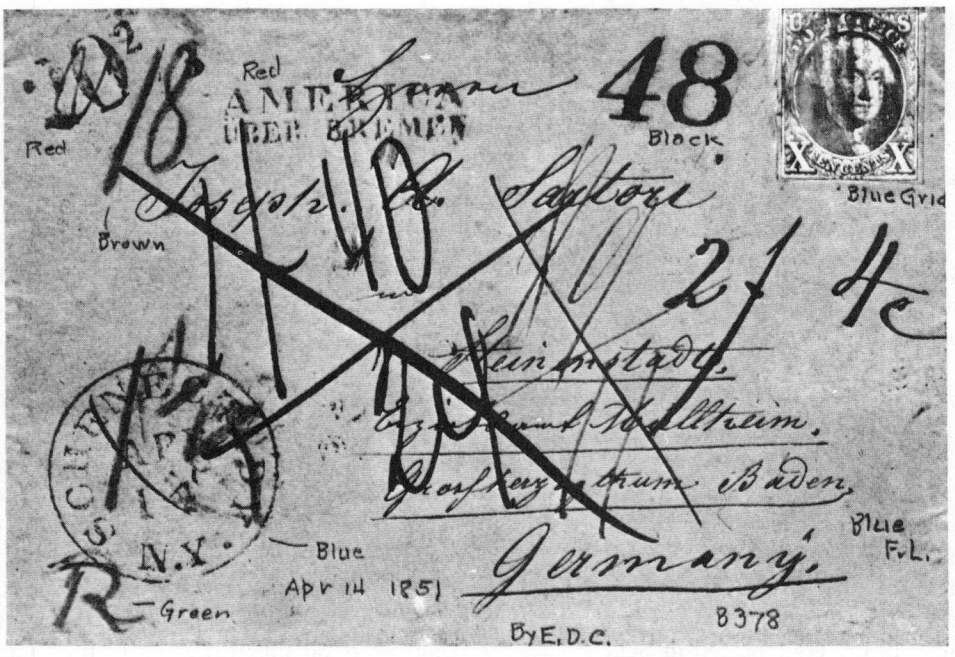

Figure 10.—Cover, from Schenectady, N.Y., to Baden, Germany, 1851. (*Ashbrook's Special Service*)

florin of Baden was worth 40¢, and there were 60 kreuzer to the florin, worth two-thirds of a cent each. Exact reconciliation of these amounts in United States currency is difficult because the Germans rounded off their small coin, creating minor discrepancies which became substantial when applied to high rates. The best that can be done is to approach an approximate agreement.

The total postage for this letter, as calculated in the United States, would have been 58¢ plus the foreign postage which was at the rate of 18¢ per quarter ounce. Since the letter weighed over half an ounce (14.18 grams), three 18¢ rates, or 54¢ foreign postage would have been charged. Hence, if the postage had been prepaid in the United States, $1.12 would have been required. On the continent, however, the quarter-ounce postage was rated at 7½ grams, and the half-ounce at 15 grams. Since this letter did not weigh over 15 grams, only two rates, or 36¢ were charged by Bremen. The total postage on this letter, as calculated by Bremen, was only 84¢.

The 20 2/3 in red at upper left means 20 2/3 silbergroschen (47.5¢) and represents the 48¢ packet postage, which is charged to Baden and must have been included in the postage collected on delivery of the letter.

The Bremen share of the postage was 18 grote for a double-rate letter, or two times 9 grote, and it is shown in red crayon to the left of the AMERICA/ÜBER BREMEN marking. This 9-grote rate appears to have been equated with 12 kreuzer, which was less than its actual value.

The manuscript 89/11 is the foreign postage beyond the limit of Bremen's share of 18 grote. The marking indicates that two postal districts participated in the total amount. The sum of 89 and 11 is 100 kreuzer, which, at 60 kreuzer to the florin, is also equal to 1 florin and 40 kreuzer.

The marking 1f40/24 expresses the preceding foreign postage over the 18-grote Bremen share expressed in kreuzer, 12 kreuzer to 9 Bremen grote.

The amount to be collected is shown at right. It is the sum of 1 florin, 40 kreuzer, and 24 kreuzer, which is 2 florin and 4 kreuzer. This is expressed in the marking 2f 4c and represents a collection of about 83¢.

If the recipient would rather pay in thaler, that amount is also shown over the Schenectady marking. At first glance it appears to be 1¼, but examination reveals that it was altered to 1⅕. This means one and one-fifth thaler, or a collection of 83¢. Since this is crossed out, the recipient evidently paid in florin and kreuzer.

Chapter 2

Negotiation of the United States-British Postal Treaty of 15 December 1848

Postmaster General Cave Johnson's instructions to Major Hobbie regarding negotiations with the British were explicit. He was to go to London and arrange for the transmission, receipt, and dispatch of the United States mail. He was to use his best efforts to secure the abolition of the 8d. ship postage imposed upon letters entering or leaving the ports of the United Kingdom by other than contract packets. If this should fail, he was empowered to use the terms upon which the Canadian mails were forwarded through the United States as a basis for further negotiation. If the British refused to abolish the ship charge on mail brought to England by American steamers, then it was to be known that the United States would impose ship postage on mail brought to the United States by the Cunard line.[1] Hobbie understood there had been some correspondence on the subject, and he anticipated little difficulty in negotiating with the British.

Hobbie later explained to the House of Representatives what happened when he arrived at Southampton. His own words present a graphic description of the affair:[2]

> On arriving at Southampton, in England, on the 15th of June, I was shown an order of the British Post Office Department, issued on the 9th of that month, imposing the British packet postage of one shilling sterling for each letter of a half ounce, and two pence for each newspaper, brought in the United States mails by the Washington. This was made chargeable as well upon those destined for France as those deliverable in the United Kingdom; and the Postmaster of Southampton was required to forward to London all mailbags left by the Washington, without being opened. The effect of this order is to subject all letters and newspapers to double postage; and those addressed to France to additional delay, by being taken out of the direct course to their places of destination. . . .
>
> Being required by [my] instructions to proceed with the Washington to Bremen, I addressed a full communication upon the subject to his excellency George Bancroft, our minister at London.

Bancroft already knew of it, for he had obtained a copy of the order on 10 June. He wasted no time in attempting to see Viscount Palmerston, British foreign secretary, but Palmerston was out on the 11th, and he was also out on the 12th. Bancroft then sought and found the British postmaster general, Lord Clanricarde, and also Colonel Maberly, secretary of the British Post Office. In his dispatch of 17 June 1847 to James Buchanan, secretary of state, Bancroft said he was frankly told by Lord Clanricarde—and Colonel Maberly reiterated it—that packet postage was imposed on American packet letters because it was intended to "protect the Cunard line of steamers, and to derive for the British Treasury a revenue out of the Mail service of our packets as well as of his own."[3]

---

[1] U.S., Congress, Senate, *Executive Document* 25, 30th Cong., 2nd sess., serial 531, p. 6.

[2] U.S., Congress, House, *Executive Document* 35, 30th Cong., 1st sess., serial 516, p. 3.

[3] U.S., Department of State, *Treaties and other International Acts of the United States of America*, vol. 5, document 133, p. 471. [*See also* U.S., Department of State, 57 Despatches, Great Britain, 28, 17 June 1847.]

Clanricarde also said he was desirous of forming a postal arrangement with the United States.

Not being able to see Lord Palmerston, Bancroft addressed a note to him on the same day. Bancroft regretted the course taken by the British, objecting to it as "contrary to equity"; it also violated the spirit of the commercial convention of 3 July 1815 between the United States and Great Britain, which placed the United States on the footing of the "most favored nation." The United States alone was discriminated against; it was a protective tariff in its most objectionable form.[4]

It is important, at this point, to note some fundamental differences that existed between the post offices of the two countries. In Great Britain the postal functions were administratively divided. The Lords of the Treasury, headed by the chancellor of the exchequer, then Sir Charles Wood, actually set postal rates. The Post Office administered postal affairs and made recommendations to the Lords of the Treasury and to the Admiralty. Contracts for sea conveyance of mail were made with the Admiralty. Postal agreements with foreign countries were of two forms: postal conventions in the form of agreements between the post offices of the contracting countries, and postal conventions resulting from diplomatic negotiations between the foreign offices of the contracting countries, which were, in fact, formal treaties. All agencies, of course, acted under laws passed by Parliament.

In the United States, the laws of Congress governed postal affairs, including the setting of rates. The Postmaster General had been given authority to make postal arrangements with foreign countries by the act of 3 March 1825, but this was conceived to mean within the context of existing law. At the time these negotiations were undertaken, the authority of the postmaster general in regard to the making of postal conventions was an unsettled question.

There was a difference in the concept of the function of postage held in the two countries. In the United States, postage rates were set at levels designed to yield revenues sufficient to cover the costs and expenses of furnishing the service. The Post Office Department was not to become a burden on the public treasury, but neither was it, except incidentally, to furnish revenue for general use. Postage was not conceived to be a basis for taxation, and this concept was applied to domestic and foreign mail services alike.

The British were far more pragmatic in their concept of the function of postage than were the Americans. While liberal policies were adopted for domestic postage in 1840, this liberal attitude did not extend to the foreign mail service. Many of Britain's foreign postal rates were set at levels designed not only to pay the cost of the service but also to produce revenue for the general treasury. Avowedly, these were looked upon as a use tax, but this was not uniformly the case. The "Colonial" packet rates produced revenues that just about covered costs, while the 8d. ship rate, for which Britain usually performed no service, was purely a tax. Foreign transit rates generally produced revenues in excess of costs. Postal rates, however, were conceived to have functions beyond those of paying for service or of producing a revenue. Postal rates could be used as an instrument in diplomacy; they could be used to promote trade; or, as in the present case, they could be used as a protective tariff.

This difference in the concept of the function of postage was clearly brought out in an interview with Lord Palmerston, reported by Bancroft in his dispatch of 11 August 1848.[5]

> On my hinting that the difficulty lay in Great Britain's demanding pay for work which the United States had done: he said, that the Postage levied on letters brought into the United Kingdom, was to be considered as a revenue duty, and not as the price paid for service rendered. If it were so considered, then England, would certainly have committed an injustice in taking the price of another's labour: but that it is a revenue impost, or tax, to be levied equally on all letters brought into the United Kingdom whether by foreign or Home packets.

On 3 July 1847, Major Hobbie arrived from Bremen, and negotiations were immediately opened for a postal convention between the two countries. At the British Post Office it was resolved to confine the negotiation to two points, namely, the reciprocal grant of closed mails, and the option as to prepayment. Hobbie was under instruction to use the transit rate on mail to or from Boston and Canada as leverage in securing a just settlement. To the British, this was not a separate issue and in any reciprocal arrangement would be covered by a general agreement concerning closed mails. At the time these negotiations were undertaken, the existing agreement was a postal convention between Great Britain and the United States, known as the *Wickliffe Agreement,* made on 14 February 1845 and dealing exclusively with the Canadian closed mail. The agreement

---

[4] Ibid, p. 471 (enclosure).

[5] Dept. of State, *Treaties,* p. 494. [*See also* Dept. of State, 58 Despatches, G.B., 84, 11 Aug. 1848.]

was not published in either country; neither an original nor a copy has been found in the archives of the Post Office Department. A copy of the original signed agreement, which is in the archives of the British Post Office, was sent to the Department of State in 1932 and is now in their files. The entire text is given in the Department of State's *Treaties and Other International Acts of the United States of America,* volume 5, pages 478–479.

The transit rate set by the convention was, peculiarly, 1 franc (18⁶⁄₁₀¢) per ounce for mail between Boston and St. Johns, Canada, during the season of steamboat navigation on Lake Champlain and Highgate, Vermont, in the remainder of the year. Notice of abrogation of this convention was sent to Bancroft on 17 July 1847, to be served on the British Post Office if no progress were made in the negotiations. Hobbie was unable to settle anything of importance; the position of the two governments remained the same, and the discriminatory charge continued to be collected on American packet mail. Bancroft, therefore, served the notice of abrogation on 16 August 1847 (effective three months thereafter). When Hobbie left England for America on 24 October 1847, on the *Washington*, negotiations had virtually ended.

The matter rested there for several months. In his annual message of 7 December 1847,[6] President Polk called the matter to the attention of Congress and referred to the report of the postmaster general [7] for a detailed account of the affair. Congress took action on the recommendation of the postmaster general on 27 June 1848 by passing the following act: [8]

> That the Postmaster General, under the Direction of the President of the United States, be, and is hereby authorized and empowered to charge upon and collect from, all letters and other mailable matter carried to or from any port of the United States, in any foreign packet ship or other vessel, the same rate or rates of charge for American postage, which the government to which such foreign packet or other vessel belongs imposes upon letters and other mailable matter conveyed to or from such foreign country in American packets or other vessels, as the postage of such government, and at any time to revoke the same....

It should be noted that British packets are not specifically mentioned, as American packets had been mentioned in the British Post Office order of 9 June 1847.

Since the United States was protesting the British charge as a violation of the "most favored nation" clause included in the commercial convention of 3 July 1815, the act of 27 June 1848 was carefully worded so that the law in no way appeared to discriminate against the British. Since, however, British packets were the only foreign packets then plying between Great Britain and the United States, the discriminatory effect was inevitable.

This law is generally known to postal historians as the "reprisal" or "retaliatory" act, and covers showing its rating marks are popular with collectors. The first letters showing a superaddition of the 24¢-packet postage to the inland postage on mail *from* the United States were conveyed by the Cunarder *Britannia* from New York on 5 July 1848, arriving at Liverpool on 17 July. The first mail so rated *to* the United States left Liverpool on the Cunarder *Caledonia* on 24 June 1848 and arrived in New York on 8 July. From this time forward until after the signing of the United States-British treaty, all packet mail between the two countries required double sea postage.

The reaction to the law in Britain was prompt. Commercial interests protested. Questions were put to the ministry in the House of Commons, and those to whom these questions were directed attempted to place responsibility on others. "Lord Palmerston seemed to think the matter belonged to the Chancellor of the Exchequer and with Lord Clanricarde. The Chancellor, on Friday last, said the matter lay with Lord Clanricarde. . . ." [9] The London *Times* invited the government to state its case by publishing its correspondence.[10]

Negotiations were reopened, and progress was now made. No useful purpose would be served by reporting the details of the vast amount of existing correspondence relating to these negotiations; the proposals, the counterproposals, and the impasses. Therefore, only those that appear to have been eventually significant will be mentioned.

The inland rates proved to be an obstacle for a time. Clanricarde proposed that the inland rate be 3¢ in each country. To this Bancroft objected on two grounds, namely, that the great expanses of the United States, as compared with the United Kingdom, would require a higher rate, and that Britain would be charg-

---

[6] *Senate Executive Document* 1, 30 Cong., 1 sess., serial 510, pp. 33–34.

[7] *House Executive Document* 35, 30 Cong., 1 sess., serial 516, pp. 748–749.

[8] U.S., 9 *Statutes at Large* 241–242.

[9] Dept. of State, *Treaties,* p. 492. [*See also* Dept. of State, 58 Despatches, G.B., 82, 28 July 1848 (Bancroft to Buchanan).]

[10] *Ibid.*

ing United States users more than her subjects were paying for the same service. Bancroft proposed that the existing inland rates in each country be used. Clanricarde objected to this on the ground that the variation in the United States rate would make it too difficult and expensive to account for international letters. Although Clanricarde was later willing to accept this proposal, Bancroft had reconsidered, for he was now thinking that the agreement should take a different form.

It was in Bancroft's mind that it would be desirable to establish uniform rates. However, his concept of the powers of the postmaster general rested upon the act of 3 March 1825 and the joint resolution of Congress of 15 June 1844, neither of which gave the postmaster general authority to vary the postal rates set by Congress. As "agent of the Post Office Department," Bancroft did not feel he had authority to establish a uniform rate. Although it was an unsettled matter, Bancroft held that a treaty, signed by the president with the advice and consent of the Senate, was the supreme law of the land and could supersede an earlier and conflicting statute. Bancroft was able to sign an agreement between the two post offices as "agent of the Post Office Department," or he could sign a treaty as "Minister." [11] If a treaty were signed, rates could be varied and arrangements made that would be impossible under existing law. It was Bancroft's decision that a treaty be sought.

Britain's decision to enter into negotiations for the formation of a treaty rested largely with the personalities involved. Sir Charles Wood had never favored the order of 9 June 1847 and welcomed the opportunity of taking a larger part in the negotiations. Although Palmerston does not appear to have favored the Post Office order, he supported Clanricarde as a member of the ministry. But Palmerston was also irritated by recent American conduct. In an unguarded moment in an interview with Bancroft, he gave vent to his feelings: [12]

> To the suggestion that the course of the British Government on this subject might produce an unpleasant impression on the public mind in America, Lord Palmerston spoke with warmth: 'That is worn threadbare,' said he, with great emphasis. 'You want us always to yield to you, in order to keep you in an amicable mood. It has always been so; and we have always yielded to you. We did so on the North-Eastern-Boundary-question; we did so on the Oregon question; and what is the Consequence? There never comes up any disturbance in this country but from one end of the United States to the other you begin an outcry against England. Your ——— (naming one of the recent orators in behalf of Ireland), and so many others, are always and on every occasion uttering all manner of evil about us.'

Palmerston did not oppose a treaty, but it is not known that he favored this form of agreement. In one of his dispatches, Bancroft referred to a note from Palmerston as "the apology of the Post Office for its unfriendly course." [13] In a long interview with Prime Minister Lord Russell, Bancroft reports him as having said he "was sensible that no fit solution of the question was expected from the London Post Office Department, and promised as one of the Lords of the Treasury, himself to give immediate attention to the subject." [14]

It is clear that the ministry was divided in its opinion of the propriety and wisdom of the Post Office order of 9 June 1847. Under this circumstance, Clanricarde did not wish to take sole responsibility for the framing of a postal convention. A treaty appealed to him because the ministry would then share the responsibility. Britain, therefore, also made the decision to form a treaty rather than a post-office agreement.

Bancroft was now able to deal with the problem of the inland rates by proposing a new formula for uniformity. In his dispatch to Buchanan of 15 December 1848, he explained the manner in which this was accomplished: [15]

> To keep just accounts under so varying rates would have been difficult. I agreed, therefore, to make an average of the inland rates in each country, . . . (California and Oregon excepted) . . . and to adopt uniformly these average rates. In England the inland rate on a letter, if paid in advance, is one penny: if not paid in advance, as most foreign letters are not, it is two pence. Three half pence, then, is a just and fair uniform British inland rate. For America an inland letter, if received at a Post Office, for delivery, and not for transmission, pays two cents; if transmitted it pays a varying rate of Five or Ten cents. The average is therefore Five and two thirds of a cent—less than six cents.

Hence, a uniform inland rate of 5¢ per single letter was adopted for all of the United States (California and Oregon excepted) regardless of distance; and for Great

---

[11] Ibid., p. 503.

[12] Ibid., p. 494 [see also Dept. of State, 58 Despatches, G.B., 84, 11 Aug. 1848 (Bancroft to Buchanan).]

[13] Ibid., p. 481.

[14] Ibid.

[15] Ibid., p. 496. [See also Dept. of State, 59 Despatches, G.B., 108, 15 Dec. 1848 (Bancroft to Buchanan).]

Britain, a uniform rate of 1½d., or 3¢, from or to any point in the United Kingdom.

Cave Johnson disapproved of it. In his letter to Bancroft of 28 November 1848, he said: [16]

> I can never give my Consent to any Postal arrangement which will authorize the letters of the Citizens of the United States, when Conveyed in the English Mails, to be Charged more than is paid by British subjects for the same service and at the same time, undertake to Convey British letters in the Mails of the United States for less than the price paid by our own Citizens.

That just about summed up the situation. A British subject in London would be able to mail a letter whose conveyance from Boston to New Orleans would cost him only 5¢, while a resident of Boston would have to pay 10¢ for the same service. At the same time, an American would have to pay 3¢ for conveyance of a letter from Liverpool to London, while a resident of Liverpool could prepay it there for 2¢. But Cave Johnson was no longer to have anything to say about what was done; neither was Clanricarde. While they would both continue to give advice, which need not be noted, the effective negotiations had passed out of their hands and into the hands of Sir Charles Wood and George Bancroft. The decision to form a treaty had made it possible to circumvent the postmasters of both countries.

The United States–British Treaty of 1848

The completed treaty was signed on 15 December 1848. The United States Senate consented on 5 January 1849, and formal ratification took place the next day. Great Britain ratified it on 23 January, and ratifications were exchanged 26 January. It was proclaimed on 15 February 1849.[17] Significant articles of the treaty are excerpted, as follows:[18]

I. For a single rate of one-half ounce, "an uniform sea rate of 8d, or 16 cents; and such postage shall belong to the country by which the packet conveying the letters is furnished."

II. For a single rate of one-half ounce, an inland postage rate of 1½d. (3¢) in Great Britain and of 5¢ in the United States.

III. Provided that the above three rates be combined into one international rate of 24¢, "of which payment in advance shall be optional in either country. It shall, however, not be permitted to pay less than the whole combined rate."

IV. Each country was at liberty to use the scale of progression in use in its own territory for charging inland postage.

V and VI. Each country granted to the other the right to send closed mails over the territory of the British North American provinces and of the United States at the rate of inland postage charged under the Convention.

VII and VIII. Reciprocally granted the right to each country to send closed mails over the territory of the other, to or from colonies, possessions or foreign countries.

IX. The rate per ounce, net weight, of closed mails was fixed at two single-letter rates "with the addition of 25 percent on the amount of postage . . ."

X. Each country was to account to the other for closed mails.

XI. Letters sent by one country, to pass in transit over the territory of the other, were to be delivered to the other country free of all postage, whether packet or inland. On letters to countries to which they cannot be forwarded unless the British postage is also prepaid, the United States is to collect and account for this postage to the British Post Office, and vice versa.

XII. Provided "that the rate of postage to be taken for transit postage between Great Britain and foreign countries shall be the same as the rate now taken, or which may hereafter be taken by the British Post Office upon letters to or from said foreign countries, when posted at the port of arrival or delivered to the port of departure of the packet conveying the mails between the United Kingdom and the United States. . . . .

> The above rate is irrespective of and beyond the inland rate to be taken in the United States on letters posted or delivered therein, when conveyed by British packet, and also above the sea rate, when conveyed by American packet. . .

An exactly similar provision secured the same conditions for letters posted or delivered in the United Kingdom.

Letters to or from France were specifically exempted from the provisions of Article XII. The contracting parties, however, agreed to invite France, without loss of time, to enter into negotiations to effect an agreement for the mutual exchange of closed mails "as may be most conducive to the interest of the three countries."

Articles for "carrying into execution the Postal Convention of December 15, 1848" were signed at Washington on 14 May 1849 and "so far as they are not already in force, shall come into operation on the 1st of July next."[19] These articles were agreed upon by

---

[16] Ibid., p. 503.
[17] Ibid., p. 470.
[18] *British and Foreign State Papers,* vol. 36, pp. 443–449.

[19] *British and Foreign State Papers,* vol. 37, p. 51.

the post offices of the two countries and take the form of what are usually called "detailed regulations." Such articles are considered to have the same force as if they had been inserted, word for word, in the original treaty. While the treaty was diplomatically negotiated and dealt with general arrangements, these articles were drawn by the post offices of the two countries and supplied the details necessary to implement the treaty. Certain of these articles will be mentioned as need arises.

Exchange Office Accounting and Accounting Marks

The exchange office was the focal point of the foreign-mail service. All mail addressed to a foreign country was routed to one of the exchange offices. These offices were established by treaty or other postal convention, and each office in the United States had an office or offices in the foreign country with which it exchanged mail. The exchange offices made up the mails to be dispatched. This was governed by the letter-bills, which were printed forms whose format had been designed in such a way as to account for the mail in the manner prescribed by the treaty provisions.

Usually, letter-bills for ordinary mail showed the number of letters, the rate, and the amount of postage, while letter-bills for closed mail also showed the net weight of the mail. Letters were wrapped in packages and banded or labeled with paper of a distinctive color, such as pink for unpaid letters, yellow for prepaid, and so forth. A copy of the pertinent letter-bill was enclosed in each package, while a letter-bill for the whole mail was separately mailed to the exchange office to which the mail was directed. Upon receipt of the mail, the exchange office checked its contents against the letter-bill, noted any discrepancies, and mailed an acknowledgment of receipt to the dispatching office. The amounts shown on the letter-bill were posted to the accounts, and account balances were settled between the countries at regular intervals prescribed by the treaty.

While the actual accounting was performed on the letter-bill, it was also prescribed that the letter be so marked as to indicate the amount of debit or credit

TABLE 4.—*Exchange Office Accounting for the Twenty-four Cent International Postal Rate*

Postage	Rate	British Packet	American Packet	British Packet	American Packet
U.S. inland	5¢	(a)	(a)	5¢	5¢
Packet	16	16¢	(a)	(b)	16
British inland	3	3	3	(b)	(b)
	24				
U.S. credit to G.B. on prepaid letters posted in U.S. (red), or British debit to U.S. on unpaid letters posted in G.B. (black)		19	3		
British credit to U.S. on prepaid letters posted in G.B. (red), or U.S. debit to G.B. on unpaid letters posted in U.S. (black)				5	21

NOTE. The above rates applied to all of the United States except California and Oregon. At the time the treaty was signed, the domestic rate to California and Oregon was 40¢. If, in the above table, 40¢ is substituted for the 5¢ United States inland postage, the rate, debits and credits, and the retentions on mail to or from California and Oregon are secured. The act of 3 March 1851, effective on 1 July, required that double postage be charged for letters conveyed in excess of 3,000 miles. This was applied to the 5¢ inland rate of the United States-British treaty and reduced the transit postage to California and Oregon to 10¢. On 1 April 1855, the domestic rate for distances in excess of 3,000 miles became 10¢ the single rate. Therefore, between 1 July 1851 and 1 July 1863, 10¢ should be substituted for the 5¢ United States inland postage in the foregoing table. On 1 July 1863, a uniform rate of domestic postage was established for all of the United States and the amounts shown in the foregoing table prevailed, no additional postage being charged on letters to or from the Pacific coast. Figure 11 illustrates some of the markings used on single-rate covers.

[a] Retained from prepayment or collection by the United States.

[b] Retained from prepayment or collection by Great Britain.

entered in the letter-bill by the dispatching office. This was necessary because letters were sometimes missent, returned, or forwarded, and once they became separated from their original letter-bill, it was impossible to know how they had originally been accounted for, unless the letter were so marked. Table 4 shows the accounting for the 24¢ international rate. It presents the amount of postage retained from prepayments or collections, and the amount of debit or credit stamped on each letter. It was required that debits be shown in black and credits in red ink. Although it was not prescribed, it was customary to show amounts to be collected in black and prepayments in red ink. Restatements of prepaid rates were always shown in red ink.

Exchange offices were established at New York and Boston in the United States and at Liverpool, London, and Southampton in Great Britain. All the British offices were to exchange mail with all the United States offices, except that Southampton was not to exchange mail with Boston. Until the Collins line began to run in 1850, therefore, Boston made up no American packet mail. Other exchange offices were added later, and they will be mentioned at the appropriate time.

International Covers between the United States and Great Britain (The Retaliatory Period)

Collectors have long been interested in covers during the period in which the Retaliatory Rate was in force and attempt to secure covers showing the 24¢, 29¢, and 34¢ rates for both incoming and outgoing letters to or from the Boston and New York offices. As an aid to those who may wish to start such a collection, the sailing and arrival dates of the Cunard and Ocean lines for this period are reported in Table 5. The Ocean line sailings given are for the entire period during which the British charged packet postage on American packet letters.

On 14 December 1848, Sir Charles Wood wrote Brancroft a note proposing that the double charge for sea postage be eliminated as early as possible. Bancroft accepted the proposal on the same day.[20] It was

---

[20] Dept. of State, *Treaties*, p. 499. [*See also* Leon Reussile, "Letters by Cunarders to the United States and There Retaliatory Rated," *Postal History Journal* 2, 1: 40.]

FIGURE 11.—DEBIT AND CREDIT MARKINGS used on single-rate covers under the United States-British treaty of 1848.

ended in Great Britain by a treasury warrant dated 22 December 1848, to become effective on 29 December,[21] and in the United States by a post office order dated 3 January 1849.[22] Between these dates and 15 February 1849, there was a period in which the former rates were restored. Since covers showing these "restored" rates are also popular with collectors, the sailing and arrival dates of the Cunard line are presented in Table 6. There were no sailings or arrivals by the Ocean line during this period, hence it is not known whether Britain would have assessed the 8d. ship rate. Sailings of the first vessels of both the Cunard and Ocean lines under the new treaty are also given.

Retaliatory Rate Covers

Figure 12 illustrates a cover prepaid with a 1s. and a 1d. stamp. The 1s. stamp paid the packet postage, while the 1d. stamp paid a late-mailing fee for a letter posted at one of the London branch offices between 6:00 P.M. and 7:00 P.M.[23] On the reverse is a Maltese-cross postmark reading LS/15SP15/1848, which is a marking of the Lombard Street office and shows the

---

[21] Edward Hertslet, ed., *Commercial Treaties*, vol. 8, pp. 935–937.

[22] *Shipping and Commercial List and New York Prices Current* 35, 3 (10 Jan. 1849): 11.

[23] W. G. Stitt Dibden, "The 6d. Fee," *Great Britain Philatelist* 4, 1 (Feb. 1964): 13.

TABLE 5.—*Cunard and Ocean Line Sailings (During the "Retaliatory Rate" Period)*

Departure date, Liverpool	Arrival date, U.S.	Ship	Port	Departure date, U.S.	Arrival date, Liverpool
1848	1848	Cunard Line		1848	1848
		Britannia	New York	5 July	17 July
		Cambria	Boston	12 July	25 July
24 June	8 July	*Caledonia*	New York	19 July	2 Aug.
1 July	12 July	*Niagara*	Boston	26 July	9 Aug.
8 July	21 July	*Hibernia*	New York	2 Aug.	16 Aug.
15 July	27 July	*Europa* M/V [a]	Boston	9 Aug.	22 Aug.
22 July	4 Aug.	*America*	New York	16 Aug.	30 Aug.
1848	1848			1848	1848/49
29 July	14 Aug.	*Acadia*	Boston	23 Aug.	6 Sept.
5 Aug.	20 Aug.	*Cambria*	New York	30 Aug.	13 Sept.
12 Aug.	27 Aug.	*Britannia*	Boston	6 Sept.	20 Sept.
19 Aug.	1 Sept.	*Niagara*	New York	13 Sept.	27 Sept.
26 Aug.	8 Sept.	*Hibernia*	Boston	20 Sept.	2 Oct.
2 Sept.	15 Sept.	*Europa*	New York	27 Sept.	10 Oct.
9 Sept.	25 Sept.	*Acadia*	Boston	4 Oct.	17 Oct.
16 Sept.	30 Sept.	*America*	New York	11 Oct.	23 Oct.
23 Sept.	6 Oct.	*Cambria*	Boston	18 Oct.	31 Oct.
30 Sept.	17 Oct.	*Britannia*	New York	25 Oct.	7 Nov.
7 Oct.	20 Oct.	*Niagara*	Boston	1 Nov.	13 Nov.
14 Oct.	28 Oct.	*Europa*	New York	8 Nov.	20 Nov.
21 Oct.	4 Nov.	*Hibernia*	Boston	15 Nov.	26 Nov.
28 Oct.	9 Nov.	*America*	New York	22 Nov.	4 Dec.
4 Nov.	19 Nov.	*Acadia*	Boston	29 Nov.	13 Dec.
11 Nov.	25 Nov.	*Cambria*	New York	6 Dec.	20 Dec.
18 Nov.	7 Dec.	*Britannia* L/V [b]	Boston	13 Dec.	28 Dec.
25 Nov.	14 Dec.	*Canada* M/V [a]	New York	20 Dec.	2 Jan.
2 Dec.	16 Dec.	*Niagara*	Boston	27 Dec.	9 Jan.
16 Dec.	30 Dec.	*Europa*	New York		
	1847/48	Ocean Line		1847/48	
	M/V [a]	*Washington*	New York	1 June	
	30 July	*Washington*	New York	23 Sept.	
	9 Nov.	*Washington*	New York	18 Nov.	
	15 Jan.	*Washington*	New York	20 Feb.	
		By Bremen treaty			
	M/V [a]	*Hermann*	New York	20 Mar.	
	7 Apr.	*Washington*	New York	20 Apr.	
Returned	22 Apr.	*Washington*	New York	25 Apr.	Sailed
	22 May	*Hermann*	New York	20 June	
	17 June	*Washington*	New York	20 July	
	4 Aug.	*Hermann*	New York	21 Aug.	
	5 Sept.	*Washington*	New York	20 Sept.	
	4 Oct.	*Hermann*	New York	20 Oct.	
	4 Nov.	*Washington*	New York	20 Nov.	

[a] Maiden voyage.
[b] Last voyage.

TABLE 6.—*Cunard and Ocean Line Sailings (During the "Restored Rate" Period)*

Departure Date, Liverpool	Arrival Date, U.S.	Ship	Port	Departure Date, U.S.	Arrival Date, Liverpool
1848/49	1849			1849	1849
		Restored Rates			
		Cunard Line			
		Europa	New York	10 Jan.	22 Jan.
30 Dec.	12 Jan.	*America*	Boston	24 Jan.	4 Feb.
13 Jan.	29 Jan.	*Canada*	New York	7 Feb.	19 Feb.
27 Jan.	11 Feb.	*Niagara*	Boston		
10 Feb.	24 Feb.	*Europa*	New York		
		First under the Treaty			
		Cunard Line			
		Niagara	Boston	21 Feb.	6 Mar.
24 Feb.	9 Mar.	*America*	Boston		
		Ocean Line			
		Hermann	New York	20 Feb.	
	13 Apr.	*Hermann*	New York		

date the mail was made up. On the following day, 16 September (a Saturday), this letter left Liverpool onboard the Cunarder *America* bound for New York where it arrived on 30 September. Since the letter was addressed to New York, it was marked for a collection of only the 24¢ packet postage. As the packet postage had already been paid in Britain, the collection of a packet postage in the United States represented the retaliatory charge authorized by the act of 27 June 1848, which required the collection of packet postage on letters conveyed by foreign (British) packets.

Figure 13 illustrates a cover posted in London, addressed to New York and prepaid with a 1s. stamp. On the reverse is a Maltese-cross marking reading ls/17no17/1848, which shows that the mail was made up at the Lombard Street office on 17 November. The letter was conveyed to Boston by the Cunarder *Britannia* which sailed from Liverpool on 18 November on her last voyage for the Cunard line. Arriving in Boston on 7 December, this letter was forwarded to New York, a distance of under 300 miles and hence was rated for a collection of 29¢ (24¢ packet and 5¢ inland postages). Again, the letter bore a double charge for sea postage.

Figure 14 illustrates a cover posted in Charleston, South Carolina, on 7 September 1848, addressed to Liverpool. It was prepaid 34¢ (24¢ packet and 10¢ U.S. inland postages) for a letter posted over 300 miles from the port of departure. The letter was conveyed to Liverpool by the Cunarder *Niagara* which sailed from New York on 13 September and arrived in Liverpool on 25 September 1848. The Liverpool office rated it for a collection of 1s. packet postage. Thus, the packet postage was collected by each country.

Figure 15 illustrates a letter posted in Liverpool, addressed to New York. This letter weighed over one half ounce and required a prepayment of 2s. in Liverpool, whence it was forwarded to Boston by the Cunarder *Acadia* which arrived there on 14 August 1848. Since New York was under 300 miles from Boston, the letter was marked for a collection of 58¢ (2 x 29¢), which represented a double-rate collection of inland and packet postages.

Restored-Rate Cover

Figure 16 illustrates a cover posted in Liverpool, addressed to Princeton, New Jersey. It was prepaid 1s. in Liverpool, whence it was forwarded by the Cunarder *Europa,* which arrived in New York on 24 February 1849. The New York office rated it for a collection of 7¢ (5¢ inland for a letter conveyed under 300 miles plus 2¢ ship postage), the 24¢ packet postage

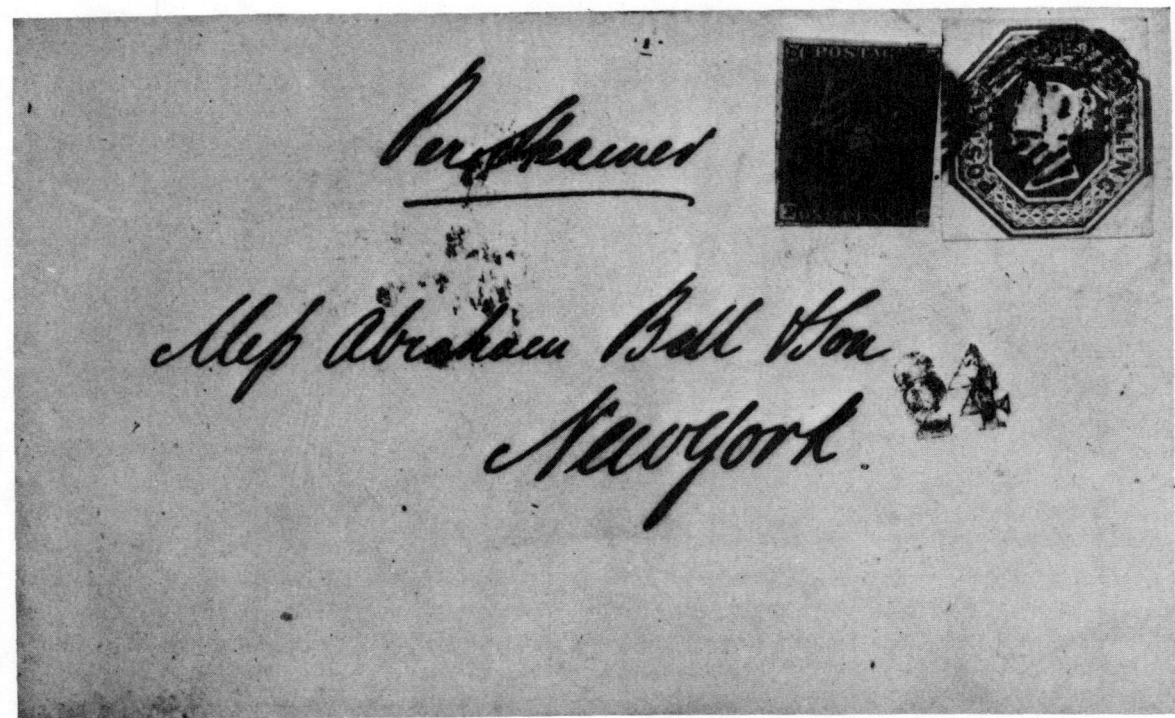

FIGURE 12.—COVER, from London to New York, 1848.

FIGURE 13.—COVER, from London to New York, 1848.

FIGURE 14.—COVER, from Charleston, S.C., to Liverpool, 1848. (*Melvin W. Schuh collection*)

no longer being assessed. This letter is an example of the last mail rated before the treaty became effective and the last mail rated according to the restored rates.

The Progression

Article IV of the treaty provided that "each country shall be at liberty to employ . . . the scale of progression in operation in its own territory for charging inland rates of postage." Immediately after the treaty was received in the United States, notice of this progression was published to the public and to postmasters through a post office announcement signed by Cave Johnson and dated 8 January 1849: [24]

> Letters posted or charged in the United States will be rated at a half ounce to the single letter, over a half ounce and not exceeding an ounce as a double letter, over an ounce and not exceeding an ounce and a half as a treble letter, and so on, each half ounce or fractional excess constituting a rate. . . .

[24] *Shipping and Commercial List*, 35, 3 (10 Jan. 1849): 11.

The scale of progression in operation in Great Britain was:

> For a letter not over one half ounce—1 rate
> Over one half, but not over one ounce—2 rates
> Over one, but not over two ounces—4 rates
> and so on, 2 rates being charged for each additional ounce or fraction of an ounce.

Since the United States progression allowed a triple rate (and further odd-numbered rates), while the British progression did not allow any odd-numbered rates after the first, attempts to apply this dual progression to the same letter produced some ludicrous situations. A good illustration would be an unpaid letter posted in Great Britain to be conveyed to the United States by British packet. It is presumed the letter weighed slightly over an ounce and, accordingly, the British Post Office would have debited the United States with four rates, or 76¢ (4×19¢). The United States exchange office, however, would only be able to charge three rates, or 72¢ (3×24¢). Thus, on one of the largest classes of mail, the United States would pay Great Britain 76¢ for each letter and only be able to collect 72¢ from the addressee.

Figure 15.—Cover, from Liverpool to New York, 1848.
(*Photograph by Smithsonian*)

Obviously, the negotiation of this article was a blunder on Bancroft's part. It evidently represents an attempt to preserve the laws of Congress in the treaty, but after the decision to form a full-fledged treaty had been reached, existing United States law no longer needed to be preserved. It is certain that Bancroft did not work out the rates under Article IV, for had he done so, he could not have allowed it to stand. Before he submitted the final treaty to Secretary of State Buchanan, he must have realized that there was a defect in this article, for he appended the following postscript to his dispatch of transmittal: [25]

P.S. By Article IV, you will observe that I have reserved for our Country the liberty, on letters over a half ounce in weight, to employ the scale of progression in operation in its own territory. But, at the same time, I cannot but recommend the adoption of the English scale of progression. It would raise the rate on scarcely one letter in a hundred; at the same time it would save the Post Office a great deal of labour on every letter transmitted. The success of the cheap postage system depends on simplifying the manual processes, and diminishing labor. Where rates are high it is proper to weigh each letter; and so to have a scale of progression by the half ounce. Where rates are uniform and low, the scale of progression should be by the ounce, so that the Post Office clerks may, without often using their scales, at once decide what rate attaches to each letter.

While the above is an excellent general discussion of the advantages of rates based upon the ounce rather than the half ounce, it did not pertain to the British progression. The first two steps in that progression were based upon the half ounce, and these two steps would include all but a few letters. It is difficult to see how the adoption of the British scale of progression would have reduced clerical time spent in rating letters. One wonders if Bancroft did not wish to confess his real reason for recommending the adoption of the British progression.

The Post Office Department, however, had to face the practical aspects of applying Article IV and shortly recommended to Congress the passage of a law that would make the British progression operative in the United States. Accordingly, the following clause was

---

[25] Dept. of State, p. 498. [*See also* Dept. of State, 59 Despatches, G.B., 108, 15 Dec. 1848.]

FIGURE 16.—COVER, from Liverpool to Princeton, New Jersey, 1849. (*Photograph by Smithsonian*)

appended to the Post Office Appropriations Act of 3 March 1849: [26]

> That to better enable the postal treaty with Great Britain to go into full effect with equal advantage to both countries, letters shall be mailed as composing one rate only where the letter does not exceed the weight of half an ounce avoirdupois; where it exceeds half an ounce but does not exceed an ounce, as composing two rates; where it exceeds an ounce but does not exceed two ounces, as composing four rates . . . and in like progression for each additional ounce, or fraction of an ounce.

While the Appropriations Act did not become effective until the beginning of the new fiscal year, 1 July 1849, Postmaster General Jacob Collamer, who had succeeded Cave Johnson, lost no time in putting the law into effect. The following appeared in the *New York Daily Tribune* of Monday, 19 March 1849:

> Hereafter, when a letter exceeds an ounce in weight, but does not exceed two ounces, it will be rated with four charges of single postage; when it exceeds two ounces, but does not exceed three, it will be rated with six charges of single postage, and so on, there being a single postage on the first half ounce, a double charge for the first ounce, and two additional charges for each succeeding ounce, or *fraction of an ounce,* beyond the first ounce. This is ordered in virtue of the Act of Congress approved March 3, 1849. . . .
>
> J Collamer, P.M. GENERAL
> P.O. Department, March 15, 1849.

Thus, the blunder in negotiating Article IV of the treaty saddled all of the United States with the British progression, domestic letters as well as those between the United States and Great Britain, under the treaty. The *American Almanac* for 1850 duly shows the domestic progression as follows:

> A letter over half an ounce in weight, but not exceeding an ounce, is rated with two charges of single postage; over one ounce, but not exceeding two ounces, with four charges.

---
[26] 9 Statutes at Large 379.

Thus, on the following sailings and arrivals, a triple rate was possible:

TABLE 7.—*Cunard and Ocean Line Sailings*

Arrival date, U.S.	Ship	Port	Departure date, U.S.
1849	Cunard Line		1849
24 Feb.	*Niagara*	Boston	21 Feb.
	Europa	New York	7 Mar.
	Ocean Line		
	Hermann	New York	20 Feb.

Article IX of the *Articles of Execution* for carrying the treaty into effect made the British progression apply to all mail exchanged under the treaty. Once this had been firmly established by treaty, Congress was able to revert to the former progression for domestic mail, and did so in the act of 3 March 1851.

Optional Prepayment

The joint resolution of Congress of 15 June 1844 authorized the postmaster general to make agreements with foreign countries in such a way that the entire postage could be paid where the letter was mailed or received. This was taken to mean that United States policy for postal agreements with foreign countries must provide for optional prepayment. Therefore, all postal conventions made by the United States during the period here considered provided for optional prepayment, at least, for the international rate. Transit rates under these agreements often required part payments or full prepayment of the entire postage.

Coupled with the provision for optional prepayment in Article III of the United States-British treaty was the clause, "It shall, however, not be permitted to pay less than the whole combined rate." Regulations issued during the life of the treaty were usually careful to point out to postmasters and to the public something similar to the following, found in the 1859 regulations: "If anything less than the whole is prepaid, no account is taken of it, and *it is entirely lost to the sender.*" This provision was evidently made to prevent the public from making partial payments which would be very difficult and expensive for the exchange offices to handle in their accounting. But what was to happen when the local office in which a letter was mailed made an error and charged a person who presented it in good faith less than the whole postage? When the exchange office discovered such an error, was the person who had mailed the letter and paid the amount demanded by the local office to suffer the loss of his prepayment? The treaty seemed to say so. The *Articles of Execution,* however, provided an "escape" clause. Article XVII states:

> If, in checking the mails transmitted to the respective offices of exchange, the amount of postage of any of the articles shall be found to differ from that entered in the letter-bill by the dispatching office, such articles shall be checked by 2 officers, and the corrected amount, which is entered by them on the verification side of the letter-bill, shall be accepted as the true amount.

Figure 17 illustrates a cover that exemplifies Article XVII. It was accepted by the Liverpool office as a letter weighing not over one ounce and, accordingly, was prepaid by a pair of 1s. stamps. When the letter arrived at the exchange office, it was found to weigh over one ounce. It was marked ABOVE *1* OZ., the *1* being filled in in manuscript. A credit of 10¢ was given for the two rates prepaid (see 10/CENTS marking), and a debit was made for the two rates unpaid (see 38/CENTS marking). At this point there are two possible explanations of the remaining markings.

One explanation is that two officers of the Liverpool office examined and corrected the letter-bill on its verification side. They then marked the cover in manuscript *Paid 24 [pence]/Un[paid] 24 [pence]* for the two rates accepted and the two rates considered unpaid. The two officers then placed their initials on the letter, *RIL* under the o of oz. and *IW* at the top of the bracket before *Paid 24*. The letter was then forwarded to Boston by the R.M.S. *Cambria,* which arrived there on 14 November 1851. A confused Boston office charged only 24¢ instead of the 48¢ to which, by this procedure, it was entitled.

The other explanation, suggested by the late Maurice C. Blake, is that after marking the letter with a credit of 10¢ and a debit of 38¢, two officers of the Liverpool exchange office corrected the letter-bill and forwarded the letter to Boston. The Boston office marked the letter in manuscript *Paid 24/Un[paid]24,* and the two officers who examined the letter and the letter-bill marked their initials upon the letter. Boston then marked the cover for a collection of 24¢.

Regardless of which of these explanations may be correct, it is agreed that the letter was rated under the provision stated in Article XVII of the *Articles of Execution,* quoted above. If the scarcity of covers of this kind is an indication, the exchange offices used the procedure sparingly.

FIGURE 17.—COVER, from Liverpool to Providence, Rhode Island, 1851.

The Packet Rate

Postmaster General Cave Johnson felt that the only *leverage* of importance held by the United States in bargaining with the British was the transit of the British mails between Boston and Canada. In his original instructions to Major Hobbie, he pointed out: "The terms upon which the Canadian mails are now transported through the United States may be made the basis of any further agreement with the British Post Office." [27] Bancroft used the transit of Canadian mails to "bargain" for a lower packet rate, but in so doing, he made an additional concession to the British.

Clanricarde had proposed a sea rate of 10d.; Bancroft thought it ought to be 7d. At this point negotiations were deadlocked, but the impasse was broken by a British proposal of an 8d. packet rate if the United States would agree to Article V and the application of the uniform 5¢ inland postage to Article IX as the transit rate for Canadian mails. Bancroft explained his acceptance of these terms in his dispatch to Buchanan of 15 December 1848: [28]

> I did not think I should be justified in refusing to take the Canada mails across our Territory at the Uniform inland rate established by Article II. It seemed to me wise to treat our Canadian neighbors liberally: A special Act of Congress on the subject of mails in transit to Canada, favors such a policy: the concession of a sea rate of Eight pence was coupled with my assent to this Fifth Article.

Thus the closed-mail transit rate for Canadian mails became 12½¢ per ounce (2 x 5¢, plus 25 percent). Bancroft could have bargained for further concessions from the British. Cave Johnson thought he should have done so, as did his successors until 1857. Had Bancroft examined Article LII of the Anglo-French treaty of 3 April 1843, he would have discovered that France was at that time paying Britain 16¢ per ounce for transit of mails between Boston and Canada, a service performed entirely by the United States.

Transit Correspondence

British Open Mail

In negotiating Articles XI and XII of the treaty, Bancroft ignored that part of the joint resolution of Congress of 15 June 1844 which pointed to optional prepayment as the United States' policy in making postal agreements with foreign countries. Article XI specifically provided for part payment of postage, a procedure not designed to satisfy American commer-

---

[27] *Senate Executive Document* 25, 30 Cong., 2 sess., serial 531, p. 7.
[28] Dept. of State, *Treaties*, p. 498.

cial interests. Although *split rates* were commonly used by the British Post Office, they had not previously had the added complication of rate variation because of the nationality of the conveying packet. In practice, this procedure proved to be confusing to the post offices in the colonies and in foreign countries.

The usual procedure used by the British in setting rates to foreign countries for mail passing through England was to add the transit postages to and from Britain to the international rate. Clanricarde, accordingly, proposed that the current transit postages to and from colonies and foreign countries be added to the 24¢ international rate to form total rates, the prepayment of which could be optional. He did, however, exempt those countries to which the prepayment of postage in Britain was compulsory, which were usually those with whom Britain had no postal convention. Since some of the postal conventions between Britain and foreign countries provided for transit rates that paid for the letter to destination in either country, Bancroft felt that, in these instances, Britain would be collecting its own inland postage twice. Bancroft proposed that the United States should have the right to bring its transit letters in its own packets to a British port and deposit them in the British Post Office, there to be treated as letters originating in England.[29] Clanricarde would not agree to this, insisting that the international rate be used. When negotiations shifted from Clanricarde to Sir Charles Wood, Bancroft's proposal was accepted.

Article XI, therefore, was developed, and provided that each country deliver to the other its transit letters free of all postage, whether packet or inland. This meant that on transit letters posted in the United States, a prepayment of 5¢ inland postage would pay a letter onboard a British packet in Boston or New York, whence it would be conveyed at British expense to a foreign destination. If the conveying packet were American, a prepayment of both the inland and packet postages of 21¢ would pay the letter to an English port where it would be deposited in the British Post Office there to be treated as a letter originating in England. In either case, the postage was split, part of it being prepaid in the United States and part of it being collected from the addressee abroad.

By Article XII, the rates to be collected abroad were to be the same rates paid by British subjects for the same service. On incoming letters, foreign postage was prepaid to Boston or New York if the conveying packet was to be British; and only to the British port of departure (then Southampton) if the conveying packet was to be American. Letters were to be rated by the exchange offices at Boston or New York for a collection of the United States postage, that is, 5¢ when brought there by a British packet, or 21¢ if the conveying packet had been American.

British Mail

Article XI also provided that on letters posted in the United States addressed to countries to which they could not be forwarded unless the British postage was prepaid, the United States was to collect and account for this postage to the British Post Office. Largely, such foreign destinations were in countries with whom Great Britain had no postal convention. Letters addressed to these destinations, therefore, required full prepayment in the United States of all postage on letters sent, and collection in the United States of all postage on letters received. On letters sent, the United States retained its share of 5¢ or 21¢ when the conveying packet was British or American, respectively, and accordingly gave Britain credit for the remainder of the postage.

By Article XII, when the packet was American, the remainder of the postage represented the then current rate being paid by British subjects to that same foreign destination, except to France, which was exempted from Article XII. When the conveying packet was British, packet postage of 16¢ was added to this rate. On letters received in the United States, Britain debited the United States for all postage, except the United States share of 5¢ or 21¢, according to the nationality of the packet by which the mail was dispatched.

The procedure just described was provided for by Articles XI and XII of the treaty, and the *Articles of Execution* supplied a list of countries falling under these provisions, together with the amounts of postage to be paid to the British Post Office, in each case 16¢ more when conveyed by British packet. There was, however, an extension of *British Mail* that evolved and was not specifically provided for in the treaty. The post offices in the British colonies, and also in foreign countries, were confused by the open-mail procedure that required prepayment abroad of one rate to the British port of embarkation or a second rate to

---

[29] Ibid.

the American frontier, according to whether transatlantic service was by the Cunard line or not. The postal officials in the colonies were not accustomed to having different rates according to the nationality of the conveying packet. Invariably they knew that the Cunarders left Liverpool every Saturday, but it is not likely they knew more about the Ocean Line than that it sailed from Southampton once a month. They did know, however, that a letter upon which postage was paid only to England could not be forwarded by the Cunard line and would have to await the next sailing of the Ocean Line, which meant that it might rest in Southampton for a month.

It is, therefore, not strange that these offices developed the custom of quoting only the rate by the Cunard line. At least, several such instances came to the attention of the United States Post Office Department. Americans traveling abroad, some of them on diplomatic service, attempted to pay letters only to England at post offices in Aden, Ceylon, and Hong Kong, only to be told that prepayment to the American frontier was required. The American travelers were anxious to have their letters conveyed by American packets, but if prepayment to the American frontier was required, the British would be collecting postage for transatlantic service. This could only mean that the United States-British treaty had not settled the problem of the British charging double sea-postage. These Americans, individually, wrote letters to the United States Post Office Department, describing a grievance that was the same in these widely separated offices.

On 6 August 1852 Postmaster General Samuel D. Hubbard wrote the British Post Office inquiring into the matter.[30] The British reply of 24 September 1852 did not specifically answer the question as to whether there was a double charge for sea postage on American packet mail. The matter was then referred to the Department of State. There ensued a considerable correspondence between J. R. Ingersoll, United States minister at London, W. L. Marcy, secretary of state, and Lord Clarendon, British foreign secretary.[31] Finally, on 25 May 1853 (and, curiously, again on 22 December 1854), William L. Maberly, secretary of the British Post Office, wrote the following note to James Campbell, United States postmaster general:[32]

> In reply to your letter of the 17th ultimo, on the subject of the treatment at this office of letters from Hong Kong, addressed to the United States, I am directed by the Postmaster General to inform you that when such letters have been paid in advance at Hong Kong, and are conveyed across the Atlantic by United States packets, it is the practice of this office to credit the post office of the United States with the sea rate of 16 cents on each single letter.

The above statement raises several questions. Was this a general policy of the British Post Office, or did it apply only to Hong Kong mail? How long had the practice been in effect? Since the procedure had not been communicated to the United States Post Office Department, how did the exchange offices at Boston and New York rate such mail for collection? No official answers to these questions have been found. No cover posted prior to 1854, showing the application of this procedure, has been seen. Numerous covers after 1854 indicate that the procedure was generally applied to letters of foreign origin addressed to the United States, prepaid to the United States frontier, and conveyed by American packet, except, of course, to letters from or through France. These covers show that the United States exchange offices rated them uniformly for a collection of 5¢ without regard to the nationality of the conveying packet.

The statement by Maberly appears to have settled the matter. Although the procedure was not authorized by treaty, the United States did not object to its use. An inkling of a possible reason for their not objecting is contained in a letter from Postmaster General Campbell to Secretary of State Marcy[33] in which he complains about the large amount of commissions that had to be allowed for the collection of postage on foreign mails. If the British were willing to collect and pay over to the United States the packet postage on such letters, commission payments to postmasters would be reduced, and a net savings to the United States Post Office Department would result.

---

[30] *Senate Executive Document* 73, 33 Cong., 2 sess., serial 756, p. 46.
[31] Ibid., pp. 45–47.
[32] Ibid.
[33] Ibid., p. 49.

Chapter 3

Postal Relations With France

Mails via England

At the time the United States-British treaty was signed on 15 December 1848, all mail between the United States and France, via England, was exchanged under provisions of Article LII of the Anglo-French treaty of 3 April 1843.[1] This article provided that France pay Great Britain 3s. 4d. (40d.) per ounce of letters for sea conveyance and transit through British territory to or from "colonies and countries beyond the sea, wherever the same may be situated." A like provision required Britain to pay France 4 francs (40 decimes) per 30 grams of letters for sea conveyance and transit through French territory. These amounts were to be paid when letters were "conveyed by private ships, by Government vessels, or by vessels freighted or maintained by order of Government."

The *Articles of Execution*[2] for carrying the treaty into effect provided that one penny (British) be considered equal to one decime (French). The weight of a single letter was to be 7½ grams in France or one-fourth ounce in Great Britain. The single-letter rate was to be arrived at by dividing the rate per ounce or per 30 grams by four. On letters from the United States, therefore, the postage from New York or Boston to the port of entry in France was 10 decimes per 7½ grams. Because the United States had no postal arrangement with France, all letters posted in the United States entered France unpaid, France collecting 10 decimes per single rate plus French inland postage from the addressee. On letters posted in France addressed to the United States, prepayment of all postage to the United States frontier was compulsory.

Until July 1849, French inland postage was determined according to the distance in a straight line between the point of posting and the point of egress from France, and vice versa on letters received.[3] The progression of the inland rates differed from the progression of the Article LII 10-decime rate.[4] The combination of these two facts makes the analysis of French due-markings during this period an exceedingly difficult task. On 1 January 1849,[5] France abandoned distance as a basis for determining domestic rates, and on 23 July 1849[6] inland postage on letters to or from the United States was set at 5 decimes for every 7½ grams, or fraction of 7½ grams.

On 31 March 1844,[7] additional articles to the 1843 treaty established a new system of accounting for mail exchanged between France and England. Essentially, this complicated system provided that the rates relating to particular places of origin and destination of mail be included under separate accounts which were called "the Articles in the Accounts." Each of these "accounting" articles was assigned a number, which was used in the preparation of the letter-bills. The numbers of the Articles in the Accounts should not be confused with the numbers of the articles in the treaty. In fact, the rates set in the treaty articles

---

[1] Edward Hertslet ed., *Commercial Treaties*, vol. 6, p. 349.
[2] *British and Foreign State Papers*, vol. 39, p. 1083.
[3] Hertslet, *Commercial Treaties* (Art. 32), vol. 6, p. 357.
[4] *British and Foreign State Papers* (Articles of Execution, Art. 50), vol. 39, p. 1102.
[5] Georges Brunel, *Le Timbre-Poste français*, p. 49.
[6] Raymond Salles, *La Poste maritime Française Historique et Catalogue*, vol. 4, p. 280.
[7] *British and Foreign State Papers*, vol. 39, p. 1164.

fell under certain *accounting* articles, and these rates were then designated by the *accounting*-article number which appeared on the letter-bill. Thus, the 3s. 4d. rate of Article LII of the treaty fell, originally, under Article 12 in the Articles in the Accounts. The Articles in the Accounts were later revised, and beginning 1 January 1846, the 3s. 4d. rate of Article LII was placed under *accounting*-article 13.

Appended to Article LII of the treaty was the provision that an additional 8d. per ounce be charged on letters forwarded from or addressed to Canada, New Brunswick, Nova Scotia, Prince Edward Island, and Newfoundland, making in all a rate of 4s. per ounce. Article LVII of the *Articles of Execution* provided the following: [8]

> In order that, the transmission of letters originating in the colonies and countries beyond the sea, forwarded by the British Post Office to the Post Office of France, there may be no confusion between letters coming from the British possessions, which are to be accounted for at the rate of 4s. per ounce, and those coming from British possessions, or countries beyond the sea, which are to be accounted for at the rate of 3s. 4d. per ounce, such letters shall be marked on their face by the British Post Office with a special stamp, indicating, as below, the heading of the letter-bill of the said Office under which they are to be respectively inscribed, namely:
> 1. North America, Canada, New Bruswick, &c. (CANADA, &c.)
> 2. Colonies and countries beyond the sea (COLONIES, &c.).

After 1 April 1844, the effective date of the additional articles of 31 March 1844, the *accounting*-article number was also included in the stamp. The British Post Office, therefore, on all letters from the United States which were forwarded to France, applied, in red-orange ink, a handstamp reading, COLONIES /&C. ART. 12, and after 1 January 1846, COLONIES /&C. ART. 13, reflecting the revision of the *accounting* articles made at that time (see markings *A* and *B* in Figure 18).

The Exclusion of France From Article XII of the United States-British Treaty

The existence of Article LII of the Anglo-French treaty of 1843 proved to be an obstacle in the negotiation of the transit rates of the United States-British

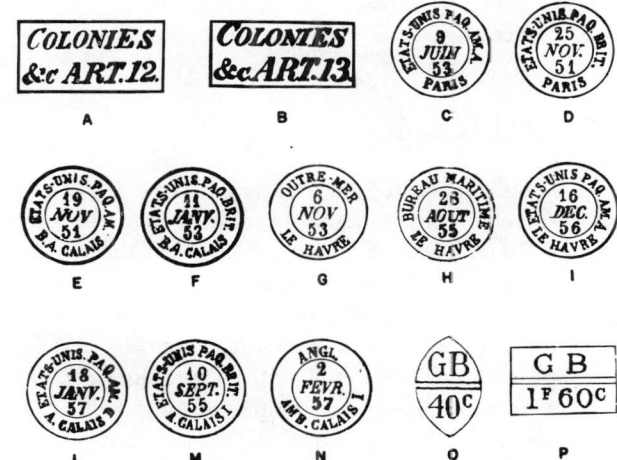

FIGURE 18.—MARKINGS on pre-treaty United States-French mail.

treaty. Bancroft explained it to Secretary of State James Buchanan as follows: [9]

> A difficulty occurred in setting the rates to be paid for letters to France, passing through England. By the 52d. Article of the British and French Postal Convention, the French pay on letters, to the British Government one uniform rate of Forty pence per ounce, British net weight, for transit through the United Kingdom and sea conveyance to and from Countries beyond the sea. There is but one and the same rate for letters, whether from Brazil or Van Diemen's Land; from Boston or Calcutta. But by our present Treaty with England this rate becomes too high on letters between France and the United States passing through the United Kingdom. The Chancellor of the Exchequer is therefore willing, on his part, to reduce rates to be paid on such letters, *and apply the principle of the Twelfth Article of the treaty to France* [italics added for emphasis]. . . . For this the concurrence of France is necessary.

Article XII of the United States-British treaty provided, in effect, that the transit rates to foreign countries via England be the rate currently charged British subjects for the same service. Although France was specifically excluded from this article, it was agreed to invite her, "without loss of time," to enter into arrangements "as are most conducive to the interests of the three countries," for the mutual exchange of closed mails. In the meantime—that is, before such agreement was reached—Britain would forward mails to and from France under the rate of Article LII of the Anglo-French treaty of 1843. France, however, was not excluded from Article XI and, hence, the open-mail

---

[8] Ibid., pp. 1106–1107.

[9] Dept. of State, *Treaties,* p. 497.

rates of 5¢ or 21¢ by British or American packet, respectively, were prepaid or collected in the United States.

The Bad Bargain

Although Bancroft held the treaty to be one of "just and fair reciprocity," it soon became evident that the United States Post Office Department felt that it was not only unfair, but also unjust and definitely biased in favor of the British. The difficulty appears to have grown out of the fact that Bancroft, wherever possible, attempted to eschew detail and to establish general principles, which were to be reciprocally applied by the two countries. The Post Office Department, however, used a different method for measuring "reciprocity." Instead of viewing the reciprocal application of principles, the amounts paid by one country to the other were examined. It did not take the department long to discover that, while the United States would pay Britain 30¢ per ounce for transit of closed mails from Liverpool to Cuxhaven, Britain would pay the United States only 12½¢ per ounce for conveying the mails between Canada and Boston or New York. In his Annual Report for 1853, Postmaster General Campbell complained: [10]

> Great Britain received for transit through that country of our Bremen closed mails, in the first quarter of the last fiscal year, thirty cents an ounce . . . whilst the United States have received but twelve and a half cents an ounce for the British and Canadian closed mails, though performing a service at least equal in point of importance.

As has been previously mentioned, Cave Johnson felt that the Canadian transit rate represented the only real "leverage" the United States held in bargaining with the British. This was bartered for a lower packet rate. It must be borne in mind that the Canadian transit rate of 12½¢ rested upon the uniform inland rate of the treaty, which Bancroft accepted in Article V as the basis for the application of the Article IX formula of taking two single-letter rates plus 25 percent for the setting of the rate per ounce on closed mails. Thus, the Canadian closed-mail rate was computed at two times 5¢ plus 25 percent of the product of 10¢. There can be little doubt that Colonel Maberly had had a hand in the maneuvering of Bancroft's acceptance of Articles V and IX.

But Bancroft accepted Article XII on his own initiative. Colonel Maberly brought Bancroft for his consideration a detailed draft of a proposal that eventually became Articles XI and XII. Bancroft cavalierly penned the following memorandum to Maberly: [11]

> Approved as far as 'the rates by sea'—what follows is superfluous and objectionable. Make your rates to your colonies and possessions and foreign countries what you please, high or low, one sea rate or a dozen, or not at all; what your people pay we are willing to pay, but not more, and *vice versa*. Our security is, that we pay what your people pay from the same place for the same benefit, and *vice versa*.
> This is the very principle agreed upon as the basis of this convention.
> The additions disagreed to are further objectionable, as introducing varying principles.

Ordinarily, such a memorandum would not be preserved, but in this instance Maberly, probably with a smile, tucked it safely away in his files, whence it was brought out on occasion to embarrass future United States postmasters general. A fundamental, more basic than the principles negotiated in the treaty, was the fact that the British used transit postage as a basis for taxation. Application of the principle of Article XII forced United States citizens to pay to Britain whatever taxes Britain imposed upon its own subjects for transit postage.

Postmaster General Samuel D. Hubbard put the matter succinctly in a letter to Edward Everett, secretary of state, dated 11 January 1853. After a recitation of the provisions of Article XII, he wrote: [12]

> Thus, while the United States mails sent through England are subject to the high rates established on correspondence between England and the continent, &c., the British mails sent through the United States have the advantage of our reduced rates.
> It appears to me it would have been more just to have secured for our mails advantages equal to those extended by the United States to the British mails.

On 8 January 1849, President Polk appointed George Bancroft and Richard Rush, minister at Paris, as envoys extraordinary and ministers plenipotentiary for the negotiation of a tripartite agreement between Britain, France, and the United States.[13] The United States felt that it was first necessary to develop a proposal with Britain which the two countries could jointly present to France. Accordingly, Bancroft

---

[10] U.S., Congress, Senate, *Executive Document* 1, 33rd Cong., 1st sess., serial 692, pt. 3; 718.

[11] *Senate Executive Document* 73, 33 Cong., 2nd sess., serial 756, p. 44.

[12] *Senate Executive Document* 32, 32 Cong., 2 sess., serial 660, p. 43.

[13] Dept. of State, *Treaties,* p. 505.

opened negotiations with the British Post Office, but was not able to secure a reply from Lord Clanricarde. In October 1849 [14] Bancroft was succeeded as minister at London by Abbott Lawrence. Up to that time, no progress had been made in the negotiations.

The United States proposed that the transit rate between Britain and France be reduced to 6d. per ounce on closed mails between the United States and France, via England; that the rate between the American and French frontiers be 2s. 2d. per ounce when conveyance was by British packet, and that only the 6d.-per-ounce transit rate be charged when conveyance was by American packet. The 6d. transit rate had no foundation in the closed-mail provisions under Articles VII, VIII, or IX of the United States-British treaty. The United States took the position that, since France had been excluded from Article XII and it had been agreed that "without loss of time" the three countries should come to an agreement mutually conducive to the interests of all, bargaining did not have to be within the context of the other treaty provisions. Further, the Americans argued acceptance of their proposal on the basis of its equity. Since Britain paid the United States only 6¼d. per ounce for transit of the Canadian mails, a rate of 6d. between England and France was equitable.

The British position was stated by Sir Charles Wood (then chancellor of the exchequer) at the time France was excluded from Article XII and before the treaty was signed. This was reported to Secretary of State James Buchanan by Bancroft in his dispatch transmitting the treaty, previously quoted, to the effect that he (Wood) was willing to "apply the principle of the twelfth article of the treaty to France." The then current rate between France and Britain was 5d. per half ounce, set by Article XXXIII of the Anglo-French treaty. To this rate the formula of Article IX of the United States-British treaty was applied. This resulted in a rate of 1s. ½d. per ounce (2 x 5d. plus 25 percent). The same formula was also applied to the 8d. packet rate, and resulted in a sea rate of 1s.8d. per ounce. Thus, the British offered a rate of 2s.8½d. per ounce by British packet and of 1s.½d. by American packet. These rates treated France as if she had not been excluded from the twelfth article. The proposal was made by Lord Clanricarde on 26 August 1850 [15]

as a counterproposal to that made by Lawrence, the new minister in London, in a letter dated 19 August 1850.[16] Shortly thereafter, the British were willing to drop one halfpenny from each of the above rates.

Until some agreement was reached between France and England, mails between the United States and France, via England, had to be dispatched under Article LII of the Anglo-French treaty. Since the sole rate of 3s.4d. per ounce applied to all mail dispatched, double sea-postage was being charged on mail conveyed by American packet. The United States, however, was not immediately aware of this fact. When Abbott Lawrence succeeded Bancroft, one of his first acts was to send John C. B. Davis, secretary of the United States legation at London, to Paris to inquire into certain aspects of the handling of the United States mail between England and France. It is significant that Lawrence did not know what rates existed in France on mail to or from the United States. These rates also had not been known by Bancroft. As one of his primary duties, Davis was charged with the responsibility of ascertaining the existing rates on letters and the division of the postage between France and England.

Davis immediately sought out M. Maurin, chief of the Bureau of Foreign Correspondence, who promptly informed him that France already knew of Clanricarde's offer, had determined to accept it, and hoped the United States would also accept it. Davis also reported as follows: [17]

> The first question I asked him was as to the present rates between here and America. He answered: '¼ oz., 1*f*.50*c*.; ½ oz., 3*f*.; ¾ oz., 4*f*.50*c*.; 1 oz., 6*f*.; of which France takes one-third, and England two-thirds. This pays the letter to New York.' Then I asked: Suppose the letter is taken to New York in an American steamer: is it subject to a new sea-rate, or does England, in her turn, account to the United States?' To this he said he did not know, but perhaps Mr. Thayer (Director General of French Posts) would be able to tell me. Then I asked how the postage would be under the proposed arrangement, (with England). He answered: '¼ oz., 1*f*.30*c*.; ½ oz., 2*f*.60*c*.; ¾ oz., 3*f*.90*c*.; 1 oz., 5*f*.20*c*.' How would it then be with the American steamers?' 'There will be such provision made that a letter going by American steamer will be required to prepay only—¼ oz., 80*c*.; ½ oz., 1*f*.60*c*.; ¾ oz., 2*f*.40*c*.; 1 oz., 3*f*.20*c*.

Upon receipt of Davis's report, Lawrence immediately wrote to the director general for French Posts, M. Thayer, asking that France delay in accepting

---

[14] *Senate Executive Document* 73, 33 Cong., 2 sess., serial 756, p. 51.
[15] *Senate Executive Document* 32, 32 Cong., 2 sess., serial 660, p. 12.

[16] Ibid., p. 8.
[17] Ibid., pp. 14–15.

Clanricarde's proposal.[18] Davis saw Thayer on 8 October 1850 and reported his reaction to Lawrence's request for delay:[19]

> America negotiates a convention with England for the regulation of the postal correspondence, in the twelfth article of which, after making provision for the correspondence passing through England to and from countries beyond, an exception is made *in favor of France,* in consequence of the existing relations with that country. Provision is made for the conclusion at some subsequent time of a triple convention between the three powers. Things go on without any official steps being taken for carrying into effect that provision; and at length England, of her own accord, offers certain concessions to France with reference to such correspondence, without requiring any corresponding ones on her part, which France determines to accept. These concessions virtually do away with the distinctions made by the convention between French and other continental correspondence, and place all on the same footing—which England, perhaps, would claim as an execution of the convention. Then America comes in, asks France not to accept, and becomes for the first time a party. . . .
>
> Now see the result. Had this been concluded, France and America would have been let at once into the benefits of it, and the latter would not have been bound by it, not being party to it, but could still have insisted on the equitable execution of the convention of 1848, and threatened to annul it in case it was not done. Now, however, America, by asking France to delay, and by opening negotiations herself, has become a party, and, if France accepts, and England does not retract, America will be bound.

Davis countered by saying that "the United States never would agree that England had executed the twelfth article in good faith by placing the French on the same basis with the other continental correspondence. The convention contemplated more." [20] It is evident that the United States felt that the convention was broader than the agreement between Bancroft and Wood. It is also evident that British policy was, in fact, the application of the principle of the twelfth article to France, which was reflected in the British offer to the United States and France. France's acceptance of this offer could not be effectually protested by the United States.

The position of the three countries remained the same until the signing of the Anglo-French treaty of 24 September 1856. The United States continued to demand that the British reduce the transit rate to France to 6d. per ounce. England and France proceeded to work out an arrangement for closed mails on terms offered by the British. On 15 April 1851, Thayer addressed Maberly with the suggestion that: [21]

> the transmission of the correspondence in question might be regulated in the following manner:
>
> The French post office to make up the correspondence for Boston and New York offices in closed mails, a statement of the contents thereof to be furnished to your department in the regular form.
>
> With regard to the return corespondence from the United States, until arrangements shall have been made with the American department for having the same forwarded in closed mails to France, it should be made up under care of the British offices, in separate parcels, addressed to the offices of Calais and Paris, marked according to the place whence the corespondence was forwarded and the route by which it had been carried.

Maberly, in his reply of 26 April 1851, accepted Thayer's proposal, and then added: [22]

> I beg leave to add, that any delay which may take place in concluding this matter is not owing to any difficulty anticipated, but to the necessity for the American minister being party to the arrangement.

This peculiar arrangement was placed in operation on 1 May 1851. From that date forward, mails from France, via England, entered the United States as closed mails, while letters from the United States to France continued to be sent in the open mail. Hence, covers from France after 1 May 1851 do not show British markings. Although France paid Britain the lowered rates, no reduction in letter postage was immediately made.

It appears that about the middle of 1851 Great Britain and France made a provisional agreement by which the rates offered by the British and already being used on closed mail from France were applied to the open mail sent from the United States to France. This agreement was placed in effect in France by French circulaire 67 (instructions to postal agents), dated 1 September 1851.[23] This circular reduced the rate on letters conveyed by American packets from 15 to 8 decimes per 7½ grams. From this time forward, mail ceased to be exchanged under Article LII of the Anglo-French convention of 1843, or under the accounting and letter-bill arrangements of Article 13 of the Articles in the Accounts. The COLONIES/&C. ART. 13 marking was, therefore, discontinued on mail from

---

[18] Ibid., pp. 7–8.
[19] Ibid., p. 16.
[20] Ibid.
[21] Ibid., p. 27.
[22] Ibid., p. 28.
[23] Salles, *La Poste maritime française,* vol. 4, p. 280.

the United States. Replacing the COLONIES marking were markings C, D, E, and F of Figure 18. Marking C was applied in red by the Paris office, while marking E was applied in black by the traveling (ambulant) post office, Calais to Paris, on American packet mail. Although the single rate by British packet remained at 15 decimes, the COLONIES marking was, nevertheless, replaced by markings D and F (see Figure 18) on mail conveyed by British packets. These markings carried out the instructions issued by Thayer.

On 19 November 1851 the French president, Louis Napoleon Bonaparte, signed a decree which became effective on 1 December 1851,[24] definitively establishing rates on letters between the United States and France, via England. This decree set a rate per 7½ grams at 1 franc 30 centimes (13 decimes) on letters between France or Algeria and the United States, when conveyed by British packet. It also repeated the existing 80-centime (8 decimes) rate by American packet set by circulaire 67 of 1 September 1851. Rates were also set for letters originating in or destined for those parts of the Mediterranean where France maintained post offices. These rates were 1 franc 80 centimes (18 decimes) when conveyance was by British packet, and 1 franc 30 centimes (13 decimes) when conveyed by American packet.

The rates reflected in the preceding decree were developed from those agreed upon between France and Great Britain in the provisional agreement. Utilizing the principle established for the setting of single-letter rates under Article LII of the Anglo-French treaty, the closed-mail-per-ounce rates were divided by four to arrive at the single-letter rates. Thus, the sea rate of 1s.8d. per ounce, plus the England–France transit rate of 1s. per ounce yielded rates as set forth in Table 8.

The United States was aware that Britain and France had agreed to send mail from France closed through England. Colonel Maberly notified the Post Office Department to this effect on 22 August 1851.[25] Neither England nor France, however, notified the United States of the provisional agreement or of the decree rates. In this regard the United States was completely ignored. The Post Office Department learned of these arrangements in a peculiar way.

In January 1853 Postmaster General Hubbard was

[24] Hertslet, *Commercial Treaties*, vol. 9, pp. 269–270. [See also Chronicle 37, (22 Sept. 1960), for English translation of the text of this decree.]

[25] *Senate Executive Document* 73, 33 Cong., 2 sess., serial 756, p. 51.

TABLE 8.—*United States and French Postal Rates via England (Under the 1851 French Decree)*

British Packet

U.S. inland postage (prepaid or collected in U.S.)	—	—	5¢
Sea postage (¼ of 1s.8d. or 40¢)	5 decimes	10¢	—
Transit postage (¼ of 1s. or 24¢)	3	6	—
French inland postage	5	10	—
Prepaid or collected in France	13 decimes	—	26
Total postage			31¢

American Packet

U.S. inland postage (U.S.-British treaty)			5¢
Sea postage			16
Prepaid or collected in U.S.			21
Transit postage (¼ of 1s. or 24¢)	3 decimes	6¢	
French inland postage	5	10	
Prepaid or collected in France	8 decimes	—	16
Total postage	—	—	37¢

NOTE: The 6¢ differential in rates is due to a reduction in sea postage on letters by British packet.

unaware of the provisional agreement or of the decree rates. He thought double sea-postage was still being charged by Britain and decided (at the wrong time) to do something about it. On 26 January 1853, the following appeared in the *New-York Tribune:*

Foreign Postage

The following official notice and order in relation to foreign postage has been issued by the Postmaster-General:
Post-Office-Department, Jan. 24, 1853.

Pursuant to authority vested in the Postmaster-General, and by and with the advice and consent of the President of the United States (which advice and consent more fully appear by an instrument in writing this day filed in the Department), it being understood that the British Post-Office charges the same rate of postage on letters and newspapers to and from France, through England, whether the same are conveyed across the Atlantic by British or United States packets: thus making a discrimination of 16 cents (sea postage) in favor of the British line,

It is hereby ordered, That on all letters to or from France, through England, the single rate of United States postage be *twenty-one cents* and on all newspapers transmitted *four cents* each, from and after the date hereof, such postage to be collected in and retained by the United States.

S. D. Hubbard, Postmaster-General

On 19 July 1853 Postmaster General James Campbell reviewed the matter for Secretary of State W. L. Marcy: [26]

> The effect of this order, it was supposed, would be to render the postage to and from France the same by both the United States and British lines. Before the order could go generally into operation, however, at the earnest solicitation of the French minister, Count de Sartiges, who promised to communicate with his government, urging a speedy settlement of the matter on a just basis, Mr. Hubbard, on the 10th of February, suspended the order for two months.

No order of suspension was found in the *New York Tribune,* or in the *Weekly New York Times.* The following news item appeared, however, on 26 February 1853 in the *New York Recorder:*

> Transatlantic Postage—The Washington papers contain an official notice from Postmaster General Hall [?], suspending for three [?] months, at the request of the French Minister, the order equalizing the rate of postage on all letters between the United States and France, via England.

The preceding is, of course, somewhat inaccurate. Nathan K. Hall had not been postmaster general since 14 September 1852, and the order was suspended for two, not three, months. The significant aspect of this news item is that its source was the Washington newspapers. Evidently, broad publicity was not given to the suspension of the order.

Any letter addressed to France, via England, posted in the United States between 24 January and 10 February 1853, that shows a prepayment of 21¢ and bears a British packet marking, would be an example of a cover sent during this "retaliatory" Post Office order. There were three sailings from the United States by the Cunard line during this period: *Arabia* from New York on 26 January (maiden voyage), *Europa* from Boston on 2 February, and *Africa* from New York on 9 February. Unfortunately, no cover addressed to France and conveyed on any of the above three sailings has been seen. The influence of the above order, however, may have extended beyond the suspension date. The order of 24 January appears to have been sent to the newspapers in the large cities, while the notice of suspension seems to have been published only in the Washington newspapers. Of course, the exchange offices were notified, and any person taking a letter for mailing to the general post offices of Boston or New York would have been informed of the order of suspension. This is attested by a cover in the Smithsonian collection which was conveyed from Boston on 16 February 1853 by Cunarder *Canada* and was prepaid with 5¢. A few persons, however, placed postage stamps upon their letters and posted them without taking them to the post-office window, and these persons may not have learned of the suspension of the order.

Figure 19 presents a cover posted in Philadelphia on 5 April 1853, addressed to Mr. Charles Toppan in Paris. The letter is signed by Samuel Carpenter. These gentlemen were members of the firm of Toppan, Carpenter, Casilear and Company, which printed the stamps appearing on the letter. These stamps represent a prepayment of 21¢, normally the required prepayment for a letter sent by American packet, but Mr. Carpenter endorsed the letter "Pr Steamer/Asia/April 6th." This endorsement indicates that reference was made to one of the notices of mail sailings, which would also have informed him that the *Asia* was a British packet. The New York British packet marking also bears the date of 6 April, the date upon which the *Asia,* according to the Cunard records, sailed from New York. Since other letters in this correspondence are endorsed to British packets and prepaid with 5¢, normally the required prepayment on British packet letters, the only logical explanation for the prepayment of 21¢ on this letter is that Mr. Carpenter thought it necessary to prepay it in that amount.

This was not the only occasion upon which Mr. Carpenter prepaid a letter to Mr. Toppan in Paris with 21¢ and endorsed it to a British packet. Lot no. 51 of the Bruce G. Daniels sale of 24 November 1959 is illustrated in the sale catalogue. That cover is similar to the one described above, except that it is endorsed "Pr Steamer/23 Feby" and bears a British packet mark of the same date. The records of the Cunard line show that the *Niagara* sailed from New York on that date. The French receiving mark clearly shows the year to be 1853. Again, the prepayment of 21¢, on this cover as well as on the one previously described, is suspected to have been influenced by the Post Office order of 24 January 1853.

On 18 February 1853 Colonel Maberly addressed a letter to the United States Post Office Department in which he stated that since the middle of 1851 a provisional arrangement had existed between Great Britain and France, by which no charge was made for

---

[26] Ibid., p. 52.

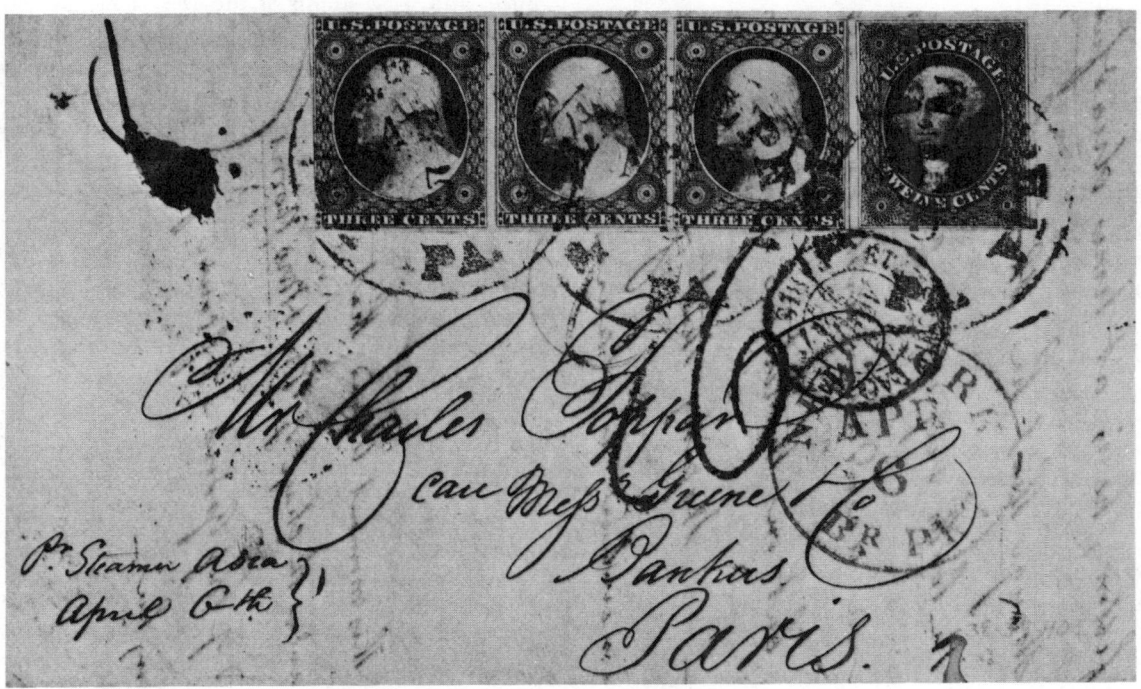

FIGURE 19.—COVER, from Philadelphia to Paris, 1853.

sea postage on letters to and from France, via England, by American packet.[27] Thus, over a year and a half after the fact, the United States Post Office learned of these arrangements between Britain and France.

On 1 May 1853[28] the Count de Sartiges also wrote the Department explaining that there was only a 6¢, not a 16¢, difference in the American and British packet rates. He further explained that the difference was the result of the lowering of the sea postage to 10¢ on British packet letters.

In his annual report for 1854 Postmaster General Campbell reviewed the situation for Congress. The British postmaster general took exception to certain statements made by Mr. Campbell. He stated that it was inconsistent on the part of the United States to complain that the British government enabled French subjects to receive their American letters at a sea rate of 10¢, while the United States demanded 16¢ from its own citizens for a like service by United States packets; and at the same time to complain that the British charges were too high.[29] In his annual report for 1855 Postmaster General Campbell answered the British postmaster general:[30]

> It is sufficient answer to say that the only controversy has been with reference to a reduction of the British transit postage, that the sea postage has not been a point of dispute, and that were our reasonable demands for a reduction of the transit postage acceded to, the reduction of the sea postage by the United States lines would follow of course, since the United States and French mails would then be treated as closed mails, and all letters between the two countries passing through England would be transmitted at a uniform rate of postage.

Citing Mr. Bancroft's memorandum to Maberly, the British pointed out that the demand by the United States for a reduction of the transit rate to France was "clearly in contradiction to the spirit of the convention of December, 1848, and to the basis on which it was negotiated . . ."[31] The memorandum clearly precluded a contest of the transit rates. It was thus that both parties rested their cases until the matter was settled by the signing of the Anglo-French convention of 24 September 1856.

---

[27] Ibid.
[28] Ibid.
[29] *Annual Report of the Postmaster General, 1855*, p. 18.
[30] Ibid.
[31] *Senate Executive Document 73*, 33 Cong., 2 sess., serial 756, p. 42 (Lord Clarendon to Mr. Ingersoll).

Covers

Figure 20 illustrates a cover posted in New York, addressed to Paris. It bears a New York postmaster's Provisional 5¢ stamp, which paid the letter to Boston, a distance of under 300 miles. The New York office canceled the stamp with a square grid, and applied a PAID in arc marking as well as a NEW YORK/5 CTS/15 DEC marking, all of which are in red. On this date (15 December 1846) the mails were made up in New York for the sailing on the following day from Boston of R.M.S. *Caledonia,* as in indicated by the endorsement. The letter was sent through Liverpool to the London office, which applied the COLONIES/&C. ART. 13 marking (see *B* of Figure 18), and forwarded the letter to the French office at Boulogne. By Article XXXII [32] of the Anglo-French convention of 1843, French territorial (inland) postage was set according to the distance in a straight line between the point at which the letter entered France and its destination. This letter is rated for a collection of 15 decimes, 10 decimes of which were paid to Great Britain under Article 13 of the Articles in the Accounts, and 5 demimes were for French territorial postage.

Figure 21 illustrates a cover posted in Boston, addressed to Paris. It is endorsed "per Steamer 'America' from Boston to Liverpool/March 6, 1850." The letter bears a 1¢ carrier stamp of the Boston Penny Post (Scott no. 3*LB*1), which paid the letter to the Boston post office, and a 5¢ stamp of the 1847 issue, which paid the United States-British treaty's open-mail rate by British packet for a letter not exceeding one half ounce. The letter was forwarded from Boston by R.M.S. *America* on 6 March, as the endorsement indicates, and arrived in Liverpool on 19 March 1850, whence it was sent to the London office. The London office applied marking *B* of Figure 18 and a packet marking on the reverse (not shown), and sent it to the French office at Calais. That office applied a double-circle 2ANGL.2/CALAIS/20/MARS/50 marking and rated the letter for a double-rate collection of 30 decimes. This collection was for a letter that weighed over 7½ but not over 15 grams. Of the 30 decimes, 20 paid the British for sea and British transit postage (including channel transit), and 10 decimes paid the French inland postage.

Figure 22 presents a cover posted in New Orleans on 25 January 1851, addressed to Paris. This letter weighed over one half but not over one ounce, and was prepaid 42¢ (2×21¢) to be sent from New York by American packet. This 21¢ single rate represented 16¢ for sea postage and 5¢ for United States inland postage. The letter was sent from New York on 5 February 1851 by the U.S.M. steamer *Arctic* of the Collins line, which arrived in Liverpool on 16 February, whence it was sent to the London office. The London office marked it with *B* of Figure 18, and sent it on 17 February to the French office at Calais (London marking on the reverse). The Calais office marked it with a 2 ANGL. 2/CALAIS/18 FEVR./51 marking and

---

[32] Hertslet, *Commercial Treaties,* vol. 6, p. 357.

FIGURE 20.—COVER, from New York to Paris, 1846. (*Courtesy of J. David Baker*)

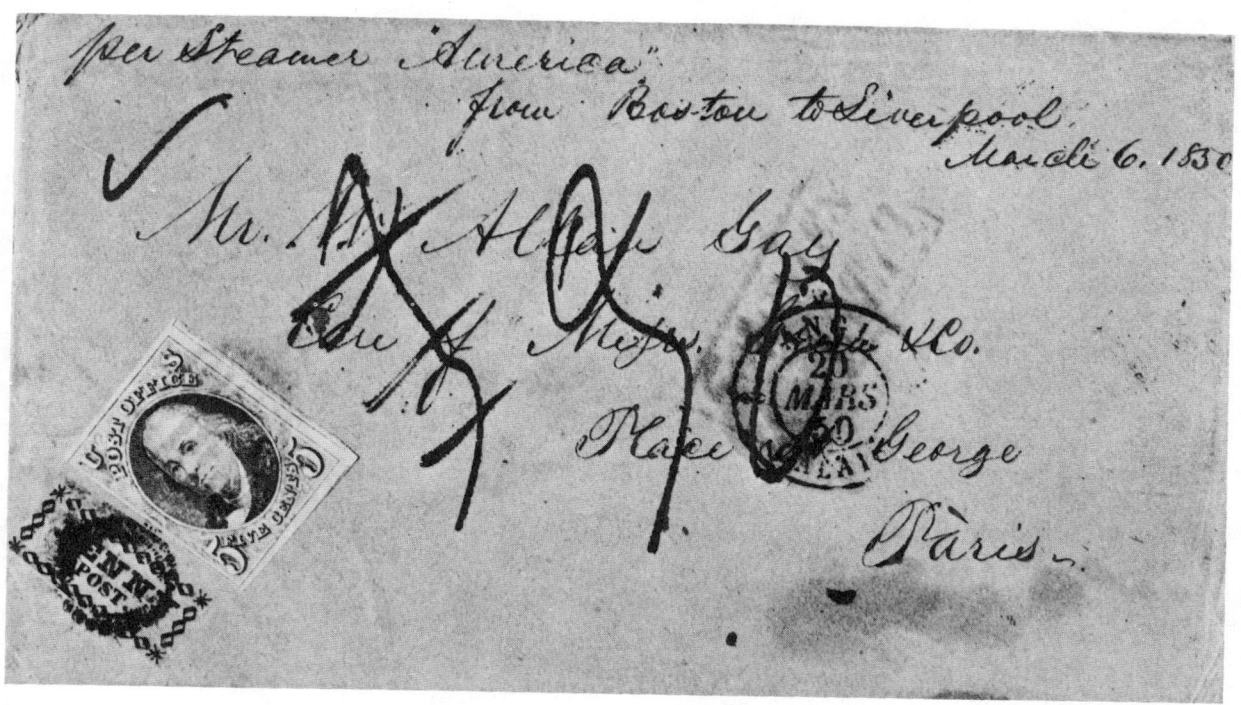

FIGURE 21.—COVER, from Boston to Paris, 1850. (*Arthur E. Beane, Jr., collection*)

FIGURE 22.—COVER, from New Orleans to Paris, 1851.

rated it for a collection of 45 decimes. This collection was for a letter weighing over 15 but not over 22½ grams. Of the 45 decimes, 30 decimes paid the British for sea and British transit postage, and 15 decimes paid the French inland postage. Since the sea postage had been paid in the United States, and charged again by France, the United States-British treaty did not settle this issue for mail to France. Clearly there was no difference made in the postage collected in France for letters conveyed by American packets.

Figure 23 illustrates a cover posted in Paris on 10 July 1851, about two months after England and France had agreed to send closed mail to the United States. The letter weighed over 7½ grams in France but not over one half ounce in the United States. A double-rate letter in France, it is prepaid 3 francs (30 decimes) by a strip of three of the "Ceres" 1ƒ. carmine (Scott no. 9). On the reverse is a double circle LIGNE-DE-CALAIS/N° 1 marking, used by the traveling post office, Paris to Calais. This office made up the mail in which the letter was included, and closed the bags and forwarded them through England to the Boston office, where they were opened for the first time after leaving France. Boston marked the letter for a single-rate collection of 5¢. The cover bears no British marking. Transatlantic conveyance was from Liverpool by R.M.S. *America* which sailed from there on 12 July and arrived in Boston on 24 July 1851. The prepayment would have been the same if the letter had been endorsed to, and sent by, an American packet. In that event, however, 21¢ would have been collected in the United States.

Figure 24 illustrates a cover posted in Charlottesville, Virginia, on 30 August 1851, addressed to Paris. It was prepaid 5¢ for British packet service. The letter weighed over 7½ grams in France but not over one half ounce in the United States. It arrived at the Paris office on 16 September 1851; the Paris office applied marking *D* of Figure 18. This marking was introduced on 1 September 1851, when the COLONIES/&C. ART. 13 marking (*B* of Figure 18) was discontinued. From 1 September to 1 December 1851, letters by British packet continued to be rated at 15 decimes per 7½ grams. This letter was conveyed from Boston on 3 September 1851 by R.M.S. *Canada,* which arrived in Liverpool on 16 September 1851 and in Paris on the same day. The Paris office marked it for a double-rate collection of 30 decimes.

Figure 25 illustrates a cover posted in New Orleans on 2 June 1856, addressed to Bordeaux. It is prepaid 5¢ for British packet service by two 1¢ stamps and a 3¢ stamp of the 1851 issue. It was conveyed from New York to Liverpool by R.M.S. *Africa,* which sailed on 11 June and arrived in Liverpool on 23 June 1856. It

FIGURE 23.—COVER, from Paris to Philadelphia, 1851.

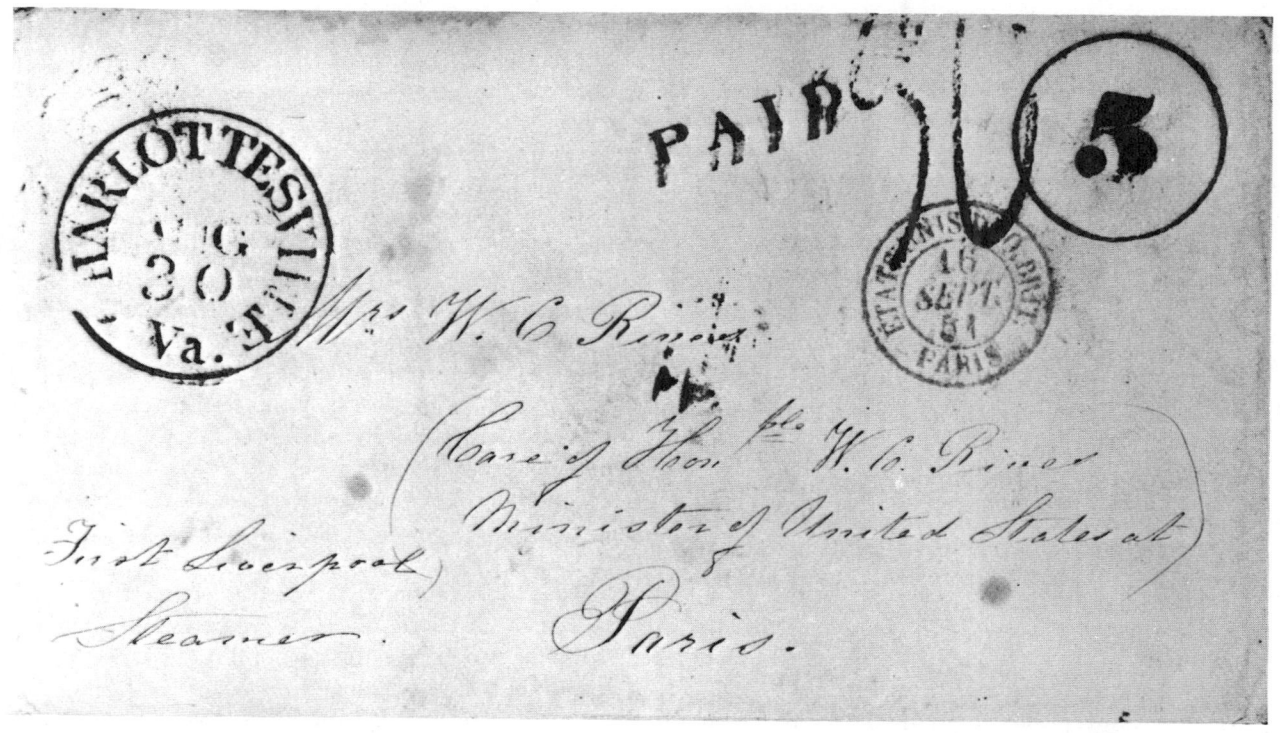

FIGURE 24.—COVER, from Charlottesville, Va., to Paris, 1851. (*Photograph by Smithsonian*)

FIGURE 25.—COVER, from New Orleans to Bordeaux, France, 1856.

was forwarded through the London office to the traveling office, Calais to Paris, arriving there on the same day, and it bears a marking similar to *M* in Figure 18, with the date of 23 June 1856. It is marked for a single-rate collection of 13 decimes, established by the decree of 19 November 1851, effective 1 December 1851, for letters conveyed by British packets.

Figure 26 illustrates a cover posted in Le Havre on 14 March 1855, addressed to New York. It is endorsed "pr str. Asia/via Calais," probably so that it would not be held for a Havre line steamer. Prepayment to the United States frontier of 130 centimes (13 decimes) was made by an 80-a 40-, and two 5-centimes imperforate "Empire" stamps. It was sent in closed mail through England, and bears no British marking. The Boston office marked it for a collection of 5¢.

Figure 27 presents a cover posted in New Orleans on 1 November 1856, addressed to Nantes. It is endorsed "Steamer/Atlantic" and is prepaid 21¢ by a strip of four 5¢ stamps issued in 1856, and a 1¢ plate II stamp (Scott no. 12 and no. 7, respectively). The New York American packet marking bears the date of 8 November (1856), and, as the indorsement indicates, the U.S.M. steamer *Atlantic* of the Collins line sailed from New York on that day. The marking of the traveling office, Calais to Paris (*L* of Figure 18), shows the date of 21 November 1856. The same office also marked the letter for a single-rate collection of 8 decimes.

Figure 28 illustrates a cover posted in Paris on 25 July 1855, addressed to Baltimore. It is prepaid by a single 80-centimes imperforate Empire stamp. It bears no French exchange-office marking, and, evidently in error, was marked with a small boxed P.P. Similar covers by American packet bear a boxed PD marking. While PD means "paid to destination," the United States frontier must have been considered "destination," for covers from France conveyed by British packets usually have this marking. It is not unlikely that, in carrying out M. Thayer's instructions for marking letters under the provisional agreement, P.P. signified *port payé partiellement,* ("postage paid for part of the transit"). The stamp is canceled with a roller cancellation, and there are no markings on the reverse of the cover. The 21/N. YORK AM. PKT marking is in black and shows the date of 8 August (1855). On that date U.S.M. steamer *Atlantic* of the Collins line arrived in New York with a closed mail from France in which this cover was included. The *21* in the New York marking indicates that 21¢ were to be collected from the addressee in Baltimore.

FIGURE 26.—COVER, from Le Havre to New York, 1855.

Figure 27.—Cover, from New Orleans to Nantes, 1856. (*Arthur E. Beane, Jr., collection*)

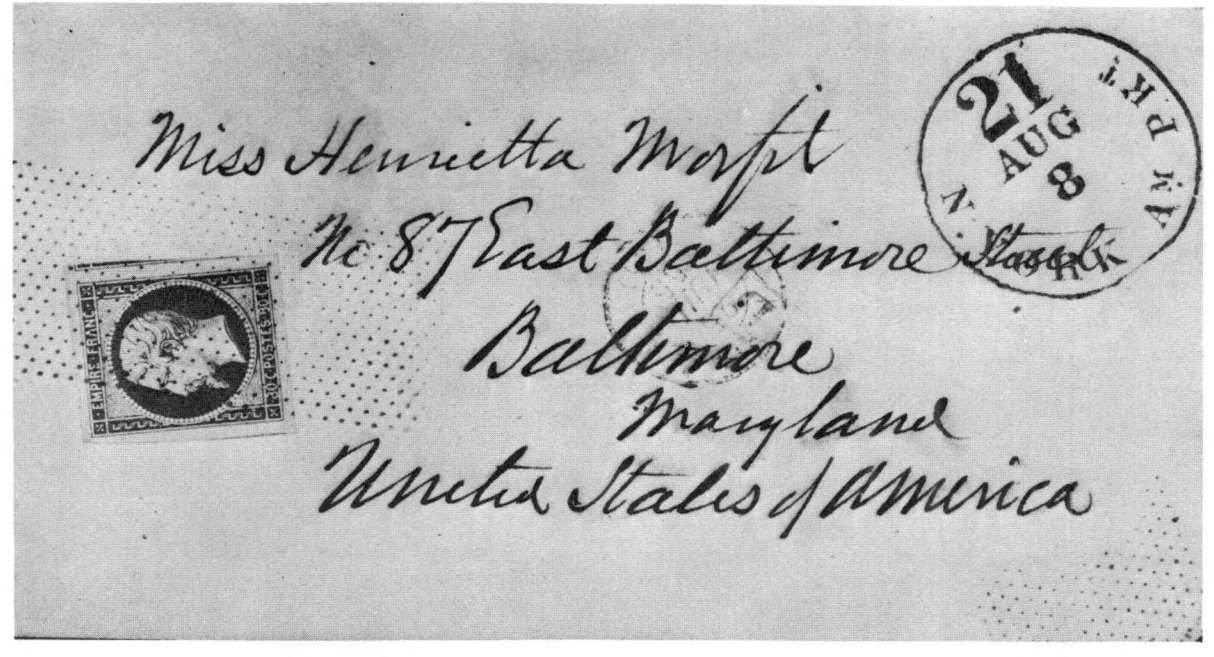

Figure 28.—Cover, from Paris to Baltimore, Maryland, 1855.

Mails Direct to France
The French Bid for a Transatlantic Service

Early in the year of 1847 the French firm of Herout et de Handel was awarded a subsidy by the French government to operate a line of steam packets between Havre and New York. For this purpose, the firm was to use four converted French steam frigates which were released from the French navy. Although these ships were termed "frigates," they were actually in the nature of supply ships rather than full-fledged vessels of war. The first sailings of the line were advertised in New York in the *Shipping and Commercial List and Prices Current* on 16 June 1847, under the name of the Transatlantic General Steam Packet Company, and in the *Journal du Havre* in France on 28 May 1847.[33]

Although Havre was to be the terminus of the line, the bassin de la Floride could not accommodate vessels with so great a draught until it was dredged,[34] and sailings were actually made from Cherbourg. Havre continued, however, to be advertised as the port, and freight, mail, and passengers were transshipped from Havre to Cherbourg. The following is an annotated list of the sailings of the line:[35]

Union, Captain Hébert, 1st voyage (formerly French frigate *Canada*):
   From France
      Sailed from Cherbourg 22 June 1847; freight and mail were transshipped from Havre to Cherbourg in the *Calibri* (4 voyages).
      Arrived in New York 8 July 1847.
   Returning
      Sailed from New York 24 July 1847.
      Arrived in Havre 7 August 1847; did not enter port; cargo was discharged by the *Colibri*.
      Arrived in Cherbourg 10 August 1847.

Philadelphie, Captain Besson, 2nd voyage (formerly French frigate *Christophe Colomb*):
   From France
      Sailed from Cherbourg 15 July 1847; freight, mail, and passengers transshipped from Havre by *Commerce-de-Lille* (2 voyages), *Courrier* (1 voyage); passengers by the *Finistère* (1 voyage).
   Returning
      Sailed from New York 15 August 1847.
      Arrived at Cherbourg 1 September 1847.

Missouri, Captain Morin, 3rd voyage (formerly French frigate *Ulloa*):
   From France
      Sailed from Cherbourg 31 July 1847; ran out of coal; put in at Halifax.
      Arrived in New York 21 August 1847.
   Returning
      Sailed from New York 31 August 1847.
      Arrived at Cherbourg 15 September 1847.

New York, Captain Pacini, 4th voyage (formerly French frigate *Darien*):
   From France
      Sailed from Cherbourg 15 August 1847.
      Arrived at New York 4 September 1847.
   Returning
      Sailed from New York 15 September 1847.
      Arrived at Cherbourg 3 October 1847.

Union, 5th voyage:
   From France
      Sailed from Cherbourg 31 August 1847.
      Arrived in New York 16 September 1847.
   Returning
      Sailed from New York 30 September 1847.
      Arrived at Cherbourg 18 October 1847.

Missouri, 6th voyage:
   From France
      Sailed from Cherbourg 30 September 1847.
      Arrived in New York 19 October 1847.
   Returning
      Sailed from New York 25 October 1847.
      Arrived at Havre 11 November 1847.

Philadelphie, 7th voyage:
   From France
      Sailed from Cherbourg 10 October 1847; ran out of coal; put in at Halifax 29 October.
      Arrived in New York 3 November 1847.
   Returning
      Sailed from New York 10 November 1847.
      Arrived at Havre 28 November 1847.

New York, 8th voyage:
   From France
      Sailed from Havre 24 October 1847; ran out of coal; put in at Newport 12 November.
      Arrived in New York 14 November 1847.
   Returning
      Sailed from New York 25 November 1847.
      Arrived at Havre 12 December 1847.

Union, 9th voyage:
   From France
      Sailed from Havre 24 November 1847; gales; put in at Cherbourg because of sea

---

[33] Raymond Rousselin, *L'Acheminement des correspondances entre Le Havre et les pays d'outre-mer*, p. 75.

[34] Bonsor, *North Atlantic Seaway*, p. 52.

[35] Rousselin, *Correspondances entre Le Havre et les pays d'outre-mer*, pp. 77–79.

damage; remained there and did not sail again.

Missouri, last voyage:
   From France
      Sailed from Havre 23 December 1847; ran out of coal; put in at Halifax on 13 January 1848.
      Arrived in New York 18 January 1848.
   Returning
      Sailed from New York 6 February 1848.
      Arrived at Havre 23 February 1848.

Not only did the ships of this line frequently run out of coal, but they also clumsily caused a number of accidents in New York harbor, most of which resulted from the helmsmen's not knowing English and being unable to understand the orders of the pilots. So many jokes were directed at the line that Frenchmen who lived in New York were piqued. They organized a mass meeting to protest the jokes, but abandoned the effort when they learned about the poor quality of food served by the line.

Albion relates an amusing incident that occurred when one of these ships put to sea with no table sugar on board.[36] When the captain discovered the oversight at breakfast, he offered to put back for sugar if the passengers desired, "but it was too late. The passengers had already become *sour*. This sugar business broke up the line." The French government evidently despaired of the enterprise when it was announced early in 1848 that the company had incurred losses of £80,000.[37] The postal administration, in circular 19, dated 18 January 1848, announced the temporary suspension of the line's service.[38] It was not revived.

No cover actually conveyed by this line has been seen by the author. Such covers, however, are reported to bear a Le Havre marking which includes the abbreviation PAQ. REG.[39] One cover endorsed to the *Philadelphie* has been seen. This cover shows a New York marking dated 14 August (1847), the day before *Philadelphie* sailed. Unfortunately, the New York office forwarded it to Boston, whence it was conveyed to Liverpool by Cunarder *Hibernia,* which left Boston on 16 August, and according to Cunard records arrived in Liverpool on 28 August. Since the cover bears a red-orange British mark dated 28AU28, as well as a COLONIES/&C. ART. 13 marking, there can be little doubt that it did not go by the *Philadelphie*.

Mails by the New York-Havre Line

When Edward Mills failed to raise sufficient capital to build the four steamships called for by the Ocean Steam Navigation Company's contract, he assigned half of it to Messrs. Fox and Livingston. The effective member of this firm was Mortimer Livingston, who, unlike Mills, had considerable experience in the shipping business. The firm of Fox and Livingston operated the Union line of Havre sailing packets and continued to do so until the early 1860s. Gibbs suggests that the letters *U.S.M.* emblazoned upon the paddle boxes of the steamers of this line stood for *Union Steam Mail*.[40] The part of the contract assigned to Fox and Livingston related to a service between New York and Havre, touching at Cowes each way. The port of Cowes was on the northern tip of the Isle of Wight in the Southampton harbor complex. The assigned subsidy was in the amount of $150,000 for twelve round voyages per annum.

Fox and Livingston organized the New York and Havre Steam Navigation Company which ordered two steamers of about 2,200 tons from Westervelt and McKay. The first of these, *Franklin,* was an improved version of *Washington,* while the second, *Humboldt,* was straight-stemmed and a reduced edition of the Collins line steamers.[41]

The service was opened by *Franklin* which sailed from New York on her maiden voyage on 5 October 1850. *Humboldt* followed on 3 May 1851. Thus, these two ships would augment the service of the Ocean line to England, making possible semimonthly sailings from New York for Southampton. When the Collins line service to Liverpool was opened in April 1850, the sailings of all the American lines were scheduled on Saturdays. As in the case of the Ocean line, the subsidy was divided by twelve and accounted for at $12,500 per voyage. Although the Havre line sailed with greater regularity than the Ocean line, some winter voyages were avoided, and it was not until 1853 that the full $150,000 was earned.

Since the United States had no postal convention with France, United States inland and packet postages

---

[36] Robert Greenhalgh Albion, *Square Riggers on Schedule,* p. 264.
[37] Bonsor, *North Atlantic Seaway,* p. 52.
[38] Ibid., p. 53.
[39] Rousselin, *Correspondances entre Le Havre et les pays d'outre-mer,* p. 79.
[40] Gibbs, *Passenger Liners,* p. 97.
[41] Ibid., p. 99.

had to be prepaid on letters sent and collected on letters received. Until 1 July 1851, the rates set by the act of 3 March 1845 prevailed in the United States. Since these 24¢, 29¢, 34¢ rates were effective for this service between 5 October 1850 and 1 July 1851, their progression was according to the British scale, then operative in the United States. On 1 July 1851, the above rates were superseded by the 20¢-per-half-ounce rate, effective from or to any point in the United States.

The French private-ship rate of 30 centimes per 7½ grams for letters posted in or addressed to the port of arrival or departure of the conveying ship, and of 60 centimes per 7½ grams if posted or received in another part of France, had been in effect since 1849. These rates were prepaid or collected in France on direct mail to or from the United States until the United States-French treaty became effective on 1 April 1857.

The rate by direct packet to France was cheaper than by American packet through England, almost as cheap as by British packet, and actually cheaper if addressed to Havre. For example, a letter that weighed 7 grams posted in New York and addressed to Paris would have incurred a total postage, if conveyed by the Cunard line, of 5¢ in the United States and 13 decimes or about 26¢ in France for a total of 31¢. If the letter had been conveyed by the Collins line, 21¢ would have been charged in the United States and 8 decimes, or 16¢, in France for a total of 37¢. If conveyed by the Havre line the postage in the United States would have been 20¢, while the French would have collected 6 decimes, or 12¢, for a total of 32¢. Thus, there was only a one-cent differential between the rate by British packet and the rate by the Havre line.

For a letter that weighed 8 grams, however, the situation was entirely different. By British packet, 5¢ would be prepaid in the United States, while 26 decimes, or 52¢, would have been collected in France for a total postage of 57¢. By a Collins line packet, 21¢ would have been paid in the United States, while 16 decimes, or 32¢, would have been collected in France for a total postage of 53 cents. By the Havre line, 20¢ would have been paid in the United States, while 12 decimes, or 24¢, would have been collected in Paris, for a total of 44¢. If, in the latter case, the letter was addressed to Havre, the total postage would have been only 32¢, that is, 20¢ United States and 12¢ French postage.

It is, therefore, evident that the American packet postage for letters above the weight of 7½ grams, but not over half an ounce, were cheaper than by British packet, and the rate by the Havre line was cheaper than the American packet rate, via England. Since all transit postage was avoided on mail by the direct route to Havre, it would have been in the best interests of the Post Office Department to have augmented this service at every opportunity. There is evidence that such an opportunity did present itself, but the United States was thwarted in its attempt to secure direct-service rating on letters for France conveyed to Southampton by the Bremen (Ocean) line by either Britain or France, or perhaps by both.

While in Paris during the fall of 1850, Mr. Davis brought the matter to the attention of Mr. Lawrence. After a long conversation with M. Maurin, chief of the Bureau of Foreign Correspondence for France, Davis, on 24 September 1850 reported the following:[42]

> The mails for France, at New York, &c., by the Southampton steamers (Ocean line), are made up *in the English bag*. They used to be made up in a separate bag; the English very shrewdly got instructions at Washington to have them made up as at present, and the result is, England gets a transit and a sea-rate on all such letters. M. Maurin suggests that this may be remedied by fresh instructions from Washington to make up the bag separately for France, and that France will take it directly from the steamer at Southampton, and, if England charges *any* postage, will discuss the matter with her.

On 24 October 1850, Lawrence wrote Daniel Webster, secretary of state,[43] that

> If the post office at New York, instead of mixing the French and English mails, (as I am told they do,) would put up the French mails by themselves, and instruct the mail-agent to put them on board the Havre steamer at Southhampton, there could be no just pretence for the English government to charge even a transit rate.

It appears that the Post Office at New York did receive instructions from Washington to have the mail for France by the Bremen line made up in a separate bag and sent closed to Havre. On 7 February 1851, Lawrence again wrote Webster,[44]

> I learn, indirectly, that, by an arrangement between the French and English governments, *our closed mails to Havre via Southampton* [italics added for emphasis] are to be exempted from the claim for postage by this [British] government. You will remember I alluded to this tax in my despatch No. 83 (quoted above). If my information is correct, one very just cause of complaint is removed.

---

[42] *Senate Executive Document* 32, 32 Cong., 2 sess., serial 660, p. 15.
[43] Ibid., p. 6.
[44] Ibid., p. 20.

Further official comment upon the matter has not been found. Mr. Lawrence must have had some information regarding the negotiation of the provisional agreement that culminated in the French circulaire 67 of 1 September 1851 and the decree of 19 November 1851. The evidence of covers, however, indicates that the advantage of the direct rate was not extended to mail conveyed to Southampton by the Bremen (Ocean) line. The author has seen only seven covers addressed to France with markings whose dates indicate service to Southampton by the Ocean line. All of these covers show a collection in France of 8 or multiple of 8 decimes. Two of them were sent in the open mail through England and bear the marking shown as C or L in Figure 18. Four of the remaining five covers have the following characteristics: (1) markings whose dates indicate service by the Bremen (Ocean) line; (2) a prepayment of 21¢ per half ounce in the United States; (3) a Havre marking inscribed ETATS-UNIS PAQ.AM.A./LE HAVRE with date in center (see marking I of Figure 18); (4) a collection in France of 8 or multiple of 8 decimes; (5) no British marking on face or reverse of the cover.

The absence of a British marking on these four covers leads to the conclusion that they were sent in a separate bag which was placed onboard a small English steamer at Southampton and sent directly to Havre.[45] Perhaps this British service between Southampton and Havre necessitated that the transit rate be charged.

A cover in the Smithsonian collection, however, indicates that all such covers were not sent directly to Havre. This cover bears the frank of Senator Underwood and is addressed to "Hon Wm C Rives/ Envoy Extraordinary etc./Paris/France." It is illustrated as Figure 29. The letter was posted on 21 May 1852 and bears no New York packet marking because that marking had not yet been introduced (earliest seen 4 September 1852). The Havre office applied marking I of Figure 18, with the date 6/MAI/52, which is obviously an error, since the letter was not posted until 21 May 1852. Evidently the postal clerk at Havre neglected to change the month in the marking from May to June. On the reverse of the cover is a blue SOUTHAMPTON/5 JU 5/1852 marking which confirms the June date. The presence of this marking indicates that this letter was sent to the Southampton

---

[45] This service is disclosed in a letter from R. Salles to the author.

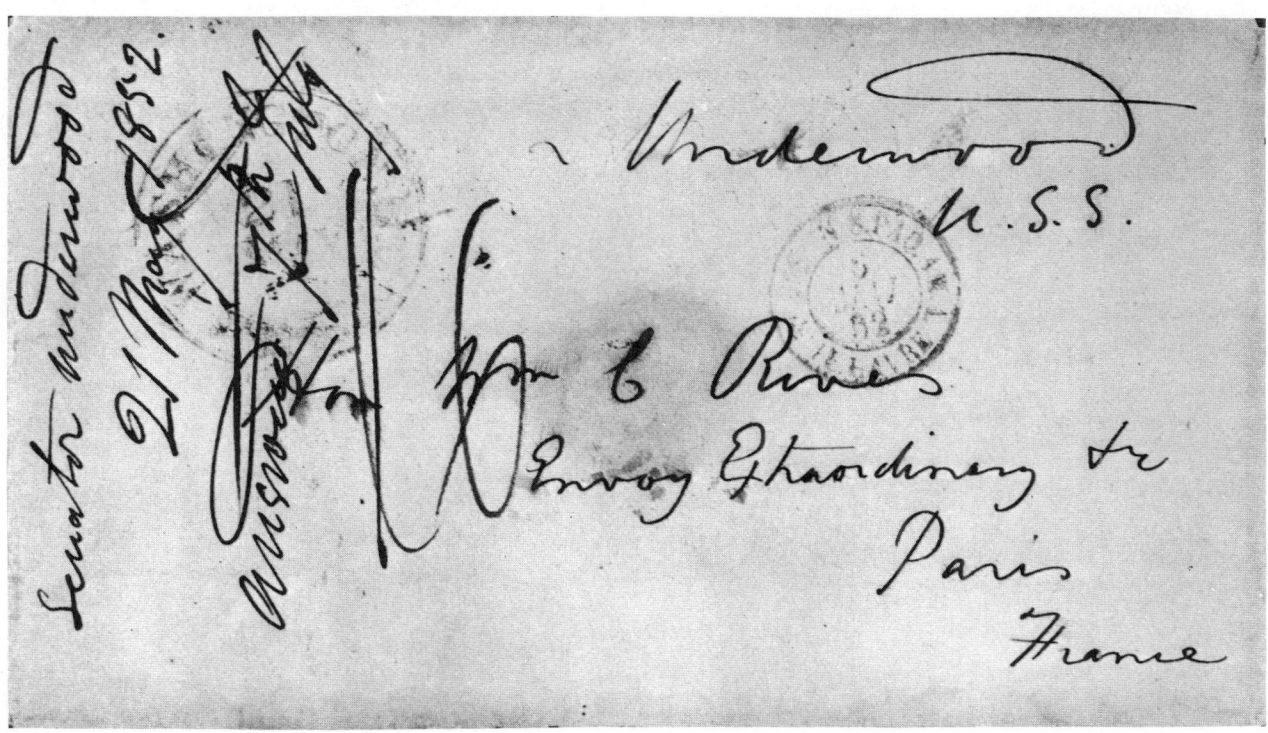

FIGURE 29.—COVER, from Washington, D.C., to Paris, France, 1852.
(*Photograph by Smithsonian*)

office, whence it was forwarded to Havre. It bears a double-rate manuscript due marking of *16* decimes. This letter was undoubtedly conveyed to Southampton by *Washington* of the Ocean line which sailed from New York on 22 May 1852. This is the only cover seen that bears marking *I* of Figure 18 and also a British marking.

It has been observed that all of the covers noted bearing marking *I* of Figure 18 were conveyed to Southampton by the Bremen (Ocean) line. This observation has also been made by M. Raymond Salles of Paris. Mr. Walter Hubbard of London has submitted a list of eleven covers compiled by M. Salles, all of which bear marking *I* of Figure 18 and were conveyed to Southampton by either the *Washington* or *Hermann*.

Of the five covers seen by the author addressed to France which bear marking *I* of Figure 18, three are stampless and two bear stamps. Figure 30 illustrates a cover posted in New Orleans on 17 January 1856, addressed to Bordeaux. The cover itself is a 3¢ stamped envelope and is additionally franked with a 12¢ and a pair of the 3¢ stamps of the 1851 issue. The New York American packet marking bears the date of 26 January (1856), and on that date *Hermann* of the Ocean line sailed from New York. The cover bears no British marking. The Havre marking (*I* of Figure 18) is dated 12/JANV./56, which is obviously an error. As in the cover shown in Figure 29, the clerk evidently neglected to change the month in the marking from January to February. The cover is marked for a double-rate collectión of 16 decimes.

A cover in the collection of Mr. Lester L. Downing bears a marking as in *I* of Figure 18. This is a printed circular that was posted in New Orleans on 3 July 1855, prepaid by a pair of 1¢ type IV stamps of the 1851 issue, addressed to Belgium. It bears no New York or British marking. Marking *I* of Figure 18 is dated 31 July 1855.

Covers by the New York-Havre Line

Covers showing direct service between New York and Havre by the ships of the Havre line prior to the United States-French convention appear to be scarce. Although such covers to France having the United States postage prepaid by stamps are much sought after, they seldom appear in auction sales. Covers showing the 24¢, 29¢, 34¢ rates of 1845 are rarely seen. There were only six sailings from New York and four sailings from Havre by the Havre line steamers prior to 1 July 1851 (Table 9).

Figure 31 illustrates a cover posted in Paris on 30 December 1850, addressed to Georgetown, D.C., and endorsed "per steamer Franklin/via Havre." On the reverse is a manuscript *6* which indicates that 6 decimes were prepaid. It was the custom of the French,

FIGURE 30.—COVER, from New Orleans to Bordeaux, France, 1856. (*Walter Hubbard collection*)

TABLE 9.—*Havre Line Sailings*

Arrival Date, N.Y.	Ship	Departure Date, N.Y.
1850		1850
	Franklin	5 Oct. 1850
17 Nov. 1850	*Franklin*	5 Dec. 1850
17 Jan. 1851	*Franklin*	5 Apr. 1851
	Humboldt	3 May 1851
19 May 1851	*Franklin*	31 May 1851
17 June 1851	*Humboldt*	28 June 1851

at that time, to indicate prepayments on the reverse and amounts due on the face of letters. Six decimes was the private-ship–beyond-the-port rate for a letter that did not weigh over 7½ grams. Also on the reverse is a marking of the maritime office at Havre, similar to H of Figure 18, but inscribed HAVRE instead of LE HAVRE, bearing the date of 31 December 1850. This marking (with HAVRE or LE HAVRE) is characteristic of all private-ship- or direct-mail-service covers forwarded from the Havre office. On the face is a boxed P.P. marking in red, which means *port payé*, and indicates that the French postage was paid. The large circular NEW-YORK/SHIP/JAN 17/29CTS black marking shows that 29¢ were to be collected at a destination under 300 miles from New York: 17 January (1851) was the date *Franklin* arrived in New York, terminating her second round voyage.

Covers showing direct service by the Havre line after 1 July 1851 went under the 20¢-per-half-ounce rate, effective on that date, to or from any part of the United States. The vessels of the Havre line sailed only once a month, with some irregularity during the winter. For the fiscal year of 1852–53, as reported by the auditor of the treasury for the Post Office Department,[46] the value of the postage on all mail conveyed from New York to Havre by this line was only $9,018.93, despite the efforts of the Post Office Department to persuade the public to favor the American lines. Few covers have been seen which bear a prepayment of 20¢. Even when letters were endorsed to be sent by this line or its ships, the usual prepayment was 21¢, since, by paying that amount, the letter could be sent by the next Collins line steamer if the Havre line ship failed to sail.

Figure 32 illustrates a very attractive Havre line cover. It bears a strip of three of the 3¢ 1851 stamps in the orange-brown shade and a single 12¢ stamp. The 3¢ stamps are of a rich color and are particularly attractive because they are canceled with a red grid. The letter was posted in New York, addressed to Lyon. It bears a red New York town postmark dated 23 August (1851), and on that date *Humboldt* sailed from New York. It should be noted that the New York American packet marking did not make its appearance until mid-1852. Characteristic of Havre line covers is a double circle OUTRE-MER/LE HAVRE marking (G of Figure 18) applied in red-orange, with date in center, in this case 4/SEPT./51. It is marked

---

[46] U.S., Congress, House, *Executive Document* 1, 33rd Cong., 1st sess., serial 692, p. 734.

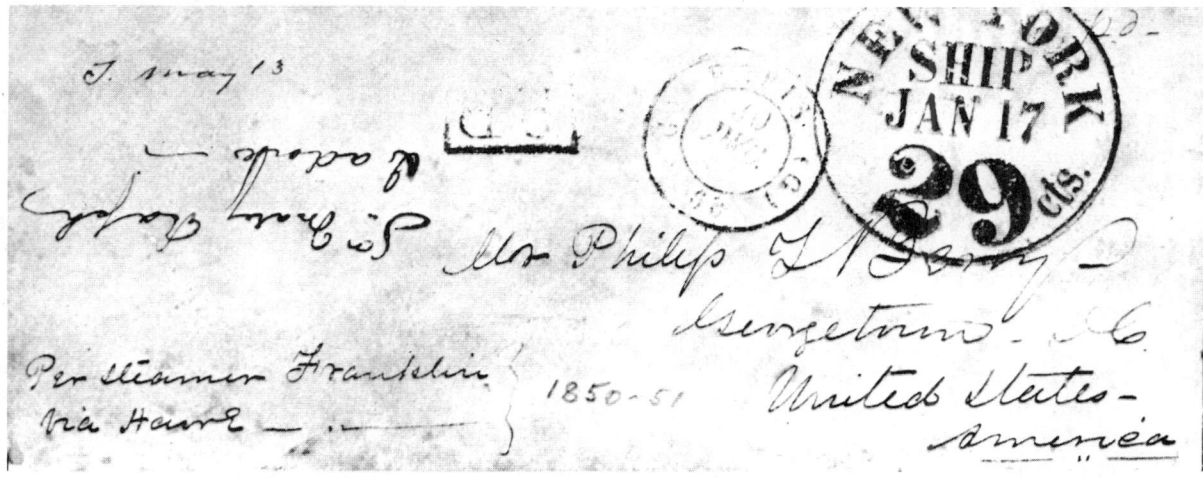

FIGURE 31.—COVER, from Paris to Georgetown, D.C., 1850.

FIGURE 32.—COVER, from New York to Lyons, France, 1851. (*Melvin W. Schuh collection*)

for a collection of the single beyond-the-port rate of 6 decimes, indicated by a *6* in manuscript.

Figure 33 illustrates a cover posted in New York, addressed to Lyons, France, and endorsed "Pr. Humboldt." It is prepaid 20¢ by a 12¢, two 3¢, and a pair of 1¢ stamps of the 1851 issue. The New York marking bears the date of 13 December and on 13 December 1851, the *Humboldt* of the Havre line sailed from New York. The OUTRE-MER/LE HAVRE marking is faintly applied, its date not being legible. This letter weighed over 7½ grams and required a double-rate collection of 12 decimes. Covers by the Havre line actually prepaid with 20¢ are seldom seen.

Figure 34 illustrates a cover posted in New Orleans on 28 December 1855, addressed to Nantes. It is endorsed to *Pacific* of the Collins line, and is prepaid 21¢ by a pair of 10¢ type III stamps and a 1¢ type IV stamp of the 1851 issue. Since *Pacific* sailed from New York on 5 January 1856, this letter evidently arrived too late to be included in its mail. It was therefore sent by the next American packet to sail, which was *Arago* of the Havre line. As is indicated by the New York packet marking, this vessel sailed from New York on 12 January 1856. The cover bears the characteristic OUTRE-MER/LE HAVRE marking (*G* of Figure 18) and shows a single rate collection of 6 decimes.

Figure 35 illustrates a cover from the Toppan-Carpenter correspondence. It was posted in Philadelphia on 8 April 1853, addressed to Paris. It is prepaid 21¢ by a strip of three of the 3¢ stamps and a single 12¢ stamp of the 1851 issue. It is endorsed "Pr Steamer Franklin/April 9," and the American packet marking bears the same date. An orange-red OUTRE-MER/LE HAVRE marking shows the date of 21 April 1853, while a Paris receiving mark on the reverse indicates it arrived at its destination on the same day. There is a manuscript marking on the face that resembles a *W*. This marking has been noted on some covers whose weight was in excess of 7½ grams. The Havre office, therefore, rated it for a collection of double the beyond-the-port postage of 6 decimes. This is shown on the face of the cover by a *12* in manuscript.

Figure 36 shows a letter posted in Sharon Springs, New York, on 29 July 1853, addressed to Paris. It is suspected that it was presented to the post office clerk with 24¢ in stamps affixed to the letter, that is, a strip of six and two single 3¢ stamps. The post office clerk determined that it weighed over half an ounce and

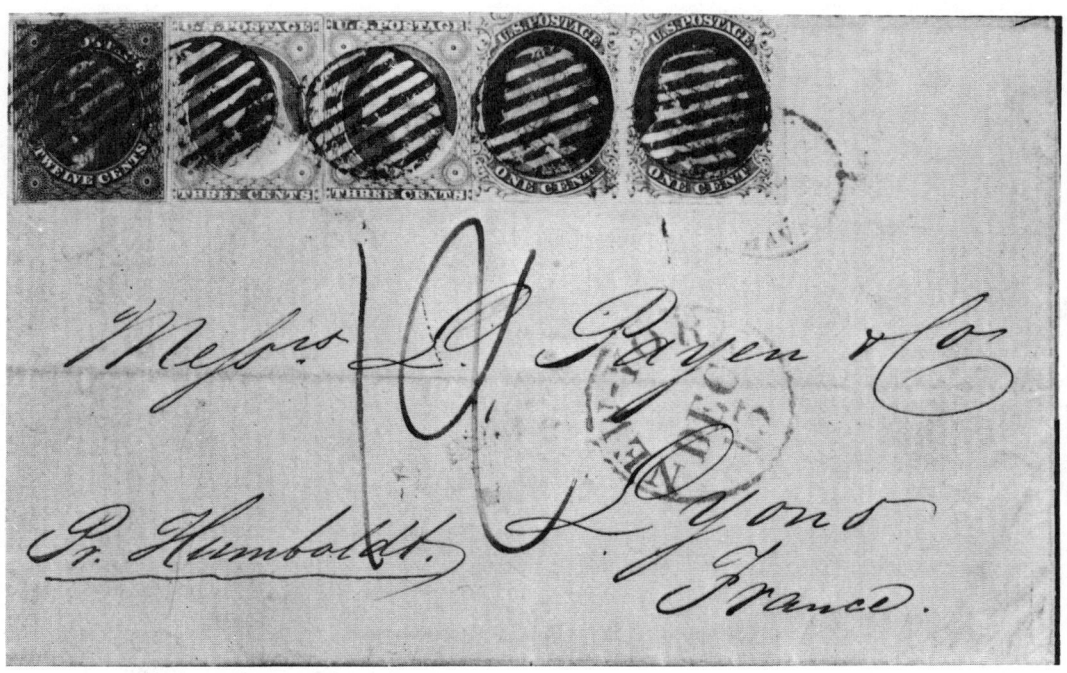

FIGURE 33.—COVER, from New York to Lyons, France, 1851. (*Walter Hubbard collection*)

FIGURE 34.—COVER, from New Orleans to Nantes, 1855. (*Arthur E. Beane, Jr., collection*)

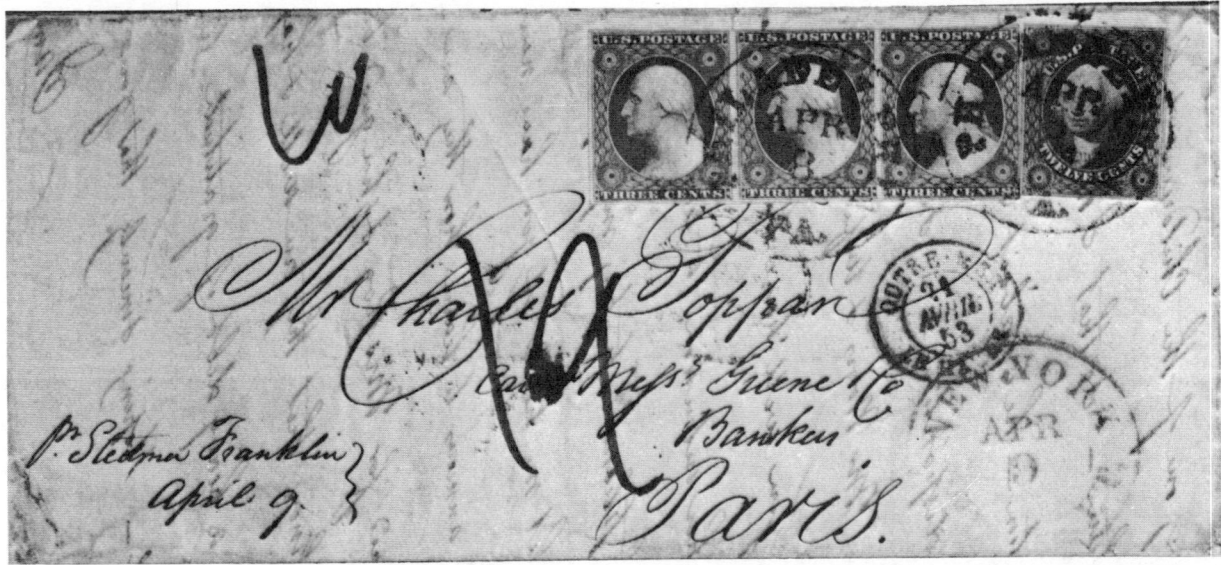

FIGURE 35.—COVER, from Philadelphia to Paris, 1853.
(*From the Toppan-Carpenter correspondence*)

thus would require two rates. It must have been known that *Franklin* of the Havre line would sail from New York on the following day, and that the rate by this route was 20¢ for a single rate. Since the required postage amounted to 40¢, the person who mailed the letter evidently paid the additional 16¢ in cash. The clerk, not finding room for the additional stamps, on the face of the cover, marked it PAID/40 and indicated the additional payment by a lead pencil *16*. Then, to clarify the matter, he marked in red ink, *Stamps 24/Cash 16/40¢*.

The letter left New York on the *Franklin* on 30 July, as is indicated by the New York packet mark, and arrived at Havre on 11 August 1853. The Havre office rated it as a letter weighing over 15 but not over 22½ grams, and marked it for a collection of 18 decimes. Although the condition of this cover leaves much to be desired, it is undoubtedly unique, not because of the triple-rate collection (the Smithsonian collection contains a cover showing 18 decimes due), but because the postage is part-paid by stamps.

Figure 37 presents a cover posted in Havre, addressed to New York. It is endorsed to *Fulton* of the Havre line which sailed from Havre on 22 October and arrived in New York on 9 November 1856, as is indicated by the BUREAU MARITIME/LE HAVRE and 20/N. YORK AM. PKT markings, respectively. The letter must have weighed over 7½ but not over 15 grams, requiring a prepayment of double the 3-decimes in-the-port rate, since it is franked with a 40- and a 20-centime imperforate Empire stamp. Twenty cents were collected from the addressee in New York.

The Three-Months' Period 1 January 1857–1 April 1857

As early as May 1853, the British and the French were attempting to negotiate a new postal convention. Lord Clarendon, at that time, suggested to Mr. J. R. Ingersoll, United States minister at London that the United States press France to accept British proposals for a reduction of rates on all mail between Great Britain and France, rather than persist in its demand that the British reduce their transit rate to France to 6d. per ounce.[47] By 1854, the British and the French had agreed upon new rates for letters passing between the two countries only, that is, new international rates. It was decided that these rates should be placed in force immediately without waiting for the completion of the negotiation of the remainder of the convention. On 12 December 1854, additional articles to the convention of 1843, which were to become effective on 1 January 1855, were signed at Paris.[48] By these articles,

---

[47] *Senate Executive Document* 73, 33 Cong., 2 sess., serial 756, p. 42.

[48] *British and Foreign State Papers*, vol. 44, pp. 43–45.

FIGURE 36.—COVER, from Sharon Springs, N.Y., to Paris, France, 1853.

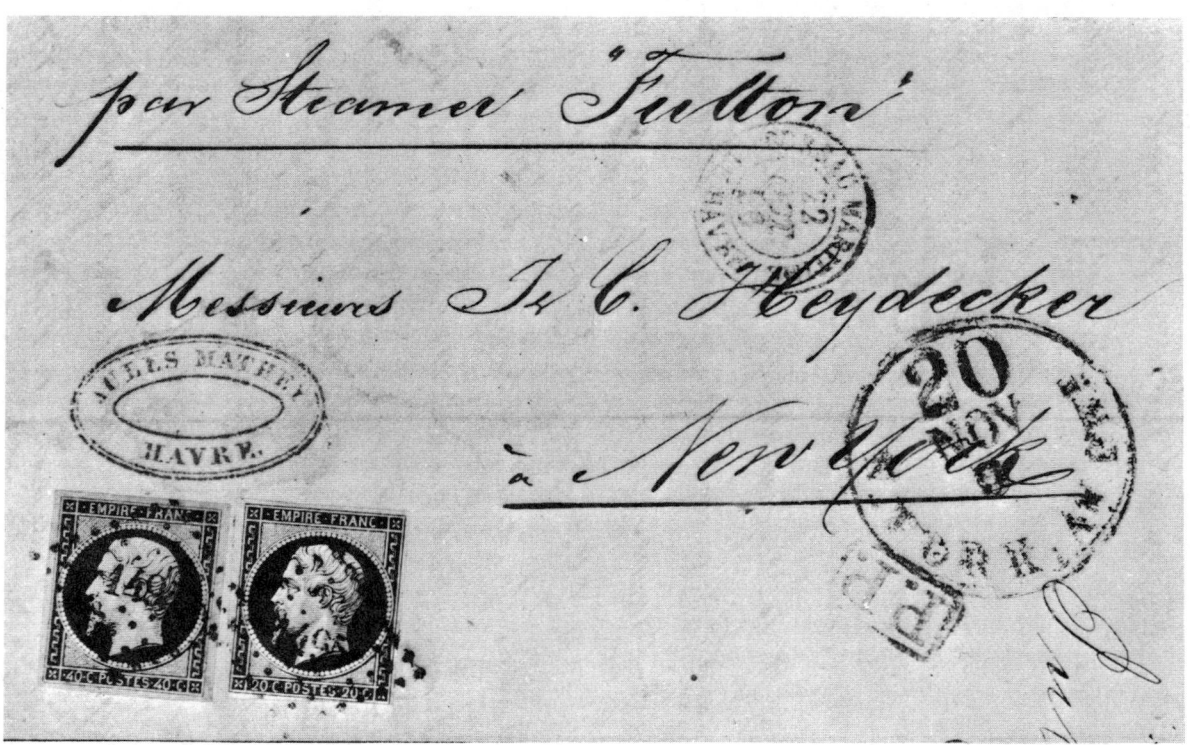

FIGURE 37.—COVER, from Havre to New York, 1856.

the international rate upon prepaid letters was reduced from 5d. in Great Britain and 50 centimes in France to 4d. in Great Britain and 40 centimes in France for single-rate letters of one-fourth ounce (British) or 7½ grams (French). Unpaid letters, however, were to be charged with double the prepaid rates. Since these articles altered only the international rates, transit mail was unaffected, and there was no change in rates charged on mail between the United States and France.

The new Anglo-French convention was finally completed and signed at Paris on 24 September 1856, ratifications were exchanged on 19 November, and the treaty became effective on 1 January 1857.[49] Articles significant in their application to mail between the United States and France are summarized as follows:

XIII. Incorporated into the convention the international rates established by the additional articles to the 1843 convention of 12 December 1854.

XIV. The French Post Office paid the British Post Office, for letters exchanged in ordinary mail, 1 franc per ounce for paid letters and 2 francs per ounce for unpaid letters.

XVII. Registered letters could be sent by the inhabitants of either country. Postage had to be prepaid and was double that of ordinary letters.

XX. Each country had the right of conveyance of closed mails over the territory of the other.

XXI. The French Office paid the British Office, for transit through England, 40 centimes per 30 grams of letters in closed mails.

XXII. The French Office paid the British Office, for sea conveyance, 1 franc, 20 centimes per 30 grams of letters in closed mails.

XXVII. Made the conditions set forth in Articles XXI and XXII apply to mail originating in or addressed to colonies and countries beyond the sea.

XXVIII. Set the letter rate for transit through France on mail passing through the Isthmus of Suez, as follows: "[that it] shall not in any case exceed 3d. per quarter of an ounce, British, or fraction of a quarter of an ounce, British."

XXXI. The two offices were to determine by mutual consent the conditions upon which open mail was to be exchanged between colonies and countries beyond the sea and between the two countries.

Detailed regulations for the execution of the convention were signed at Paris on 27 October 1856[50] and became effective with the convention on 1 January 1857. Following is an excerpt from a significant article of these regulations:

XXXII. Ordinary unpaid letters "charged with transit or sea rates, which shall be exchanged in ordinary mails between the Post Office of France and the Post Office of Great Britain, shall receive, in some conspicuous part of the address, the impression in black ink of a stamp intended to show the rate at which the dispatching office shall have delivered those letters and printed papers to the other office."

Illustrated[51] in the article were eleven marks to be used by the French Post Office and seven similar marks for use by the British Post Office on letters exchanged. Marks to be used on printed papers were also illustrated. Each of these marks had an outer frame line of a distinctive and different shape. All were divided horizontally by double lines at about the center, and in the upper portion of each were the letters F.R. (on those for use by the French Office) or G.B. (on those to be used by the British Office). Each bore in its lower portion an amount expressed in French currency showing the rate per 30 grams or per ounce at which the mail containing the letter had been dispatched. Collectors have variously called these "currency marks," "partitioned marks," or "tray marks." It has been suggested that the reason for having a mark of distinctive shape for each rate was to enable postal clerks to recognize the rate without reading what was written on the mark. This undoubtedly speeded the sorting of and accounting for mail, especially in those colonies and countries where native clerks did not ordinarily read English or French.[52]

Only two of these markings were used on mail from the United States regularly during this three-month period and occasionally thereafter on letters missent or intentionally forwarded in the open mail. To letters charged with transit postage only, that is, those conveyed by American packet, the British Post Office applied a marking showing G.B. at top and 40^c at bottom (see marking O of Figure 18). To letters charged with both transit and sea postage, that is, those conveyed by British packet, the British Post Office applied a marking bearing G.B. at top and 1^f 60^c at bottom (see marking P of Figure 18).

---

[49] Ibid., pp. 195–224.
[50] Ibid., vol. 52, pp. 1123–1141.
[51] Ibid., pp. 1133–1135. [See also George E. Hargest, "Unpaid and Part-Paid Rates Between the United States and France," Postal History Journal 7, 1 (June 1963): 4–6, for reproduction of these markings.]
[52] W. Skrine, and F. W. Webb, "Anglo-French Currency Handstamps, 1857–75," The Philatelist 27, 9 (June 1961): 222.

Mail from France to the United States had to be prepaid to the United States frontier when conveyed by British packet, or to the British port of embarkation when conveyed by American packet. In either case postage was prepaid through Great Britain, and unpaid currency stamps were, therefore, not applied.

Article XXI of the detailed regulations provided that ordinary mails passing through Great Britain, to or from France and Algeria and countries enumerated in an appended Table I, would be exchanged between the post offices of the two countries in accordance with conditions set forth in that table. For single-rate (7½ grams) letters from or to the United States, Table I prescribed that the amount to be collected in France and Algeria on unpaid letters received or on prepaid letters sent was to be 80 centimes when conveyance was by British packet, and 50 centimes when the letter was conveyed by American packet.

Since the post offices of the two countries were able, under Article XXXI of the treaty, to establish by mutual consent the rates to be used for the exchange of open mail, it would appear that they had agreed to apply the rates set forth in Articles XXI and XXII of the treaty to open mail as well as to closed mail. Because mail originating in France, addressed to the United States, was closed through England, the application of the closed-mail rates to open mail originating in the United States and addressed to France continued the practice established by the provisional agreement and the decree rates established in 1851. Table 10 shows the method by which the British and French Post Offices arrived at the amounts of postage to be prepaid or collected in France on letters between the United States and France, via England.

TABLE 10.—*United States and French Postal Rates via England (1 January–1 April 1857)*

	Rate per 7½ grams	
	British Packet	American Packet
Article XXI—Transit postage of 40 centimes per 30 grams. Single rate, ¼ thereof	10c	10c
Article XXII—Sea postage of 1 franc 20 centimes per 30 grams, single rate, ¼ thereof	30	—
French inland postage, single rate	40	40
Prepaid or collected in France	80c	50c

From 1850 the United States had been demanding that the British reduce their transit rate to France to 6d. per ounce. Although the Anglo-French convention of 1856 reduced this transit rate to only 4d. per ounce, the United States did not avail itself of the reduction. By the effective date of the Anglo-French convention, 1 January, 1857, the United States and France were nearing agreement on a postal convention between the two countries, and it is suspected that they did not wish to make an interim arrangement for what they anticipated would be a very short period of time. By Article XLIV of the detailed regulations of the Anglo-French convention, provision was made for closed mail between the United States and France, via England. It would appear that the French negotiated this article with the United States-French convention in mind.

Whatever the reason the United States may have had for delay, the rates of the new Anglo-French convention had a devastating effect upon American packet mail-service between the United States and France, via England. It will be noted in Table 10 that sea postage by British packet was only 30 centimes per 7½ grams, or 6¢ in United States currency. The United States, however, continued to require a collection on American packet letters received, or a prepayment on American packet letters sent, of 21¢, which included a sea postage of 16¢. Thus, the rate by British packet was 10¢ lower than by American packet. It is small wonder that few people elected to send letters by American packet during this three-month period.

The scarcity of covers showing American packet service, via England, during the three-month period may also be attributed to a decline in Collins line service. *Arctic* had been lost in 1854 and *Pacific* "went missing" in early 1856. Because it was believed that *Pacific* had struck an iceberg, the line's management decided to fit the remaining two ships with watertight compartments. For this purpose, *Baltic* was out of service from 6 February to 15 August 1857, while *Atlantic* went into drydock on 5 March and did not sail again until 11 April.[53] Ever since 1855, the line had been using some chartered vessels which were definitely inferior to the original ships. Although the line continued to use *Ericsson*, it did not, at this time, charter additional ships, and its service was necessarily curtailed. During this period (from January to March) there were only five sailings by American pac-

[53] *Shipping and Commercial List and New York Prices Current,* 11 Mar. 1857.

kets which conveyed mail via England. They are presented in Table 11.[54]

To the date of this writing, only five covers showing American packet service, via England, during this three-month period have been noted. Three of them bear stamps, two are stampless, and all five are by Collins line ships.

Figure 38 illustrates a cover showing markings characteristic of American packet letters, via England, during the three-months period. Posted in New Orleans on 25 December 1856, addressed to Garonne, France, it was prepaid with 21¢ by a pair of 10¢ type II stamps and a 1¢ type II of the 1851 issue. The New York American packet mark bears the date of 3 January, the date *Baltic* sailed on the first voyage conveying mail to France under the rates of the new Anglo-French convention. On its reverse is a circular British marking applied in dark brown bearing the date of 17 January 1857, while on its face is a GB/40¢ currency mark applied in black ink by the London office, indicating that the letter was included in a mail dispatched to France charged only with transit postage of 40 centimes per 30 grams, bulk weight, of such mail. The French exchange office marking (see marking *L* of Figure 18) is that of the travelling office, Calais to Paris and reads ÉTATS-UNIS PAQ. AM./A. CALAIS D/18/ JANV./57, meaning "From the United States by American packet through the abulant office from Calais, the mail being processed by a mail crew (brigade) identified by the letter *D*." This cover is owned by Walter Hubbard of London, England, and is reproduced through his kindness.

Figure 39 illustrates a cover showing dissimilarities in the British and French exchange office markings. Originating in New Orleans on 7 January 1857, addressed to Bordeaux, this letter was prepaid 21¢ by seven 3¢ stamps of the 1851 issue, a strip of six (95 to 100L4) and a single (94L4). The New York packet mark is dated 17 January, indicating conveyance to Liverpool by *Ericsson*, then under charter to the Collins line. The London marking on the reverse is of the usual circular type applied in orange ink, and bears the date of 2 February. The French exchange office mark reads ANGL./AMB. CALAIS [?]/2/FEVR./57, and is in black ink. This marking was used on mail dispatched by British exchange offices to France without regard to the mail's origin (see marking *N* in Figure 18). This cover is owned by Mr. Tracy W. Simpson of Berkeley, California, and is reproduced with his kind permission.

A third cover bearing 24¢ in stamps (3¢ overpaid) and markings identical with those shown on Figure 38 is in the collection of Dr. Robert de Wasserman of Brussels, Belgium. It is illustrated in *Chronicle* 39, April 1961.

Covers showing British packet service during these three months are scarce. The Cunard line made sixteen voyages with mails rated under terms of the new 1856 Anglo-French convention. They are listed in Table 12. Since the United States was not a party to this convention, no change was made in the prepayment or collection of postage in this country. Those letters from the United States, addressed to France, that arrived at the London exchange office on or after 1 January 1857 were forwarded by that office to France under conditions and rates set forth in the new Anglo-French convention and its detailed regulations. Regular use of these conditions and rates on mail between the United States and France was terminated when the United States-French convention became effective. While the rates of this convention came into operation on letters posted in either the United States or France on 1 April 1857, the effective date on letters received in each country is indefinite. Letters posted in New York on 1 April were rated and marked according to the United States-French convention by the New York exchange office and were dispatched on that same day by the *Africa* (see Table 12). Those posted in places remote from New York or Boston as late as 31 March, however, may not have arrived

TABLE 11.—*American Packet Sailings via England (1 January–1 April 1857)*

Arrival Date, New York	Ship	Departure Date, New York
1856/57	Collins Line	1857
25 Dec.	*Baltic*	3 Jan.
13 Jan.	*Ericsson*	17 Jan.
23 Jan.	*Atlantic*	31 Jan.
6 Feb.	*Baltic* Up [a]	14 Feb. Dns.[b]
5 Mar.	*Atlantic* Up [a]	14 Mar. Dns.[b]
25 Feb.	*Ericsson*	14 Mar.
	Ocean Line	
20 Jan.	*Washington*	21 Feb.

[a] Sailing announced at New York.
[b] Did not sail.

[54] *Shipping and Commercial List,* appropriate issues.

FIGURE 38.—COVER, from New Orleans to Garonne, France, 1856. (*Walter Hubbard collection*)

FIGURE 39.—COVER, from New Orleans to Bordeaux, 1857. (*Tracy W. Simpson collection*)

at one of these exchange offices in time to catch the sailing of *Europa* from Boston on 8 April, or possibly that of *Asia* from New York on 15 April. The last sailing shown in Table 12 is based upon the latest cover noted at this time. It is possible that one showing a later date will be found.

Markings characteristic of letters conveyed by British packets during this three-month period are found on the cover illustrated in Figure 40. The letter was posted in New Orleans, addressed to Bordeaux, on 10 March 1857. It was forwarded from New York on 18 March 1857 by R.M.S. *Persia,* as is indicated by the date in the New York packet marking. Since Liverpool was not an exchange office for Anglo-French mail, the bags were sent directly to the London office. That office applied a GB/1^{F}60^C marking in black (see *P* in Figure 18) to the face of the cover and a marking on the reverse (not shown), and dispatched it to the traveling office, Calais to Paris, which applied marking *N* of Figure 18 on 30 March 1857 and also marked the cover for a single-rate collection of 8 decimes. The letter is franked with a single 5¢ imperforate stamp issued in 1856 (Scott no. 12). The New Orleans post office appears to have been well

TABLE 12.—*Cunard Line Sailings*
(*December 1856–April 1857*)

Departure Date, Liverpool	Arrival Date, U.S.	Ship	Port	Departure Date, U.S.	Arrival Date, Liverpool
1857	1857			1856/57	1857
		Africa	New York	24 Dec.	4 Jan.
		Canada	Boston	31 Dec.	13 Jan.
		Europa	New York	7 Jan.	18 Jan.
		Niagara	Boston	14 Jan.	26 Jan.
		Asia	New York	21 Jan.	2 Feb.
3 Jan.	16 Jan.	*America*	Boston	28 Jan.	11 Feb.
10 Jan.	24 Jan.	*Persia*	New York	4 Feb.	14 Feb.
17 Jan.	30 Jan.	*Arabia*	Boston	11 Feb.	21 Feb.
24 Jan.	6 Feb.	*Africa*	New York	18 Feb.	2 Mar.
31 Jan.	16 Feb.	*Europa*	Boston	25 Feb.	8 Mar.
7 Feb.	22 Feb.	*Asia*	New York	4 Mar.	16 Mar.
14 Feb.	2 Mar.	*Niagara*	Boston	11 Mar.	23 Mar.
21 Feb.	6 Mar.	*Persia*	New York	18 Mar.	29 Mar.
28 Feb.	14 Mar.	*America*	Boston	25 Mar.	6 Apr.
7 Mar.	24 Mar.	*Africa*	New York	1 Apr.	12 Apr.
14 Mar.	29 Mar.	*Europa*	Boston	8 Apr.	20 Apr.
21 Mar.	4 Apr.	*Asic*	New York		
28 Mar.	11 Apr.	*Niagara*	Boston		
4 Apr.	18 Apr.	*Arabia*	New York		

NOTE. Sailings taken from incomplete records of the Cunard line by Lester L. Downing, completed and confirmed by the author from appropriate issues of *Shipping and Commercial List and New York Prices Current*.

FIGURE 40.—COVER, from New Orleans to Bordeaux, 1857. (*Lester L. Downing collection*)

supplied with this stamp. It has been noted that more covers posted in New Orleans addressed to France during this three-month period are franked with 5¢ stamps than are franked with any other combination of stamps. This is not, however, intended to imply that such covers bearing a 5¢ stamp are not scarce.

Covers from France addressed to the United States during this period are difficult to find. No cover showing a prepayment of 50 centimes in France and a collection of 21¢ in the United States has been seen by the author. Only two covers showing a prepayment of 80 centimes in France and a collection of 5¢ in the United States have been noted. These covers, however, have been collected for their rates by only a few collectors and are not offered as such in auction sales. That they are scarce is not doubted, but it is not believed they are as rare as is indicated by the preceding statement.

Figure 41 illustrates a cover posted in Bordeaux on 25 March 1857, addressed to New York. It is franked with two 40-centimes imperforate Empire stamps. It is struck with a boxed P.P. marking indicating that postage was "prepaid for some part of the distance beyond the territory of the dispatching office."[55] Since mail from France was closed through England there is no British marking. A circular BOSTON BR. PKT./5/APR/11 in black on the face of the cover indicates that 5¢ were to be collected in New York. The date of 11 April shows that it was conveyed by R.M.S. *Niagara* (see Table 12).

---

[55] *British and Foreign State Papers*, vol. 52, p. 1136. Detailed regulations for the execution of the convention of 24 Sept. 1856, Article 34. Although this statement appears in the article for the first time, covers indicate that the marking was used to indicate a payment of postage for part of the distance when the Anglo-French provisional agreement became effective in 1851.

FIGURE 41.—COVER, from Bordeaux to New York, 1857.

Chapter 4

The United States-French Postal Convention of 2 March 1857

As early as 1849, the United States was attempting to negotiate a postal convention with the French. The negotiations, however, remained stagnant for years because the French refused to consider the adoption of rates based upon the weight of half an ounce, and also because no way could be found of circumventing the existing high transit-rate between Great Britain and France. Another obstacle was the French inland rate, which was high on domestic letters but even more expensive on foreign correspondence.

In his annual report for 1854, Postmaster General Campbell said, "No satisfactory progress has been made, since my last report, toward effecting a postal convention with France."[1] In the following year, however, he reported:[2]

> One of the obstacles to an arrangement with France consisting of the unwillingness of the French government to adopt the half instead of the quarter-ounce scale for letters passing between the two countries, in the month of May last I embraced a favorable opportunity to propose that, rather than the negotiation should fail, I would yield my objection to the quarter-ounce scale. To this proposition . . . I have received no reply.

But the acceptance by the United States of the quarter-ounce scale settled only one of the impediments to agreement. There still remained the high Anglo-French transit and French inland rates. The former had to await the signing of the Anglo-French convention of 24 September 1856 and the latter a willingness on the part of the French to reduce their inland rate before final agreement could be reached. As previously mentioned, the French negotiated the final provisions of the Anglo-French treaty with the United States-French convention in mind. By admitting the United States to its closed-mail provisions as set forth in Article XLIV of the detailed regulations, the "via England" provisions of the United States-French convention became possible.[3]

The final draft of the United States-French postal convention was signed at Washington on 2 March 1857,[4] and according to Article XVII was to become effective on the following first day of April. The provisions of this convention are laboriously detailed, probably because sea and French inland postages differed according to the routes established. Following is a résumé of the articles of the convention:

I. The United States and French Post Offices would exchange correspondence by means of the following:
   A. By packets and other steam vessels performing regular service between the ports of the United States and France
   B. By United States mail packets plying between the ports of the United States and Great Britain
   C. By British packets and other British steam vessels plying between the ports of Great Britain and the United States

---

[1] "Report of the Postmaster General, 1854," U.S., Congress, Senate, *Executive Document* 1, 33rd Cong., 2nd sess., serial 747, p. 631.

[2] *Report of the Postmaster General*, 1855, p. 19.

[3] *British and Foreign State Papers*, vol. 52, p. 1139.

[4] U.S., 16 Statutes at Large 871.

II. The French Post Office was to pay all expenses of direct conveyance of the mails, except for mail transported directly in United States packets, and was also to pay the following:
   A. The expenses of transportation of mail between France and England
   B. The transit charges due the British Post Office on said mails
   C. The expenses of sea transportation by means of British packets and other British steam vessels

   The United States Post Office would pay as follows:
   A. The expenses of direct conveyance by United States mail packets
   B. The expenses of conveyance between the United States and Great Britain in United States mail packets

III. Established exchange offices in France, as follows:
   A. Havre
   B. The travelling office from Calais to Paris
   Established exchange offices in the United States, as follows:
   A. New York B. Boston C. Philadelphia D. San Francisco

IV. All United States and French exchange offices were to correspond with each other by the routes mentioned in Article I.

V. Refers to an appended table which set forth the manner in which the exchange offices were to correspond with each other: by what steamship lines and according to the origin and destination of which mail.

VI. Established for France and Algeria an international rate of 80 centimes for a single letter of $7\frac{1}{2}$ grams, or fraction of $7\frac{1}{2}$ grams.

Established for the United States an international rate of 15¢ for a single letter of one quarter ounce, or fraction of one quarter ounce.

Prepayment was made optional, but the whole postage to destination was to be prepaid, if prepayment was desired.

VII. The rates of postage to be paid by the French Post Office to the United States Post Office on prepaid letters sent from France and Algeria, as well as on unpaid letters received in France and Algeria were fixed as follows:
   A. At 3¢ per single rate for *each* letter conveyed between the French and American frontiers at French expense
   B. At 9¢ per single rate for *each* letter conveyed between the American and British frontiers at United States expense
   C. At 12¢ per single rate for *each* letter conveyed between the American and French frontiers direct, or when touching only at one intermediate English port without passing through England, at United States expense

   The rates of postage to be paid by the United States Post Office to the French Post Office on prepaid letters sent from the United States as well as on unpaid letters received in the United States were fixed as follows:
   A. At 3¢ per single rate for *each* letter conveyed between the American and French frontiers direct, or when touching only at one intermediate English port without passing through England, at United States expense
   B. At 6¢ per single rate for *each* letter conveyed between the American and British frontiers at United States expense
   C. At 12¢ per single rate for *each* letter conveyed between the American and French frontiers at French expense

VIII. Referred to tables which set forth the rates, via France, to certain designated foreign countries. (These rates will be presented later, in Table 17, the exchange office accounting for the rates, in Table 18.)

IX. Badly addressed and undeliverable letters were to be returned for the sum that the sending office allowed the other office, if prepaid, or charged with the postage that should have been paid by the addressee, if unpaid.

Letters addressed to persons who had changed their residence would be delivered or returned, charged with the postage which should have been paid by the person addressed.

X. Provided that letters be marked by the sending office with the amount credited to, or charged to, the corresponding office, debits to be made in black and credits in red ink.

XI. Provided that the United States exchange offices mark PAID in red ink on prepaid letters dispatched to France; the French offices were to mark PD in red ink on prepaid letters sent to the United States.

XII. The exchange offices were to mark letters received by them with a stamp indicating the date of receipt and the way by which the mail had been forwarded to them. The stamp that was to be placed upon letters that had been conveyed between the American and French frontiers at French expense was to bear, independently of the name of the exchange office of destination, the characters SERV. FR. or BR. ("French or British service"). This stamp was to be placed in blue ink on letters transmitted directly, and in red ink on letters transmitted by way of England.

On letters to be conveyed between the American frontier and the French frontier, or the British frontier, at United States expense, a similar stamp bearing the characters SERV. AM. ("American service") was to be used. It was to be applied in blue ink to letters that had been transmitted directly and also upon the mails of or for the office of Havre that had been conveyed by packets of the New York-Bremen line, or by packets that plied between Havre and Southampton without touching British territory. It was to be applied in red ink to letters that had been transported by the aid of the British Post Office.

It will be noted that Article VII sets forth the specific amount to be debited or credited for each service provided for in Articles I and II. There is no statement as to the division of the international rate into inland, sea, and transit postages. Such a division, usually stated in postal conventions, was carefully avoided because these postage amounts were different for direct mail and for mail via England. Postal historians have deduced the division of the rate from the total figures included in Article VII. It has been deduced that inland postage was 3¢ in each country; that sea postage was 6¢ on mail via England and 9¢ on direct mail; and that transit postage was the residual of 3¢ on mail via England. Although this division has worked very well for purposes of explaining the debit and credit markings, it is incorrect as far as mail via England is concerned. The above division does not give consideration to the amounts paid by France to Great Britain under the closed-mail provisions of the Anglo-French convention of 1856, which governed mail exchanged between the United States and France, via England.

While correspondence or other documentary evidence regarding the negotiation of the via-England rates has not been found, certain facts are known. Miller[5] states that the United States-French postal convention was made possible by the Anglo-French convention of 1856 and points to Articles XXI and XXII as the pertinent provisions. As previously mentioned, under Article XXI, France paid Great Britain 40 centimes per 30 grams of closed mail for British transit, and by Article XXII, 1 franc 20 centimes per 30 grams for sea postage. Applying the prescribed procedure for ascertaining the single rate of 7½ grams, these postages when divided by four yielded a transit rate of 10, and a sea rate of 30, centimes, respectively. Since France paid Great Britain on the basis of the bulk weight of mail, but accounted to the United States on the basis of the individual letter, she must have attributed single-letter rates of 10 centimes for transit postage and 30 centimes for sea postage.

How the international rate of 15¢ in the United States or 80 centimes in France was arrived at is not known. It is suspected that the direct-mail provisions of the United States-French convention had been agreed upon before the Anglo-French convention was signed. For direct mail, the debits and credits established by Article VII indicate that an inland postage of 3¢ was set for either country, while sea postage was to be 9¢. It is also suspected that it was decided that the rate by all routes be made uniform and hence the 15¢ or 80-centime rate agreed upon for direct mail was also applied to mail via England.

The direct rate allowed the French only 3¢ for inland postage, which was less than their 20 centimes prepaid domestic rate. A possible reason for this concession on the part of France was the determination of Emperor Napoleon III to establish a line of French packets to the United States. Although then nonexistent, provision was made for French packets in Articles VII and XII of the convention. In the event that such a line were established, it would have been of advantage to the French to have the packet postage as high as possible. In other words, if a total rate had been agreed upon, it would have been to their advantage to sacrifice some inland postage and account for the sacrificed portion as an addition to packet postage.

It will be noted that only the total international rate of 80 centimes is expressed in French currency. All debits and credits were to be made in United States cents. Although this, at first glance, appears to have been a concession to the United States, it operated to the advantage of France. A rate of 15¢ in the United States and 80 centimes in France made the United States cent equal to $5\frac{1}{3}$ centimes and the French centime equal to 0.1875 of a cent. The Anglo-French convention, however, equated 10 centimes (French) with 1d. (British), while the United States-British treaty equated 1d. (British) with 2¢ (American). Thus, the United States Post Office normally held the French decime (10 centimes) to be worth 2¢. These exchange differences operated to conceal the amount France was receiving as inland postage on the via-England route. The division of the 80-centime rate for mail via England was as is shown in Table 13.

TABLE 13.—*Division of French Rate*

Postage	Rate, centimes
U.S. inland ($3 \times 5\frac{1}{3}$ centimes)	16
Sea (per single rate; paid to Britain)	30
Transit (per single rate; paid to Britain)	10
French inland (residual of rate)	24
Total rate	80

Considering the differences in conversion under the applicable treaties, the division in United States cents (rounded to the whole cent) was as follows:

---

[5] U.S. Department of State, *Treaties and Other International Acts of the United States*, p. 506.

TABLE 14.—*Division of United States Rate*

Postage	Rate, cents
U.S. inland (U.S.-French Convention)	3
Sea (Anglo-French Convention)	6
Transit (Anglo-French Convention)	2
French inland (residual of rate)	4
Total rate	15

It matters little whether an extra cent is added to the transit and deducted from the inland postage, as the French were realizing at least 4¢ for their share of the postage. Actually, they were receiving a greater amount, for it is certain that the number of letters per 30 grams would average more than four. It was undoubtedly this situation that led Postmaster General Creswell in 1869, at a time when the United States was attempting to negotiate a new convention with France, to say of the 1857 convention, "In its details and practical operation it is very unequal, giving unfair advantages to the French post department."[6] No inequity is apparent if the rate division allows each country an inland postage of 3¢.

The division of the direct rate in centimes and in cents was as follows:

TABLE 15.—*Division of United States and French Rates*

Postage	Rate, cents	Rate, centimes
U.S. inland	3 (3×5⅓ centimes)	16
Sea	9 (9×5⅓ centimes)	48
French inland	3 (3×5⅓ centimes)	16
Total rate	15	80

The exchange office accounting for the preceding rates is presented in Table 16. The time-honored division of the rates via England is altered to reflect the amounts actually paid by France to Great Britain.

From its inception, the United States Post Office Department found the United States-French convention an unsatisfactory instrument. While mail via England was exchanged between France and the United States in closed bags and France paid Great Britain on the basis of the bulk weight of the mail, the accounting between France and the United States was on the basis of the individual letter. Neither the United States nor France was able to avail itself of the simplified accounting procedures made possible by closed mail. In addition to the cumbersome accounting procedures, the making up of the mails was further complicated by extremely detailed instructions regulating the forwarding of mail between the exchange offices by prescribed packet routes. The complicated nature of the accounting procedure, as well as the inflexibility of the regulations, led the exchange offices to establish schedules by which the time required for making up French mails was planned in advance. Some mail packets leaving New York or Boston, therefore, did not carry French mail. As the volume of mail increased during the late 1860s, these French-mail omissions were noted in the *U.S. Mail and Post Office Assistant*.

The convention was deficient because it did not provide for the exchange of newspapers, pamphlets, or printed papers of any kind. These continued to be forwarded under the United States-British and Anglo-French conventions, via England, or direct, paid only as far as the French frontier. The United States-French convention was also deficient because it made no provision for the registration of mail.

The rates to foreign countries beyond France were set forth in an appended Table *B*, as provided in Article VIII of the convention. The format of this table has been revised and is presented here as Table 17, while the exchange office accounting for the rates is set forth in Table 18. It will be noted that a simple schedule of only four rates was developed for mail to points ranging from Luxembourg to China. France had postal conventions, either directly or indirectly, with most of the countries with which it exchanged mail, that is, with the country itself or with one that, in turn, held a convention with the country in question. It is obvious that so simple a schedule of rates for mail in transit through France would not agree with the many rates contained in these conventions. It is suspected that these rates were arrived at by an averaging process.[7]

The international rate of 15¢ or 80 centimes was basic to all French-mail rates. To the international rate one of the four transit charges was added to arrive at the total rate. Since all postage beyond France was at French expense, on prepaid letters posted in these foreign countries addressed to the United States only

---

[6] *Report of the Postmaster General,* 1869, p. 14.

[7] *See* George E. Hargest, "French Mail Rates," *Chronicle* 45 (July 1963): 27.

TABLE 16.—*Exchange Office Accounting for the French Mail International Rate*

Postage	Via England				
	Rate	British Packet	American Packet	British Packet	American Packet
U.S. inland	3¢	(a)	(a)	3¢	3¢
Sea	6	6¢	(a)	(b)	6
Transit	2	2	2¢	(b)	(b)
French inland	4	4	4	(b)	(b)
Single rate	15	—	—	—	—
U.S. credit to France on prepaid letters posted in U.S. (red); or French debit to U.S. on unpaid letters posted in France (black)		12	6		
U.S. debit to France on unpaid letters posted in U.S. (black); or French credit to the U.S. on prepaid letters posted in France (red)				3	9

	Direct				
	Rate	French Packet	American Packet	French Packet	American Packet
U.S. inland	3¢	(a)	(a)	3¢	3¢
Sea	9	9	(a)	(b)	9
French inland	3	3	3	(b)	(b)
Single rate	15	—	—	—	—
U.S. credit to France on prepaid letters posted in U.S. (red); or French debit to U.S. on unpaid letters posted in France (black)		12	3	—	—
U.S. debit to France on unpaid letters posted in U.S. (black); or French credit to U.S. on prepaid letters posted in France (red)				3	12

a Retained out of prepayment or collection by the United States.
b Retained out of prepayment or collection by France.

the international rate of 15¢ was usually restated by the United States exchange officers. Several exceptions to this procedure, however, have been noted on mail processed by the Philadelphia office. For the same reason, only the United States share of the international rate was debited to France on unpaid letters posted in the United States and addressed to these same countries. On prepaid letters posted in the United States, addressed to foreign countries, the transit postage from France to destination was added to the basic credit for the international rate, as presented in Table 18. Only on unpaid letters addressed to the United States are the totals of these four rates reflected in the United States postmarks, and a collection of them makes an interesting exhibit.

Since it appears that an averaging process was used to arrive at these four rates, it is certain that France lost on some and gained on others. For example, the rate between France and Belgium was of such amount that only 2 decimes were added to the 8-decime international rate, hence, only 1 franc was collected in Belgium on an unpaid letter posted in the United States, or was prepaid in Belgium on a letter addressed to the United States. Since 1 franc was worth only 19¢,

Table 17.—*French Mail Rates to Countries Beyond France*

Rate	Destination of Letters Posted in U.S.	Prepayment	Limit of Prepayment	Rate per ¼ ounce
1	France and Algeria (international rate)	Optional	Destination	15¢
2	Great Britain, Belgium, Low Countries, Luxemburg, Switzerland, Sardinia, and German States (except Austria)	Optional	Destination	21
	Spain, Portugal, and Gibraltar	Obligatory	Behobia	21
3	Denmark, Austria, Servia, Tuscany, Roman states, Parma, and Modena	Optional	Destination	27
	Ionian Islands	Obligatory	Trieste	27
4	Russia, Poland, Two Sicilies, Malta, Greece, Alexandria, Jaffa, Beyrout, Tripoli in Syria, Latakia, Alexandretta, Messina, Rhodes, Mitylene, Dardanelles, Gallipoli, Constantinople, Tunis, Tangiers, Pondicherry, Karikal, Yanaon, Mahé, and Chandernagor	Optional	Destination	30
	Aden, East Indies, Ceylon, Mauritius, Réunion, Penang, Singapore, Hong Kong, Shanghai, China, and Batavia, via Suez	Obligatory	Seaport to which English packets ply	30
	Countries beyond the seas, other than those designated:			
	Letters from U.S.	Obligatory	Port of arrival	30
	Letters for U.S.	Obligatory	Port of departure	30
5	Sweden and Norway	Optional	Destination	33

NOTE: Postage on letters to or from Moldavia, Wallachia, or Turkey in Europe, via Austria, was always paid by the inhabitants of Moldavia, Wallachia, or Turkey in Europe.

Table 18.—*Exchange Office Accounting for French Mail Rates to Countries Beyond France*
(*Prepaid Letters Posted in the United States*)

	Rate	Direct		Via England	
		French Packet	American Packet	British Packet	American Packet
		(Credit)	(Credit)	(Credit)	(Credit)
International rate	15¢	12¢	3¢	12¢	6¢
21c rate:					
Excess over international rate	6	6	6	6	6
Rate and credit	21	18	9	18	12
27c rate:					
Excess over international rate	12	12	12	12	12
Rate and credit	27	24	15	24	18
30c rate:					
Excess over international rate	15	15	15	15	15
Rate and credit	30	27	18	27	21
33c rate:					
Excess over international rate	18	18	18	18	18
Rate and credit	33	30	21	30	24

the rate *from* Belgium to the United States was 19¢, while the rate *to* Belgium was 21¢. The bajocchi of Rome was worth about one cent in United States currency. The rate from Rome to the United States was 32 bajocchi, while the rate from the United States to Rome was only 27¢. The rate from Sardinia to the United States was 1 lira 20 centesimi (23¢), and from the United States to Sardinia, 21¢. France broke even on letters prepaid in Switzerland where the rate to the United States was 11 decimes (21¢), and the rate from the United States to Switzerland was also 21¢. In these calculations, 8 decimes are equal to 15¢, and additional decimes are taken at 2¢ each.

Article VIII contained a clause allowing the rate to foreign countries to be altered if "the conventions which regulate the relations of France with the foreign countries . . . should be modified in such manner as to affect the (stated) conditions of exchange." Relatively few changes in the original rates were made. All changes in rates to European countries were made within the context of the four original rates, that is, 27¢ rates were changed to 21¢ or 30¢, or mandatory prepayment was changed to optional prepayment, but rates of new and different amounts were not introduced.

A word about optional prepayment on French mail letters: When regulations indicated, through published tables of postal rates to foreign countries, that prepayment was optional to a particular foreign country, if the sender elected to prepay the postage, the whole rate had to be prepaid. A partial payment was ignored, the letter being forwarded as an unpaid letter with the whole postage to be collected upon delivery. Prepayment of only the international rate of 15¢ was not recognized. For example, the rate to Switzerland was 21¢, either prepaid or unpaid, prepayment being optional. A prepayment of only 15¢ would not pay the letter through France, and if prepayment were made in that amount, it would be entirely lost to the sender. This differed from the procedure used under the Bremen and Prussian closed-mail conventions. Under those agreements, nonrecognition of a partial payment applied only to the international rate.

French Mail Covers

Because the United States-French convention was in effect for nearly thirteen years, covers showing use of the 15¢ international rate are relatively common today. The markings presented in Figure 42 are typical

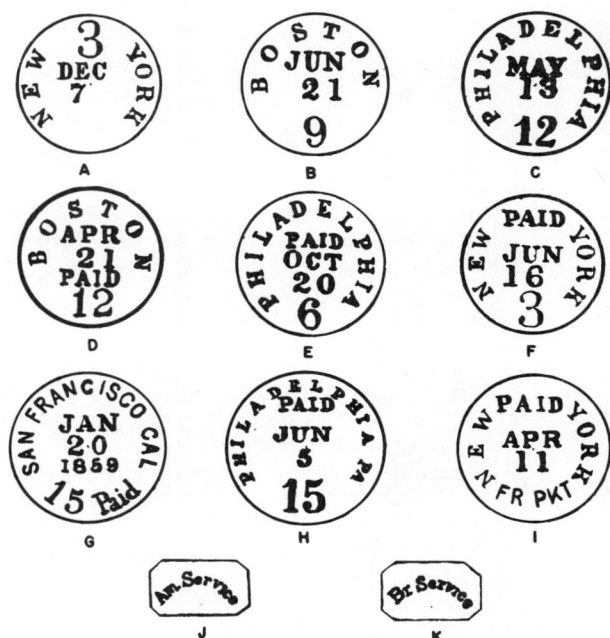

FIGURE 42.—MARKINGS on French mail by United States exchange offices.

of those used by the original United States exchange offices. Markings *A, B,* and *C* were applied in black to unpaid letters posted in the United States and reflect debits to France for mail conveyed on the three routes presented in Table 16. Markings *D, E,* and *F* were applied in red to prepaid letters and reflect the credits to France made by these exchange offices to letters conveyed on the same routes, that is, markings *A* and *D* by British packet; *B* and *E* by American packet through England; and *C* and *F* by direct service to France.[8]

When San Francisco officially became an exchange office for United States-British mail on 19 October 1863,[9] it was specifically provided that it should handle incoming mail addressed to California, Oregon, Washington territory, the Sandwich Islands, British Columbia, and Vancouver Island. It was not, however, to dispatch mails to the British offices. The United States-French convention restricted the San Francisco office to the exchange of mail to or from California and the territories of Oregon and Washington, but it

---

[8] For more complete illustrations of the exchange office markings used by the U.S. offices see Tracy W. Simpson, *United States Postal Markings and Related Mail Services 1851–1861,* pp. 91–108.

[9] 16 Statutes at Large 830.

did not restrict that office only to the receipt and distribution of mail. The evidence of covers, however, indicates that the San Francisco office did not, in fact, make up and dispatch French mail, for no cover seen shows a debit or credit to France. Marking G of Figure 42 (also showing 30 PAID) was applied in red to stampless prepaid letters dispatched by San Francisco in French mail, but these letters usually also bear a New York exchange office marking.

Prepaid letters dispatched by the French exchange offices, regardless of their rate and point of origin, usually bear a United States exchange office marking in red, showing a restatement of the 15¢ rate. Restatements of the 21¢, 27¢, 30¢, or 33¢ rates are rarely seen. Since all postage beyond France was at French expense, there was no need for the United States offices to indicate any amount other than the 15¢ international rate. Marking H shows a restatement of the international rate applied by the Philadelphia office.

All of the United States offices applied either marking J or K of Figure 42 to incoming French-mail letters. Marking J was applied in blue to letters arriving by the direct route, in red to American packet letters through England. Marking K was applied in red to those received by British packet. After about the middle of 1864, many prepaid incoming letters do not show either marking J or K.

After the French line between Havre and New York started to run in 1864, markings showing French packet service appear. Marking I of Figure 42 is an example of one of these markings which were applied to incoming letters.

Some markings used by the French exchange offices are illustrated in Figure 43.[10] It should be noted that, until the French line between Havre and New York started to run in 1864, all French exchange office markings applied to French mail had somewhere in their inscriptions the abbreviation SERV. for "service." Both the French and United States exchange offices had special handstamps available for use on 1 April 1857. A double-rate unpaid letter is endorsed *p Arago* and bears a marking similar to A of Figure 42, but with a debit of 24¢, and is dated 4 April. It also bears a marking (A of Figure 43) dated 18 April 1857. This was the first direct sailing from New York after the convention became effective on 1 April 1857.

---

[10] For a more complete listing of French exchange office markings *see* Raymond Salles, "La Poste maritime française historique et catalogue," vol. 4, pp. 224–298.

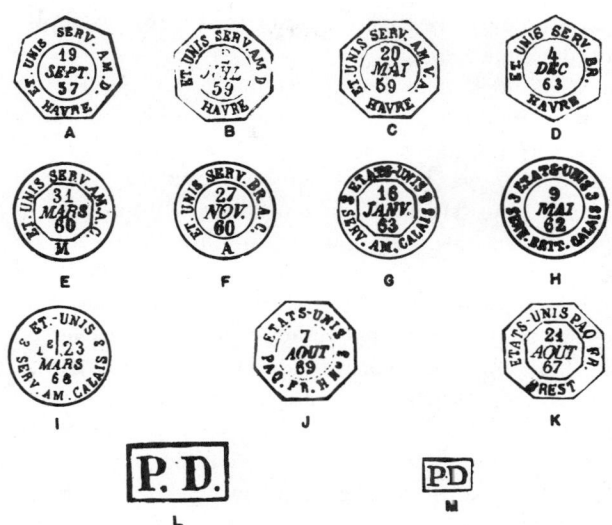

FIGURE 43.—MARKINGS on French mail by French exchange offices.

Marking A of Figure 43 was applied in indigo ink to letters received at the Havre office by direct service until late in 1858 or early in 1859, when it was superseded by marking B which was applied in blue ink. All direct service ceased in November 1861 when the Havre line ships *Arago* and *Fulton* were taken over by the United States for the duration of the Civil War. The Vanderbilt European line and the North Atlantic Steamship Company had ceased to run their ships at an earlier date. The direct service by American packets of the Havre line was revived in November 1865 by *Arago* and *Fulton*. In 1867 the Havre line fleet was augmented by *Mississippi* and *Guiding Star,* but at the end of 1867 the line discontinued operations. During this period of revival, marking B of Figure 43 was again used on mail conveyed to Havre by these ships, but was applied in red instead of blue. The D in markings A and B abbreviates "direct." Prepaid letters by direct service also bear marking M in red.

The Havre office also applied markings C and D of Figure 43 to letters received at that office by way of England. The inscription in marking C, ET. UNIS SERV. AM. V.A. means "From the United States by American packet via England," while the inscription in marking D means "From the United States by British service." It would appear that marking C was intended to be used on mail conveyed by American packet and passing through England to Havre, while marking D was to be used on mail conveyed by British packet and forwarded from England to Havre. If this is so, the Havre office made an exceedingly large number of errors in applying these markings.

M. Salles [11] considers that marking *C* (Figure 43) was reserved for mail originating in the United States and entering Havre by way of Southampton, while marking *D* was used on mail conveyed only by the Cunard line. He notes that marking *C* was used on mail conveyed by several Inman line ships, but he also remarks that through error it was struck on letters conveyed by several ships of the Cunard line. The author records marking *C* used on a cover conveyed by the *Bremen* of the North German Lloyd and rated in the United States at the direct rate; he also notes marking *D* on a cover conveyed by *Hansa* of the North German Lloyd and rated in the United States as by American packet through England. Marking *D* has been noted on two covers conveyed by the ships of the Inman line. All of these markings were applied in red. The instructions for marking letters included in Article XII of the convention contain the phrase "It was to be applied in red ink upon letters which had been transported by the aid of the British Post-Office." It may be that marking *D* did not refer only to transatlantic service.

Markings *E* and *F* of Figure 43 were used by the travelling post office, Calais to Paris. The A. C. in these markings abbreviates "ambulant Calais." An octagonal center indicates day service, while the double-circle mark refers to night service. The letters at the base of these markings identify the mail crew (brigade) that processed the mail.

Paris became an exchange office for French mail on 1 April 1861. While there are no markings inscribed PARIS, the Paris office applied markings *G* and *H* in red to mail arriving by way of Calais. Marking *G* is known in blue as well. These were used from 1861 to 1866.[12] Marking *I* was also applied by the Paris office in blue from 1867 to 1869.

Marking *J* was applied by the mail agents on board the steamers of the Compagnie Générale Transatlantique, Ligne *H*, plying between Havre and New York.[13] Four mail agents were assigned to the line by the French Post Office. The markings appear with *N° 1, N° 2, N° 3,* and *N° 4,* and were applied in black or red. The dates of these markings coincide with the dates in the New York packet markings, and indicate the date of sailing from New York. From June 1865 the ships of this line called at Brest, and marking *K* is a receiving mark used at that port.

Figure 44 illustrates a cover posted in New Orleans on 17 November 1857, addressed to La Rochelle, France. The 15¢ international rate is prepaid by a strip of three of the 5¢ red-brown stamps issued in 1857. The New York exchange office marking bears a credit to France of 12¢ (type *F* of Figure 42), while the French exchange office marking (type *F* of Figure 43) shows British packet service. The date of 25 November in the New York marking shows that this letter was dispatched to Liverpool by R.M.S. *Arabia* of the Cunard line which sailed from New York on that date. A strip of three of 5¢ stamps was a common method of prepaying the 15¢ international rate.

Figure 45 presents the front (*A*) and back (*B*) of a cover posted in Baltimore on 2 November 1960, franked with a 30¢ stamp issued in 1860 for a double-rate letter. It was addressed to Miss M. M. Tompkins, care of Dr. J. S. Wellford, Poste Restante, Paris, France. The New York exchange office marking shows a credit to France of 12¢ (2 x 6¢) for a double-rate letter to be conveyed to England by an American packet. The date of 3 November in the New York exchange office marking indicates that the letter was forwarded to Liverpool by *City of Washington* of the Inman line. The French exchange office marking is of type *E* of Figure 43 and shows that the letter arrived at the ambulant office on 19 November. A Paris POSTE RESTANTE marking indicates it was at the Paris office on 20 November. Miss Tompkins, however, had evidently returned to the United States. Somone called for and secured the letter, crossed out the address on its face, and wrote at the top, *Regardez l'autre côté* ("see the other side"). This expression would not have been written by a French postal official, for its connotation would lead a Frenchman to look at the edge, rather than the reverse, of the letter. A French postal official would simply have written *Au dos* ("to the back"). The person who retrieved the letter turned it over and readdressed it on the reverse to Miss Tompkins who was now in Richmond, Virginia. A small note was also penned at lower left.

Article IX of the convention provided that letters addressed to persons who had changed their residence would be returned "charged with the postage which should have been paid by the persons addressed," that is, the postage on unpaid letters. Article XV provided that letters which cannot be delivered for any cause would be returned. "Those which shall have been

---

[11] Salles, *La Poste maritime francaise,* p. 295.
[12] Ibid., p. 291.
[13] Ibid., p. 233.

FIGURE 44.—COVER, from New Orleans to La Rochelle, France, 1857.

delivered prepaid to destination . . . shall be returned without charge or deduction." Thus, this letter was started on its return trip, the Paris office marking it at upper right on its reverse with the postmark of that office dated 20 November 1860. On the face is the marking of the ambulant office PARIS A CALAIS with the date of 21 November 1860. Since the letter was being returned without charge, the ambulant office made no debit to the United States. The letter was forwarded to Liverpool, whence it was conveyed to New York again by *City of Washington* which arrived on 6 December. Unaccountably, the letter was sent to the Boston office. As a returned letter no charge should have been made. While the Paris office overlooked the note penned on the reverse, "Emmy has received your letter today Nov 20 & will write soon—," the Boston office considered this a message and therefore marked the letter for a collection of 30¢. Thus, there is on the face of this cover markings characteristic of a prepaid letter to France, and on the reverse, the markings of an unpaid letter from France (except that there is no debit to the United States).

Figure 46 presents a cover posted in New Orleans on 12 June 1860, addressed to Bordeaux, France. The 15¢ international rate is prepaid by a 3¢ and a 12¢ stamp of the 1857 issue, a common combination for paying the 15¢ rate. The New York office forwarded the letter directly to Havre by *Vanderbilt* of the Vanderbilt European line which sailed from New York on 16 June 1860, the date in the New York postmark. This cover shows the markings characteristic of direct service to Havre by French mail, that is, a United States exchange office marking with a credit of 3¢ (usually New York, but rarely Boston or Philadelphia), a French exchange office marking of type *A* or *B* of Figure 43, and a small PD marking of type *M* of Figure 43.

Figure 47 presents a cover to a point beyond France at the 21¢ rate. This letter was posted in Highland, Illinois, on 1 June 1860, addressed to Neuchâtel, Switzerland. The 21¢ rate was prepaid by a pair of the 10¢ type *V* stamps and a single 1¢ type *V* stamp of the 1857 issue. The New York office forwarded it to Liverpool by R.M.S. *Persia* which sailed from New York on 6 June 1860. Because this ship was a British packet, the New York office credited France with 18¢ (see Table 18). The letter arrived at the travelling office, Calais to Paris, on 17 June 1860, and that office applied a marking in black similar to *F* of Figure 43.

Figure 48 illustrates a cover posted in Boston, addressed to Rome. The 27¢ French mail rate to Rome was prepaid by a pair of 12¢ and a single 3¢ stamp of the 1861 issue. These stamps bear a black grid with PAID in center. Although Boston used a number of simi-

Figure 45, Face of cover (*above*), from Baltimore to Paris, 1860. Reverse of same (*below*), redirected.

FIGURE 46.—COVER, from New Orleans to Bordeaux, France 1860.
(*Photograph by Smithsonian*)

FIGURE 47.—COVER, from Highland, Illinois, to Neuchâtel, Switzerland, 1860.
(*Photograph by Smithsonian*)

FIGURE 48.—COVER, from Boston to Rome, Italy, 1862. (*Melvin W. Schuh collection*)

lar grid markings, this particular one was reserved for use on foreign mail.[14] The Boston packet marking bears the date of 25 March (1862), and on this day the mails were made up at Boston for the sailing of R.M.S. *Africa* on the following day from New York. Because this ship was a British packet, the Boston office credited France with 24¢ (see Table 18). The letter arrived at the travelling office, Calais to Paris, on 8 April 1862, and that office applied a marking in black similar to *F* of Figure 43 and a boxed P.D. marking similar to *L* of Figure 43, which indicated that the letter was paid to destination. In 1862 there was an additional 46¢-per-half-ounce rate to Rome by Prussian closed mail and a 28¢-per-half-ounce rate by Bremen-Hamburg mail, both of which paid the letter only to the Roman frontier. Only the 27¢-per-one-fourth-ounce rate by French mail paid the letter to destination. It has been observed that French mail letters bear a diagonal manuscript line that was applied at Rome, and was evidently intended to indicate that no additional postage was due.

Figure 49 illustrates a cover addressed to a point beyond France to which the rate was 30¢. This cover was posted in New Orleans on 19 May 1858, addressed to Palermo (Sicily). It is prepaid by a strip of three of the 10¢ stamps of the 1857 issue (positions 2, 12, and 22*RI*), a combination of two type II and a type III stamp. The single-letter rate to the kingdom of the Two Sicilies by French mail was 30¢, prepayment compulsory, from 1 April 1857 until January 1862, shortly after Sicily and Naples were incorporated into the kingdom of Italy, when the rate was reduced to 21¢, prepayment optional. The New York office forwarded this letter directly to Havre by *Fulton* of the New York-Havre Line, which sailed from New York on 29 May 1858. France was given credit for 18¢ by use of a manuscript marking in red ink (see Table 18). The cover bears markings characteristic of those by direct service, as in markings *A* and *M* of Figure 43, which were applied by the Havre office on 13 May 1858. On the reverse is a 20 GIU° 1858 straight-line marking in magenta indicating that the letter arrived in Palermo on 20 June 1858. Covers between Sicily and the United States prior to Sicily's unification with the kingdom of Italy are seldom seen.

Figure 50 presents a cover to a point beyond France to which the single French-mail rate was 33¢. This letter was posted in Boston, addressed to Norway, and was prepaid by a pair and single of the 10¢ type *V*, and a single of the 3¢ type II stamp of the 1857 issue. As on the cover illustrated in Figure 48, the stamps are canceled with a grid with PAID in center. The Boston packet marking bears the date of 8 June (1860). On that date the mails were made up at Boston for the sailing of *Glasgow* of the Inman line from New York on the following day. Since the Inman line was under con-

---

[14] M. C. Blake and W. W. Davis, *Postal Markings of Boston, Massachusetts, to 1890*, marking 625, Plate 35, p. 133.

FIGURE 49.—COVER, from New Orleans to Palermo (Sicily), 1858. (*Photograph by Smithsonian*)

FIGURE 50.—COVER, from Boston to Laürvig [Larvik], Norway, 1860.
(*Melvin W. Schuh collection*)

tract to the United States Post Office and, although British-owned, considered an American packet, the Boston office gave France a credit of 24¢ (see Table 18). The letter arrived at the travelling office, Calais to Paris, on 23 June 1860. That office, in error, struck the letter with marking F of Figure 43, then, discovering that it had marked it for British service, superimposed marking E over the marking F originally applied. Marking L (Figure 43) was also applied, indicating that the letter was paid to destination.

Some New Light upon the Negotiation of the U.S.-French Convention of 2 March 1857

From Mr. Tracy W. Simpson, RA 5, and former editor of the *Chronicle*, I received the following copy of an article that appeared in the *New York Daily Tribune*, Monday, January 12, 1857. Since I had available to me a complete file of the *New York Daily Tribune*, I can offer no excuse for not finding it at the time I wrote my book, "The History of Letter Post Communication Between the United States and Europe, 1845–1875." It was the very thing I was looking for, and I must have examined the issue of 12 January 1857 without seeing it. It was tucked away between political notices from Washington and a story about the Philharmonic Society. Nevertheless, it represents a *careless* piece of research on my part. Following is the text of this news item:

As yet, the proposed Postal arrangement between France and the United States has not been completed. On the 27th of December Count Sartiges submitted the *projet* of a treaty, containing seventeen articles, which has since then been the subject of several conferences between him and the Postmaster-General. In general terms, it proposes to substitute 15 cents as the rate of postage for each letter of one-quarter of an ounce, transmitted between France and Algeria, and the United States, and *vice versa*, divided as follows:

	cents		cents
United States inland	3	European rate	6
Atlantic sea rate	6		
Total			15

When conveyed across the Atlantic, either by British or French packet, the expenses thereof to be paid by France, the United States accounting to France at 12 cents per letter; and when conveyed by United States packet, the United States accounting to France at 6 cents per letter. On a letter, therefore, conveyed by British packet via England, the division is understood to be as follows:

	cents		cents
United States inland	3	British transit	3
Sea	6	French inland	3
Total			15

If conveyed by United States packet, via England, as follows:

	cents		cents
United States inland	3	British inland	3
Sea	6	French inland	3
Total			15

If conveyed to or from France direct by United States packet, as follows:

Unites States inland	3 cents
Sea	6 cents
French inland	6 cents
Total	15 cents

The last division is regarded as objectionable by the Postmaster-General, and he proposes a modification to this effect: When the letter is conveyed to or from France direct by United States packet, the division shall be as follows:

French inland and sea	12 cents
United States inland	3 cents
Total	15 cents

The foregoing is the material point of difference between the two Governments, and will probably be accommodated, as France is about putting on a new line of steamers between Havre and New York. Objection is also taken against the suggested mode of extinguishing balances, by which France claims payment at the rate of five francs thirty centimes to the dollar. On our side it is proposed to settle these balances on a par basis, and to divide equally any premiums or discounts in the settlements between the two countries.

The postmaster-General also insists that Philadelphia shall be incorporated as one of the exchange offices on an equality with New-York and Boston. Exception was taken to the limitation of a quarter of an ounce as the weight, the Postmaster-General desiring the adoption of half an ounce as the one to which our people are more accustomed. This point, was however, yielded for other considerations, and the thin paper used in France and on the Continent will probably be much adopted in American correspondence with foreign countries. Count Sartiges has substantially agreed to recommend these modifications, and they will go out by the first steamer. No serious difficulty or delay is now apprehended on either side, and the arrangement will be closed before the exodus of the Administration, furnishing an important contribution to the commercial intercourse between the United States and France, and such countries as the postal arrangements of the latter are connected with.

The timing of this *projet* of the French for a postal convention is important. The Anglo-French treaty was signed on 24 September 1856, ratifications were exchanged at Paris on 19 November 1856,[1] and the *projet* was presented on 27 December 1856. Since it would have required two weeks for it to be conveyed across the Atlantic, the French must have been working on the details of the proposal before the ratifications were exchanged. The French were aware of the fact that Postmaster General Campbell was anxious to conclude a convention with France before he left office on 3 March 1857 and time was a factor which favored the French. If the French had demanded that their domestic rate of 20 centimes for a 7½ grams letter be included in the convention, it would have made French inland postage 4c, while U.S. inland was only 3c per single rate. It is doubtful that the Postmaster General could have agreed to this arrangement, or whether the President would have supported him if he had agreed. On the other hand, France could not easily make the postage on foreign letters cheaper in France than it was on domestic letters. Since the rates were based upon those included in the Anglo-French treaty of 1856, France had to pay England for all mail passing in transit through that country. Cleverly, the French raised the transit rate by one cent more than it cost them, and accepted an inland postage of one cent less than their domestic rate. Regardless of how the division was stated, France received four cents on each letter sent, via England. While the table presented on page 74 of my book[2] shows the amounts paid to England for transit postage, and the amounts received by France, this is evidently not the division understood to exist by the Americans.

If I had seen this news item before I wrote Chapter 4 of my book, what changes would I have made? Did the United States have knowledge of, or understand, the transit provision included in the Anglo-French treaty of 1856 as stated in Article XXI?[3] There is evidence that they did not. Chapter III deals with the long struggle between the United States and England over the transit rate to France, which the United States demanded the British reduce. This transit rate was reduced from one shilling to 40 centimes per ounce on 1 January 1857, and yet the United States did not accept the closed mail provisions of the provisional agreement between France and England, which would have drastically reduced the postal rate to France. It was assumed in Chapter III that the reason for the failure of the United States to do so was because negotiations for a U.S.-French convention were nearing completion. This news item indicates that negotiations between the Post Offices of the two countries were not being carried on, and the *projet* sent to Count Sartiges, who was French minister to the United States, was sent through diplomatic channels and not between the Post Offices. If the United States Post Office Department had knowledge of Article XXI of the Anglo-French treaty of 1856, why did they not prepare to accept the provisional agreement between France and Great Britain as soon as the ratifications were exchanged on 19 November 1856, something they had promised to do if the British transit rate were reduced? They had no knowledge that a *projet* for a treaty would be forthcoming in December. It is not unlikely that the United States Post Office Department did not know what the transit rate between France and England was at the time the U.S.-French convention was signed. Although the convention itself stated only gross debits and credits to be made on letters by each route, France must have disclosed that the transit rate was on the basis of bulk weight and amounted to about three cents. Or, did the Post Office Department know the transit rate, and Postmaster General Campbell decided to accept the offer in order to conclude the convention? One thing is now certain; it was the French who suggested a division that included a three cent British transit rate. It was not postal historians who deduced it. It was also the French who demanded that the accounting be on the basis of the individual letter, instead of accounting on the basis of the bulk weight of closed mail. This insured them of a return of four cents per letter. The French probably did not expect the United States to accept the direct mail division of six cents for sea postage and a French inland of six cents. But Postmaster General did allow France a total of 12 cents for French inland and sea postage.

At the time the convention was signed on 2 March 1857, just one day before Postmaster General Campbell left office, it could not be foreseen how important these divisions of the rates were to become. After 14 June

1858, American vessels were paid the U.S. sea and inland postages accruing on the letters they conveyed, while foreign vessels were paid the sea postage only. In the convention, 12 cents was also allotted for United States sea and inland postage for vessels plying directly between New York and France. Thus, the Vanderbilt, Havre, and other direct U.S. lines received 12 cents per quarter ounce for conveying the direct mail. This kept the Vanderbilt line on the run to Havre long after it ceased to run on the less profitable run to Bremen.

This news item also shows that the direct rate was the last to be negotiated, when it had been assumed to be the first agreed upon. Although Postmaster General Campbell objected to the settlement of balances on the basis of five francs, thirty centimes to the dollar, Article XVI of the convention gives these amounts as the basis upon which the United States would settle accounts with France. The French won this point also. The news item is in error on the division of mail by United States packet, via England. It is stated that British *inland* postage is 3 cents. Since all mail, via England, was closed through England, and Great Britain was not a party to the U.S.-French convention, Great Britain could not charge or receive an inland postage; they did charge and receive a transit postage.

Since the *projet* submitted by Count Sartiges and the completed convention both contain seventeen Articles, it does not appear that many changes were made in the original text. The divisions were *understood* to be as presented in the news item, but whose understanding was it? Was it as Count Startiges explained it, or was it the way Postmaster General Campbell presented it to the *New York Daily Tribune?*

---

[1] *British and Foreign State Papers,* vol. XLVI, p. 195.
[2] Hargest, George E., *The History of Letter Post Communication Between the United States and Europe, 1845–1875,* p. 74.
[3] *Ibid.,* p. 64.

Chapter 5

The Prussian Closed-Mail Convention

Shortly after the American Collins and Havre lines began to run in 1850, the Bremen closed mail (discussed in Chapter 1) was sent only by these lines. Cunard line service to Germany was available only on letters sent in the British open mail, and much mail was sent by this route. The London office usually forwarded open mail addressed to the northern German states in the Anglo-Prussian closed mail, via Belgium, which was faster than the direct route from England to Cuxhaven or Bremerhaven. Mail addressed to the southern German states was usually sent through France.

Although the route through Belgium was faster than the direct route, which was the route used for the Bremen closed mail, it was also more expensive, because of the high British and Belgium transit rates. These high rates were set by the Anglo-Prussian convention of 1846 and are presented in Table 2, Chapter 1.

As with all British open mail, the burden of high transit charges fell upon the correspondent in the foreign country. Regardless of what the charges abroad might be, Americans paid only 5¢ for a letter conveyed by British packet, or 21¢ when transatlantic service was by American packet. In this particular case, the Germans either prepaid these high transit rates on letters posted in Germany, or the rates were collected from them upon delivery of letters posted in the United States. Prussia had good reason to seek a postal convention with the United States that would more equitably distribute postage costs between correspondents in the two countries.

On 1 July 1850, a new posal convention between the states of Germany brought into existence the German-Austrian Postal Union, and greatly simplified and reduced rates between these countries. Prussia now worked for an agreement that would utilize the reduced rates, as well as make use of the Cunard line, and the Anglo-Prussian closed mail, via Belgium. Such a service would supersede the slower Bremen closed mail. By mid-1851 a closed mail agreement between the two countries which included the above features was all but complete. On 21 June 1851, Postmaster General Nathan K. Hall wrote Secretary of State Daniel Webster: [1]

> Articles of agreement between this department and the post office of Prussia have been prepared, providing for the reciprocal receipt and delivery of letters and packets in closed mails between the United States and Prussia, to be conveyed through England; but their final execution has been postponed for several months, in the confident hope and expectation that the British government would finally yield to the reasonable demands of the contracting parties for a reduction in their transit postage, and thus facilitate the communication so much desired by either side.

Mr. Lawrence, United States minister at London, addressed a note to Lord Palmerston on 8 August 1851, in which he explained: [2]

> by the German-Austrian convention which went into operation on the first of July, 1850, it is understood that the rates of postage throughout Prussia, Austria, and indeed in most, if not all, the States of Germany, have been greatly reduced, and that it is represented that the high transit rate through England is the only obstacle in the way of rendering that convention available to parties corresponding between the United States and those countries.

The British did indeed reduce the transit rate through a new postal convention with Prussia. Al-

---

[1] U.S., Congress, Senate, *Executive Document* 32, 32nd Cong., 2nd sess., serial 660, p. 31.
[2] Ibid., p. 34.

though Mr. Lawrence was not aware of it at the time he addressed the above note to Lord Palmerston, a new Anglo-Prussian convention was then in the process of negotiation. It was completed early in 1852, signed at London on 2 July, at Berlin on 7 July, and became effective on 1 August of that year.[3] It established a reduced international rate between the two countries which was, by Articles II and III, also set for transit mail, via Belgium, to or from colonies or foreign countries. The single-letter rate for the weight of one-half ounce (British), or of one zoll loth (Prussian), was set at 8d. (British) and 7 silbergroschen (Prussian). The rate was divided as shown in Table 19.

TABLE 19.—*Division of the British and Prussian Rates*

Postage	Rate	
	British penny	Prussian silbergroschen
British	3½	3
Belgian transit	½	½
German	4	3½
Total rate	8	7

The rates set by this convention were evidently acceptable to the Prussian and United States post offices, for the United States-Prussian closed-mail convention was signed at Washington on 17 July and at Berlin on 26 August 1852.[4] Prussia and the United States utilized provisions of both the United States-British and the new Anglo-Prussian conventions to complete the pending agreement. Articles I, VIII, and IX of the United States-British treaty were used to fix the rate for sea postage. By Article I, sea postage was 8d., or 16¢ for a single letter of half an ounce; by Article VIII, the United States had the privilege of sending closed mails over British territory; and by Article IX, closed mails were paid for by the ounce at a rate determined by taking the postage of two single-letter rates plus 25 percent. Thus, a sea rate of 40¢ per ounce was set (2 x 16¢ plus ¼).

British transit postage was established by applying the same formula to the British postage included in the international rate set by the Anglo-Prussian convention. The postage was 3½d. per single rate and yielded a transit postage per ounce of 8¾d., or 17½¢ (2 x 3½d. plus ¼). These rates were directly incorporated into Article VI of the Prussian closed-mail convention. Strangely, the Belgian transit postage, which Prussia held at ½ silbergraschen and Great Britian at ½d. for a single rate, was to cost 8¢ per ounce.

At the time the convention was framed, one Prussian silbergroschen was worth about 2.3¢ in United States currency. The rate within the German-Austrian Postal Union had been uniformly established at 2 silbergroschen by the German-Austrian convention, effective on 1 July 1850. In setting the German inland postage, 2 silbergroschen were rounded to 5¢. The United States also adopted an inland postage of 5¢.

Article II established an international postage of 30¢ for a single rate of half an ounce (American) or one loth (German). In setting this rate, "the Article stated, sea and British and Belgian transit postage, will be . . . 20¢." Article VII stated that letter rates were established "on the supposition that four letters to the ounce will be about the average number," and it was agreed that if the number proved to be less, rates were to be adjusted accordingly. The rate per ounce for sea, British, and Belgian transit postages totaled 65½¢ (sea, 40¢; British transit, 17½¢; and Belgian transit, 8¢). This amount divided by four yields only 16.4¢, whereas the convention set an undivided postage of 20¢ for these services. Thus, a "cushion" was built into the rate in case the average number of letters was fewer than four to the ounce.

The accounting between the post offices was set forth in Article VI, as follows:

The Prussian Post-Office is to account to the United States Post-Office in respect to all letter postages collected by Prussia from closed mails, as follows, viz.:

On mails sent from the United States, for each unpaid letter weighing half an ounce or less, twenty-three cents

And also on mails sent from Prussia, for each prepaid letter of half an ounce or under, twenty-five cents

And, in addition thereto, the Prussian office is to account to Belgium for its transit rate on all letters received in said closed mails from the United States

The United States Post-Office, when it collects the postage on letters sent in the closed mails, is to account to the Prussian Post-Office, as follows, viz.:

On mails sent from the United States, for each prepaid letter weighing half an ounce or less, seven cents

And also on mails sent from Prussia, for each unpaid letter of half an ounce or under, five cents

And the United States Post-Office is to account to the British Post-Office for British transit postage at the rate of fifty-seven and one half cents per ounce when mails are conveyed by British packets across the Atlantic, and at the rate of seventeen and one half cents per ounce when conveyed by United States packets across the Atlantic, in

---

[3] *British and Foreign State Papers,* vol. 59, p. 893.
[4] U.S., 16 Statutes at Large 963.

either direction; in addition to which, the United States Post-Office is to account to the British Post-Office for Belgian transit postage, at eight cents per ounce, on all letters in said closed mails *from* Prussia; that is, whenever, in all of the above cases, the British and Belgian conveyances are used.

Thus, the United States paid the British Post Office 40¢ per ounce for all Prussian closed-mail letters conveyed by British packet; it also paid the British Post Office 17½¢ per ounce for transit through England on all letters conveyed in the Prussian closed mail; additionally, it paid the British Post Office 8¢ per ounce for transit through Belgium on all letters posted in Prussia addressed to the United States. Prussia made no payments to the British Post Office, but paid Belgium directly for transit through that country on all letters posted in the United States addressed to Prussia. The Belgian transit postage was 2¢ for a single rate and was evidently arrived at by dividing the 8¢-per-ounce rate by four. The exchange office accounting for Prussian closed mail is set forth in Table 20.

Article I established exchange offices at Boston and New York in the United States and at Aix-la-Chapelle (Aachen) in Prussia. Article IX stated:

> The closed mails will be made up at the office of New York or Boston, in the United States, respectively, as the conveyance may be directed by the United States Post-Office from either of said ports, to Aix-la-Chapelle (Aachen), in Prussia, and at Aix-la-Chapelle (Aachen) to New York or Boston, according as the conveyance may be directed as aforesaid.

It was the British Post Office, however, who exercised the option of sending the closed bags by British or American packet.[5] In his annual report for 1853, Postmaster General Campbell complained bitterly about British discrimination against the Collins line steamers in this regard. He pointed out that from 16 October 1852 to 30 June 1853, sea postage charged against the United States on Prussian closed mail dispatched from Great Britain was eight times more than that earned by the Collins line steamers which performed half as many voyages as the Cunard line. During this same period, the postage on Prussian closed mails disptached by the United States, considering the difference in the number of voyages performed, was about equally divided between the Cunard and Collins line services.

By Article II, prepayment of the 30¢ international rate was made optional, but

> it shall not, however, be permitted to pay less than the whole combined rate. If the letter is of the weight of half an ounce or under, the combined rate is 30 cents. Above half an ounce and not over an ounce, 60 cents. Above one ounce, but not exceeding two ounces, $1.20. And the postage will increase in this scale of progression, to wit: An additional 60 cents for each ounce, or fraction of an ounce.

A partial payment of the international rate was not recognized, but the letter was forwarded as an unpaid letter. The nonrecognition of a payment of less than the whole rate, however, applied only to the in-

---

[5] Since the Aachen office made up mails to be sent by either British or American packet and, accordingly, made out the letter-bills for one or the other service, the British office furnished the Aachen office schedules of sailings by which it would disptach Prussian closed mails to the U.S.

TABLE 20.—*Exchange Office Accounting for Prussian Closed Mail*

Postage	Rate	Letters from U.S.		Letters from Prussia	
		Unpaid	Prepaid	Unpaid	Prepaid
U.S. inland	5¢	5¢	(a)	(a)	5¢
Sea and British transit	18	18	(a)	(a)	18
Belgian transit	2	(b)	2¢	(a)	2
Prussian inland	5	(b)	5	5¢	(b)
International rate	30	—	—	—	—
Debit to Prussia by U.S.	—	23	—	—	—
Credit to Prussia by U.S.	—	—	7	—	—
Debit to U.S. by Prussia	—	—	—	5	—
Credit to U.S. by Prussia	—	—	—	—	25

a Retained from collection or prepayment by the United States.
b Retained from collection or prepayment by Prussia.

ternational rate. Tables of postal rates to foreign countries were published in the United States from time to time, in postal guides, almanacs, postal directories, and in post office broadsides, as well as in editions of the Postal Laws and Regulations. After October 1860 these tables were published monthly in the *U.S. Mail and Post Office Assistant,* a private publication having official sanction. Prussian closed-mail rates included in these tables to countries beyond the German-Austrian Postal Union indicated the amount of postage to particular countries and whether prepayment was optional. When prepayment was optional, it was possible to pay only the 30¢ international rate, which paid the letter to the border of the German-Austrian Postal Union; it was forwarded from there with the remaining foreign postage to be collected from the addressee. These letters were rated and marked by the Aachen office which also applied special handstamps to indicate that the postage was paid only to the border of the postal union. Marking Q of Figure 51 is an example of one of these markings. It is inscribed FRANCO/PREUSS. RESP. VEREINS/AUSGANGS-GRENZE. This translates literally as "Paid/Prussian, and so forth, Union/Exit-Border." A free translation would be "Paid to the point of exit on the border of the German-Austrian Postal Union."

Information as to whether a rate paid to destination in or to the frontier of a particular country is not disclosed by the published tables of postages. In regard to Prussian closed mail, where optional prepayment is shown, the rate usually paid the letter to its destination. In those cases where prepayment was compulsory, the rate usually paid the letter only to the frontier of the country of destination.

The convention does not mention German currency, or any equivalent in United States money. All of the rates were expressed in, and all of the accounting was to be performed in United States currency. Since there was a welter of currencies circulating throughout Germany, it is doubtful that any particular currency could have been used. In general, the Prussian closed-mail rate was 13 silbergroschen in the northern states and 45 kreuzer in the southern states. There was, however, a special fee for delivery which was collected from the addressee. This charge appears to have varied in amount. Unpaid letters from the United States show a superaddition to the 13-silbergroschen rate, sometimes expressed as a fraction of a silbergroschen, and sometimes expressed in pfennige. Smith states: [6]

> The existence of this charge was found to be specially unfortunate in regard to foreign letters, since its collection was regarded by foreign administrations as an addition to the ordinary postage and consequently an evasion of the terms of the agreements under which foreign rates had been fixed.

Beginning in 1862, this fee was to be gradually abolished and by 1864 was no longer to exist.[7] There was, however, a fee for rural delivery which was not abolished until 1 January 1872.[8]

As already mentioned, the Prussian closed-mail rate in the southern German states of Baden, Bavaria, and Württemberg appears to have been 45 kreuzer. The currency in these states was based upon 60 kreuzer to the florin or gulden, either of which was worth about 40¢ in United States currency, and each kreuzer was, therefore, worth about two thirds of a cent. Until 1858 the florin of Austria was worth 48¢, and its kreuzer about four fifths of a cent. An 1851 almanac (its title page is missing and full citation cannot be given) in a table entitled "Value of Silver Coin &

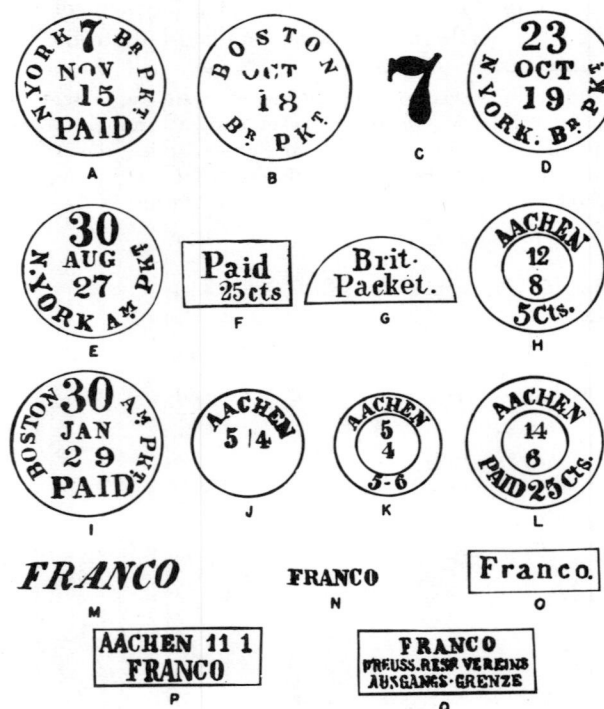

FIGURE 51.—MARKINGS on Prussian closed-mail covers.

---

[6] A. D. Smith, *Development of Rates of Postage,* p. 107.
[7] Ibid.
[8] Ibid., p. 110.

Foreign Currencies" shows 20 kreuzer to be equal to 16¢. The Prussian closed-mail rate in Austria was, therefore, 38 kreuzer. In 1858 Austria increased the number of kreuzer to the gulden from 60 to 100.

It was the custom of the Aachen office to show the Union and foreign postages on letters prepaid in Germany or on unpaid letters from the United States. The Union postage was 2 silbergroschen, or 6 kreuzer, while the remaining postage was 11 silbergroschen, or 39 kreuzer. One, and sometimes both, of these amounts appear on letters prepaid in Germany. Unpaid letters from the United States usually show a 2, or a 6, applied in manuscript or by use of a handstamp.

Prussia paid the postage on letters to or from places beyond the German-Austrian Postal Union. When the postage to these places was prepaid in the United States, the exchange offices increased the credit to Prussia above the 7¢ applicable to the 30¢ rate by the amount of postage beyond the border of the Union. Thus, a letter to Switzerland would bear a credit of 12¢, the postage beyond the border being 5¢, and the total postage set at 35¢.

The effective date of the convention as provided by Article XX was to be one month from the time notice was received of its being concluded. The annual report of Postmaster General Campbell for the year ended 30 June 1853 gives the effective date as 16 October 1852. This was undoubtedly determined by the sailing date of the first American packet at the expiration of one month after notification was received. The Collins line steamer *Atlantic* sailed from New York on that date, and it is presumed she carried the first Prussian closed mail dispatched from the United States.

Prussian Closed-Mail Markings and Covers

Because the Prussian closed mail was sent in closed bags between New York or Boston and Aachen through England and Belgium, its covers do not bear British or Belgian markings. At least as early as 12 January 1853, the New York office used a marking on letters prepaid in the United States similar to *A* of Figure 51, applied in red. The Boston office applied marking *C* in red to the face and a marking similar to *B* of Figure 51 (with either BR. or AM. PKT.) in black to the reverse of prepaid letters forwarded from that office. At a later date (uncertain) a marking similar to *A* of Figure 51, but inscribed BOSTON instead of N. YORK was introduced.

The Aachen office marked prepaid letters received from the United States with markings showing the word FRANCO. The earliest and latest uses of these markings noted to the date of this writing are as follows (letters in parentheses refer to Figure 51):

Marking	Earliest	Latest
Large FRANCO (**M**)	24 Jan. 1853	12 Dec. 1854
Small FRANCO (**N**)	26 Dec. 1854	5 Apr. 1855
Boxed *Franco* (**O**)	19 Jan. 1855	(one seen)
Boxed AACHEN/FRANCO (**P**)		
In red	29 Apr. 1854	1 Dec. 1863
In blue	10 Mar. 1865	22 Apr. 1867

Until marking *P* of Figure 51 came into use, the Aachen office applied either marking *J* or *K* to the reverse of prepaid letters received at that office.

Unpaid letters posted in the United States show a debit of 23¢ for a single rate in black ink on the face of the letter. Marking *D* of Figure 51 is typical of these markings.[9] To these unpaid letters the Aachen office applied either marking *J* or *K* of Figure 51 to the reverse of the cover.

Markings *F* and *G* were applied to early prepaid letters posted in Germany, addressed to the United States. A marking similar to *G* of Figure 51 shows AMERIC for American packet service, instead of the BRIT illustrated. These markings were applied in red, marking *F* to the face, and *G* to the reverse of such letters. At a later date (uncertain) markings *F* and *G* were superseded by marking *L*. It must be noted that, since all postage beyond the German-Austrian Postal Union was at Prussian expense, all Prussian closed-mail prepaid letters sent by the Aachen office, regardless of their point of origin, bear a credit to the United States of 25¢ per single rate. Prepaid letters received by the New York or Boston offices usually show a restatement of the 30¢ international rate marked in red ink. Marking *I* is a typical marking showing a restatement of rate.

Unpaid letters forwarded by the Aachen office to the United States show a debit of 5¢ per single rate, usually similar to marking *H* applied in black. To these unpaid letters, the United States offices applied black markings indicating a collection of 30¢ per

---

[9] For a more complete presentation of postal markings used on Prussian closed mail *see* Tracy W. Simpson, *"United States Postal Markings and Related Mail Services, 1851 to 1861,"* pp. 91–109. For markings of the Boston office *see* M. C. Blake and W. W. Davis, *"Boston Postal Markings of Boston, Massachusetts, to 1890,"* pp. 157–189.

single rate. Marking *E* is a typical marking indicating the postage to be collected.

Figure 52 presents a very early Prussian closed-mail cover. It is the only cover seen by the author which has the 30¢ rate prepaid by stamps and which bears the large FRANCO marking (*M* of Figure 51). Posted in Baltimore, Maryland, on 7 January 1853, it was forwarded to the New York office where marking *A* of Figure 51 (with the date of JAN/12) was applied in red. This letter was placed in a bag which was closed at the New York office and forwarded to Liverpool by R.M.S. *Asia* of the Cunard line which sailed from New York on 12 January 1853. The Liverpool office forwarded the closed bag through London and Ostend directly to the Aachen office where the bag was opened. On the reverse of this letter is an Aachen marking in orange ink (marking *J* of Figure 51) which bears the date of 24/1, indicating that it arrived at the Aachen office on 24 January. As is true of many Prussian closed-mail letters, there is nothing in either the United States or German markings to indicate the year. In this case, however, the cover is a folded letter whose heading shows the year to be 1853.

Figure 53 illustrates a letter posted in Warsaw, Illinois, on 17 July (1857), prepaid 30¢ by a strip of three of the imperforate 10¢ stamps of the 1851 issue, positions 1L, 2L (type II), and 3L (type III) of plate I. The letter was forwarded to the New York office which applied marking *A* of Figure 51 in red ink, with the date of JUL/22. Since there is nothing on the cover to indicate the year, it is necessary to determine it from the New York postmark. The marking shows British packet service, and this means service by the Cunard line. The date of 22 July, therefore, could be a Tuesday if the packet sailed from Boston on 23 July, or it could be a Wednesday if the packet sailed from New York on 22 July. In 1855 all sailings were from Boston, *America* sailing from there on 18 July. Thus, the year was not 1855. In 1856 *Africa* sailed from New York on 23 July, which eliminates 1856. In 1857 *Arabia* sailed from New York on 22 July, which indicates that this is the year in which the letter was mailed. Marking *P* of Figure 51 was applied in red by the Aachen office, and this marking shows the date of 4/8, which means that it arrived there on 4 August. The letter was, therefore, thirteen days in transit from New York to Aachen. Surface mail is seldom faster than that today.

Figure 54 illustrates an unpaid letter posted in Columbia, Maine, on 8 October (1853), addressed to

FIGURE 52.—COVER, from Baltimore to Munich, Bavaria, 1853.
(*Melvin W. Schuh collection*)

Figure 53.—Cover, from Warsaw, Illinois, to Osnabrück, Germany, 1857.
(*Mortimer L. Neinken collection*)

Figure 54.—Cover, from Columbia, Maine, to Weimar, Germany, 1853.
(*Photography by Smithsonian*)

Weimar, Thuringia. The cover is a 3¢ Nesbitt envelope (seal of *G. F. Nesbitt/N.Y.*, on reverse) which prepaid the letter with 3¢. Since this was a partial payment of the 30¢ rate, the New York office did not recognize it (see Article II, above, page 87) and marked the letter with the unpaid debit of 23¢. The New York marking shows British packet (Cunard line) service and the date of 19 October. This indicates that the letter was forwarded to Liverpool by R.M.S. *Arabia* which sailed from New York on 19 October 1853. On the reverse is an orange Aachen marking (*K* of Figure 51) bearing the date of 1/11 (1 November). There are several other transit marks and a Weimar receiving mark showing the date of 2 November.

Of particular interest are the foreign rate markings. At left is a blue manuscript *45* which shows that the letter was rated for a collection of 45 kreuzer, the equivalent of 30¢. This is crossed out in red crayon, and it is marked with 13 $\overline{9}$, which indicates that 13 silbergroschen and 9 pfennige were to be collected. In Thuringia both the silbergroschen and the kreuzer were in circulation, and the recipient evidently preferred to pay in silbergroschen. The Prussian closed-mail rate, however, was only 13 silbergroschen, and this letter shows a surcharge of 9 pfennige. The surcharge evidently represents the delivery fee previously mentioned in this chapter. The 45 kreuzer represented the rate to be charged while the letter was held in the post office, but when delivery was made, the additional 9 pfennige were added. This cover is illustrated as photo 22 in the first section of the late Stanley B. Ashbrook's Special Service. Mr. Ashbrook indicated that the circular marking with 23 in the center was a Prussian marking. It may be; the author does not know whether it is. On the reverse is a blue manuscript *11*, which indicated the foreign portion of the 13-silbergroschen rate, the remaining 2 silbergroschen representing the Union postage.

Figure 55 illustrates a cover posted in Munich, addressed to New York. It is prepaid 45 kreuzer by a strip of three and a pair of 9 kreuzer Bavarian stamps (Scott no. 6). The date in the Munich postmark is 4 October, while an Aachen marking (*L* of Figure 51) shows that it passed through that office on 7 October. The Aachen office indicated the foreign postage in silbergroschen by marking it *11* in red crayon. The New York office restated the 30¢ rate by striking it with a marking similar to *I* of Figure 51, but showing

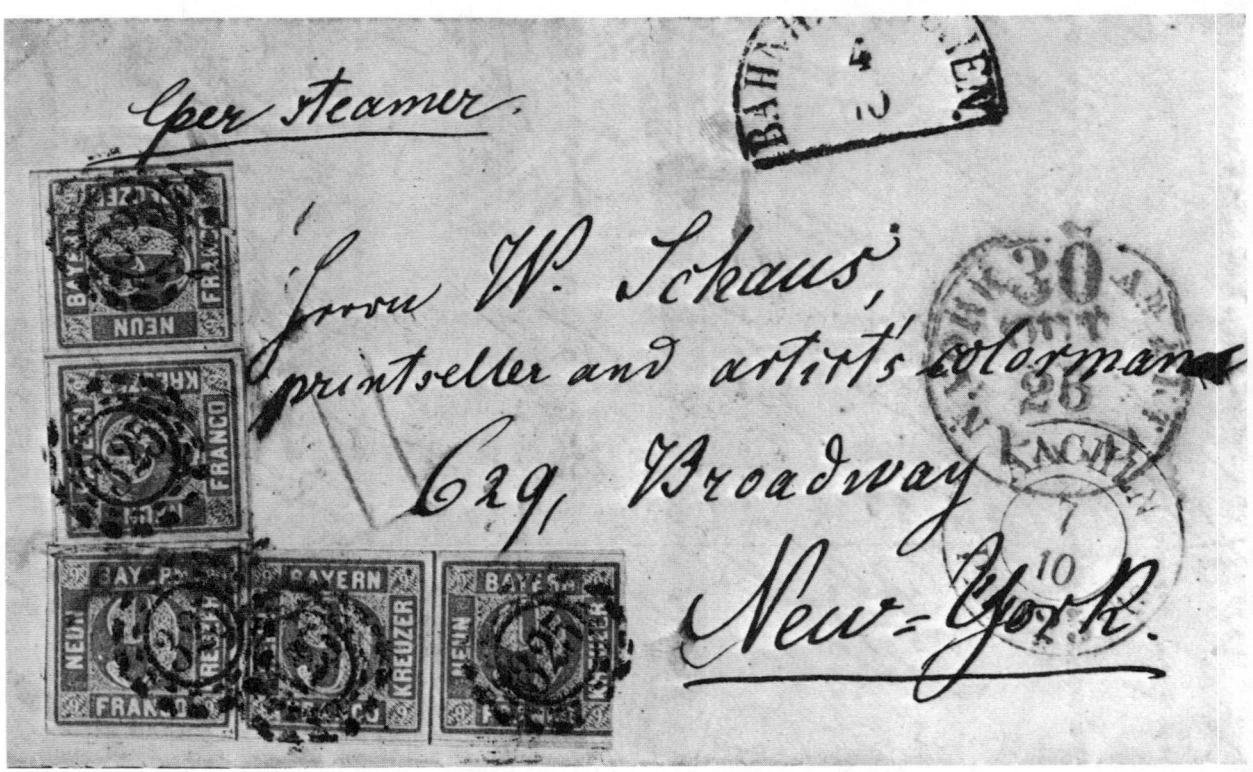

FIGURE 55.—COVER, from München to New York, 1856. (*Photograph by Smithsonian*)

N. YORK instead of BOSTON. The date in this marking is OCT/25, and steamer *Ericsson,* then in Collins line service, arrived in New York on 25 October 1856.

Figure 56 illustrates a double-rate cover to Norway by Prussian closed mail. This cover was posted in San Francisco on 18 April 1862, prepaid 92¢ by a pair of 1¢ and a single 90¢ stamp of the 1861 issue. The Prussian closed-mail rate to Norway at that time was 46¢, prepayment optional, for a single rate. The foreign postage, that is, postage in excess of the 30¢ international rate, was 16¢ per single rate. The single-rate credit for the international postage of 7¢, therefore, should be augmented by 16¢, and the total single-rate credit should be 23¢. Thus, the New York office marked this cover in red manuscript with a *46,* representing a double-rate credit to Prussia. At the time Mr. J. David Baker illustrated this cover in the *Chronicle,*[10] he asked, "Is this the only 90¢ cover known used to Norway?" To the date of this writing no other has been reported.

Covers by British Open Mail

From 1849 until 1856 tables of postages to foreign countries published in United States official and semi-official sources show the open-mail rates of 5¢ by British packet or of 21¢ by American packet as being available for letters addressed to the various German states and to most of the countries in central and eastern Europe. The table included in the 1857 edition of the *Postal Laws and Regulations* deletes the open-mail rates to most of those destinations and introduces rates by French mail. The deletion does not mean that open-mail rates to those countries were no longer available for use by the United States exchange offices; it simply means that the Post Office Department no longer recommended this route for mails addressed to those destinations. After the Prussian closed-mail convention became effective on 16 October 1852, little mail between the northern German states and the United States was sent in the British open mail. The few covers seen were forwarded by the London office to the Prussian office at Aachen in the Anglo-Prussian closed mail under terms of the Anglo-Prussian convention of 2/7 July 1852. This route proceeded from London through Ostend and Verviers to Aachen, and thence to the second Prussian exchange office for Anglo-Prussian closed mail at Cologne. Letters from the United States were usually put off at Aachen, while letters to the United States usually entered the closed mails at Cologne. The United States-Prussian closed mail also followed this route, but Aachen was the exchange office for mail sent in either direction.

Prior to the effective date of the United States-

[10] *Chronicle of the U.S. Classic Issues* 17, 1 (Oct. 1964): 37.

FIGURE 56.—COVER, from San Francisco to Thronjem [Trondhjem—Trondheim], Norway, 1862
(*Courtesy of J. David Baker*)

French convention, 1 April 1857, mail addressed to the southern German states, Switzerland, and the northern Italian states was usually sent in the British open mail through France or in the Prussian closed mail. Bremen rates, and after 1 July 1857, rates by the Bremen and Hamburg services, were also available to these destinations. After the United States-French convention became effective, open-mail covers to these destinations are seldom seen.

Figure 57 illustrates a cover posted in Rochester, New York, on 14 February 1853, addressed to Berlin. It is prepaid 21¢ by a strip of seven 3¢ stamps of the 1851 issue. A New York American packet marking dated 19 February indicates service to Liverpool by U.S.M. (United States Mail) steamer *Atlantic* of the Collins line. The cover bears on its face markings *B*, *C*, and *E* of Figure 58. Marking *B* is the British debit to Prussia for British and Belgian transit postage (see page 86. This marking does not appear on several covers used during 1856, and it is not known whether the use of the marking was discontinued, or whether it was omitted on covers in error. Marking *E* is in blue manuscript and indicates that 7 silbergroschen were to be collected (see page 86). On the reverse of the cover is a circular British marking BX/3 MR 3/1853 applied in orange-red ink, and marking *A* of Figure 58 dated 4/3, that is 4 March. These markings are characteristic of open-mail letters forwarded by the London office in the Anglo-Prussian closed mail.

Figure 59 illustrates a cover posted in Mainz on 29 April 1856, adderssed to New York. The letter is prepaid 47 kreuzer by a strip of five of the 9-kreuzer and two single 1-kreuzer stamps (Scott nos. 46 and 42, respectively, of the Southern District of Thurn and Taxis posts of Germany). On the face is a P. in a circle and a PD marking which indicated that the postage was paid to destination, in this case, the United States frontier.

On the reverse is a double circle COELN/5–6 marking with date of 30/4 (30 April) in the center. This indicates that the letter entered the Anglo-Prussian closed mail at the Cologne office on 30 April 1856. The Cologne office marked the letter *10¾ gn* in manuscript in red ink to show a credit to Great Britain of 10¾ groschen. This was for sea postage which was 8d. under the United States-British treaty, and was evidently held at 7¼ silbergroschen, plus 3½ silbergroschen for British and Belgian transit (see page 86). These same rates in British pence were 8d. and 4d., respectively, and the London office, which performed the accounting, marked the letter 1s. in red manuscript. The German postage was also 3½ silbergroschen or 4d., which would make the total postage to the United States frontier amount to 32¢ (24¢ British and

FIGURE 57.—COVER, from Rochester, N.Y., to Berlin, Prussia, 1853. (*Melvin W. Schuh collection*)

Figure 58.—Markings on open-mail covers to Germany and Switzerland.

8¢ German). Since 1 kreuzer was equal to about two thirds of a United States cent, 47 kreuzer were equal to about 31⅓¢, the discrepancy undoubtedly being due to rounding off the rates and coin.

The London office marked the letter PAID and forwarded it to Liverpool on 2 May 1856 (see circular PAID/2 MY 2/1856 on face of cover). The New York office marked the letter in black with a circular 5/N. YORK BR. PKT. marking dated MAY/16. The R.M.S. *Asia* of the Cunard line arrived in New York on that date, confirming the endorsement to that ship. Five cents were collected in New York.

Figure 60 illustrates a most unusual cover. It was posted in New Orleans on 27 December 1856, addressed to Basle, Switzerland. It is endorsed "p. first Steamer via Liverpool/p. prussian closed mail." Since the first steamer to Liverpool may not have carried a Prussian closed mail, the two portions of the endorsement were ambiguous. The single rate by Prussian closed mail to Switzerland was 35¢. This letter is prepaid 70¢ by stamps of the 1851 issue, which apparently indicates that the mailer's intention was to send it in the Prussian closed mail, and that the letter weighed over half an ounce, requiring two rates. For a reason upon which it is futile to speculate, the New York office sent the letter in the British open mail to Liverpool, instead of in the Prussian closed mail. A New York American packet marking dated 17 January signifies service to Liverpool by steamer *Ericsson*, then running for the Collins line. Since this was an American packet, only 42¢ of the 70¢ prepayment was utilized. On the reverse is a London marking FD/2 FE 2/1857 applied in orange-red. The London office evidently intended to send the letter through France, but, after applying a GB/40¢ marking (*O* of Figure 18), changed the routing and sent it in the Anglo-Prussian closed mail to Aachen. On the face of the cover is marking *C* and on the reverse, marking *A* of Figure 58 dated 3/2 (3 February).

Rates for transit mail were established by Articles II and III of the Anglo-Prussian convention. Transit letters were to be liable for the 8d. or 7 silbergroschen international rate and "be further liable to the rates which are now or which shall hereafter be taken from

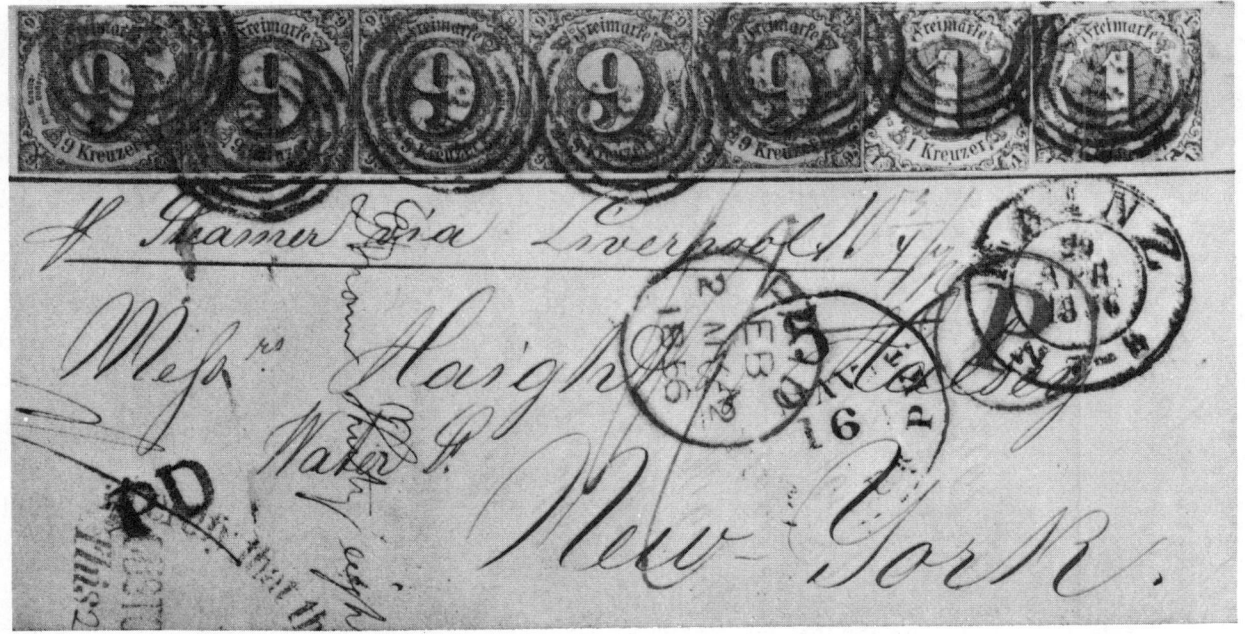

Figure 59.—Cover, from Mainz [Germany], to New York, 1856.

Figure 60.—Cover, from New Orleans to Basle, Switzerland, 1856.
(*Hugh J. Baker, Jr., collection*)

British subjects, upon letters . . . passing in transit through any of the States of the German Postal Union, and also the United Kingdom"; the foreign rates "are to be calculated from the port of departure or arrival of the packet." Article II refers to an appended table which gives the rate to Switzerland as 5d. foreign postage and 4d. British and Belgian transit for a total of 9d. Since 1d. (British) was equal to 10 rappen (Swiss), a double-rate letter should be rated for a collection of 180 rappen in Switzerland. On the face of the cover (Figure 60) is a red crayon *180,* and since it was the custom of the Swiss to show postage due in red crayon, it is presumed that this marking indicated the amount to be collected. Also on the face of the cover are blue manuscript markings which are presumed to be German. The author has not been able to determine the nature of these markings in regard to either the currency they represent or their significance.

Figure 61 illustrates an open-mail cover that was forwarded through France. This letter was posted in Philadelphia on 21 November 1851, addressed to Nuremburg [*sic*], Bavaria. It is prepaid 21¢ for American packet service by a strip of four and a strip of three of the 3¢ stamps in the orange-brown shade. The Philadelphia postmark is in blue as are also the grids canceling the stamps. The New York American packet marking had not yet been introduced, but it is presumed this letter was conveyed to Liverpool by U.S.M. steamer *Baltic* which sailed from New York on 22 November 1851. Although the provisional agreement between France and England which culminated in the decree of 19 November 1851 fixed rates only between England and France and those places on the Mediterranean where France had post offices, the COLONIES/&C. ART. 13 was no longer used on mail in transit through France from the United States. On this cover, marking *E* of Figure 18 with the date of 6 December 1851 was applied in black. Marking *E* was introduced at the time the COLONIES/&C. ART 13 (*B* of Figure 18) was discontinued on mail from the United States. The cover bears a manuscript *1/30* marking, which it is presumed signified that one florin thirty kreuzer were to be collected in Bavaria. This was equal to 60¢ in United States currency and to 90 Bavarian kreuzer. The southern German states charged postage on the quarter-ounce basis, and it is suspected that this represented a collection of two single rates of 45 kreuzer.

Figure 62 illustrates a most unusual cover which was sent through France in the open mail as late as 1865. This letter originated in a town named Mishicott, but the name of the state is off the letter. There was a town by the name of Mishicot (spelled with one *t*) in Wisconsin, and this is the only town by that name

Figure 61.—Cover, from Philadelphia to Nuremburg [Nuremberg], Bavaria, 1851. (*Melvin W. Schuh collection*)

that has been found in any of the listings to which reference has been made. The state of origin is, therefore, uncertain. If the state was Wisconsin, however, much about the cover can be explained. As will be more fully examined later, the additional articles to the United States-French convention, effective 1 April 1861, which created an exchange office at Detroit, provided that all French mail originating in Wisconsin be sent to that office, whence it was to be forwarded by the Allan line from Portland or River du Loup. The Detroit office could not send French mail to Boston or New York for transmission, but it could send British mail to the offices at Boston or New York to be included in mails made up at those offices. The Detroit office made up no mails for conveyance to Europe that were not to be forwarded by the Allan line.

It is assumed that this letter was sent by the Mishicott office to the office at Detroit prepaid with 21¢ in stamps and without the required endorsement if it were to be sent by French mail. Although the table of postages to foreign countries does not show the open-mail rates as being available on mail to Switzerland, they were available to the exchange offices, and the public was admonished to endorse its letters to be sent by French mail, or they might be sent in the open mail to Liverpool.[11]

Whether it was the intention of the person who mailed this letter to send it by French mail is not known. The Detroit office determined that it weighed over one-fourth ounce and would require two French mail rates of 21¢ to be prepaid. If it were sent by French mail it would have to be forwarded as an unpaid letter, the 21¢ prepaid not being recognized. Since the letter was not endorsed to be sent by French mail, it was sent in the British mail, directed to the New York office. At the New York office it was included in the Liverpool mail and entered on the letter-bill as an open-mail letter addressed to Switzerland. The New York packet marking was applied lightly in red over the Mishicott marking and shows the date of 4 November. On 4 November 1865, the *City of New York* of the Inman line sailed from New York for Queenstown with the British mail, and it is assumed she carried this letter to Liverpool. Since Liverpool was not an exchange office

[11] *U.S. Mail and Post Office Assistant* on page 4 under "Foreign Miscellany." All issues from October 1860 through December 1867.

Figure 62.—Cover, from Mishicott [state unknown] to Martigny, Switzerland, 1865.

for Anglo-French mail, this letter was forwarded to the London office, whence it was forwarded to France on 17 November 1865 (London marking bearing this date on reverse of cover). The London office also marked the cover with the GB/40^c marking (*O* of Figure 18), showing that it was forwarded to France charged with transit postage only. The ambulant office, Calais to Paris, marked the letter with marking *N* of Figure 18 dated 17 November 1865. The Paris office (marking on reverse, date 18 November 1865) forwarded the letter to a French border exchange office designated by the marking F./27.

Maury [12] lists thirty-nine such markings, each with the single letter *F.* and a numeral, and having a border of a different shape. He notes that they were introduced in 1857 and that they were applied by the French exchange offices on letters passing in transit through France (see marking *D* of Figure 58). On the reverse of the letter is a marking of the Swiss AMBULANT-CIRCULAIRE dated 19 November 1865 and a Martigny town marking of the same date. On the face at upper left is a small manuscript *2* signifying a double-rate letter, and a *140* in red crayon. This latter marking indicates that 140 centimes were to be collected in Switzerland. Very few letters were sent in the open mail to points on the continent *through France* as late as 1865.

---
[12] Author Maury, *Catalogue descriptif de toutes les marques postales de la France,* pp. 48–50.

Chapter 6

Postal Relations With Belgium 1844–1868

On 19 October 1844, a postal convention between Great Britain and Belgium was signed at London.[1] This convention governed the exchange of mail between the United States and Belgium, via England, until after the United States-British treaty became effective in 1849. During this period, mails to or from the United States were sent in the ordinary or "open" mail. The rates to be charged in Belgium on letters to or from "colonies and countries beyond the sea" were set forth in Article XXIV, as follows:

1. Eightpence per single letter, for transit through the territory of the United Kingdom.
2. The packet rate the inhabitants of Great Britain have to pay on letters coming from or addressed to colonies and countries beyond the sea.

The detailed regulations, in an appended table,[2] specifically provided a rate for the United States of 1s. 8d., which was to be prepaid in Belgium on letters sent, or collected there on letters received. Since this rate covered only British transit and packet postages, it paid the letter no farther than the frontiers of the two countries. Inland postage in either country was required to be prepaid on letters sent, or collected on letters received. The inland postage to be prepaid or collected in Belgium was set by Article XIX at 4 decimes, or 4d.

Article X of the detailed regulations established the progression of the Belgian postage, as follows:

1. Under 10 grams, one single rate
2. From 10 grams to 15 grams inclusively, one rate and a half
3. From 15 grams to 20 grams inclusively, two rates
4. From 20 grams to 30 grams inclusively, two rates and a half, and so on; one half rate being added for every 10 grams

The British postage was calculated upon the progression then in force in Great Britain, which was:

1. For every letter not exceeding half an ounce in weight, one single rate
2. Above half an ounce, but not exceeding one ounce, two rates
3. Above one ounce, but not exceeding two ounces, four rates . . . and so on, two rates being added for every ounce, or fraction of an ounce.

Article I of the detailed regulations required that the Belgian office at Ostend exchange mails with the British offices at Dover and London. The Belgian office at Antwerp was to exchange mails only with the British office at London. By additional articles signed at London on 18 June 1845,[3] the office at Antwerp was also to correspond with a new British office at Hull.

The advent of the American contract packets of the Ocean Steam Navigation Company in June 1847 created a number of problems for the British Post Office. As explained in Chapter 2, it was the desire of the United States Post Office that letters conveyed by American packets be delivered to the British Post Office at Southampton to be forwarded from that office as letters originating in the United Kingdom. It was hoped that the British would relinquish their 8d. ship letter fee on these letters. Had the British Post Office acceded to this American wish, the inhabitants of the United Kingdom would have paid no packet postage

---
[1] *British and Foreign State Papers,* vol. 32, pp. 66–77. (According to a letter from Jacques Stibbe of Brussels this convention was placed in force in Belgium on 1 Dec. 1844.)
[2] Ibid., pp. 78–85.
[3] Ibid., vol. 33, p. 35.

on letters conveyed by the American steamers. Under XXIV of the Anglo-Belgian convention (previously outlined), no packet postage, under this circumstance, would have been levied in Belgium on letters conveyed by the American line. Implementing Article XXIV of the convention, the detailed regulations, however, provided a sole rate of 1s. 8d. for mail to or from the United States. This provision would have required amendment so that it applied only to mail conveyed by British packets, and an additional rate of 8d. for letters by American packet would have to have been introduced. It will be remembered that the Anglo-Prussian convention of 1 October 1846 and the Anglo-French convention of 3 April 1843 also provided for sole open- or closed-mail rates between the frontier of the United States and the frontiers of Prussia or France.

On 9 June 1847, the British Post Office solved its problem. As will be remembered from Chapter 2, on that date the British Post Office issued an order requiring the inhabitants of the United Kingdom to pay the 1s.-packet postage on letters conveyed by the American line. Thus, the inhabitants of Belgium were also required to pay it, and the sole rate of 1s. 8d. prevailed.

In issuing this order, the British Post Office was primarily, and avowedly, motivated by a desire to protect the Cunard line of contract packets. It cannot be doubted, however, that a desire to maintain the existing mail arrangements the British Post Office held with the corridor countries on the continent was also an influencing factor.

While the United States "retaliatory" act of 27 June 1848 required that 24¢-packet postage be collected in the United States on letters conveyed by the Cunard line, it had no effect on the postage prepaid or collected in Belgium. After the United States-British treaty was signed on 15 December 1848, and before it became effective on 15 February 1849, it will be remembered, the former rates were restored; in Britain on 29 December 1848 by a treasury warrant, and in the United States on 3 January 1849 by a post office order. Between 29 December 1848 and 15 February 1849, therefore, the 1s. charge for packet postage on mail between the Belgian and United States frontiers, when conveyed by American packets, should have been dropped. Since there were no sailings by the American Ocean line between 20 November 1848 and 20 February 1849,[4] the British Post Office did not have to face this issue.

[4] *Shipping and Commercial List and New York Prices Current,* arrival and clearance dates reported in appropriate issues.

From 1844 until the United States-British treaty became effective on 15 February 1849, therefore, there was a sole rate of 1s. 8d. between the United States and Belgian frontiers, whether the letter was conveyed by a British or an American packet. When the United States-British treaty became effective in Great Britain, the packet rate was reduced to 8d., and according to Article XXIV of the Anglo-Belgian convention, should have immediately reduced the rate between the United States and Belgian frontiers to 1s. 4d. by British packet, and to 8d. by American packet. No covers passing between the United States and Belgium during this period, however, have been seen, and it is not known whether this reduction was immediately recognized.[5]

Figure 63 illustrates a letter posted in Charleston, South Carolina, on 21 February 1848, addressed to Gand, Belgium, and endorsed to Cunard steamer *Hibernia*. The inland rate from Charleston to New York, a distance of over 300 miles, was 10¢, which was prepaid by use of a pair of 5¢ stamps of the 1847 issue. The letter was conveyed by *Hibernia*, which sailed from New York on 26 February and arrived in Liverpool on 11 March 1848. Since Liverpool was not an exchange office for Anglo-Belgian mail, this letter was sent directly to the London or Dover office, probably the foreign office at Lombard Street, London.

FIGURE 63.—COVER, from Charleston, S.C., to Gand [Ghent], Belgium, 1948. (*Photograph by Ashbrooke. Courtesy of Creighton C. Hart*).

[5] A letter from Stibbe states that the reduction in rate following the U.S.-British treaty was placed in force in Belgium after 29 Mar. 1849. An official circulaire concluded: "A new convention between Great Britain and the United States of America has reduced the rate on correspondence exchanged, via England, between the United States and the continent. This correspondence can be sent by English or American packets, at the choice of the senders. However, those intended to be sent by the latter, must bear in the upper part of the address the words: 'Par paquebot des États Unis'.... Followed by the postage to the benefit of Great Britain."

The back of the cover is not shown, but it should bear a British exchange office marking showing a date of 11 or 12 March. The British exchange office debited Belgium with 1s. 8d., which is indicated by the manuscript *1/8* on the face at right. The letter was then forwarded to either the Ostend or the Antwerp office, which marked it for a collection in Belgium of 24 decimes. This is shown by the manuscript marking in blue, which looks something like *9N*, but is the way the Belgians and the French wrote *24*. The 1s. 8d., of course, was equal to 20d., or 20 decimes, to which was added 4 decimes for Belgian inland postage.

Figure 64 presents a cover to which the late Stanley B. Ashbrook devoted considerable space in his *Special Service*.[6] As Mr. Ashbrook pointed out, this letter originated in Charleston, South Carolina, on 28 October 1848, during the retaliatory period, and required a prepayment of 10¢ inland (for a distance beyond 300 miles), and a packet postage of 24¢, for a total of 34¢. This postage was prepaid by use of a strip of three of the 10¢ stamps and a single 5¢ stamp of the 1847 issue. Thus, the letter was 1¢ overpaid. It was conveyed, in some manner not apparent on the cover, to New York, where it was posted and the stamps canceled with the well-known square grid. It is endorsed to steamer *Niagara*, which sailed from Boston on 1 November and arrived in Liverpool on 13 November 1848. Mr. Ashbrook photographed the back of the cover (not shown here), and this bears what appears to be a London marking with the date of 14 November 1848, indicating the date it was dispatched from that office. Shown is an Ostend marking dated 15 November and a Gand receiving mark bearing the date of 18 November. On the face of the cover is a manuscript 1/3 in black ink, indicating the British debit to Belgium.

Also on the face of the cover is a rectangular box marking, bearing three lines of type. Because the impression is somewhat blurred, these cannot be read from the photograph, but Mr. Ashbrook was able to decipher them from the original. They read (with a literal translation), as follows: DÉBOURS ÉTRANGER ("Foreign disbursement") 1/8 [inserted]/TAXE RÉDUITE ("Rate converted") 20 [inserted]/PORT BELGE ("Belgian postage") 4 [inserted].

The inserted figures show the British postage of 1s. 8d. and its equivalent of 20 decimes brought down. The Belgian postage of 4 decimes indicates that the letter weighed under ten grams. This marking was undoubtedly developed to assist in computing and explaining the amount to be collected, which, because of the differences in the British and Belgian progressions, would become complicated on letters above ten grams in weight. Also on the face is a manuscript *24*, which indi-

---

[6] S. B. Ashbrook, *Special Service,* issue 20, pp. 137–144.

FIGURE 64.—COVER, from Charleston, S.C., to Gand [Ghent], Belgium, 1848. (*Photograph by Ashbrook. Courtesy of Creighton C. Hart*)

cated that 24 decimes were to be collected from the addressee in Gand [Ghent].

The covers illustrated in Figures 63 and 64 both show the same rate to be collected in Belgium, as would any cover whose weight was under ten grams, sent from the United States to Belgium, via England, between 1844 and 15 February 1849. The photographs of these covers were taken from the late Stanley B. Ashbrook's *Special Service,* and are presented here through the courtesy of Mr. Creighton C. Hart.

On 27 November 1849,[7] an additional postal convention between Great Britain and Belgium was signed at London. Although this convention was considered as additional to the convention of 19 October 1844, many changes in the original arrangements were made.

Article I reduced the Belgian inland postage to 2 decimes, or pence, and changed the progression for the Belgian postage to the following:

1. Under 7½ grams, one single rate
2. From 7½ grams to 15 grams exclusively, two rates
3. From 15 grams to 22½ grams exclusively, three rates, and so on, one rate being added for every 7½ grams

Article V set the rates for ordinary transit correspondence as follows:

1. Fourpence per single letter for transit through the territory of the United Kingdom, when the letter shall be posted in or addressed to Belgium . . .

---
[7] *British and Foreign State Papers,* vol. 37, pp. 11–19. (According to a letter from Stibbe this convention became effective in Belgium on 1 Feb. 1850.)

2. The packet rate which the inhabitants of Great Britain have to pay on letters coming from or addressed to colonies and countries beyond the sea

Article VIII made the rates established in Article V apply to closed mails.

For a letter that weighed less than 7½ grams, therefore, the rate to be prepaid or collected in Belgium was the sum of 2 decimes for inland, 4 decimes for British transit, and 8 decimes for packet postages. Thus, a total of 14 decimes would have paid such a letter posted in Belgium to the United States frontier when conveyance was by a British packet. On such a letter, Belgium would have given Great Britain a credit of 12 decimes, the equivalent of 1s. After 1854, if the British Post Office elected to send the above letter by an American packet, it would have given the United States a credit of 16¢ for packet postage (see Chapter 2, p. 39).

Figure 65 illustrates a cover posted in Deep River, Connecticut, on 28 April 1856, addressed to Antwerp. It is prepaid 21¢ by a single 1¢ type IV stamp, and a pair of 10¢ type II stamps of the 1851 issue. It was sent to the New York exchange office which forwarded it on 3 May 1856 to Southampton by the *Arago* of the Havre line. From Southampton it was sent to the London office which applied a straight-line U.S. P^{KT} marking in black (*C* of Figure 58, Chapter 5) and debited Belgium in black manuscript with *4* (pence) transit postage. The Ostend exchange office applied a rectangular marking to the face of the letter, similar to that shown

FIGURE 65.—COVER, from Deep River, Ct. [Connecticut], to Antwerp, 1856. (*Courtesy of John A. Fox*)

in Figure 64. The manuscript insertions (in blue ink) in this marking are: DÉBOURS ÉTRANGER 4 [inserted]/ TAXE RÉDUITE 4 [inserted]/PORT BELGE 2 [inserted]. Below this marking is a blue manuscript 6 which signifies a collection of 6 decimes (4 decimes transit and 2 decimes inland postage). The inland postage of 2 decimes was for a letter that weighed under 7½ grams.[8]

A new postal convention between the post offices of Great Britain and Belgium was signed at London on 28 August 1857.[9] This convention was preceded by one signed at London on 8 January 1857,[10] which simply gave the post offices of the two countries the right to make a postal convention. The previous conventions, signed by the British secretary of foreign affairs and the Belgian minister at London, were diplomatically negotiated, but the two post offices were allowed to settle matters of detail. Evidently, a quirk of Belgian law required special permission for its postal authorities to make a postal convention.

Article II established Belgian exchange offices at (1) Ostend, local office and travelling office; (2) Antwerp; (3) travelling office on railway between Ghent and Mouscron; (4) travelling office between Brussels and Quiévrain. The British offices remained (1) Dover, (2) London, and (3) Hull. Others could be established by agreement between the two post offices.

Article VII set the international rate at 40 centimes, or 4d., which included Belgian postage of 20 centimes, or 2d., and British postage of 20 centimes, or 2d., for prepaid letters. Unpaid letters were at double the above rates, and insufficiently prepaid letters by means of postage stamps were charged double the amount of the deficiency. Dr. Robert de Wasserman of Brussels has kindly submitted a copy of Belgian Post Office order 413 which explains by several examples how the amount due on insufficiently paid letters was to be computed. One example will suffice. It translates:

A single-rate letter, addressed from Belgium to England, and prepaid by postage stamps to the value of 10 centimes, will arrive at destination marked by the Belgian exchange office for a collection of 6d. (60 centimes), as follows:

One single rate	40
Value of postage stamps	10
Insufficiency	30
Double the insufficiency	60

[8] This cover is in the collection of L. L. Downing.
[9] *British and Foreign State Papers,* vol. 56, pp. 989–997. (According to a letter from Stibbe this convention became effective in Belgium on 1 October 1857.)
[10] Ibid., vol. 47, pp. 9–11.

Article VII also established the progression for both countries as that used in Great Britain, as follows:

1. For every letter of which the weight shall not exceed 15 grams (half an ounce), one single rate
2. Exceeding 15 grams (half an ounce) and not exceeding 30 grams (1 ounce), two rates
3. Exceeding 30 grams (1 ounce) and not exceeding 60 grams (two ounces), four rates, and so on, adding two rates per 30 grams or fraction of 30 grams (1 ounce or fraction of 1 ounce)

Article XI set the rates for ordinary letters to or from colonies or countries beyond the sea, as follows:

1. For transit over the territory of the United Kingdom, 2d. per single letter
2. The sea rate paid by the British public upon letters originating in or addressed to the colonies or countries beyond the sea

Article XV applied the rates of Article XI to closed mail. By a table appended to the detailed regulations, special rates for letters between Belgium and the United States were fixed at 10 decimes by British packet, and 2 decimes by United States packet.[11] These rates were required to be prepaid and accounted for by the Belgian office to the British office on correspondence originating in or addressed to British colonies, possessions, or foreign countries. The above rates were made applicable to unpaid letters forwarded by the British office to Belgium by Article XI of the convention.

Thus, on letters posted in Belgium, addressed to the United States, a prepayment of 12 decimes, that is, 2 decimes Belgian inland, 2 decimes British transit, and 8 decimes sea postage, would pay the letter to the United States frontier by a British packet. By an American packet the prepayment would be only 4 decimes (2 decimes Belgian inland and 2 decimes British transit postages). Letters posted in the United States, addressed to Belgium, would require a prepayment of 5¢ in the United States and a collection in Belgium of 12 decimes, if conveyed by British packet. If conveyance was by American packet, a prepayment of 21¢ in the United States was required, and 4 decimes would be collected in Belgium. Letters posted in Belgium prepaid with the British packet rate of 12 decimes, if sent by American packet by the British Post Office, would receive a credit to the United States from the British Post Office of 16¢ for the packet postage.

[11] Ibid., vol. 56, p. 611.

Article XVI provided for mails which were to be sent by way of France:

> The mails which shall be exchanged in conformity with Article II of the present convention between the Belgian Post Offices established on the lines of railway from Ghent to Mouscron, and from Brussels to Quiévrain, on the one side, and the British Post Offices of London and Dover, on the other side, shall be forwarded through the medium of the Post Office of France.
>
> In addition to the rates fixed by Article VII of the present Convention the correspondence, whether paid or unpaid, which the public of the two countries may wish to send by the route of France, shall be subject to a supplementary rate of 2 decimes, or pence, per single letter.

Figure 66 illustrates an open-mail cover from the United States to Belgium by American packet. Posted in San Antonio, Texas, on 10 June (1859), addressed to Mons, Belgium, this letter is prepaid with 21¢ in stamps. It was forwarded from New York by steamer *Fulton* of the Havre Line, which sailed on 25 June 1859 for Cowes (Southampton) and Havre. The letter was sent through the Southampton office to London or Dover, and thence to Belgium. The back of the cover is not shown, but it must bear both British and Belgian markings. On the face appears what looks like a *24*. It is, however, composed of two markings, a *2* and a *4*. If the cover had been marked for a collection of *24* in Belgium, the marking would appear as it does on Figures 63 and 64. The *2* in the marking on this cover is not written as the Belgians or the French would have written it, but it is the way the British would have written a *2*. The *2*, therefore, is the British debit of 2d., while the *4* indicates that 4 decimes were to be collected on delivery. The photograph of this cover is taken from the late Stanley B. Ashbrook's *Special Service*[12] and is presented here through the courtesy of Mr. Creighton C. Hart.

Figure 67 presents a cover posted in Antwerp on 28 July 1863, addressed to New York. It is prepaid by one 20- and three 40-centime perforated stamps issued in 1863 for a total of 140 centimes. At upper left it is endorsed "Via Calais," indicating it was to be sent by the route of France which required the prepayment of an additional 20 centimes. The 140-centime rate is, therefore, divided into: Belgian inland, 20 centimes; French transit (paid to France), 20 centimes; British transit, 20 centimes; and packet postage, 80 centimes. To the right of the endorsement is a red manuscript *10*, which is the Belgian credit to the British Post Office for the British transit and packet postages. The letter arrived at the London office prepaid with the postage required for transmission by a British packet. The London office, however, included it in mail to be sent by an American contract packet, and credited the United States Post Office with the packet postage of 16¢. This is shown by a red crayon *16* on the face.

---

[12] Ashbrook, *Special Service,* issue 53, p. 420.

FIGURE 66.—COVER, from San Antonio, Tex., to Mons, Belgium, 1859.
(*Photograph by Ashbrook. Courtesy of Creighton C. Hart*)

Figure 67.—Cover, from Antwerp to New York, 1863.

On 29 July the London office sent the letter to Liverpool, whence it was conveyed by *Glasgow* of the Inman line which arrived in New York on 11 August 1863. The New York office marked it for a collection of 5¢ United States inland postage.[13]

The United States-Belgian Convention of 21 December 1859

As early as 1854 the United States and Belgium were attempting to form a postal arrangement.[14] Satisfactory progress toward this end was not made until the railway lines connecting Antwerp with the principal cities of Belgium, the Netherlands, and the western states of Germany had been completed in 1855.[15] The attractiveness of Antwerp as a trading port for goods and emigrants led to the formation of the Compagnie Transatlantique Belge for the purpose of operating a line of steamships between Antwerp and New York. Two iron screw steamers were ordered from the van Vlissingen yards at Amsterdam, a firm with little experience in building this class of vessel.

In his annual report for 1855, Postmaster General James Campbell stated:

In view of the establishment of a line of steamships between New York and Antwerp, I have intimated my readiness to conclude the pending convention with Belgium by fixing the rate of postage for letters between any part of the United States and any part of Belgium at fifteen cents, which rate shall combine five cents United States to two cents Belgium inland, and eight cents sea postage.

The convention, however, was not concluded. The poor performances of *Belgique* and *Constitution*, both of which had to be extensively rebuilt, forced delays and irregularities in sailings. Between November 1856 and September 1857, the above two ships and *Leopold I* made about ten round voyages for the line before the service was withdrawn. The firm, having suffered heavy financial losses, went into liquidation.

Belgium and the United States finally concluded a convention on 21 December 1859[16] which provided for closed mails through England as well as for a direct service in the event that a direct line of steamers should be established between the two countries. The principal articles of this convention are summarized as follows:

I. Provided for a regular exchange of mails between the United States and Belgium in closed mails, via England, or by the direct route. All mail between the two countries was to be sent in the closed mails, via England, unless the letters were endorsed to be sent by another service.
II. Provided that Belgium was to pay Great Britain the charges for transit over British territory in conformity with the Anglo-Belgium convention of 14–28 August 1857, while the United States was to bear the expense of sea transportation across the Atlantic by United States or British packets (closed-mail provisions of the United States-British treaty of 1848).
III. Established United States exchange offices at New York and Boston; Belgian offices were set up at the local office at Ostend, the travelling Ostend office, and at Antwerp. By Article IV, others could be established by mutual consent.
V. Provided for optional prepayment of postage, but no account was to be taken of a payment of less than the whole rate.
VI. Established the progression for letters not exceeding 15 grams (half an ounce) at a single rate; over 15 grams (half an ounce), but not over 30 grams (1 ounce), 2 rates; over 30 grams (one ounce), but not over 60 grams (two ounces), 4 rates; and so on, adding two rates for every 30 grams (one ounce, or fraction of an ounce).
VII. Set the closed-mail postage for prepaid or unpaid letters for a single rate at 1 franc 40 centimes in Belgium, or 27¢ in the United States, divided as shown in Table 21.

---

[13] According to Stibbe, letters from Belgium for the U.S. could not be prepaid by postage stamps but had to be paid in money. After 1857 letters found in the boxes were tolerated if prepayment by postage stamps was correct. Beginning 1 June 1864, prepayment by postage stamps was compulsory on all letters, and insufficiently paid letters were sent to the dead-letter office.
[14] U.S., Congress, Senate, *Executive Document* 1, 33rd Cong., 2nd sess., serial 747, p. 631.
[15] N. R. B. Bonsor, *North Atlantic Seaway*, p. 107.

[16] U.S., *Statutes at Large,* vol. 16, pp. 899–905.

TABLE 21.—*Division of United States and Belgium Rates*

Postage	Rate, cents
United States	5
Sea	15
British transit	4
Belgian	3
Total rate	27

IX. Provided that each office account to the other for letters exchanged in closed mails for the actual postage set forth in Article VII and according to the progression set by Article VI, "letter by letter."

X. Provided for transit mail through Belgium or through the United States.

XXIII. Provided that in the event of a direct line or lines of steamships between the United States and Belgium being established the postage for a single rate, according to the progression set by Article VI, was to be 15¢ divided as shown in Table 22. (Article XXIV):

TABLE 22.—*Division of United States and Belgium Rates*

Postage	Rate, cents
United States	5
Sea	7
Belgian	3
Total rate	15

It will be noted that Article IX required that the accounting between the two offices be on the basis of the individual letter and not on the basis of the bulk weight of mail. This was made necessary because Belgium paid Great Britain for the British transit postage on the basis of the individual letter, but it destroyed the advantage of simplified accounting procedures usually accompanying the exchange of closed mails. The Prussian closed-mail convention, on the other hand, did provide for the settling of accounts on a bulk-weight basis. This may point to the reason for the United States not availing itself of the transit-mail privileges offered by Article X. Until the expiration of the convention on 31 December 1867, the only transit mail exchanged under its provisions was mail to the Netherlands after July 1866.

Although this convention was made between the post offices of the two countries, the formalities of exchanging ratifications and of proclamation were observed. Article XXVIII stated that it was to be placed in operation one month after the exchange of ratifications. Dr. Robert de Wasserman has called the author's attention to the fact that the convention was placed in force at an earlier date. While he notes that the ratifications were not exchanged until 19 October 1860, and the convention was proclaimed in the United States on 20 October 1860, he finds in the *Recueil administratif des Lois, Arrêtés et Décisions concernant le Chemin de fer, Postes & Télégraphes* no. 472, that it was placed in force in Belgium on 1 March 1860. According to the annual report of Postmaster General Holt for 1860, it was placed in force in the United States on 24 January 1860. This was the date the mails were made up in New York for the sailing on the following day of the *Europa* from Boston.

The exchange office accounting for Belgian closed mail is presented in Table 23. The United States paid Great Britain 40¢ per ounce for mail conveyed by British packet. Foreign steamships under contract to the United States were paid the actual sea postage on mail conveyed, while American vessels under contract to the United States received the sea postage and also the inland postage.

Prussian closed-mail service was never made available to Belgium. A rate by Bremen-Hamburg mail was not introduced until February 1867. The rate by this route was 18¢ per half ounce, prepayment optional; no cover showing it has been noted. French mail between Belgium and the United States became available on 1 April 1857, at a rate of 21¢ per quarter ounce in the United States and of 1 franc per 7½ grams in Belgium.

Belgian Closed-Mail Covers

Although the Belgian closed mail was in operation between 24 January 1860 and 31 December 1867, covers showing its use are very scarce. They are rare when prepaid with stamps of the 1860 issue, and none is illustrated here. One is illustrated on p. 101 of *United States Postal Markings . . . 1851 to 1861* by Tracy W. Simpson, to which the reader may make reference.

Figure 68 presents a Belgian closed-mail cover which was forwarded to Brazil. Posted in Philadelphia on 31 August 1865, the letter was prepaid 27¢ by a 24¢ red lilac and a 3¢ rose stamp of the 1861 issue. The letter is addressed to Lieut. B. J. Cromwell/U.S.S.

TABLE 23.—*Exchange Office Accounting for Belgian Closed Mail*

Postage	Rate	Letters from U.S.		Letters from Belgium	
		Prepaid	Unpaid	Prepaid	Unpaid
U.S. inland	5¢	(a)	5¢	5¢	(a)
Sea	15	(a)	15	15	(a)
British transit	4	4¢	(b)	(b)	4¢
Belgian inland	3	3	(b)	(b)	3
Total	27	—	—	—	—
Credit to Belgium by U.S. (red)	—	7	—	—	—
Debit to Belgium by U.S. (black)	—	—	20	—	—
Credit to U.S. by Belgium (red)	—	—	—	20	—
Debit by Belgium to U.S. (black)	—	—	—	—	7

a Retained from prepayment or collection by the United States.
b Retained from prepayment or collection by Belgium.

Shawmut/Care American Consul/Antwerp/Belgium. Since Philadelphia was not an exchange office for Belgian closed mail, the letter was sent to New York where it was marked in red with a circular N. YORK AM. PKT./7 PAID marking of the New York exchange office, and indicated a credit of 7¢ to Belgium. The date in this marking in 2 September, and on that date *City of Baltimore* of the Inman line sailed from New York to Liverpool. The closed-mail bag was sent directly to Ostend where the letter was marked on its reverse with a circular ETATS-UNIS PAR OSTENDE/8 11/16 marking in black which showed that it arrived at the Ostend office between eight and eleven o'clock on 16 September. The Ostend office also applied a straight line AM. PACKET marking in black. These two markings, together with a New York or Boston exchange office marking showing a credit of 7¢, are characteristic of the Belgian closed mail. Also on the reverse is an Antwerp (Anvers) receiving mark dated 16 September. The remaining markings on the cover relate to its conveyance from Antwerp to Brazil.

By the time the letter arrived, *Shawmut* had evidently sailed for Brazil. The American Consul's office readdressed the letter to "Rio de Janeiro/Barsil" and posted it. It bears two travelling post office markings: BELG. À QUIÉVRAIN and FRANCE PAR AM3T MIDI 1, both of which bear the date of 17 September. There are two Paris markings, one applied upon receipt, the other on

FIGURE 68.—COVER, from Philadelphia to Antwerp, Belgium, forwarded to Brazil, 1865.

dispatch of the letter, and each bears the date of 18 September. Paris forwarded the letter to Bordeaux, whence it was sent to Brazil by a steamer of the *Messageries Impériales*. On the reverse is an octagonal marking inscribed POSTE FRANÇAISE/NAVARRE with the date of 18 October 1865 in the center.[17] This indicates that the letter was conveyed to Brazil by steamship *Navarre*. The line ran from Bordeaux, via Lisbon, St. Vincent (Cape Verde Islands), Bahia, and Pernambuco, to Rio de Janeiro. On the face of the cover is a manuscript *240,* which indicates that 240 reis were to be collected from the addressee. It is indeed unusual to find these markings on a cover from the United States.

French-Mail Covers to Belgium

Covers showing French-mail service to or from Belgium are seldom seen. Figure 69 illustrates a letter posted in New York, addressed to Brussels and endorsed to "Steamer Fulton" of the Havre line. It is prepaid 21¢ by a pair and single of the 3¢ stamps and a single 12¢ stamp of the 1857 issue. It bears a NEW PAID YORK/9 exchange office marking in red which

[17] Raymond Salles, *La Poste Maritime Française Historique et Catalogue,* vol. 3, p. 17 (Fig. 1.008). [*See also* V. Bourselet et al., *Les Paquebots français et leurs cachets, 1780–1935,* pp. 29–31.]

FIGURE 69.—COVER, from New York to Brussels, 1858.

shows the date of 6 February, the date *Fulton* sailed from New York in 1858. The Havre exchange office marking, applied in indigo ink, is of the type shown as *A* in Figure 43 (Chapter 4), and the small boxed PD marking, also applied by the Havre office, is type *M* in Figure 43. The Havre marking shows the date of 22 February 1858, as does also a LE HAVRE À PARIS marking on the reverse. Also on the reverse is a Paris marking with the date of 23 February. It was forwarded by the travelling post office AMB. DU MIDI NO. 2 on the same day and arrived in Brussels on 25 February 1858. The 9 in the New York marking represents a credit of 3¢ for the international rate plus 6¢ postage from France to destination in Belgium.

Chapter 7

Amendments, New Conventions, and the Operations of the Steamship Lines

Additional Articles to the United States-Bremen 1847 Convention

As one of the measures taken to strengthen the authority of the German Confederation (the Bund), under the aegis of Admiral Brommy a navy was created in 1849. Subsequent disagreement between the Frankfurt parliament and Prussia over schemes for the unification of the German states,[1] forced the parliament to dissolve, and the navy was disbanded.[2] At the auction of its ships, a Bremen syndicate, headed by W. A. Fritze and Company and Karl Lehmkuhl, purchased two frigates for £26,250.[3] One of these was *Hansa*, which had been Admiral Brommy's flagship (formerly *United States* of the Black Ball line), and the other was *Erzherzog Johann* (formerly Cunard's *Acadia*).[4] Lehmkuhl's interest appears to have been primarily financial, with little activity in management. At least, a painting of the two ships clearly shows the Fritze house flag and the iron cross repeated on their paddle boxes.[5] *Hansa* was allowed to retain her name, but *Erzherzog Johann* was rechristened *Germania*.

Senator Arnold Duckwitz was interested in strengthening transatlantic communication, and above all, of preserving and augmenting, if possible, the service rendered by the Ocean Steam Navigation Company. He proposed to W. A. Fritze and Company that they place their two ships, *Hansa* and *Germania,* on the Bremen–New York run. At about the same time, the Bremen senate requested its resident minister in Washington, R. Schleiden, to try to have the Ocean Steam Navigation Company augment the service of *Washington* and *Hermann* by two additional steamers with the same specifications as those of the Fritze ships. If the United States postmaster general would not agree to this, Schleiden was then to attempt to secure a reduction in postage on mail conveyed directly between New York and Bremen. This was felt to be a necessary measure if the direct service was to compete equitably with the Prussian closed mail.[6]

Whether the Ocean line was, at that time, prepared to build new ships is not known. They were prepared to do so in 1856 when their subsidy was threatened. Postmaster General Campbell then reported: "The present contractors state that they are prepared to build new and swifter ships than those now on their lines, provided their contract is renewed."[7] Additional ships, however, would have meant an additional subsidy, which the postmaster general could recommend but only Congress and the President could grant.

No documentary evidence relating to these negotia-

---

[1] William L. Langer, *An Encyclopedia of World History,* pp. 675–677.
[2] Frank C. Bowen, *A Century of Atlantic Travel: 1830–1930,* p. 72.
[3] C. R. Vernon Gibbs, *Passenger Liners of the Western Ocean,* p. 195.
[4] N. R. P. Bonsor, *North Atlantic Seaway,* p. 79.
[5] Gibbs, *Passenger Liners,* p. 195.

[6] Christian Piefke, *Geschichte der Bremischen Landespost,* Chap. 22.
[7] U.S., Congress, Senate, *Executive Document* 5, 34th Cong., 3rd sess., serial 876, pt. 2: 772.

tions has been found. Piefke, however, states:[8] "The diplomatic measures of the wise and energetic Bremen business leader resulted in the production of a short written agreement, by which steamers *Germania* and *Hansa* were to take over the Atlantic traffic." This must be the agreement referred to in Article IX of the formal Additional Articles signed at Washington on 4 August 1853,[9] which referred to "this arrangement, which supersedes the temporary arrangement of July 6, 1853." While a copy of this temporary arrangement has not been found, its terms must have been similar to those of the final formal arrangement.

It will be remembered that the 1847 postal arrangement with Bremen dealt only with procedures for handling mail. The rate structure was included in the regulations. The Additional Articles of 4 August 1853 altered only Article VI of the 1847 arrangement, which dealt with the compensation of the Bremen mail agent. Primarily they were concerned with a complete revision of the rate structure originally included in the regulations. The provisions of the Additional Articles of 4 August 1853 are summarized as follows:

 I. Established exchange offices at New York and Bremen.
 II. Set an international rate for letters between all of the United States (including its territories) and Bremen
    For a letter not exceeding half an ounce   10¢
    Above half an ounce but not over one ounce 20¢
    Above one ounce but not over two ounces   40¢
    And 20¢ for each additional ounce or fraction thereof
    Prepayment was optional, but a partial payment of the international rate was not to be recognized.
 III. All of the states of the German Austrian Postal Union were to have the advantage of the 10¢ rate whenever their postage to or from Bremen was reduced to 5¢ or less. On correspondence between Bremen and those states that did not reduce their postage to 5¢ or less, the international rate for a single letter became 15¢.
 IV. The postage from or to countries beyond the United States or Bremen was to be added to the applicable international rate as set forth in Article II, or in Article III. The two post offices were to furnish each other with lists stating the foreign countries to which the foreign postage, and the amount thereof, must be absolutely prepaid, or left unpaid. Until such lists were furnished, mail to or from these countries was not to be exchanged.
 VI. Established the accounting as follows: The Bremen office was to pay the United States office per single-letter rate for unpaid letters posted in the United States, or prepaid letters posted in Bremen, when conveyed
    Under Article II, by U.S. steamer   9¢
    Under Article II, by Bremen steamer   5¢
    Under Article III, by U.S. steamer   14¢
    Under Article III, by Bremen steamer   5¢

[8] Piefke, *Bremischen Landespost,* Chap. 22.
[9] U.S., 16 *Statutes-at-Large,* 953–956.

The United States office was to pay the Bremen office per single rate for unpaid letters posted in Bremen, or for prepaid letters posted in the United States, when conveyed
   Under Article II, by U.S. steamer   1¢
   Under Article II, by Bremen steamer   5¢
   Under Article III, by U.S. steamer   1¢
   Under Article III, by Bremen steamer   10¢
"It is understood and agreed that, of the portion of the postage for which the United States office is to account to Bremen, as well as of what Bremen may collect, all but one cent a single letter is to go to the benefit of the proprietors of the Bremen line of steamers."
 VII. Arranged for the settlement of accounts between the two post offices. It also provided that: "the 20 per cent commission to the postmaster of Bremen, stipulated in Article VI of the arrangement of 1847, is to cease from and after the date these articles take effect."
 VIII. Provided for the mutual conveyance of dead and returned letters, and of official communications between the two post offices, free of charge.
 IX. The arrangement, which superseded the temporary arrangement of 6 July 1853, was to go into effect on 15 August 1853, and was to continue in force unless annulled by mutual consent or three months notice by either party; "and it may also cease whenever the Bremen steamers cease running."

Article VI shows only the gross debits and credits to be made by the two offices. The division of these rates between inland and sea postages has to be deduced. For the 10¢ international rate the division was apparently 5¢ for United States inland, 4¢ for sea postage, and 1¢ for Bremen inland. In the event that the international rate became 15¢ when a German state did not reduce its Bremen transit postage to 5¢, the additional 5¢ postage included in the international rate belonged to the country that furnished the packet. The exchange office accounting for these rates is presented in Table 24.

In all of the countries which did not reduce their transit postage to or from Bremen to 5¢ or less, the rate was 7¢. All of the states made the reduction with the exception of Baden, Wurttemberg, and the Thurn and Taxis posts. In most of these states the monetary unit was the kreuzer and the florin. The 22¢ rate, therefore, was equated to 33 kreuzer, of which 9 kreuzer represented the transit and 24 kreuzer was attributed to sea and other postages.

The only state to have a transit postage of less than 5¢ was Oldenburg. When this arrangement became effective, the transit rate between Bremen and Oldenburg was 3¢.

As pointed out in Article VI, the steamship line was to receive as compensation all but one cent of the

TABLE 24.—*Exchange Office Accounting for United States-Bremen Mail*
(*Under the 1853 Convention*)

Postage	Rate	Unpaid from U.S.		Prepaid in U.S.	
		American Packet	Bremen Packet	American Packet	Bremen Packet
International Rate of Ten Cents					
When addressed to Bremen:					
U.S. inland	5¢	5¢	5¢	(a)	(a)
Packet	4	4	(b)	(a)	4¢
Bremen inland	1	(b)	(b)	1¢	1
International rate	10	—	—	—	—
U.S. debit to Bremen	—	9	5	—	—
U.S. credit to Bremen	—	—	—	1	5
When addressed to rest of German-Austrian Postal Union:					
U.S. inland	5	5	5	(a)	(a)
Packet	4	4	(b)	(a)	4
Bremen inland	1	(b)	(b)	1	1
International rate	10	—	—	—	—
Union transit	5	(b)	(b)	5	5
Rate	15	—	—	—	—
U.S. debit to Bremen	—	9	5	—	—
U.S. credit to Bremen	—	—	—	6	10
International Rate of Fifteen Cents					
When addressed to those countries falling under Article III:					
U.S. inland	5¢	5¢	5¢	(a)	(a)
Packet	9	9	(b)	(a)	9¢
Bremen inland	1	(b)	(b)	1	1
International rate	15	—	—	—	—
Union transit	7	(b)	(b)	7	7
Rate	22	—	—	—	—
U.S. debit to Bremen	—	14	5	—	—
U.S. credit to Bremen	—	—	—	8	17

a Retained from prepayment by United States.
b Retained from collection by Bremen.

Bremen share of the postage. The agreement between Duckwitz and W. A. Fritze and Company provided that the sailing dates for *Hansa* and *Germania* be fitted in with those of *Washington* and *Hermann* so that a ship would leave every fourteen days from New York and Bremen.[10] This schedule could not be maintained. *Germania* left Bremen on 3 August 1853 and did not arrive in New York until 26 August. *Hansa* left Bremen on 31 August 1853 and arrived in New York on 20 September. Since the normal run for the Ocean line ships was seventeen days, these long passages required that the schedule be readjusted. It appears that the Fritze Company did not maintain sailings for the purpose of carrying mail; they merely carried mail when they did sail. At the request of Postmaster General Campbell, *Hansa* made a round voyage during November–December 1853,[11] after which the ships were laid up. Duckwitz expected a sailing in February which did not materialize, and only after repeated efforts was he able to induce Fritze and Company to establish a schedule of five sailings during 1854, beginning with a sailing of *Germania* in June and ending with a sailing of the same ship in October.[12] On 26 October 1854, the Bremen City Post Office announced that the scheduled trip of *Germania* on that day would not be under-

---

[10] Piefke, *Bremischen Landespost*, chap. 22.

[11] Ibid.

[12] Ibid. Piefke states there was a schedule of 4 sailings, 3 of which were made. *The Shipping and Commercial List* shows 4 sailings actually made (see Table 25, this work).

taken "due to changing circumstances," and further sailings of the Bremen steamships would not take place that year. Piefke explains: [13]

> Fritze himself had decided this, because the *Germania* was once again in need of repair and the *Hansa* had no cargo of goods or passengers. To add to the serious embarrassment of the New York-Bremen Line, the steamers *Washington* and *Hermann* had discontinued trips for the winter months.[14] A way out was found; unpaid letters went by the Prussian-American Line,[15] paid letters went via England to Liverpool to New York by American steamers,[16] and foreign letters were despatched by sailing vessels.

It is suspected that the United States sent unpaid letters posted during this period as unpaid in the Prussian closed mail; letters prepaid with Bremen rates and endorsed to go via Bremen were sent as fully prepaid in the Prussian closed mail. At least, they were treated in this manner in other years when the Ocean line ships failed to sail in winter.

In January 1855 the two Fritze ships were chartered to the British Government as troopships for the duration of the Crimean War. Upon their return, it was intended that the line and its mail service be revived. *Germania* was scheduled for a sailing in March 1857, which it did not make. *Hansa* made a round voyage during April–May and was scheduled to make another during June, which was canceled. In October 1857 they were chartered to the British East India Company as troopships for service in the Indian Mutiny. Upon her return to Bremen *Hansa* was sold, and as *Indian Empire* opened the Galway line's service to New York; *Germania*, now unseaworthy, was broken up on the Thames.[17] The sailings of this line are presented in Table 25.

Figure 70 illustrates a cover posted in Oxford, Ohio, on 14 September 1853, addressed to Hamburg. It is prepaid 15¢ by a strip of five 3¢ stamps of the 1851

---

[13] Ibid.

[14] There was no sailing from New York by the Ocean line between the *Washington* on 4 Nov. 1854 and the *Hermann* on 27 Jan. 1855. The *Washington* arrived in New York on 24 Dec. 1854, and the next arrival was by the *Hermann* on 18 Mar. 1855.

[15] This must refer to Prussian closed mail.

[16] It is not clear whether this was a revival of the Bremen closed mail, or use of the open mail. The U.S. did not use either of these routes for mail sent to Bremen.

[17] Bonsor, *North American Seaway*, p. 80.

TABLE 25.—*W. A. Fritze & Company Sailings*

Arrival Date, New York	Ship	Departure Date, New York
	1853	
26 Aug.	*Germania*	19 Sept.
20 Sept.	*Hansa*	3 Oct.
17 Nov.	*Hansa*	29 Nov.
20 Nov.	*Germania*	3 Dec.
	1854	
10 July	*Germania*	20 July
6 Aug.	*Hansa*	26 Aug.
21 Sept.	*Germania*	3 Oct.
9 Oct.	*Hansa*	17 Oct.
	1857	
Dna.[a]	*Germania* Up [b]	10 Apr. Dns[c].
2 May	*Hansa*	7 May
Dna.[a]	*Hansa* Up [b]	29 June Dns[c].

[a] Did not arrive.
[b] Sailing scheduled in *Shipping and Commercial List*.
[c] Did not sail.

issue. The New York marking is of type *A* of Figure 71 and shows a credit to Bremen of 10¢, indicating that the United States retained 5¢ for its inland postage. The date in the New York packet marking is 19 September, which coincides with the date of sailing from New York of W. A. Fritze and Company's *Germania* (see Table 25), which conveyed the first mail to Bremen under the convention of 1853. In accordance with the mail arrangements established by the convention of 1847, and not disturbed by the convention of 1853, the New York exchange office made up a separate bag for mail addressed to the city of Hamburg, which passed through the Bremen office as closed mail. This cover, therefore, bears no Bremen markings, not even marking *J* of Figure 71, which usually appears on covers in transit through Bremen. Upon the reverse of the cover are two oval markings, ST.P.A./9 OCT. 53 and ST.P.A./10 OCT. 53 which are markings of the Hamburg City (state) Post Office (see *N* of Figure 71). There is also a double circle marking HAMBURG/2–3/20/10, which is a marking of the Hamburg local office dated 20 October. Evidently, the addressee had departed from Hamburg before the letter arrived. Delivery was attempted on 9 October, and on the following day the letter was sent to the

Figure 70.—Cover, from Oxford, O. [Ohio], to Hamburg, Germany, 1853.

Hamburg local office where it waited until a forwarding address was received. On 20 October it was forwarded to *Post restante, Berlin,* charged with the transit rate of 3 silbergroschen. There is a *3* in blue manuscript on the face of the cover. Only on letters conveyed by the Fritze Company ships does the credit of 10¢ to Bremen appear.

Figure 72 presents a cover posed in Columbia, South Carolina, on 29 November 1853, prepaid 15¢ in stamps of the 1851 issue. It bears marking *A* of Figure 71 with the date of 3 December which indicates that it was sent by *Germania* on its 3 December 1853 sailing from New York (see Table 25). This cover passed in transit through the Bremen office and bears marking *J* of Figure 71 applied in red.

Abandonment of Steamship Mail Subsidies by Congress

After intensive and very expensive lobbying by E. K. Collins,[18] Congress, on 21 July 1852, increased the subsidy granted the Collins line from $385,000 to $858,000 a year. During the next two years, opposition to the increased subsidy began to make itself evident. In his annual report for 1854 Postmaster General Campbell called the attention of Congress to the great discrepancy between the subsidy granted to the Collins line and those given the other United States transatlantic lines, but rapid crossings of the Collins steamers were at the time inflating American prestige, and nothing was done about it.

In his annual report for 1855, however, Campbell made specific recommendations to Congress. He asked that the six months' notice required by the act of 21 July 1852 be given and the increase in the Collins line subsidy withdrawn. He felt that Congress had already dealt very liberally with the line. He pointed out that Congress had relieved the line of the necessity for maintaining four passed midshipmen, which had been specified in the contract; that the Post Office Department had not sent out mail agents, whom the line was bound to accommodate and subsist. The Collins line was receiving $858,000 a year for performing only twenty-six trips, while the British gave the Cunard line $866,700 for performing fifty-two. He considered the increased compensation a mere gratuity, destroying all competition, attended by the most pernicious influences, and creating a monopoly having injurious effects upon the commercial interests of the country. In the following year the increase in the subsidy was withdrawn.

Since all of the transatlantic lines ran to New York, commercial interests in other eastern and in southern

---

[18] Robert G. Albion, *Square Riggers on Schedule,* pp. 327–328.

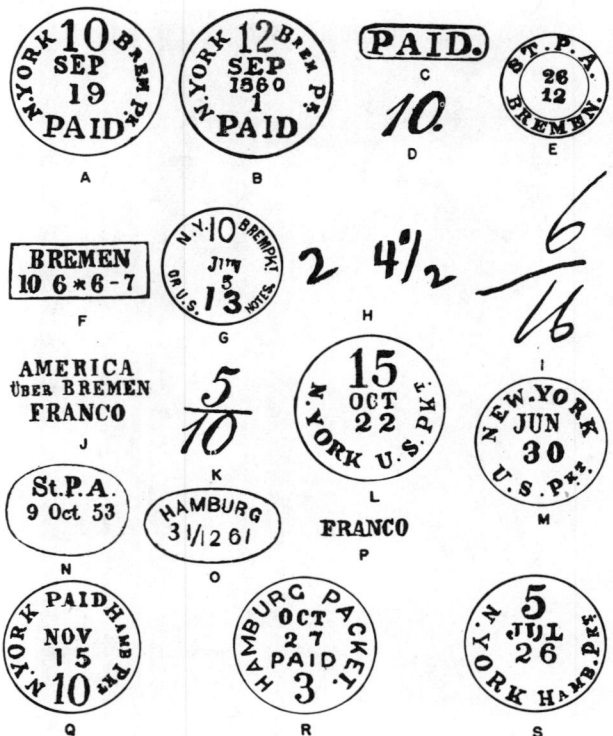

FIGURE 71.—MARKINGS on Bremen-Hamburg mail.

ports felt that the subsidies were inflating the importance of the port of New York to their detriment. While it was believed that subsidies were necessary to maintain the lines, it was also felt that some of them should run to other ports. This feeling was reflected by Postmaster General Campbell in his report for 1856. He first called the attention of Congress to the fact that the contracts with the Bremen and Havre lines would expire on 1 June 1857. If these services were to be continued, he should be authorized to advertise and take such steps as were necessary to have them continued. He then went on to say:

> In relation to these mail lines to foreign ports . . . no reason is perceived why one port of the United States should be preferred to the exclusion of others. From the port of New York there now run four lines, embracing the branch from New Orleans to Havana, which receive from the treasury the yearly sum of one million four hundred and ninety-eight thousand dollars, and appropriations continue to be asked for other lines running from the same port. The establishment of steam lines from any port adds considerably to its trade and importance, and the advantages arising therefrom should be distributed equally, as far as practicable, among the different States of the Union.

In expressing this opinion, Campbell was reflecting the growing jealousy of the ports of Boston, Philadelphia, and Baltimore, as well as those of the southern states.

Congress did not renew the contracts of the Bremen and Havre lines. The Collins line contract, which was with the Navy Department, was to run until 1860. The appropriations bill for paying the annual mail subsidies for 1858, including that of the Collins line, touched off a long congressional debate. It was during this debate that Congress changed its policy regarding the subsidization of mail steamship lines.

It was alleged in the Senate by Toombs of Georgia and in the House by Davis of Mississippi that the subsidized mail lines to California, that is, the U.S. Mail Steamship Company running from New York to Aspinwall and the Pacific Mail Steamship Company plying between Panama and San Francisco, had paid Cornelius Vanderbilt $40,000 a month for not competing with them, in other words, for not placing his ships on the Panama run after he closed his Nicaragua Transit. The payments were said to have been made to Vanderbilt during a year, beginning in May 1856, at the end of the year the payments increasing to $56,000 a month.[19] While these were only allegations (they were not substantiated until 1860), they were believed. Although the standard of business and political ethics of that time did not allow great condemnation of Vanderbilt for his "blackmail" (for example, Toombs said he admired him),[20] the allegations led Congress to believe that mail subsidies were no longer necessary. If these steamship companies could pay over to Vanderbilt their entire subsidy and still operate at a profit, there was no need for the Treasury to support them.

Although Vanderbilt's "blackmail" pertained to the lines carrying the California mail, the attitude created by the allegations carried over to the transatlantic lines. Fifty years later, during the "muckraking" period, Gustavus Myers wrote:[21] "There were indications that for years a secret understanding had been in force between Collins and Vanderbilt by which they divided the mail subsidy funds. Ostensibly, however, in order to give no sign of collusion, they went through the public appearance of warring upon each other." Myers does not document this statement, and no evidence of the existence of such an agreement has been found. Senator Toombs, however, intimated that such

---

[19] U.S., Congress, *Congressional Globe*, 1857–58, pt. 3: 3029.

[20] Ibid., p. 2843.

[21] Gustavus Myers, *History of Great American Fortunes*, p. 284.

Figure 72.—Cover, from Columbia, S.C., to Bremervorde ?), Hannover, 1853. (*Melvin W. Schuh collection*)

collusion might exist.[22] It was in an atmosphere of suspicion and jealousy, perhaps of revulsion, that Congress acted. Little of the nationalism that had had so much to do with the creation of the subsidies was evident. Senator Toombs said, in effect, that if foreign steamers would carry the United States mails cheaper than American steamers, they should be allowed to do it.[23] This point was not debated. A clause, however, was inserted in the act that would force the postmaster general to prefer American over foreign steamers if they departed from the same port for the same destination within three days of each other.

On 14 June 1858, Congress passed the Appropriations Act, which provided (in addition to the clause just cited) that it would be unlawful for the postmaster general to make any steamship or other new contract for carrying the mail on the sea for a longer period than two years, or for any compensation other than the sea and inland postages on the mails so transported, when conveyed in American steamers.[24] The compensation was limited to the sea postage only when conveyance was by a foreign steamer. The compensation for steamship lines provided by this act had been recommended by Postmaster General Aaron V. Brown in his annual report for 1857, and was already being used on contracts with Cornelius Vanderbilt and the New York and Havre Steamship Company.

The Vanderbilt European Line

When Congress failed to renew the contracts of the Ocean and Havre lines in 1857, the postmaster general was faced with the problem of maintaining the United States packet service to Europe. In his annual report for 1857, he explained how he met the situation. He called attention to the fact that the contracts expired on 1 June 1857, but it did not appear to him that Congress intended the service to Europe to be discontinued after their expiration. He, therefore, deemed it his duty to make temporary arrangements for the continuation of the service until Congress could take action. He then stated:

> The temporary contract for service on the Breman line is with Cornelius Vanderbilt, and upon the Havre line with the New York and Havre Steamship Company. Each contract provides for thirteen round trips annually; and the compensation to be paid is limited to the United States postages, sea and inland, accruing from the mail conveyed. . . . Moreover, it appeared a fit occasion to inaugurate a system of self-sustaining ocean mail service; and I shall esteem it fortunate if the present temporary arrangements lead, as I trust they may, to the adopted of this as a permanent system.

In 1855 Commodore Vanderbilt placed his *North Star,* which had served as his private yacht in 1853,

---

[22] *Congressional Globe,* 35 Cong., 1 sess., 1857–58, pt. 3: 2844.
[23] Ibid., 2841.
[24] 11 *Statutes at Large* 364.

and *Ariel* on the run to Havre, via Southampton. He then attempted to secure a subsidy for a fortnightly service to Liverpool to alternate with the sailings of the Collins line.[25] He failed in this attempt and discontinued his sailings to Havre in the summer of 1856. On 13 June 1857 *Ariel* sailed from New York for Breman, via Southampton and Havre, carrying the first mail under Vanderbilt's contract. Although his contract provided for the conveyance of mail between New York and Breman, his ships also carried British and Prussian closed mail to Southampton, and French mail direct to Havre. Vanderbilt must have found the returns on the run to Havre satisfactory, but the run from Havre to Breman appears to have been unprofitable. *North Star* and *Ariel* carried steerage passengers, something that the Collins line never did and that the Cunard line, up to this time, had refused to do.[26] His new ship, *Vanderbilt,* one of the largest and speediest of her time, was not allowed to carry steerage passengers, was not allowed to sail in winter, and only on one occasion was allowed to make the run to Bremen.

Vanderbilt had competition on the run between Bremen and New York during 1857. The British-owned European and American Steam Shipping Company ran steamers *Queen of the South, Indiana, Argo,* and *Jason* between Bremen and New York, via Southampton, for eleven round voyages between May and October 1857. At the end of that time these ships were taken over as troop transports in the Indian Mutiny. Postmaster General Brown explained to Congress the decrease of $5,491.74 in postage on the Bremen line as "owing to the fact that much of the time there have been several foreign steamers running and carrying ship letters on this line." [27]

The Vanderbilt European line maintained its scheduled sailings from New York from June through December 1857, but in January 1858 the service collapsed. *Ariel* sailed from New York on 28 November 1857 and suffered sea damage on the run to Bremen. She did not return to New York until 4 May 1858. *North Star* sailed from New York on 26 December 1857, had similar difficulties, and did not arrive back in New York until 13 February 1858, so badly in need of repair that she did not sail again until 17 April 1858. The scheduled sailings of 23 January and 20 February 1858 were not made. It also appeared that the scheduled sailing of 20 March would not be made. When Vanderbilt refused to run *Vanderbilt* to Bremen, the postmaster general, in exasperation, made a trip contract with the Inman line for steamer *Kangaroo* to carry the Bremen mail to Liverpool.[28] Letters prepaid with Bremen rates were sent in the Prussian closed mail as fully paid. If Vanderbilt was fined for this default, no record of it has been found.

Piefke gives the Bremen reaction to this situation:[29]

> So the Bremen-United States line was dependent upon the inferior Vanderbilt steamers, which were soon driven by sea damage into this or that harbor of refuge—and suddenly, at the start of winter, their runs ceased altogether. As a consequence of these constant troubles one could not talk of a regular postal service. Even the American Postmaster General confided to the Bremen Minister Resident that Vanderbilt had cheated him. Due to a sea accident of the *Ariel,* Post Director Dr. Bartsch announced that on the return journey to New York a large mail would, lacking other means, have to be sent as 'closed mail' by the Hapag steamer *Hammonia*.[30] Bartsch spoke of the 'necessity caused by Vanderbilt's breaking his word' and concluded, 'the weight presses on our breast in this moment, and each day brings new trouble.' From a letter of Burgomeister Duckwitz we find how 'odious' the thought has been that the Bremen mail had to be sent by a Hapag steamer.

Not only does the above explain how the Bremen mail was sent to New York during this crisis, but it also gives some insight into the intense rivalry existing between Bremen and Hamburg.

Figure 73 illustrates a cover posted in Baltimore, Maryland, on 19 March 1858, addressed to Prussia. It was prepaid 15¢, which is indicated by a PAID applied in red and a red crayon 15. It is endorsed "Via Bremen Steamer," which clearly shows that the mailer of the letter intended that it be sent by the Vanderbilt line to Bremen. The Vanderbilt ships, however, had not sailed from New York since 26 December 1857 and would not again sail until 17 April 1858. The New York office sent this letter as fully prepaid in the Prussian closed mail. This route is evidenced by the New York packet marking, similar to *A* of Figure 51, but showing American packet service and the boxed Aachen marking (*P* in Figure 51). The credit of 7¢ in the New York marking shows that the United States

---

[25] Bonsor, *North Atlantic Seaway,* p. 104.
[26] Gibbs, *Passenger Liners,* p. 106.
[27] *Senate Executive Document* 11, 35 Cong., 1 sess., serial 921, pt. 3: 969.

[28] U.S., Congress, House, *Executive Document* 2, Report of the auditor of the Treasury for the Post Office Department, 35 Cong., 2 sess., serial 1,000, p. 862.
[29] Piefke, *Bremischen Landespost,* chap. 22.
[30] The *Hammonia* arrived in New York 1 Apr. 1858. [For definition of "Hapag" see p. 119.]

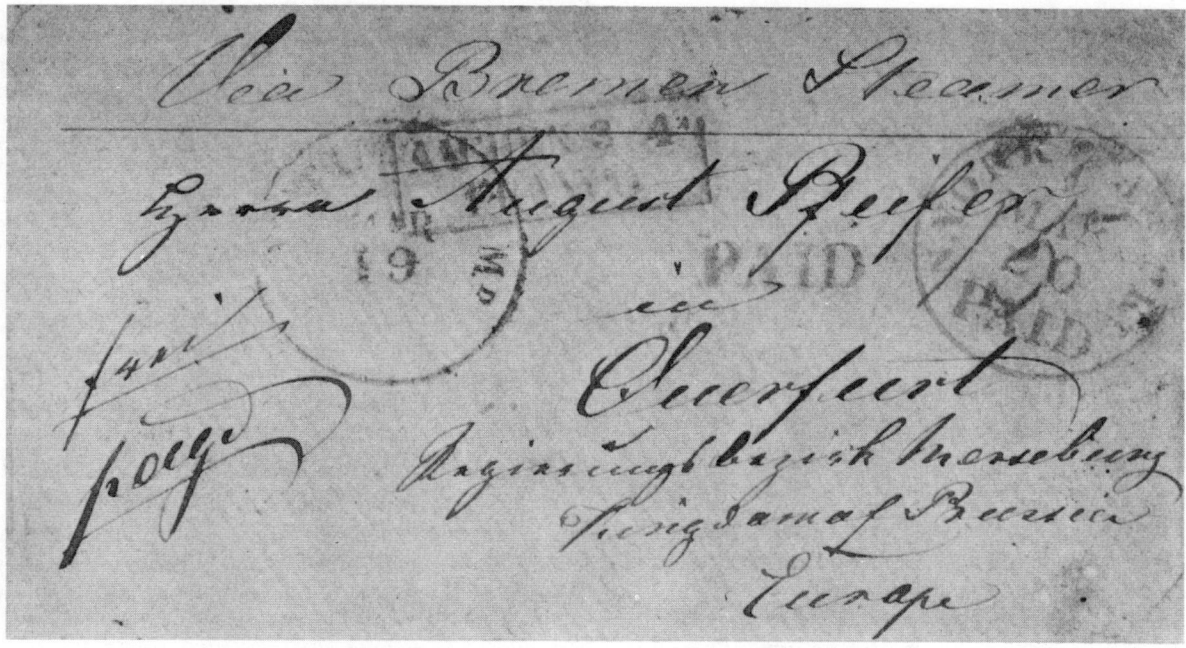

FIGURE 73.—COVER, from Baltimore, Md., to [?], Prussia, 1858.
(*Melvin W. Schuh collection*)

accepted it as a fully paid Prussian closed-mail letter. The date in the New York marking is 20 March, the date *Kangaroo* sailed with a special mail intended to be sent via Bremen but forwarded as Prussian closed mail. While the auditor of the Treasury for the Post Office Department lists *Kangaroo* among the Bremen steamers for that year, this letter shows that she carried a Prussian closed mail to Liverpool.

During the summer of 1858, not only were the scheduled Vanderbilt sailings made, but additional sailings were added, the fleet being augmented by steamer *Northern Light*. In the fall, however, Vanderbilt decided to quit the Bremen run. On 2 October 1858, *Vanderbilt* sailed from New York on her only trip to Bremen. On 30 October 1858, *Ariel* sailed with the last mail conveyed to Bremen by the Vanderbilt European line. The voyage, however, was not completed. Piefke explains: [31]

> Although the captain had to deliver the mail to the Weser, he landed her in Le Havre, 'because there was no hope of finding passengers in Bremen for the return trip.' Due to his arbitrary action, the letter bag had to be sent by rail via Belgium and Aachen to Bremen. Since the captain had no legitimate reason for his conduct, the company was liable for the high transit costs.

[31] Piefke, *Bremischen Landespost,* chap. 22.

During 1857 steamer *Vanderbilt* made six round trips to Havre. Five of them were made in head-on competition with the Collins line steamers, *Vanderbilt* leaving New York on the same day as the Collins line ships. The postmaster general appears to have been extremely cooperative with Vanderbilt, for despite the fact that a heavy subsidy was being paid to the Collins line for carrying the mail, nevertheless, mails were sent to Southampton and Havre by *Vanderbilt*. During 1858 *Vanderbilt* made five round voyages to Havre. During 1859, after the Bremen run was discontinued, there were fifteen round voyages to Havre by *Vanderbilt, Ariel,* and *Ocean Queen*. During 1860 Vanderbilt ran *Vanderbilt* and *Illinois* to Havre for eleven round voyages. At the end of October he decided to quit the run and placed *Illinois* on the Panama service. The Post Office had scheduled a mail by *Illinois* to sail from New York on 3 November 1860. This mail was sent to Southampton by *Borussia* of the Hamburg-American Line.[32] *Illinois'* mail on the return trip was brought by *Saxonia* which arrived in New York on 6 December 1860.

[32] Report of Treasury auditor for Post Office Dept. appended to *Annual Report of the Postmaster General for 1861.*

Problems of the Postmaster General During 1858

In his annual report for 1858, Postmaster General Brown explained his difficulties. He stated that since the expiration of the Bremen and Havre line contracts the United States mail service to Europe had not been established on a permanent basis. The Collins line contract was with the Navy Department and he, therefore, had no power to enforce fulfillments or to annul the contract. Since the Navy Department had taken no action, and the temporary contracts for service to Southampton, Bremen, and Havre had expired on 1 June 1958, it was out of his power to engage other than temporary service by the single trip, "and the result has been that all service performed has been entirely of a temporary character." Commenting on the terms of the act of 14 June 1858, he asked:

Can the service be obtained upon these terms? I believe it may be. If deemed expedient to employ foreign vessels, it is certain that parties now stand ready to take the mails for the sea postage. But shall this service be relinquished entirely to foreign steamers? and if not, will American lines contract under existing law? . . . Save during the winter months, there would be no difficulty in getting the mails carried on these terms; but for a period so short as two years, it is hardly probable that contracts with American lines could be obtained to carry regularly the year round. . . . The want of regularity heretofore has had the effect to give the advantage to the British lines. . . . Why may not the same regularity be established and maintained by American ships? Let this be done, and no good reason is perceived why they may not carry an equal proportion of the mails, the postage of which would afford a fair compensation for the service.

To supply a substitute service for the defunct Collins line, Postmaster General Brown made up what he called a "miscellaneous line." The lines, ships, and sailings utilized by him for this purpose are presented in Table 26. Examination of the list shows that the

TABLE 26.—*Collins Line and "Miscellaneous Lines" Sailings*

Arrival Date, New York	Ship	Departure Date, New York	Comments
1857/58		1858/59	
7 Dec.	*Baltic*	16 Jan.	Last outward voyage for Collins line
1858			
18 Feb.	*Baltic*		Last inward voyage for Collins line
3 Feb.[a]	*Edinburgh*	13 Feb.	Glasgow & New York Steam Ship Company
5 Mar.[a]	*New York*	13 Mar.	Glasgow & New York Steam Ship Company
30 Mar.[a]	*City of Baltimore*	10 Apr.	Inman (Dales) line—to Liverpool
13 Apr.[a]	*City of Washington*	24 Apr.	Inman—to Liverpool
30 Apr.	*Kangaroo*	8 May	Inman—to Liverpool
12 May	*City of Baltimore*	22 May [a]	Inman—from Liverpool
9 May [a]	*Vanderbilt* [b]	22 May	Vanderbilt line—to Southampton
23 May	*City of Washington*	5 June	Inman—N.Y. & Liverpool
9 June	*Kangaroo*	17 June [a]	Inman—from Liverpool
19 June	*Vanderbilt* [b]	3 July	Vanderbilt—N.Y. & Southampton
6 July	*City of Washington*	17 July	Inman—N.Y. & Liverpool
1 Aug.	*Vanderbilt* [b]	14 Aug.	Vanderbilt—N.Y. & Southampton
18 Aug.	*City of Washington*	28 Aug.	Inman—N.Y. & Liverpool
13 Sept.	*Vanderbilt* [b]	2 Oct.[a]	Vanderbilt—from Southampton
	Vigo	25 Sept.	Inman—first voyage
27 Sept.	*City of Washington*	9 Oct	Inman—N.Y. & Liverpool
12 Oct.[a]	*City of Baltimore*	23 Oct.	Inman—to Liverpool
26 Oct.	*Vigo*	6 Nov.	Inman—N.Y. & Liverpool
9 Nov.	*Kangaroo*	20 Nov.	Inman—N.Y. & Liverpool
23 Nov.	*City of Baltimore*	4 Dec.	Inman—N.Y. & Liverpool
12 Dec.	*City of Washington*	18 Dec.	Inman—N.Y. & Liverpool
26 Dec.	*Kangaroo*	1 Jan.	Inman—N.Y. & Liverpool

[a] Not designated by the auditor of the Treasury for the Post Office Department as carrying mail on this trip.

[b] The *Vanderbilt* continued to Havre and may have carried French mail to that port on trips not designated as carrying mail to Southampton.

only American ship to serve in this "line" was *Vanderbilt*. The list also shows the increasing reliance he placed upon the British-owned Inman line (called Dales line in the United States). By 1860 this line was matching the mail sailings of the Cunard line to and from Liverpool under contracts with the United States Post Office Department. By the time the Civil War began, the United States mail service to Europe was entirely in the hands of foreign steamers.

The United States-Hamburg Convention

The Hamburg Amerikanische Paketfahrt Aktien Gesellschaft was organized in 1847 for the purpose of running a line of sailing packets between Hamburg and New York. From its inception it was known in Germany as "Hapag," a contraction formed by the first letter of each word in its official name. In the United States and Great Britain it was called the Hamburg-American line. In 1853 the line decided to convert to steam, and after many delays ordered two iron screw steamers of about 2,000 tons from Caird & Co. of Greenock.[33] The first of these, *Borussia*, sailed from Hamburg for New York on 1 June 1856, followed in the next month by the second ship, the *Hammonia*. The impending stringency in packet service led Postmaster General Campbell to seek an agreement that would allow these ships to carry mail. In his annual report for 1856 he stated:

> An informal arrangement has been entered into with the free city of Hamburg for the exchange of mails, by the direct line of Hamburg steamers plying between that city and New York. The single rate of postage for letters is ten cents; no mails for places beyond Hamburg being transmitted by this line.

The auditor of the Treasury for the Post Office Department reported that during the fiscal year ended 30 June 1857, the Hamburg line carried a total of 10,606 letters, 1,504 of which were sent to Hamburg, while 9,102 were received from Hamburg.[34] Since the ships of this line, at that time, did not call at Southampton, all the letters were between the city of Hamburg and the United States. On 12 June 1857, a formal postal convention was signed in duplicate at Washington.[35] In his annual report for 1857, Postmaster General Aaron V. Brown announced that a convention had been concluded between the United States and Hamburg, and further stated that it was "similar in all respects to that existing between the United States and Bremen—the rates of postage under both being the same. It was finally executed in June last, and went into effect on the first of July."

While the rate structure of the two conventions was identical, they differed in one major and in two minor respects. The clause that provided for paying the proprietors of the steamship line, included in Article VI of the United States-Bremen convention, was omitted in the United States-Hamburg convention. Under this clause the proprietors of the Bremen steamship line were to receive all but one cent a single letter of the postage accounted for by the United States to Bremen, as well as of the postage collected by Bremen. The omission of the clause from the United States-Hamburg convention can only mean that the compensation of the Hamburg-American line rested upon a different kind of financial arrangement between the line and Hamburg.

Minor differences resulted from the insertion of Article IX in the United States-Hamburg convention. This article provided that the sailing days of the Hamburg-American ships were not to conflict with those of the Bremen and Havre lines. Article VII of the United States-Bremen convention had a clause that rescinded the twenty percent commission of the Bremen mail agent. This clause, of course, was excluded from the convention with Hamburg. In all other respects the United States-Hamburg convention was a verbatim copy of the United States-Bremen convention.

What was the nature of the informal agreement that existed between the United States and Hamburg from June 1856 to 1 July 1857? Did New York apply a Hamburg packet marking? Was there an accounting between the post offices of the two countries? Prepaid covers addressed to Hamburg or unpaid letters marked for collection in the United States could explain how the New York office handled this mail. Unfortunately, none has been seen.

The North German Lloyd

The North German Lloyd had been plying between Bremen and London since 1856. In 1858 it announced a service between Bremerhaven and New York. This service, however, had been contemplated for some time. In 1857 Postmaster General Brown gave as one

---

[33] Bonsor, *North Atlantic Seaway*, p. 111.
[34] *Senate Executive Document* 11, 35 Cong., 1 sess., serial 921, p. 1118.
[35] *16 Statutes at Large* 958–960.

of his reasons for concluding a temporary arrangement with Vanderbilt the fact that he "had official information of the intention of a Bremen company to put on a line of semi-monthly steamers, so as, in connexion with an increased American line, to secure a weekly communication with the United States."[36]

On 19 May 1858, the Bremen authorities notified the German-Austrian Postal Union that the North German Lloyd steamers *Bremen, Hudson, New York,* and *Weser* would carry the mails every fourteen days to New York at the same low rates as the American steamers.[37] On 19 June 1858, *Bremen* sailed from Bremerhaven inaugurating the service. She arrived in New York on 4 July 1858 and was scheduled to sail for Bremen on 10 July, but the sailing was postponed until 30 July, when she sailed from New York with the first mail conveyed by the Lloyd to Bremen. *New York* left Bremen on 14 August 1858 and arrived in New York on 28 August. She sailed from New York for Bremen on 11 September 1858.[38]

Article IX of the United States-Bremen convention provided that it might be terminated "whenever the Bremen steamers cease running." The agreement was not terminated, however, when *Germania* and *Hansa* stopped running. This is verified by the fact that additional articles to the convention were signed in 1860 and in 1864. What arrangements were made with the North German Lloyd in regard to its compensation are not known. Certain it is they were not the same as those made with W. A. Fritze and Company.

The evidence of numerous covers carried by the ships of the North German Lloyd indicates that the United States reduced its inland postage from 5¢ to 3¢. It had been generally believed, however, by the author as well as by others,[39] that the United States retained 3¢ on prepaid letters, but charged 5¢ on unpaid letters. This is now known not to be true. Evidence shows that the United States inland postage was 3¢ on unpaid as well as on prepaid letters.

Since the United States-Bremen convention remained in force, the reduction of the United States inland postage to 3¢ had the effect of increasing the sea postage from 4¢ to 6¢ the single rate. This increase was the result of no reduction being made in the 10¢ internatioanl rate, and all but 1¢ of the Bremen share of the postage was to go to the benefit of the proprietors of the Bremen line of steamships.

There are no additional articles to the 4 August 1853, United States-Bremen convention that would allow this change. Whatever was done to create it was arranged by correspondence, or by agreement between the Bremen resident minister and the United States postmaster general. No documentary evidence of such an agreement and no correspondence relating to this change have been found. Certain facts, however, should be mentioned.

The United States-Bremen convention was the only postal convention entered into by the United States that prescribed the method of paying the steamship line that conveyed the mail. United States packets were paid according to contracts made between the Post Office Department and the American steamship line. The provisions relating to inland and sea postage contained in the postal conventions determined the amounts to be settled between the post offices of the contracting countries. A contract with a steamship company was a separate agreement, not necessarily affected by the postal convention governing the mails conveyed by the steamship line. Bremen contracted with the North German Lloyd for the direct mail service between New York and Bremen. The United States, however, contracted with the same line for a service between New York and Southampton, and under that agreement the Lloyd conveyed British treaty mail, Prussian closed mail, Belgian closed mail, and French mail. The compensation was the sea postage accruing on these mails.

On 21 December 1857, steamship *Borussia* of the Hamburg-American line arrived in New York from Southampton, the line having introduced an intermediate call at this port.[40] The postmaster general, however, did not immediately contract with the line for a service to England. He did not do so until May 1861. On 4 May 1861 *Bavaria* sailed from New York carrying the first United States mail to Southampton. With this sailing, the line changed its sailing dates to Saturdays, alternating with those of the North German Lloyd so that the two lines maintained a weekly service to that port. Direct mail from Hamburg for New York did not show debits or credits on letters dispatched to the United States. Normally, postal conventions prescribed the manner in which letters

---

[36] *Senate Executive Document* 11, 35 Cong., 1 sess., serial 921, pt. 3: 968.

[37] Piefke, *Bremischen Landespost,* chap. 22.

[38] *Shipping and Comercial List* appropriate issues.

[39] See George E. Hargest, "The U.S.-Bremen Postal Convention of 1853 and the North German Lloyd Line," *Chronicle,* 17, 1 (Oct. 1964): 35.

[40] Bonsor, *North Atlantic Seaway,* p. 111.

were to be marked so that proper charges could be made, or credits taken, on dead or returned letters. The actual accounting for the mails was performed on the letter-bills, whose format was usually prescribed in the convention or in its regulations. Under the 4 August 1853 United States-Bremen and the United States-Hamburg conventions, letter-bill forms were not prescribed, and the conventions were mute on the matter of markings. Since Article VIII of each of these conventions provided for the mutual conveyance of dead or returned letters *free of charge,* there was, in reality, no reason for marking the letters with debits or credits.

The Bremen and Hamburg offices did mark letters with amounts of postage that would assist them in their accounting and in the preparation of letter-bills. Some time during 1864 the Hamburg office introduced packet marks that showed debits or credits to the United States office, but this procedure was not adopted by the Bremen office.

The 15¢ rate, which included 5¢ transit postage, was equated with 6½ silbergroschen, or with 22 kreuzer. The 10¢ rate was equated with 10 grote in Bremen, and with 6 schillings in Hamburg. It was the custom of the Bremen and Hamburg offices to mark the letters with the German-Austrian Postal Union (transit) postage and with the postage representing the international 10¢ rate. On prepaid letters dispatched by the Bremen office to the United States, markings C and D of Figure 71 were applied in red. Marking D indicated the international rate of 10 grote (10¢), which was the only part of the 15¢ rate in which the United States participated. Additionally, when the currency was silbergroschen, marking H was usually applied in red or blue ink or crayon. This set forth the Union postage of 2 silbergroschen and the international postage of 4½ silbergroschen as separate items. Marking I expresses the same division in kreuzer. The Union postage of 6 kreuzer is written over the international postage of 16 kreuzer. Sometimes the amount indicating the international postage is preceded by an F which abbreviates the word FRANCO ("paid").

There was considerable irregularity in these markings. Frequently letters will show only the Union postage and sometimes only the international postage. In some cases, markings H and I (Figure 71) appear on the same letter. Usually letters prepaid in Germany do not bear a United States marking, and it is seldom possible to say whether they were conveyed by an American or German packet.

Unpaid letters originating in the city of Bremen addressed to the United States bear a black *10* (*D* of Figure 71), and a Bremen marking (*E* or *F* of Figure 71). Many of these covers do not show a United States marking, the *10* already on the letter being allowed to indicate the amount to be collected. After depreciated currency markings were introduced, the New York office applied markings in black similar to G of Figure 71. Markings D, F, and M of Figure 71 are the only ones that appear on a letter originating in Bremen addressed to San Francisco. This letter was conveyed by steamer *Ariel* of the Vanderbilt European line which arrived in New York in the evening of 29 June 1858, its mail being processed the following day.

An unpaid letter originating in Syke, Prussia, on 1 October 1858, is addressed to Louisville, Kentucky. It bears a circular BREMEN/2/10 marking in blue, showing that it arrived at the Bremen office on 2 October. It also bears the marking of the Bremen City Post Office (*E* of Figure 71) with the date of 2/10, showing that it was dispatched from that office also on 2 October. The Bremen City Post Office applied marking K of Figure 71 in blue ink. This shows the 5 grote (5¢) Union postage over the 10 grote (10¢) international rate. The Bremen office also applied a *2* in red crayon, indicating the Union postage in silbergroschen. The New York office marked the letter as in L in Figure 71 to indicate that 15¢ were to be collected in Louisville. This letter was conveyed by steamer *North Star* of the Vanderbilt European line which arrived in New York on 22 October 1857.

Figure 74 illustrates a cover posted in New York, addressed to Bremen. It is franked with a 10¢ type V stamp of the 1857 issue. The New York office applied a marking similar to A in Figure 71, but with a credit 7, which shows that the United States retained only 3¢ out of the 10¢ rate for inland postage. There is no other marking on the cover. This cover is endorsed to steamer *Bremen* which sailed from New York on 29 September 1860.

Figure 75 presents a cover posted in New York addressed to Hamburg. It is franked with a 10¢ type V stamp of the 1857 issue. The New York office applied a marking similar to Q of Figure 71, but showing a credit 5, which indicates that the United States retained 5¢ out of the 10¢ prepayment as its inland postage. On the reverse is a marking of the Hamburg City Post Office (*N* of Figure 71) with the date of 16 December 1860. The letter is endorsed to *Teutonia* of the Hamburg-American line which sailed from New York on 1 December 1860.

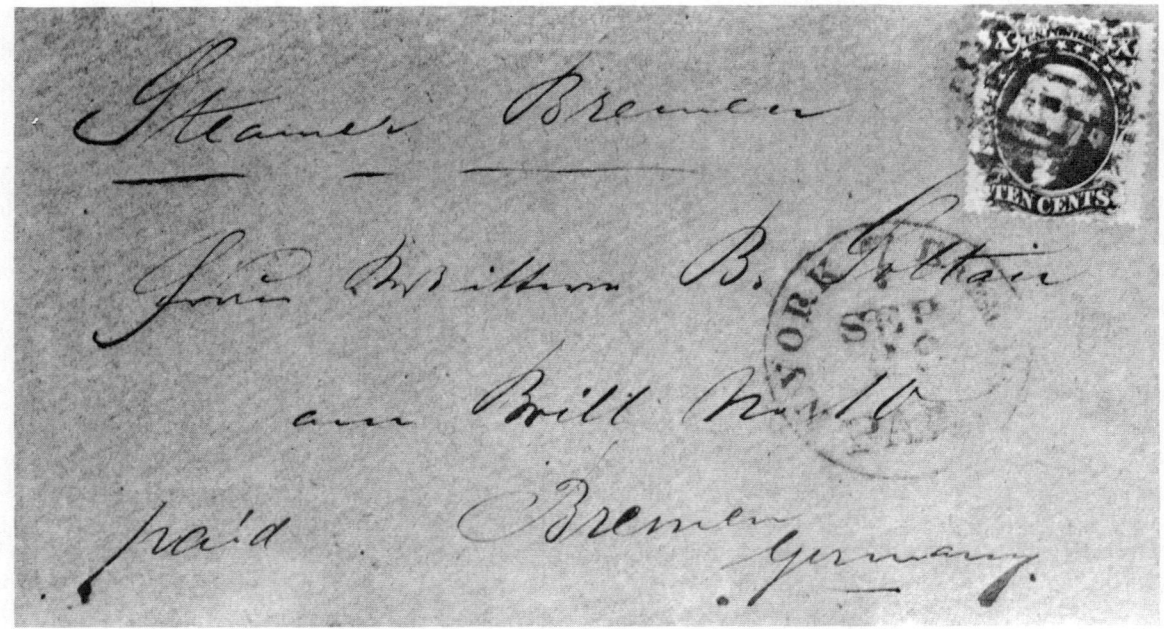

FIGURE 74.—COVER, from New York to Bremen, Germany, 1860.

FIGURE 75.—COVER, from New York to Hamburg, Germany, 1860.

Figure 76 illustrates a cover posted in Allentown, Pennsylvania, on 6 May 1862, addressed to Hanover. It is franked 15¢ by a 10¢ type *I* stamp and a 5¢ brown-yellow stamp of the 1861 issue. Although it is endorsed "p. Hamburg Steamer," the New York office sent it by a steamer of the North German Lloyd. It bears a marking similar to *B* of Figure 71 but is dated 10 May, without the year. On 10 May 1862, steamer *Bremen* sailed from New York. The Bremen office applied marking *J* of Figure 71 in blue ink. Figure 74 does not bear this marking because it was addressed to Bremen and did not pass in transit through the Bremen office. The credit of 1 2 in the New York marking shows that the United States retained only 3¢ for its inland postage.

Figure 77 illustrates a cover prepaid with the rare 22¢ rate. It was posted in Staunton, Virginia, addressed to Hesse. Since the Grand Duchy of Hesse utilized the services of the Thurn and Taxis posts, which had not yet reduced their transit rate to that duchy to 5¢, the transit rate remained at 7¢, and the international rate became 15¢ under the provisions of Article III of the convention. Thus, the international rate of 15¢ plus 7¢ transit postage yielded a total rate of 22¢ (see Table 24). The letter is franked by a 12¢ stamp and a 10¢ type II stamp of the 1857 issue. The New York office applied a marking in red similar to *Q* of Figure 71 but with a credit 1 7 and the date 1 March.

There is nothing on the cover to indicate the year date. Since the steamers of the Hamburg-American line sailed on the first of each month from 1858 to 1861, neither the year date nor the name of the steamer that conveyed this letter can be determined.

Figure 78 presents a cover posted in Clermont, New York, addressed to Hanover. It is franked with a 10¢ type III stamp of the 1851 issue, and is endorsed "via Bremen." It bears a N. YORK 1 U.S. PKT/PAID marking dated 19 April. On 19 April 1856, the *Washington* of the Ocean line sailed from New York, and it is presumed that she conveyed this letter to Bremen. The New York office credited Bremen with 1¢ of the 10¢ rate and marked the letter PAID TO BREMEN. Since the rate to Hanover was 15¢, this letter shows that the nonrecognition of a partial payment applied only to the 10¢ international rate. The gute groschen of Hanover was worth 3¢ in United States currency, and there were 12 pfennige to the gute groschen. The Bremen office applied an AMERICA/ÜBER BREMEN marking to the letter, and rated it for a collection of 1⅔ gute groschen in red crayon. The Hanover office crossed this out and marked it in blue crayon *1–8,* meaning 1 gute groschen 8 pfennige, which, of course, was equal to 1⅔ gute groschen or 5¢ in United States currency. Covers showing a credit of 1¢ to Bremen (see Table 24) are seldom seen.

FIGURE 76.—COVER, from Allentown, Pa., to Hannover [Hanover], Germany, 1862.

124

FIGURE 77.—COVER, from Staunton, Va., to Hessen, Germany, (*Melvin W. Schuh collection*)

FIGURE 78.—COVER, from Clermont, N.Y., to Hanover, 1856. (*Melvin W. Schuh collection*)

Revival of American Packet Service to Bremen

After the Vanderbilt European line stopped its runs to Bremen in 1858 there was no American packet service to Bremen until 1866. In 1865 the Ruger Brothers of New York organized the North American Lloyd to operate a line of steamships between New York, Southampton, and Bremen. Their fleet was made up, for the most part, of steamers that had been released from service in the Civil War, and included the ex-Collins line steamers *Atlantic* and *Baltic;* the *Ericsson,* which had been chartered by the Collins line; and *Mississippi* and *Merrimack,* sister ships, which, like *Western Metropolis,* had served as troop transports.

While primarily interested in the emigrant trade, the Ruger Brothers also sought and secured a mail contract. The *Shipping and Commercial List and New York Prices Current* listed their sailings as by "U.S.M." steamers. Some of their sailing dates coincide with those listed in the *U.S. Mail and Post Office Assistant* as by the Bremen line, under contract to the United States. The mail sailings of this line are presented in Table 27, as reported by the *Shipping and Commercial List and New York Prices Current.*

The North American Lloyd suspended operations in the fall of 1866, and evidently was reorganized by the Ruger Brothers as the New York and Bremen Steamship Company.[41] In March of 1867, the *U.S. Mail and Post Office Assistant* listed sailings by the North German Lloyd and by a Bremen line. The sailing for 7 March 1867, listed in the *U.S. Mail* as by a Bremen line, coincides with a scheduled sailing of *Western Metropolis* of the New York and Bremen Steamship Company. The *Shipping and Commercial List,* however, does not show this scheduled sailing of *Western Metropolis* as by a U.S.M. steamer. If the postmaster general made a trip contract with the New York and Bremen Steamship Company for this voyage, he was disappointed, because the ship failed to sail. Although this line continued to operate until 1870, there is no evidence that its ships carried mail after March 1867.

Figure 79 illustrates a cover posted in New York, addressed to Schwartzburg-Sonderhausen, Thuringia. The 15¢ rate under the United States-Bremen convention of 4 August 1853 is prepaid by a 15¢ stamp issued in 1866. The proper credit of 6¢ is included in the New York postmark (see Table 24). This N. YORK 6 U.S. PKT./PAID marking bears the date of 20 September, but there is nothing on the cover to indicate the year of use. There was, however, no sailing by an Ocean line ship from New York on 20 September in any year after 1850, and no ship of the Vanderbilt European line sailed from New York on 20 September in any year. As is indicated in Table 27, *Baltic* of the North American Lloyd sailed from New York on 20 September 1866, which determines the year date of this cover. Since it has been thought that all American packet service ceased in 1858, this cover could have been, at some time in the past, condemned as fraudulent.

The Galway Line

The Irish migration to the United States during the 1850s led to the demand that steamship service between the United States and a port in Ireland be established. Situated as it was on the west coast of Ireland, 300 miles nearer New York than Liverpool, the port of Galway attracted the attention of a group of businessmen who, in 1850, sought to run a line

TABLE 27.—*North American Lloyd Sailings*

Arrival Date, New York	Ship	Departure Date, New York
1866		1866/67
F/V [a]	*Atlantic*	22 Feb.
F/V [a]	*Ericsson*	15 Mar.
9 Apr.	*Atlantic*	12 Apr.
F/V [a]	*Baltic*	26 Apr.
F/V [a]	*Mississippi*	10 May
F/V [a]	*Merrimack*	17 May
2 May	*Ericsson*	24 May
27 May	*Atlantic*	31 May
9 June	*Baltic*	14 June
F/V [a]	*Western Metropolis*	28 June
12 July	*Western Metropolis*	Returned
16 July	*Atlantic*	19 July
6 Aug.	*Baltic* Dns. [b]	9 Aug.
6 Aug.	*Baltic* Dns. [b]	16 Aug.
12 July	*Western Metropolis*	30 Aug.
6 Aug.	*Baltic*	20 Sept.
25 Sept.	*Atlantic*	4 Oct.
(c)	*Western Metropolis* Dns. [b]	7 Mar.

[a] First voyage for the line.
[b] Scheduled; did not sail.
[c] Scheduled for the New York & Bremen Steamship Company; date shown in *U.S. Mail.*

---
[41] Ibid., p. 240.

FIGURE 79.—COVER, from New York to Schwartz[burg-]Sondershause[n], Thuringen [Thuringia, Germany], 1866.

of steamers between Galway and New York. Although their efforts in this regard have been described as "farcical," [42] they did succeed in securing the completion of the Midland and Great Western Railway which connected Galway with Dublin.

In 1858 John Orr Lever, a Manchester business man, and a group of associates, organized the Atlantic Steam Navigation Company for the purpose of operating a line of steamships between Galway, Halifax, and New York.[43] From its inception the company was known as the Galway line. Lever's plans extended far beyond the emigrant traffic. Since the steaming time from New York to Galway was twenty-four hours less than to Liverpool, he hoped by the use of steamers of the highest speed and excellent accommodations to outstrip the Cunarders. Also involved in his scheme was a call at St. Johns, Newfoundland, whence the latest news could be telegraphed to the United States. He planned that the passage time from Galway to St. Johns would be only six days.[44]

By various means he secured financial backing, and through the support of Irish Nationalists, a mail contract from the British government. Under the terms of this contract, there would be sailings twice a month from Galway, to Boston or New York, alternately. The passage time to Newfoundland was to be six days, and New York was to be reached in another six days. The contract was to become effective in June 1860.[45]

Although four vessels were ordered built by the company, it was decided to start operations with chartered tonnage. *Hansa* (formerly the *United States*), chartered from W. A. Fritze and Company, was renamed *Indian Empire,* and made the initial sailing for the line. She sailed from Galway on 19 June 1858 and required twelve instead of the forecasted eight days to reach Halifax. The next voyage was taken by *Prince Albert,* which required ten days to reach Halifax. Altogether eleven vessels were chartered, most of which made only one or two voyages for the line, and none were able to meet the time-schedule prescribed by the contract.

The first of the four vessels ordered by the company, the *Connaught,* was not delivered in time to make a scheduled sailing on 26 June, and did not sail until 10 July 1860. Her speed was disappointing, since she required eight instead of six days to reach St. Johns. On her second voyage she was destroyed by fire in mid-

---

[42] Gibbs, p. 141.
[43] Bonsor, p. 161.
[44] Gibbs, p. 141.

[45] *Ibid.*

Atlantic.[46] The speed of the remaining three vessels, *Hibernia, Columbia* and *Anglia,* was equally disappointing. In March 1861 the company purchased ex-Collins liner *Adriatic,* then running for the North Atlantic Steamship Company. *Adriatic* proved to be the only ship in the company's fleet able to meet the terms of the mail contract, but she arrived on the scene too late. In June 1861 the British postmaster general announced that he had canceled the mail contract of the Galway line.[47]

In August 1863 the British Post Office revived the mail contract of the Galway line. Although Liverpool was to be the British terminal port, the vessels were to call at Galway outwards and homewards. The revived sailings continued until the company, always in financial difficulties, collapsed in February 1864.

Figure 80 illustrates a cover posted in Boston addressed to Tunis. It is prepaid 33¢ by a strip of three of the 10¢ type V stamps and a 3¢ stamp of the 1857 issue. On the reverse is a BOSTON BR. PKT/AUG/7 marking in black. Of particular interest is the endorsement "pr Galway Line." The London marking on the face shows the year to be 1860.

In 1860 there were two available routes and rates to Tunis: (1) British mail, via Southampton, to Marseilles, and thence by French packet to Tunis at a rate of 33¢ for a quarter-ounce letter, prepayment compulsory; (2) French mail at a rate of 30¢ per quarter ounce, prepayment optional. The United States-French convention of 2 March 1857 provided for mail by British packet from Boston or New York to Liverpool, but made no provision for mail from New York to Galway. French mails were therefore not made up for conveyance by the ships of the Galway line.

Since this cover is endorsed to the Galway line, it could be sent only at the British mail rate. The Boston office retained the United States inland postage of 5¢ and gave Great Britain credit for the remainder of the prepayment. This is indicated by a red crayon *28* on the face. The date of 7 August in the Boston marking on the reverse indicates that it was conveyed across the Atlantic by *Connaught* on its only eastward voyage.

TABLE 28.—*The Mail Sailing of the Galway Line*

Arrival Date, U.S.	Ship	Port	Departure Date, U.S.
		1860	
9 July	*Parana*	New York	16 July
23 July	*Connaught*	Boston	7 Aug.
4 Aug.	*Prince Albert*	New York	14 Aug.
18 Aug.	*Parana*	Boston	27 Aug.
9 Sept.	*Prince Albert*	New York	12 Sept.
7 Nov.	*Prince Albert*	New York	20 Nov.
		1861	
	Adriatic	New York	13 Mar.
15 Mar.	*Prince Albert*	New York	26 Mar.
27 Apr.	*Columbia*	Boston	30 Apr.
2 May	*Adriatic*	New York	13 May
18 May	*Parana*	Boston	28 May
		1863	
	Hibernia	Boston	8 Sept.
11 Sept.	*Adriatic*	New York	21 Sept.
26 Sept.	*Anglia*	Boston	6 Oct.
12 Oct.	*Columbia*	New York	19 Oct.
23 Oct.	*Hibernia*	Boston	3 Nov.
10 Nov.	*Adriatic*	New York	17 Nov.
		1864	
3 Jan.	*Adriatic*	New York	12 Jan.
	Columbia	Boston	25 Jan.
3 Feb.	*Hibernia*	New York	9 Feb.

[46] Bonsor, p. 163.
[47] Gibbs, p. 142.

Irregularities in Sailings of the Steamship Lines

Some irregularities in the sailings of the steamship lines and the resultant effect on the carriage of mail have already been noted. There were, however, other sailing irregularities, failures, and changes of sailing dates that should be mentioned. These will be considered as nearly as possible in chronological order.

R.M.S. *Hibernia* of the Cunard line arrived in Boston on 16 August and sailed for Halifax and Liverpool on 29 August 1849. Maginnis notes "*Hibernia* on this trip sprang a leak, and returned to Halifax and left passengers and mails; then she came to New York for repairs, and sailed on 29 September for Liverpool direct with 19 passengers."[48] How the mails were forwarded from Halifax to Liverpool is not known, and Cunard records are not helpful on this point.

On 7 December 1850, *Atlantic* of the Collins line sailed from New York for Liverpool. On her return voyage, when far out in the Atlantic, she fractured her paddle shaft and was forced to return to Queenstown under sail.[49] As a result of this accident, she was long

[48] Arthur J. Maginnis, *The Atlantic Ferry, Its Ships, Men and Working,* footnote, p. 26.
[49] Bonsor, *North Atlantic Seaway,* p. 56.

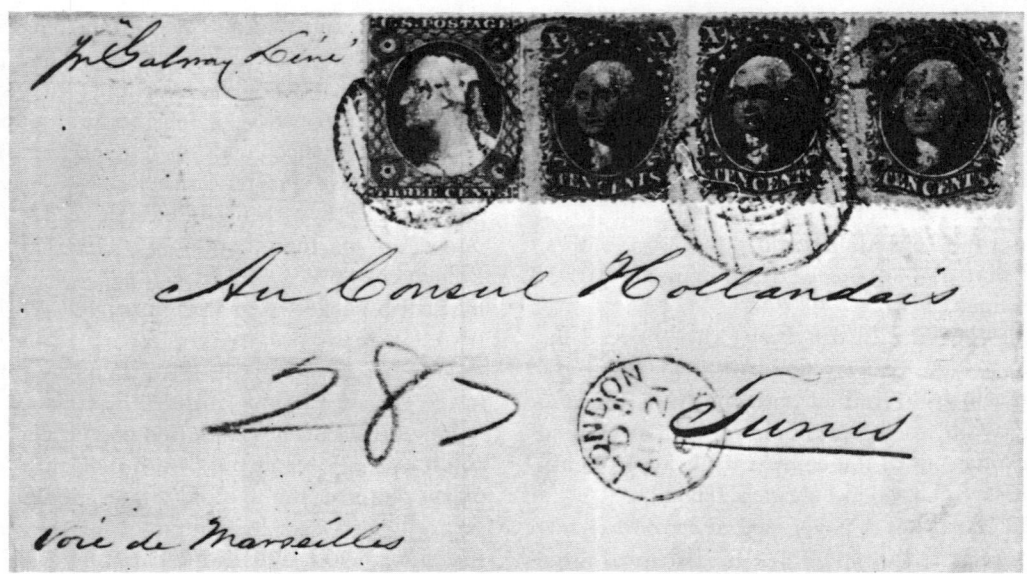

FIGURE 80.—COVER, from Boston to Tunis, 1860.
(*Robert de Wasserman collection*)

overdue in New York, and as time passed with no word of her safety, concern mounted. It was feared she had suffered the fate of *President,* which had sailed from New York on 11 March 1841 with 136 passengers and crew and "went missing," that is, she disappeared and was never heard of again. When the news that *Atlantic* and her passengers were safe in Queenstown was finally received, there was great rejoicing in New York. So moved was a New York musician by the name of Johann Munck that he composed a schottische and entitled it "Atlantic's Return," dedicating the piece to Captain James West, skipper of *Atlantic.* Jaques and Brother, who published it, had William Endicott and Company of New York prepare a lithograph of *Atlantic* to be used as the front cover of the selection. This was reproduced in black and white but was finished by hand-coloring. It is presented here as Figure 81.

Atlantic did not arrive back in New York until 3 August 1851. During her absence, the mail service of the Collins line had to be maintained by *Pacific, Baltic,* and *Arctic.* A rearrangement of scheduled sailings was made. Sailing days were changed from Saturdays to Wednesdays for the following trips: *Baltic,* 8 January; *Pacific,* 22 January; *Arctic,* 5 February; *Baltic,* 5 March; *Pacific* 19 March; *Arctic,* 2 April; and *Baltic,* 16 April 1851. With the sailing of *Pacific* on 10 May 1851, sailing days were returned to Saturdays. It will be noted that a second voyage in February was omitted. Unfortunately, the American packet marking of the New York office was not introduced until 1852 (earliest seen, 2 September 1852), and covers by the sailings listed here can usually be identified only by their arrival dates or by endorsements to one of the above ships.

During the Crimean War, many of the Cunard ships were taken over by the Allies as troop transports. The Cunard line, therefore, discontinued its service to New York after the sailing of *Niagara* on 20 December 1854 and did not revive it until the sailing of *Africa* from New York on 6 February 1856. During this period, the Cunard line maintained its fortnightly sailings from Boston with steamers *Asia, Africa, Canada,* and *America.* As soon as the Cunard line discontinued its New York runs, the Collins line, perhaps by prearrangement, changed its sailing days from New York to Wednesdays. In this way a weekly service to Liverpool on Wednesdays was maintained. The first Wednesday sailing from New York by the Collins line was taken by *Pacific* on 27 December 1854, while the first Saturday sailing after the Cunard line returned to the New York service was also by the *Pacific* on 5 January 1856, on her last outward voyage.

In regard to American packet covers prepaid with 21¢ in postage stamps, and used during the year of 1855: those showing dates in their American packet markings that indicate a Saturday sailing were con-

FIGURE 81.—LITHOGRAPH of the Collins line ship, *Atlantic*. (*Courtesy of James E. Schofield*)

veyed either by the Havre line or by the Ocean (Bremen) line. Those conveyed by the Havre line bear French markings for direct service to Havre, while those conveyed by the Ocean (Bremen) line were rated by France for American packet service through England. Most of the American packet covers seen which can be attributed to Collins line service were used during 1855 and show American packet marks whose dates indicate a Wednesday sailing.

On 1 November 1856, steamship *Hermann* of the Ocean line sailed from New York for Southampton and Bremen. The following appears in the 21 January 1857 issue of the *Shipping and Commercial list and New York Prices Current* under a section headed "Gales and Disasters": [50]

> Southampton, December 20 (1856)—The Hermann, United States Mail Steamship, Captain Higgins, put back to Southampton, Sunday, December 14th. with center shaft broken, side lever carried away, and port engine damaged and useless.—The starboard engine remained available, the hull was not much damaged, but the repairs of the engine will require at least six weeks. The accident took place about 1000 miles from Southampton. She was laboring heavily, and only just able to make headway in the recent gales.

Hermann did not arrive back in New York until 12 March 1857. *Washington* sailed from New York on 29 November 1856, arrived back in New York on 20 January 1857, and did not sail again until 21 February 1857. There was no sailing by the Ocean line during December 1856 or January 1857.

What happened to the Bremen mail during this period is explained by the cover illustrated in Figure 82. This letter originated in Taunton, Massachusetts, on 12 December 1856, addressed to Halle, Prussia. It was prepaid 15¢ by a 3¢ and a 12¢ stamp of the 1851 issue. The prepayment indicated that the letter was intended to be sent by the Ocean (Bremen) line, the only route to Germany to which a 15¢ prepayment pertained. It was known, however, that the Ocean line ships would not sail until *Washington* returned some time in January. The letter was, therefore, sent as fully paid in the

---

[50] *Shipping and Commercial List and New York Prices Current,* 11 Feb. 1857.

FIGURE 82.—COVER, from Taunton, Ms. [Massachusetts], to Halle, Prussia, 1856. (*Melvin W. Schuh collection*)

Prussian closed mail by *Atlantic* of the Collins line which sailed from New York on 20 December 1856. The New York American packet marking shows a credit of 7¢, which was all that the Aachen office considered; proper prepayment by stamps was regarded as the problem of the American exchange office. The Aachen office applied the boxed AACHEN/FRANCO marking, characteristic of Prussian closed-mail covers. This bears the date of 3 January (3/1), and a circular AUSG. (*Ausgabe*) marking on the reverse was applied on 4 January (4/1). Thus, the person who mailed this letter, inadvertently had the advantage of a 30¢ rate for a 15¢ prepayment, and of much faster service than the letter would have received if the Ocean line ships had been running. It also demonstrates that the post office relied on the Prussian closed mail when the Ocean line service failed, as the Bremen closed mail had been previously relied upon for the same reason. It also brings into question the saying, Do not buy a cover if the rate is not right, which is a perfectly good rule to follow if the buyer has sufficient knowledge.

The original fleet of the North German Lloyd consisted of *Bremen, New York, Hudson,* and *Weser.* On 4 December 1858, *Weser* sailed from Bremen for New York on her maiden voyage. She encountered heavy seas, was forced to put back to Queenstown for repairs, and did not arrive in New York until 18 March 1859. She made two further voyages for the Lloyd after which she was sold to France.[51] On the night of 2 November 1858, *Hudson* was destroyed by fire at her pier at Bremerhaven.[52] Thus, by the end of 1859 the North German Lloyd fleet was reduced to *Bremen* and *New York,* and these two ships were maintaining a monthly service. *Bremen* sailed from New York on 24 December 1859, broke a shaft on the run to Bremen, and did not arrive back in New York until 25 July 1860. During the period in 1860 in which *Bremen* was out of service, *New York* made the following voyages: arrived in New York on 17 January and sailed 21 January; arrived 11 March and sailed 17 March; arrived 1 May and sailed 12 May; arrived 25 June and sailed 7 July. On 25 July *Bremen* arrived again in New York and sailed on 4 August 1860, restoring the monthly service.

Piefke relates how Bremen sent the mail during this period:[53]

> During this period it was impossible . . . to forward the mails regularly. These sad events caused Post Director Dr. Bartsch to utter the lament, 'What will they think of us in

---

[51] Ibid., p. 182.
[52] Ibid.
[53] Piefke, *Bremischen Landespost,* chap. 22.

America when we, disregarding our public announcements and promises, delay letters . . . for six weeks?' There remained only one unlovely way out—the same used when the Vanderbilt ships failed—to use the Hapag Line.

The report of the auditor of the Treasury for the Post Office Department, appended to the annual report of the postmaster general for 1860, discloses that the postage on letters sent from Bremen by the Hamburg-American line amounted to $3,837.69, whereas no mail from the United States is reported as being sent to Bremen by the Hapag ships.

Figure 83 illustrates a cover posted in Augusta, Georgia, on 12 January 1860, prepaid 27¢ by two 12¢ stamps and a 3¢ stamp of the 1857 issue, and addressed to Switzerland. At the time the letter was posted, the rate to Switzerland by Bremen or Hamburg mail was 27¢ per half ounce. It is not unlikely that this letter arrived at the New York office before *New York* arrived on 17 January 1860, and, in any event, it was uncertain as to when she would sail. There was no scheduled sailing by the Hamburg-American line during January 1860.[54] The letter was, therefore, sent in the Prussian closed mail as fully paid. The Prussian closed-mail rate to Switzerland was 35¢. The basic credit of 7¢ for the 30¢ international rate was increased by the postage of 5¢ beyond the 30¢ rate, making a total credit of 12¢. The New York office, therefore, marked the letter P.D. ("paid to destination"), with a red 12 next to it, and forwarded it in the Prussian closed mail to Aachen. The Aachen office applied marking *P* of Figure 51, which indicated that the letter was paid, and that it was received at that office on 31 January. It also marked the letter in blue manuscript *f 2*, showing that the postage beyond the German-Austrian Postal Union border of 2 silbergroschen (5¢) had been paid. These markings are typical of those applied to Prussian closed mail. If the letter had been sent in the Hamburg mail, the credit would have been 22¢, or if in the Bremen mail, 24¢ would have been credited to Bremen.

Early in 1860 the North Atlantic Steamship Company acquired the services of ex-Collins liners *Adriatic* and *Atlantic* and placed them on the run from New York to Havre, via Southampton. Their sailing dates were set on Saturdays so that they augmented the service of Vanderbilt steamers *Illinois* and *Vanderbilt*. The postmaster general made trip contracts with this line for service to Southampton and Havre. The sailings of the line are presented in Table 29.

---
[54] Sailing data reported in *Shipping and Commercial List* (appropriate issues) disclose that there was no sailing from New York during any January until 2 Jan. 1861.

FIGURE 83.—COVER, from Augusta, Ga., to Geneva, Switzerland, 1860.
(*Melvin W. Schuh collection*)

TABLE 29.—*North Atlantic Steamship Company Sailings*

Arrival Date, New York	Ship	Departure Date, New York
(New York, Southampton, and LeHavre)		
1860		1860/61
F/V [a]	*Adriatic*	14 Apr.
15 May	*Adriatic*	2 June
1 July	*Adriatic*	14 July
11 Aug.	*Adriatic*	25 Aug.
24 Sept.	*Adriatic*	6 Oct.
F/V [a]	*Atlantic*	17 Nov.
5 Nov.	*Adriatic* Dns.[b]	29 Dec.
19 Dec.	*Atlantic* Dns.[b]	29 Dec.[c]
5 Nov.	*Adriatic* Dns.[b]	9 Mar.[d]
5 Nov.	*Adriatic*	13 Mar.[e]

[a] First voyage for line.

[b] Scheduled; did not sail.

[c] Announced as substituted for the *Adriatic*; did not sail; mail sent by *Etna* of the Inman line.

[d] *Adriatic* sold to Galway line; mail rerated and sent by the *Edinburgh* of the Inman line.

[e] *Adriatic* sailed as British steamer for delivery to Galway line.

Figure 84 presents a cover (face only) in the Smithsonian collection that shows the transfer of *Adriatic* to the Galway line. It was posted in New Orleans on 1 March 1861 (when Louisiana was a Confederate state) prepaid 15¢ to be sent by French mail. It is franked by a 10¢ type V and a 5¢ type II stamp of the 1857 issue. New York first applied marking F of Figure 42, bearing the date of 9 March and a credit of 3¢ for direct service to Havre. This marking was obliterated by a red grid, and a second marking similar to F of Figure 42 was applied bearing the same date, but with a credit of 6¢ for service to France, via England. *Adriatic* was scheduled to sail on 9 March 1861 as a United States mail steamer. With the exception of the sailing of *Adriatic* on 13 March 1861, all of the sailings reported in Table 29 are designated in the *Shipping and Commercial List* as either "U.S.M. steamer *Adriatic*," or "U.S.M. steamer *Atlantic*." The sailing on 13 March 1861 is shown simply as "steamer *Adriatic*" among the ship clearances for that day.

What happened is evident on the face of the cover. After *Adriatic* was scheduled to sail and after her mails were made up, she was sold to the Galway line.[55]

---

[55] Bonsor, *North Atlantic Seaway*, p. 163. Dates from *Shipping and Commercial List*.

Since she would not again sail for Havre, her mails were rerated. The presence of the date of 9 March in the second application of the New York marking indicates that the mail was sent on that day (the same day as the scheduled sailing by *Adriatic*) by a different ship. The only mail steamer to sail from New York on 9 March 1861 was *Edinburgh* of the Inman line, and it is presumed that she conveyed this letter to Liverpool. This would verify the use of the credit of 6¢ in the second New York marking. The letter was evidently sent from Liverpool through the Southampton office to Havre. The Havre office applied marking D of Figure 43 bearing the date of 28 March 1861.

The "Miscellaneous line" developed by the postmaster general for 1859 [56] discloses that he contracted with the Cunard line for one trip to Liverpool by steamer *Lebanon* which sailed from New York on 26 February 1859, conveying United States mail. *Lebanon* was a freighter and was not used by the Cunard line as a mail carrier. This was her only transatlantic mail voyage.

After the loss of *Indian* on 21 November 1859 and *Hungarian* on 20 February 1860, the Allan line had difficulty in maintaining its service between Liverpool and Portland or Rivier du Loup (Quebec). After the collapse of the European and Australian line, Allan chartered that line's screw steamer *Australasian* for one voyage. She arrived in Portland, Maine, on 23 April 1860, and sailed on 5 May conveying the last mail of the winter of 1859–60 from Portland;[57] on the following voyages the ships ran to Quebec. Late in 1860 *Australasian* was purchased by the Cunard line. The Allan line chartered *Melita* from the Cunard line for one trip to Liverpool. Since *Melita* was a freighter, she sailed from Quebec on 6 July 1860, on her only mail voyage to Liverpool.[58]

In October 1863 *Africa* of the Cunard line was disabled off Cape Race. H.B.M.S. *Vesuvius* came to her rescue. The *Africa* was scheduled to sail from Boston with a mail on 28 October 1863, but of course did not arrive to take the sailing. H.B.M.S. *Vesuvius* arrived in Boston on 21 October 1863 with *Africa*'s mail. The *Olympus* of the Cunard line arrived in New York on 22 October 1863 and sailed for Boston on 25 October

---

[56] *Senate Executive Document* 3, 36 Cong., 1 sess., serial 1025, p. 1498.

[57] *Shipping and Commercial List* (appropriate issues).

[58] Report of Treasury auditor for Post Office Dept. appended to *Annual Report of the Postmaster General for 1861*, p. 124.

Figure 84.—Cover, from New Orleans, La. [then a Confederate State], to France, 1861. (*Photograph by Smithsonian*)

1863. On 28 October 1863, *Africa's* scheduled sailing date, *Olympus* sailed from Boston for Liverpool with *Africa's* mails.[59] Since *Olympus* normally carried freight and steerage passengers, this was her only mail voyage. Also, the bringing into Boston of *Africa's* mails by H.B.M.S. *Vesuvius* is the only instance in which a naval vessel carried mail for the Cunard line.

The Additional Exchange Offices Under the United States-British Treaty of 15 December 1848

Additional articles to the United States-British treaty of 15 December 1848 were signed at London on 25 November and at Washington on 12 December 1853, which created an exchange office at Philadelphia.[60] These article were to come into operation on 1 January 1854. The Philadelphia office was to correspond with the British exchange offices at Liverpool, London, and Southampton. Mails sent in transit through England were to be directed to the London office when conveyed from Boston or New York by mail packets to Liverpool, or to the Southampton office when conveyed by United States mail packets plying between New York and Southampton. The mails made up at the three British offices were to be forwarded in separate bags addressed to the Philadelphia office and were to comprise all correspondence for the city of Philadelphia. It was not specified, however, that mails dispatched by the Philadelphia office comprise only mails originating in the city of Philadelphia.

Figure 85 illustrates a cover posted in Philadelphia on 14 October 1857, addressed to Liverpool. It is endorsed "per City of Washington/from N.York to Liverpool." The subsidized Collins line had taken *Baltic* and *Atlantic* out of service temporarily so that they could be fitted with watertight compartments, and had delayed the maiden voyage of *Adriatic* for the same purpose. *Ericsson* and *Columbia,* chartered by the line, were attempting to maintain the fortnightly schedule, together with the Collins line ships as they were returned to service. However, there had been no sailing by the line in February and only one sailing in each of the months March, April, and May. *Atlantic,* which was scheduled to sail on 10 October

---

[59] *Shipping and Commercial List* (appropriate issues).
[60] *16 Statutes at Large* 814.

FIGURE 85.—COVER, from Philadelphia to Liverpool, 1857. (*Melvin W. Schuh collection*)

1857, did not arrive back in New York until that day, and did not sail until 24 October 1857. There was, therefore, to be only one sailing by the line during October.

Although there is nothing relating to it in the report of the auditor of the Treasury for the Post Office Department, this cover indicates that the postmaster general made a trip contract with the Inman line for the services of *City of Washington* to convey the mail to Liverpool. The credit 3 in the Philadelphia packet marking indicates American packet service by a contract packet. This marking is dated 14 October, and *City of Washington* sailed from New York on Thursday, 15 October 1857. Since the cover bears an endorsement, the sailing must have been publicly announced. This is the earliest cover noted by the author showing service by an Inman line ship as a contract packet.

In June 1857 the provincial government of Canada arranged with the Montreal Ocean Steam Ship Company (Allan line) for a weekly conveyance of mail to Liverpool. In order to increase the service from fortnightly to weekly, new steamships had to be built. An annual subsidy of £42,000 was granted, and shortly thereafter it was increased to double that figure. The line was plying between Liverpool and Quebec between April and October, inclusive, and between Liverpool and Portland, Maine, during the remainder of the year when the St. Lawrence River was closed to navigation. The weekly service came into operation in April 1859.[61]

In his annual report for 1859 Postmaster General Joseph Holt said of the Allan line:

This line is hereafter to run weekly, Portland being the terminus on this side during the winter, and Quebec during the summer season; and in connexion with the Grand Trunk railway, over the Victoria bridge at Montreal, now completed, it will afford the means of the most direct and probably the most expeditious communication between Chicago and Liverpool. Arrangements have been made with the Canadian post office department to transport, for the sea postage, any mails it may be desirable to send by this line; and, in order to give them as much expedition as possible, it is intended to have Chicago and Detroit, as well as Portland, constituted offices of exchange for United States and British mails. Bags will then be made up at each of these offices, and will not be opened until they reach Liverpool. The running time from Chicago to Portland, *via* Detroit, Toronto, &c., is not to exceed forty-eight hours; and either from Portland or from the contemplated terminus of the railway, near the mouth of the St. Lawrence, where the mails are to be transferred to and from the steamships, the distance to Liverpool is several hundred miles less than from New York.

Additional articles to the United States-British treaty of 15 December 1848 creating Portland, Maine, an exchange office were signed at Washington on

---

[61] Bonsor, *North Atlantic Seaway*, p. 84.

11 January and at London on 3 February 1859.[62] Significant portions of these articles are summarized as follows:

I. Established an exchange office at Portland for the exchange of United States and European mails with the British offices of Liverpool and London by means of United States, British, or Canadian mail packets plying between Liverpool and Portland.
II. Provided that the offices of Boston, New York, and Philadelphia might exchange mails with the offices of London and Liverpool, respectively, by way of Portland, in the same manner as mails are now being exchanged by United States and British packets plying between New York and Liverpool, and Boston and Liverpool.
III. The mails forwarded by the Portland Office to the Liverpool office were to comprise the correspondence for all parts of the United Kingdom, except the city of London and its suburbs.
   The mails for London would comprise all correspondence for that city and its suburbs, and for countries in transit through the United Kingdom.
IV. Mails forwarded from the offices of London and Liverpool to Portland would comprise all the correspondence for the United States, except the cities of Boston, New York, and Philadelphia.
   The mails forwarded by the offices of London and Liverpool to Boston, New York, and Philadelphia would comprise the mails destined for each of those cities, respectively.

Although the reports of the auditor of the Treasury for the Post Office Depatrment show that the Canadian (Allan) line carried much American packet British mail after 1860, Portland exchange office markings are scarce. The above mail arrangements point to the reason for their scarcity.

The offices of Boston, New York, and Philadelphia could make up a mail, direct it to one of the British offices, and send it to Portland for conveyance to Liverpool. The mail so sent was not confined to that originating in the respective city, and would bear the marking of the office that sent it to Portland. The only mail made up at Portland was mail specifically directed to that office by the local offices. On the other hand, mails received from the British offices at Portland and directed to the New York, Boston, or Philadelphia offices contained only the mail addressed to those cities. Mail addressed to other parts of the United States passed through the Portland office and bore a Portland marking. This may explain why Portland markings are more frequently seen on incoming than on outgoing mail.

Additional articles to the United States-British treaty were signed at London on 25 November, and at Washington on 14 December 1859,[63] creating exchange offices at Chicago and Detroit in the United States and at Cork, Dublin, and Galway in the United Kingdom. These offices were to exchange mails with each other by means of British, United States, and Canadian mail packets. It was not prescribed that the packet ply between Liverpool and Portland or River du Loup. The Portland office was also to exchange mails with the offices at Dublin, Cork, and Galway, but was henceforth to exchange mails with the offices at London, Liverpool, and Cork only by means of the Canadian mail packets (Article III).

Article IV provided that the "description of letters, &c., of the mails exchanged shall be arranged by correspondence between the British and United States Post-Offices." What these arrangements were is not known. The very few British mail covers seen which bear a Chicago or Detroit packet marking originated in midwestern towns. It has been noted, however, that some British mail covers posted in Chicago were sent to Boston or New York and bear markings of those exchange offices. It is evident, therefore, that letters posted in the midwestern towns and sent in British mails did not have to be conveyed by the Canadian (Allan) line.

At the time these articles were signed, the Allan line did not call at Queenstown, the port for the city of Cork. Mails exchanged between Portland and Cork, therefore, were routed from Liverpool to Holyhead, and thence across the Irish sea by the packets of the City of Dublin Steam Packet Company, a twice-a-day service, to Kingstown (near Dublin)[64] and thence by rail to Cork. Both the Inman and Cunard lines introduced a call at Queenstown in 1859.[65] In June 1860 the Allan line started to call at Moville, the port for the city of Londonderry, which was made an exchange office on 21 July 1860.[66] In 1861 a direct Allan line service to Glasgow was inaugurated. In anticipation of this announced service, additional articles creating an exchange office at Glasgow were signed at London on 13 August and at Washington on 1 September 1860.[67]

On 26 September at London and on 19 October 1863 at Washington, additional articles to the United States-British treaty were signed creating an exchange

---

[62] 16 *Statutes at Large* 824.
[63] Ibid., 825.
[64] Thomas Rainey, *Ocean Steam Navigation and the Ocean Post*, paper by Pliny Miles, appendix, p. 193.
[65] Bonsor, *North Atlantic Seaway*, pp. 16 and 63.
[66] 16 *Statutes at Large*, 826.
[67] Ibid., p. 827.

office at San Francisco,⁶⁸ which was to receive and distribute mails. It was not, however, to dispatch mails to the British offices. There are, therefore, no San Francisco markings that show debits or credits to Great Britain.

In the boom days immediately following the Civil War, the Baltimore and Ohio Railroad availed itself of the opportunity of purchasing from the United States Navy four vessels whose services the Navy no longer required. According to Bonsor, these ships were renamed *Somerset, Carroll, Worcester,* and *Allegany* after four Maryland counties.⁶⁹ Although built for coastal service, the Baltimore and Ohio Railroad organized the Baltimore and Liverpool Steamship Company with a view to placing these 1,250-ton wooden screw steamers on the transatlantic ferry for the purpose of carrying freight and mail, if a mail contract could be secured.

The Post Office Department appears to have given the line its full cooperation, for not only was a mail contract awarded, but Baltimore was made an exchange office by additional articles to the United States-British treaty, signed at Washington on 11 November 1865.⁷⁰ Staff reports a British Post Office order of 23 April 1866, which notes the establishment of the new line of packets and states that sailings would be at "irregular intervals." ⁷¹ Of greater interest, however, it the fact that all correspondence addressed to the city of Baltimore, the District of Columbia, and all southern, southeastern, and central states bordering the Mississippi—nineteen in all—would be sent by this line, "if not specifically addressed to be otherwise sent."

During 1865 *Allegany* was placed on the New York-Baltimore run and was wrecked off Long Island on 5 December 1865. When the mail service was inaugurated, therefore, it was maintained by the three remaining ships. During 1866 twelve round voyages were made between Liverpool and Baltimore, but during 1867 only seven were made, and in 1868 the service was discontinued.⁷² Numerous covers posted in the area to be served by this line have been noted. Most of them bear an endorsement indicating that they were to be sent through New York or Boston. Even when such letters were not so endorsed, their early dispatch required that they be sent to New York or Boston. As a result, covers showing a Baltimore exchange office marking for British mail service are rare, and none is illustrated here.

Although there were no additional articles to the United States-French convention of 2 March 1857, creating Baltimore an exchange office, the *U.S. Mail and Post Office Assistant* in repeated issues during 1867 notes Baltimore as an exchange office for French mail. That it was an exchange office at least for the receipt and distribution of French mail is attested by Figure 86. This double-rate letter was posted in Paris on 25 June 1867, addressed to New Orleans. It bears a double-rate credit of 18¢ for American packet service through England. The BALTIMORE AM. PKT./PAID/JUL/9/1867 marking (which ties the French stamps) is in red. On 9 July 1867, *Worcester* of the Baltimore and Liverpool Steamship Company arrived in Baltimore from Liverpool. This is the only cover known to the author whose conveyance can definitely be attributed to this steamship line.

The Additional Exchange Offices Under the United States-French Convention of 2 March 1857

Additional articles to the United States-French convention of 2 March 1857 were signed at Washington on 22 February and at Paris on 8 March 1861.⁷³ The modifications made by these articles to the arrangements included in the original convention were extensive.

Article I provided for the exchange of correspondence "by Canadian mail packets plying between Liverpool and Portland, or between Liverpool and River du Loup."

Article II provided that the articles of the convention which applied to letters exchanged between the French and United States post offices "by means of British packets and other British steam-vessels performing regular service between the ports of Great Britain and the ports of the United States, shall apply to letters which shall be exchanged between the two post-offices" when conveyed by Canadian packets. This article created the peculiar situation of treating French

---

⁶⁸ Ibid., p. 830.
⁶⁹ Bonsor, *North Atlantic Seaway,* p. 233.
⁷⁰ 16 *Statutes at Large,* p. 832.
⁷¹ Frank Staff, *The Transatlantic Mail,* pp. 152–153.
⁷² Cedric Ridgely-Nevitt, "The Baltimore and Liverpool Steamship Line," *Steamboat Bill* 95 (Fall 1965): 85.

⁷³ 16 *Statutes at Large* 890.

FIGURE 86.—COVER, from Paris to New Orleans, 1867. (*James E. Schofield collection*)

mail conveyed by the Canadian (Allan) line as being conveyed by British packets, while British and Prussian closed-mail letters conveyed by the same line were treated as being conveyed by American packets.

Article III established an additional exchange office at Paris, for France, and created offices at Portland, Detroit, and Chicago, for the United States. The office at San Francisco was discontinued.

Article IV provided that the three French offices correspond with the offices at New York, Boston, and Philadelphia by means of United States, British, and Canadian packets; and with the offices of Portland, Detroit, and Chicago *by means of the Canadian packets only.*

Article V referred to an appended table which described the origin and destination of mails and the packet lines by which the mails were to be exchanged. The packet lines included were: New York and Havre; Bremen and New York, via Southampton; Liverpool and New York; Liverpool and Boston; and Liverpool and Portland or River du Loup. It should be noted that the New York and Hamburg packet line is not included. It was provided, however, that these arrangements could be modified by correspondence between the two post offices.

Although the mail arrangements set forth in the table are exceedingly complicated, the relations between the French offices and the offices at Portland, Detroit, and Chicago may be summarized as follows:

The French exchange offices were to correspond with the offices at Detroit by means of Canadian packets for mails originating in or destined for the States of Michigan, Ohio, Indiana, and Kentucky; with the office at Chicago by means of Canadian packets for mails originating in or destined for the States of Illinois, Wisconsin, Minnesota, Iowa, and Missouri, and the Territories of Kansas and Nebraska; and with the office at Portland by means of Canadian packets for mail originating in or destined for all of the United States and its territories (except those mentioned above as related to the offices of Detroit and Chicago, and mails to or from the cities of New York, Boston, and Philadelphia, as well as mails to or from California, Oregon, and the territory of Washington, which were to pass through the New York office).

The mails sent from or received at the Boston Office, via Portland or River du Loup, were to comprise of the mails of the city of Boston only; the mails sent from or received at the Philadelphia office, via Portland or River du Loup, were to comprise of the mail of the city of Philadelphia only; the mails sent from or received at the New York office, via Portland or River du Loup, were to comprise of the mails of the city of New York, California, Oregon, and the territory of Washington.

By Article VI these articles were to come into operation on 1 April 1861.

The Additional Exchange Offices Under the United States-Prussian Closed-Mail Convention

Additional articles to the United States-Prussian closed-mail convention were signed at Washington on 28 December 1860, and at Berlin on 24 April 1861, creating United States exchange offices at Portland, Detroit, and Chicago which were to correspond with the Prussian office at Aachen by means of Canadian mail packets.[74] By Article II, "The description of letters, &c., which shall comprise the closed mails (exchanged between the above offices) . . . shall be from time to time arranged by correspondence between the Post-Office Departments of the two countries." By Article III, the two post offices were to account to each other for the mail exchanged by means of Canadian packets, "precisely in the same manner as if the sea transportation were performed by a United States packet between New York and Liverpool." By Article IV, these articles were to "go into effect in each country at the expiration of fifteen days from the time notice is received of their being concluded." The exact date upon which these articles went into effect is not known, but considering the preceding provision, they probably went into effect in the United States about the middle of May 1861.

What arrangements were made between the post offices of the United States and Prussia regarding the origin and destination of mail exchanged between the offices of Portland, Detroit, and Chicago and the office at Aachen are not known. It must be emphasized, however, that by Article I, the exchange of Prussian closed mails between these offices could only be effected by Canadian mail packets. In his annual report for 1861, Postmaster General Montgomery Blair mentioned the additional articles to the United States-French convention, and then went on to say, "Additional articles to the postal convention with Prussia, of the same character, have been agreed upon with the general post office at Berlin. . . . These arrangements have greatly expedited the transmission of European correspondence to and from the western States." This leads one to conclude that it is not unlikely that similar conditions for mail originating in or destined for the same places as set forth in the United States-French convention were applied to the Prussian closed mail.

---

[74] Ibid., 978.

Covers Conveyed by the Allan Line

Figure 87 illustrates a cover posted in Bath, Maine, addressed to Liverpool. It is prepaid 24¢ by two 12¢ stamps (Plate III) issued in 1860. The postal clerk evidently had difficulty in canceling the black stamps, struck the left stamp twice, and then struck the postmark at bottom center of the cover. This cover passed through the Portland office in British mail and received a PORTLAND ME. AM. PKT./3/MAR/16/1861 marking in red. The 3 in this marking indicates a credit to Great Britain for her inland postage, the United States retaining 16¢ packet and 5¢ inland postages. *North Briton* of the Allan line sailed from Portland on 16 March 1861, and it is presumed that this ship conveyed the letter to Liverpool.

The Allan line packets sailed from Portland or River du Loup on Saturdays. According to the French mail arrangements, Boston could send a bag to Portland which was to include only mail originating in that city. The Boston exchange office markings for mail thus sent show Saturday dates. These markings, of course, show credits indicating British packet service by French mail. When Boston forwarded French mail by the Cunard line, its markings bear Wednesday dates when the ship sailed from Boston, or Tuesday dates when the ship sailed from New York. A Boston marking showing a credit that indicates British packet service by French mail and a Saturday date, therefore, discloses that the cover was sent by Boston to Portland for conveyance by the Allan line. Few covers endorsed to Allan line ships have been noted, and all of them were posted during the "winter" season when the ships ran from Portland.

Figure 88 illustrates a cover which originated in Boston, addressed to Paris. It is prepaid 15¢ by stamps of the 1861 issue, and is endorsed to *Norwegian* of the Allan line. The Boston marking shows a single-rate credit of 12¢ to France, indicating British packet service. The date in the Boston marking is 26 April (1862), a Saturday, and the *Shipping and Commercial List and New York Prices Current* discloses that *Norwegian* sailed from Portland on that date.

Figure 89 illustrates a cover posted in Fond du Lac, Wisconsin, on 26 August 1861, addressed to Switzerland. It is prepaid 21¢, the single rate *via* French mail, by two 10¢ stamps and a 1¢ stamp of the 1861 issue. This is a very early use of the stamps on a cover to a foreign country. The Fond du Lac post office sent the letter to the Detroit exchange office, complying with the requirement that letters from Wisconsin to be sent

Figure 87.—Cover, from Bath, Me. [Maine], to Liverpool, England, 1861.

in French mail be forwarded to that office for transmission by Canadian packets. The Detroit office applied in red a DETROIT MICH/PAID 18/AUG/29 exchange-office marking, the 18 indicating the correct credit to France for a single-rate letter conveyed by British packet. The exchange office marking did not show whether conveyance was by British or American packet, and, in order to emphasize that the letters were rated as by British packet, the boxed BR. SERVICE marking (K of Figure 42) was applied in red. This marking was designed for use on incoming letters, and it is unusual to find it on a letter forwarded from the United States. The date of 29 August (1861) in the exchange office marking shows the date on which the mails were made up at the Detroit office for the sailing of *Bohemian* from River du Loup on 31 August 1861.

Figure 90 illustrates an unpaid letter posted in Kanalle Depot, Illinois, on 11 November 1865, addressed to Paris. As was required by regulations, the postal clerk marked the rate on the letter by use of a handstamp containing the figure 15 in an oval, but applied it in blue instead of the required black ink. He also wrote *France* upon the letter. Since this letter originated in Illinois, it was sent to the Chicago exchange office. The Chicago office ascertained that the letter weighed over a quarter ounce, and the rating by the Kanalle Depot post office was, therefore, incorrect. Not having a stamp inscribed *insufficiently rated*, it was marked INSUFFICIENTLY/PREPAID in blue ink. Since a partial payment was not recognized, this marking would not confuse the French. The letter was also struck with an exchange office marking inscribed CHICAGO ILL/6, which bears no date and is in blue. The 6 in this marking indicates a double-rate debit to France of 6¢ for British packet service. The French exchange office marking (H of Figure 43) was applied at Paris, and that office rated the letter for a collection of two 8-decime rates by applying a *16* in black.

Figure 91 illustrates an unpaid letter posted in Ottawa, Illinois, on 1 December 1862, addressed to Wiborg, Finland. The postal clerk at the Ottawa post office endorsed the letter *via Prussian Close mail,* and, complying with regulations, applied a 30 to indicate the 30¢ international rate for a single-rate Prussian closed-mail letter. Both the Ottawa postmark and the 30 are in blue ink. The letter was forwarded to the Chicago exchange office for the required transmission by Canadian packet. The Chicago office applied an exchange office marking inscribed CHICAGO ILL AM. PKT./23 in blue ink. As is the case with the exchange office marking shown on the cover illustrated in Figure

FIGURE 88.—COVER, from Boston to Paris, 1862.

89, this marking also shows no date. While one may speculate upon the reason for this omission, no evidence has been found that explains it. The 23 in this marking is the single-rate debit to Prussia for an unpaid letter by Prussian closed mail. The manuscript *12/2* on the face of the cover is in blue ink and represents the Prussian debit to Russia (Finland) of 12 silbergroschen foreign and 2 silbergroschen Union postage (about 33¢). On the reverse is a manuscript *56* in red ink which indicated that 56 kopeck were to be collected in Finland (about 40¢).

Changes in the Prussian Closed-Mail Rates

The significant provisions of the Anglo-Prussian additional postal convention of 2–7 July 1852 have been presented in Chapter 5, dealing with the Prussian closed-mail convention. On 13 June at Berlin and on 20 June 1859 at London, Great Britain and Prussia signed an additional postal agreement [75] which reduced the international rate from 8d. to 6d. in Great Britain and from 7 to 5 silbergroschen in Prussia on *prepaid* letters originating in or destined for the states of Prussia, Austria, Bavaria, Saxony, Württemberg, Mecklenburg-Strelitz, Oldenburg, Luxembourg,

Brunswick, or Lübeck. Unpaid letters remained at the former rates. Under this agreement, Belgian transit postage of ½d. was to be paid to Belgium by the British, but was to be repaid to Great Britain by Prussia (Article IV). Prussia was then to pay Britain 3d. for every single-rate prepaid *letter,* which included ½d. for Belgian transit. The net British transit postage thus became 2½d. per single rate of half an ounce, representing a reduction of 1d. from the former rate.

Although the above agreement became effective on 1 July 1859 (Article X), it was over two years before there was an adjustment in the United States-Prussian closed-mail rate. The *U.S. Mail and Post Office Assistant* contains the following announcement: [76]

> A reduction of one penny (two cents) the single rate having been made by Great Britain on prepaid letters mailed in the United Kingdom and addressed to Prussia, Austria, Bavaria, Saxony, Wurtemberg, Mecklinburg-Strelitz, Luxemburg, Brunswick, Lubeck, Hamburg, or Bremen, the British office has consented to extend the benefit thereof to the *paid* correspondence between the United States and those countries respectively, transmitted through England in the United States and Prussian closed mail, by reducing the British territorial transit rate in respect to such prepaid letters, from 8¾d. to 6¼d. per ounce.

The 6¼d.-per-ounce rate was arrived at by applying the formula of Article IX of the United States-

---

[75] *British and Foreign State Papers,* vol. 59, p. 900.

[76] *U.S. Mail and Post Office Assistant* 2, 1 (Oct. 1861): 2.

FIGURE 89.—COVER, from Fond du Lac, Wis., to Fribourg, Switzerland, 1861.

British treaty to the 2½d. single-letter rate for British transit postage. Article IX, it will be remembered, set the closed-mail rate per ounce at two single-letter rates plus 25 percent. The British transit rate, therefore, became 6¼d. per ounce (2 x 2½d. plus ¼). In terms of United States currency this represented a reduction from 17½¢ to 12½¢ per ounce.

An additional agreement signed at Berlin on 8 March 1862 between Prussia and Great Britain applied the reduced prepaid rate "from the 1st of April . . . to correspondence exchanged via Belgium, between the postal district of the Prince of Thurn and Taxis and the United Kingdom of Great Britain and Ireland." [77] Further additional articles signed at Berlin on 12 April 1862 extended the privilege of the reduced prepaid rate to Mecklenburg-Schwerin after 1 May 1862.[78] A United States Post Office Department announcement dated 17 May 1862 and published in the June 1862 issue of the *U.S. Mail and Post Office Assistant*, stated that the 28¢ rate on prepaid letters was extended to all of the German states, except Baden, via Prussian closed mail.

A new postal convention between Great Britain and Prussia was signed in duplicate at London on 13 October 1862.[79] This convention consists of forty articles, the first twelve of which largely consolidate the scattered additional articles already in effect into a single agreement. One change worthy of note, however, was the substitution of the travelling office between Verviers and Cologne for Aachen as an exchange office. The route taken by the Anglo-Prussian and the United States-Prussian closed mails extended from Ostend to Verviers, Belgium, and thence through Aachen to Cologne. Prior to this agreement these mails were put off at the Aachen office. From 1 November 1862, when this portion of the convention became effective, the United States-Prussian closed mail continued to be put off at Aachen, but the Anglo-Prussian closed mail was sorted en route between Verviers and Cologne.

Also of particular interest are those articles dealing with the expansion of correspondence in transit through the German Postal Union. Article XIX granted the British office the transit of closed mails through the German Postal Union from the frontier of Belgium to any part of the German frontier or vice versa, as well as conveyance by German mail packets for mail exchanged with India, Australia, Russia, or Russian Poland, Norway, Sweden, Denmark, Constantinople, Smyrna, or the Ionian Islands; also, "the transit of

---

[77] *British and Foreign State Papers,* vol. 59, p. 903.
[78] Ibid., p. 904.
[79] Ibid., vol. 52, p. 1148.

Figure 90.—Cover, from Kanallee Depot, Ill., to Paris, 1865.

British closed mails through the territory of Turkey, whether by land or water, or partly one and partly the other, so long as German closed mails can be sent through Turkish territory."

Articles XXVII to XXX provided for the use of British packets to or from the port of Trieste for the conveyance of closed mails, while Article XXVI provided for an exchange of letters between the Austrian Post Office at Alexandria (Egypt), and the British post offices of Aden, Bombay, Calcutta, Madras, Point de Galle, Port Louis, Penang, Singapore, Hong Kong, King George's Sound, Adelaide, Geelong, Melbourne, Hobart Town, Launceston, Sydney, Brisbane, Auckland, and Wellington.

Article XL provided that the convention come into operation on 1 November 1862, but that none of the provisions relating to transit mail (mentioned above)

> ... shall take effect until each of the Contracting Parties has announced to the other that satisfactory arrangements arising out of the Convention, on the side of the British office with the Post Offices of Austria, Hamburg, Bremen, and the United States, and on the side of the Prussian office with the Post Offices of Austria and the United States, have been concluded.

The pending agreement between the British and United States post offices just referred to, consisted of additional articles to the United States-British treaty which were signed at London on 26 December 1862 and at Washington on 12 March 1863.[80] These articles provided that the transit rate for closed mails, either through the United States or through the United Kingdom, be at the rate of 8¢ or 4d. per ounce. "and they [these articles] shall be carried into effect as soon as the British Post-Office has announced to the United States Post-Office that the negotiations now pending between the British Post-Office and the German Post-Offices, on the subject of the mutual exchange of closed mails, have been satisfactorily concluded."

Although Article XL of the Anglo-Prussian convention of 13 October 1862 provided that it become effective on 1 November 1862, an agreement signed at London on 22 October and at Berlin on 25 October 1862 deferred the date until 1 January 1863.[81]

Evidently, all negotiations were completed and all announcements made before 1 May 1863, for the May issue of the *U.S. Mail and Post Office Assistant* carried the following:[82]

> We are requested to state that the reduced postage charge of two cents the single rate on prepaid letters, will, in future, be extended to the entire correspondence exchanged in the United States and Prussian closed mails, so that letters to or from Baden, Russia (including Poland), Sweden, Norway, Denmark, and all other countries beyond Germany, will have the benefit of the reduced rate.

---

[80] 16 *Statutes at Large* 829.
[81] *British and Foreign State Papers*, vol. 52, p. 1161.
[82] *U.S. Mail* 3, 8 (May 1863): 2.

FIGURE 91.—Cover, from Ottawa, Ill., to Wiborg, Finland, 1862.

Henceforth, to most places served by Prussian closed mail, the prepaid rate was two cents cheaper than the unpaid rate. To some places in the Far East, to some Turkish towns, and to Rome, prepayment of postage was compulsory. Beginning in June 1865, on mail to Norway and Sweden the differential between prepaid and unpaid rates became 4¢ instead of 2¢. In March 1867, for a reason unknown to the author, the rate to all Turkish towns became 35¢. To some towns prepayment was compulsory, but to others prepayment was optional, there being no difference made between the prepaid and unpaid rate.

Covers

Few covers posted prior to May 1863 that show a prepayment of the 28¢ rate have been seen. A possible reason for this may rest upon the manner in which the rate was presented in the tables of postages to foreign countries published in the *U.S. Mail and Post Office Assistant*.[83] Using Saxony as an example, these tables, beginning with the October 1861 issue, presented the rates as follows:

Saxony, Kingdom of, Prussian closed mail   *30
   do.   do.   do.   when prepaid 28

---

[83] This explanation was suggested by C. J. Starnes in a letter to the author.

The asterisk indicates that prepayment was optional. This presentation was ambiguous, and it is feared that few referred to the second line. While the individual states were separately listed, the entry for the German states until June 1862 was as follows:

German States, Prussian closed mail   *30

There was no reference to the prepaid rate. The May issue, however, placed all information on a single line:

German States, Prus. closed mail (if prepaid, 28¢) *30

After this rate announcement appeared, covers showing a 28¢ prepayment are more frequently seen.

Figure 92 illustrates a cover posted in New York, addressed to Brunswick. It is prepaid 28¢ by stamps of the 1861 issue and is endorsed "via Boston./per Str. Europa." The New York exchange office marking shows the date of 2 September (1862), and on that date the mails were made up at New York for the sailing from Boston of *Europa* on 3 September 1862. Since the reduction in rate occurred in the British transit postage, there was no change in the 7¢ credit to Prussia. On incoming letters, prepaid in Germany, however, the credit to the United States was reduced from 25¢ to 23¢.

Figure 93 illustrates a cover posted in Virginia City, Nevada Territory, on 7 August 1863, addressed to

Figure 92.—Cover, from New York to Brunswick, Germany, 1862.
(*Melvin W. Schuh collection*)

Geneva, Switzerland. It is prepaid 30¢ by a 30¢ stamp of the 1861 issue. This paid the letter only through the German-Austrian Postal Union. The New York office credited Prussia with 7¢ and forwarded the letter on 29 August 1863, by *City of Washington* of the Inman line. Although the person who mailed this letter may not have known it, 28¢ would have been sufficient postage. The Aachen office received the letter on 12 September (12 9 in marking *P* of Figure 51) and also applied marking *Q* of Figure 51, indicating that postage was paid only to the point of exit from the German-Austrian Postal Union. The Aachen office also marked it in blue manuscript *0/6*, indicating that there was no postage due to the border but that 6 kreuzer were due in Switzerland. At this time, the prepaid rate from the United States to Switzerland by Prussian closed mail was 33¢, or 5¢ in excess of the 28¢ prepaid international rate. The 6 kreuzer charged by Aachen was worth slightly more than 4¢. The Swiss marked the letter for a collection of 20 rappen, which was also equal to slightly more than 4¢.

Changes in Progression

The postal conventions of 4 August 1853 with Bremen and of 12 June 1857 with Hamburg provided for use of the "British" progression, which allowed no triple rate. On 23 August 1860, identical additional articles to both of these conventions were signed at Washington, providing that the progression be one rate for every half ounce, or fraction of a half ounce.[84]

As has been previously mentioned, the progression used on letters between the United States and Great Britain after 15 March 1849 was also the British progression, which allowed no triple rate. In 1864 the British Post Office began to adopt the progression of one rate for every half ounce, or fraction of a half ounce, on mail between certain of its colonies and some foreign countries and the United Kingdom. On 3 March 1866 a British treasury warrant provided that on letters from the United Kingdom addressed to the United States (among other countries), the progression was to be one rate for every half ounce, or fraction of a half ounce, on and after 1 April 1866.[85] Simultaneously, the April 1866 issue of the *U.S. Mail and Post Office Assistant* announced the same progression for letters from the United States. Since the United States-British treaty of 15 December 1848 remained in force for only another twenty-one months, covers showing a triple rate, either from or to the United States, are very scarce.[86]

Figure 94 illustrates a triple-rate cover from the United States. This letter was posted in Philadelphia

---

[84] 16 *Statutes at Large* 956, 960.

[85] Hertslet, *Commercial Treaties*, vol. 12, p. 121.

[86] Stanley B. Ashbrook, *Special Service* 5: 29. Mr. Ashbrook considered triple rate covers to England rare.

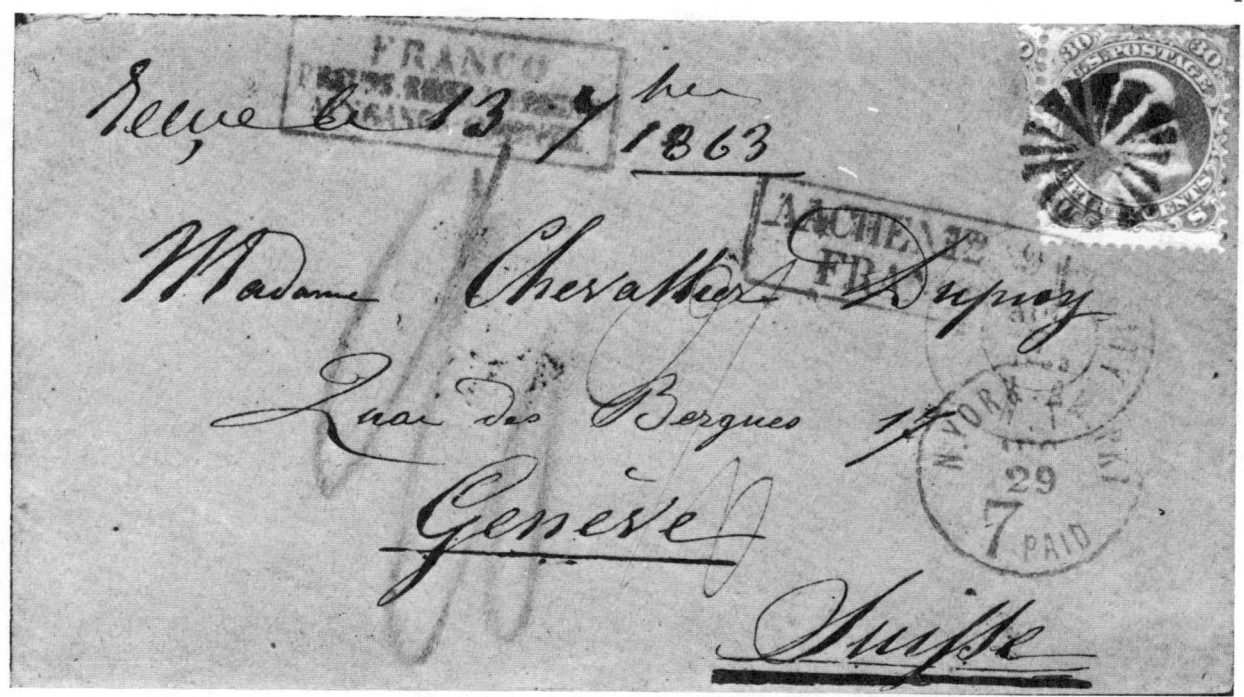

FIGURE 93.—COVER, from Virginia City, Nevada Territory, to Geneva, Switzerland, 1863.

FIGURE 94.—COVER, from Philadelphia to London, 1866. (*Photograph by Smithsonian*)

and passed through the Philadelphia exchange office on 8 June 1866 (the exchange office marking is indistinct, but the date is decipherable). It is prepaid 72¢ by a block of three 24¢ stamps (Scott's no. 78), for three times the 24¢ rate. The Philadelphia exchange office marked it *9/3* in red manuscript. The *9* in this marking indicates a credit of three times 3¢, the credit for a single rate by American packet. The *3* shows the number of rates. On 9 June 1866, the *City of London* of the Inman line sailed from New York for Liverpool as an American contract packet, and it is presumed she conveyed this letter to England. The London marking on the face shows that it arrived at that office on 21 June 1866.

Figure 95 illustrates a triple-rate cover from England to the United States. It was posted in Liverpool (466 in killer), prepaid three 1s. rates, and passed through the Liverpool Packet Letter Office on 11 July 1866, which is indicated by a circular (18-mm) 2C/LIVERPOOL/11 JY 66 P.L.O. marking on the reverse. The letter is endorsed "p City of Paris/via Queenstown," a ship of the Inman line under contract to the United States. The Liverpool office credited the United States with 63¢ (3 x 21), a proper credit for service by American packet. The cover bears a PAID in arc marking which is in brown and was apparently applied at New York.

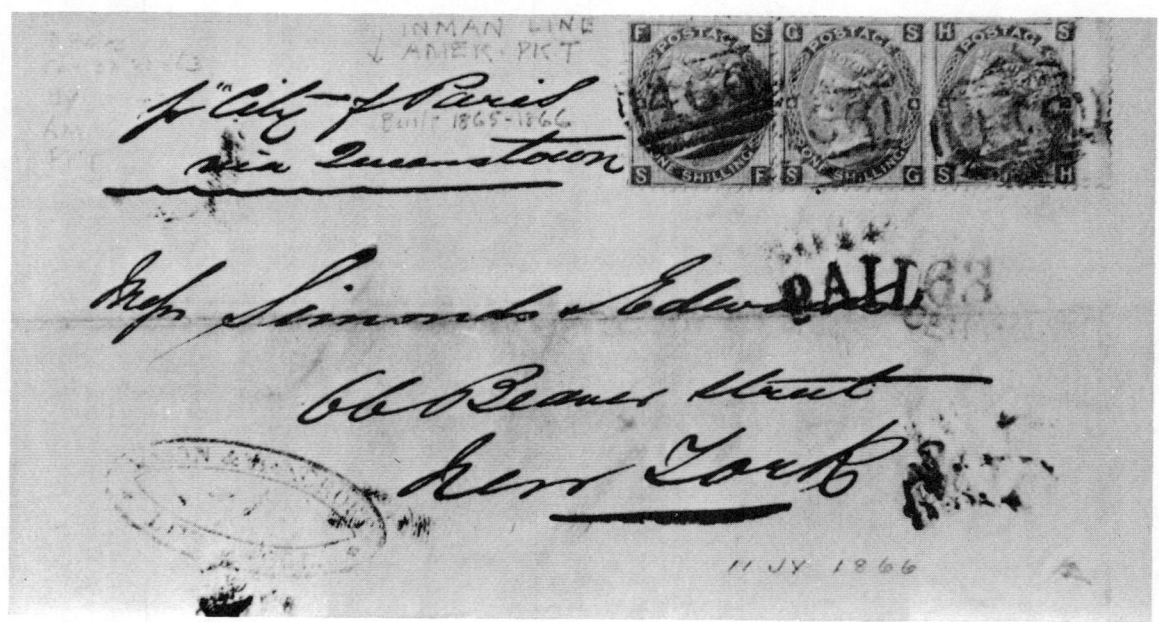

FIGURE 95.—COVER, from Liverpool to New York, 1866.

Chapter 8

Postal Conventions Effective After 1 January 1868

The Paris Conference

Sir: Many embarrassments to foreign correspondents exist in this, and probably in other postal departments, which can be remedied only by international concert of action. The difference in postal principles, as well as postal details or arrangement, in the several countries of both continents contributes to the result. Great diversity in rates prevails between the same points, in some instances as many as six different rates, according to the route of transit. Mistakes are perpetually recurring, arising from the complexity of present arrangements, and operate to serious delay and expense of correspondents. . . .

It is believed that a conference between fit representatives delegated by the several post departments of the principal corresponding countries of Europe and America, and to meet at some convenient point in Europe, would greatly facilitate the postal arrangements in which they are respectively interested. . . .

Thus did Postmaster General Montgomery Blair write to Secretary of State William H. Seward on 4 August 1862.[1] As a result of this letter a call for an international conference was issued, and on 11 May 1863, delegates from eighteen postal administrations assembled at Paris. After a general exchange of ideas and much deliberation, a list of thirty-one rules (or principles) was agreed upon.[2] Only those sections that relate to letter mail are here summarized:

2. Prepayment should be optional, but unpaid letters must bear a moderate additional charge.
3. Letters insufficiently prepaid by postal stamps must be rated as unpaid, deducting, however, the value of the stamps affixed.

6. Letters prepaid to destination shall not be charged with any additional rate whatever on delivery.
7, 8, and 9. The single rate upon international letters shall be applied to each standard weight of 15 grammes (metric system) or fractional part of it, to the exclusion of all other weight systems.
12. The weight stated by the despatching office must be accepted by the receiving office, except in case of manifest error.
16. The rates upon international letters should be the same, by whatever route the mails may be conveyed.
17. Where different routes exist, the sender may indicate the route desired on the address, or by the rate prepaid. In the absence of such indication the despatching office will determine the route most advantageous to the public interest.
18. Unpaid letters addressed to a country to which prepayment is compulsory, shall be returned as wrongly sent.
21. International post offices shall account to each other by the piece of letters in open mails, and by the net weight of correspondence in closed mails.
25. The transit charge should never be higher than one-half of the interior rate of the transit country, and for countries of small territorial extent this transit charge should be even less.
26. The cost of sea conveyance claimed by one country from another shall in no case be higher than the rate charged upon its own correspondence by the country by whose vessels the conveyance shall be effected.

"I deem it proper," said Postmaster General Blair, "in concluding my remarks on this subject [the Paris conference], to make known the fact that the public owes the suggestion to invite this international con-

[1] *Annual Report of the Postmaster General for 1862*, p. 165.
[2] Ibid., 1863, pp. 11–13.

ference to the Hon. John A. Kasson, who represented our government in it."[3] Although the letters relating to the call for an international conference bear Blair's signature, there can be little doubt that Kasson was the moving force in initiating it. He had been a first assistant postmaster general, and as a member of the American equivalent of the "permanent establishment" was intimately familiar with the problems related to foreign mails. Kasson remainded in Europe after the Paris conference closed and negotiated postal conventions with Belgium[4] and the new Kingdom of Italy,[5] neither of which were effective. In February 1867 it was learned through the State Department that the government of the French emperor, Napoleon III, was desirous of forming a new postal convention with the United States.[6] Kasson was again appointed a special commissioner of the Post Office Department and sent to Paris. Although he was unable to reach agreement with the French, he remained in Europe and negotiated new postal conventions with Great Britain,[7] the North German Union,[8] Belgium,[9] the Netherlands,[10] Switzerland,[11] and Italy.[12]

The New Postal Conventions Effective in 1868

In all of the new conventions of 1868 Kasson attempted to negotiate the principles adopted by the Paris conference. There was also an additional principle which was introduced for the first time: a recognition of the reciprocal nature of letter mail, which Postmaster General Alexander W. Randall expressed succinctly in his annual report for 1867: "the principle that every letter receives an answer, and that the labors of each office are substantially equal." Although each of these conventions had articles which were adapted to the peculiar conditions of the country with which the convention was negotiated, many of the articles were common to all. The common elements of these articles are here discussed as a unit, while those that were unique to particular conventions are considered separately.

In all of the conventions the United States adopted 15 grams (metric system) as the standard weight for a single-rate letter and a progression of one additional rate for each additional standard weight or fraction thereof. Before this provision could be included in these conventions, however, it was necessary that Congress pass a law authorizing the use of the metric system of weights in the United States, which it did on 28 July 1866.[13] Since the local post offices in the United States were not equipped to weigh in grams, all of these 15-gram rates were stated as rates per half ounce when they were published to postmasters and to the public. Because the half ounce weighs only 14.18 grams, a discrepancy in rating occurred between the local offices and the exchange offices which weighed in grams. For example, a letter that weighed 14.30 grams (over one half ounce) would have required a payment of two rates at a local office, but the exchange office, since the letter weighed less than 15 grams, could have forwarded it for a single rate. Thus, there was a built-in provision for overpayment of postage on marginal-weight letters, a condition that exists today. Except on letters to France after 1 January 1870 (which will be discussed later), this discrepancy caused no difficulty because all of the conventions provided that the weight stated by the dispatching office be accepted, except in the case of manifest mistake. Of all the countries with whom these conventions were made, only Great Britain refused to adopt a standard weight of 15 grams, steadfastly adhering to a single rate per half ounce.

Each country was to make its own arrangements for the dispatch of mail, and at its own cost pay for intermediate transportation. But the country that secured the best pecuniary arrangement was to pay for the service and be compensated by the other country. Sea postage was to belong to the dispatching country.

While none of the countries was willing, at that time, to go as far as to allow each country to retain the postage it collected, the reciprocal nature of letter mail was, nevertheless, recognized. All of the conventions provided that the postage on international mail be divided equally between the post offices of the two contracting countries, except in the conventions with Switzerland and the Netherlands, in which the division

---

[3] Ibid., p. 13.
[4] 16 *Statutes at Large* 918.
[5] Ibid., p. 1005.
[6] *Annual Report of the Postmaster General for 1868*, p. 18.
[7] 16 *Statutes-at-Large* 833.
[8] Ibid., 979.
[9] Ibid., 923.
[10] Ibid., 1063.
[11] Ibid., 1031.
[12] Ibid., 1009.

[13] Irving S. Kull, and Nell M., *An Encyclopedia of American History*, p. 231.

was three-fifths to the United States and two-fifths to the other country. Thus, debit and credit markings were no longer necessary on international letters. Such markings, however, continued to be used on transit letters.

In all cases prepayment was optional, but unpaid letters were subject to a fine per letter of 5¢ in the United States and of 2d. in Great Britain; 2 silbergroschen in the North German Union; 30 centesimi in Italy; 25 centimes in Switzerland; 30 centimes in Belgium; and 15 cents (Dutch) in the Netherlands. All fines were to be retained by the office collecting them. Insufficiently paid letters were subject to deficient postage as well as the unpaid-letter fine.

The United States-British Postal Conventions

On 25 June 1866,[14] the British Government served notice to the United States of its intention to terminate the postal convention of 15 December 1848 on 1 January 1868, simultaneously with the expiration of the mail subsidy contract with the Cunard line.[15] A new convention was completed and signed at London on 18 June 1867, the provisions relating to letter mail to become effective on 1 January 1868.[16]

Before this convention came into operation, however, the British, on 13 December 1867, served notice of their intention to terminate it on 31 December 1868.[17] This notice was accompanied by the announcement that the British Post Office would send Mr. Anthony Trollope to Washington in the spring of 1868 with full powers to negotiate a new convention.[18] The new convention was signed at London on 7 November and at Washington on 24 November 1868, and became fully effective on 1 January 1869.[19] It was agreed to consider a further reduction of the international rate at the expiration of twelve months from the date the convention came into operation.

Much of the second convention was a verbatim copy of the first, but the few changes made were significant. the convention of 18 June 1867 stated that the single international rate "shall not exceed 6d. in the United Kingdom, or 12 cents in the United States." This was changed to "shall be" 6d., or 12 cents. The convention made in 1867 held that "the charge for sea conveyance of letters across the Atlantic shall be computed on the basis of 4d., or 8 cents, per single letter rate." The convention made in 1868 provided that "the charge for sea conveyance of letters in closed mails across the Atlantic shall be computed at 20 cents per ounce, or per 30 grammes."

An anomalous situation, however, was created by Article XIV of the convention of 18 June 1867:

> The amount of postage chargeable by The United States Post Office, on its own account, upon every single letter sent through the United Kingdom in ordinary mails addressed to The United States, shall be 3 cents, and the amount chargeable by the British Post Office, on its own account, upon every single letter sent through The United States in ordinary mails addressed to the United Kingdom shall be 1d.

It is not clear what postage the above amounts represented. If it was intended to be inland postage, the United States would receive a credit of 3¢ on incoming letters, but would only retain 2¢ on outgoing letters. Regardless of how it was computed, the United States retained 10¢ as its share of the total postage on letters posted in the United States addressed to foreign countries and sent in transit through England. It is suspected that this amount was arrived at by subtracting the British postage of 1d. (2¢) from the 12¢ international rate. On letters posted in foreign countries addressed to the United States, via England, the British Post Office credited the United States with 3¢ per single rate.

The above arrangement was changed by Article XV of the convention of 7–24 November 1868 to the following:

> The British Post Office shall account to The United States' Post Office for the sum of two cents upon every single paid letter sent through the United Kingdom in ordinary mails addressed to The United States, and The United States' Post Office shall account to the British Post Office for the sum of 1d. upon every single paid letter sent through The United States in ordinary mails addressed to the United Kingdom.

After this convention became effective on 1 January 1869, the British Post Office credited the United States with only 2¢ per single rate. On outgoing letters, however, the United States continued to retain 10¢ as its share of the total postage. Only during the year of 1868, therefore, do incoming letters show a British credit to the United States of 3¢, and these are far from common.

---

[14] *Annual Report of the Postmaster General for 1866*, p. 6.
[15] Ibid.
[16] 16 *Statutes at Large* 837.
[17] *Annual Report of the Postmaster General for 1868*, p. 17.
[18] Ibid.
[19] 16 *Statutes at Large* 851.

Total rates were arrived at by adding to the 10¢ United States postage whatever postage was paid by the inhabitants of Great Britain on letters to or from a particular foreign country. Thus, on letters to or from those places to which the 6d. (12¢) "Colonial" rate prevailed, the total rate in the United States was 22¢ and in the foreign country, 11d (or its equivalent). The foreign postages (between Great Britain and particular destinations) were listed in a table appended to the detailed regulations.

The United States-North German Union Postal Convention

On 23 August 1866, the Treaty of Prague brought to a close the Seven Weeks' War between Prussia and Austria, Bavaria, Saxony, Hanover, and several other German states.[20] Victorious Prussia directly absorbed the duchies of the Elbe, Hanover, Electoral Hesse, the Grand Duchy of Hesse, Nassau, and Frankfort on-the-Main.[21] Early in 1867 a North German Confederation (Union) was formed through treaties made between Prussia and the remaining German states north of the Main. A federal constitution, primarily the work of Bismarck, established a federal council (Bundesrat), effectively controlled by Prussia, and a lower house (Reichstag), which shared the legislative function equally with the Bundesrat. The presidency was held by the King of Prussia, represented by a chancellor (Bismarck), who was responsible only to the King.[22] Prussia assumed control of the posts in the absorbed territories which had formed a large part of the Thurn and Taxis system. While this system had provided a unified postal service for Germany, and had avoided the problem of arranging such a service between the various states, the formation of the confederation made this function of the Thurn and Taxis posts no longer necessary. Additionally, these posts had been considered an infringement upon the sovereignty of the states they served. Prussia, therefore, negotiated with the Taxis family for a transfer of the whole system to Prussia for a money payment of three million marks.[23] The sum was voted by the Prussian legislature without debate, and on 1 July 1867 the Thurn and Taxis administration was amalgamated with the ordinary Prussian posts. The postal administrations of Prussia and the other states of the North German Union were then organized into the North German Postal District, in which uniform rates and services were established. This was achieved by a law passed on 4 November 1867, which became effective on 1 January 1868.[24]

When John A. Kasson entered into negotiations in 1867 for a postal convention between the United States and the North German Union, he negotiated with the Prussian Post Office which acted for the Union. The completed convention was signed at Berlin on 21 October 1867,[25] but the regulations were arranged with the new post office of the North German Union and were not signed until 30 June at Berlin and 22 July 1868 at Washington.[26] Because the United States, in maintaining its postal communication with Europe, placed great reliance upon the German steamship lines, this convention was fully as important to the Post Office Department as were those held with the British.

In addition to the provisions held in common with the other conventions, which have already been discussed, there were articles which were unique to this convention, or were related to transit mails which have not previously been considered. These may be summarized as follows:

Exchange offices in the United States were established at New York, Boston, Philadelphia, and Chicago; and in the North German Union at Bremen, Hamburg, and the Travelling Post-Office No. 10, between Cologne and Verviers, which was to correspond only with New York, via England and Belgium. Bremen and Hamburg were to correspond with all of the United States offices.

The international rates for single letters of 15 grams were:

Direct, between Bremen or Hamburg and the United States:
On letters from the United States, 10 cents
On letters from Germany, 4 silbergroschen
Closed mail, via England:
On letters from the United States, 15 cents
On letters from Germany, 6 silbergroschen

All of the conventions, except that with the British, provided the same procedure for setting the rates on open-mail letters. In this convention it is stated in Article XII:

Such letters [open-mail letters] were to be charged with the direct international rate, augmented by the postage

---

[20] William L. Langer, *An Encyclopedia of World History*, p. 686.
[21] A. D. Smith, *The Development of Rates of Postage*, pp. 354–55.
[22] Langer, *World History*, p. 686.
[23] Smith, *Rates of Postage*, p. 355.

[24] Ibid.
[25] *16 Statutes at Large* 979–982.
[26] Ibid. 984–985.

due to foreign countries, and by any other tax for exterior service.

Thus the international rate was basic to all open-mail rates, the postage between the North German Union and the particular foreign country merely being added to it. The international postage was retained by the dispatching office, and finally accounted for by dividing the total collected in both countries equally between the two post offices. On letters posted in the United States, the North German Union was given credit for the foreign postage. Appended to the regulations was a table which set forth the amount of the foreign postage (in silbergroschen) to be paid by the United States to the North German Union on letters addressed to a number of destinations. The regulations also provided that credits were to be made, on prepaid letters, in the currency of the dispatching country, and in doing so the cent (U.S.) was to be considered as equivalent to five pfennige (German).

The total rates on letters sent in closed mails, via England, were also arrived at by adding to the 15¢ international rate the postage beyond the North German Union. In the *U.S. Mail and Post Office Assistant* tables of postages to foreign countries, these rates are shown for the particular countries as "via North German Union, direct," and "via North German Union, closed mail, via England." In each case the latter rate was 5¢ higher than the former.

The regulations provided that letters be marked to show the office of origin. Correspondence fully paid to destination was to be marked PAID ALL in the United States, and FRANCO in the North German Union. All of the conventions, except that with the British, provided for the marking of prepaid letters with PAID ALL. Correspondence insufficiently paid was to be marked INSUFFICIENTLY PAID in the United States, and UNZUREICHEND FRANKIRT in the North German Union. The amount of deficient postage was to be expressed in black figures on the face in the currency of the receiving office. The treatment prescribed by the regulations for insufficiently paid transit letters differed from that to be used on international letters. Insufficiently paid transit letters were to be sent as wholly unpaid, partial payments not being recognized. But if one or more full rates were prepaid, the number of rates fully prepaid was to be recognized.

The exchange offices were to mark in red ink in the upper part of the address of prepaid letters sent in transit in the open mail the amount of postage due to the foreign office of destination, and in black ink on unpaid transit letters the amount of postage due to the office of origin. Although this procedure was prescribed only for open-mail letters, covers indicate that it was also used on letters sent in closed mails, via England.

While it was not prescribed by the regulations, the exchange offices customarily placed their mark upon letters when they were received. Until 1 July 1870, letters sent from the United States in closed mail, via England, bear the marking of the travelling post office, Verviers to Cologne. This marking was inscribed (in four straight lines) VERVIERS, B./[date]III/COELN/FRANCO and was applied in red to prepaid letters. A similar marking without FRANCO was applied in blue to unpaid or insufficiently paid letters. The Hamburg office used rectangular boxed markings of at least two types inscribed HAMBURG/[date]/FRANCO applied in red. The Bremen office also used a boxed marking inscribed BREMEN/[date]/FRANCO which was applied in purple until early 1869, and thereafter in red. The United States offices applied to incoming North German Union mail a variety of circular markings inscribed with the name of the office, the date, and PAID ALL OR PAID.

To prepaid letters dispatched by the New York office to the travelling office, Verviers to Cologne, a circular marking inscribed NEW YORK PAID ALL/[date]/BR. TRANSIT was applied in red. Letters sent to the offices of Bremen or Hamburg bear circular markings showing the United States exchange office, the date, and PAID ALL. Those from the New York and Boston offices are also inscribed DIRECT.

Although the United States offices marked prepaid transit letters with the amount of credit to the North German Union for the foreign postage in United States cents, the German offices also marked the letters with the same amount in silbergroschen. These German markings are usually preceded by the letter *f*, abbreviating *franco* (meaning "paid") or by *Wfr*, abbreviating *weiterfranco* (literally meaning "paid beyond").

Rates and Special Provisions of the Other Conventions Effective in 1868

The conventions with Belgium, the Netherlands, Switzerland, and Italy provided that the single rate of postage on direct correspondence exchanged between the two administrations be 15¢ in the United

States on prepaid letters. The corresponding rates in the other countries were: Belgium, 80 centimes; the Netherlands, 40 cents (Dutch); Switzerland, 80 centimes; and Italy, 80 centesimi. In relation to these rates, the conventions speak of *direct* correspondence. Formerly, the term "direct" referred to mail conveyed by direct steamer between New York and a European port without passing through England. The term "direct" as here used takes on a new meaning. The tables of postages to foreign countries included in the *U.S. Mail and Post Office Assistant* for January 1868 show the rates to Belgium and the Netherlands as follows:

Belgium *15
Netherlands *15

* Indicates optional prepayment, and rates are for letters not exceeding one-half ounce in weight.

While the Belgian and Netherlands conventions became effective on 1 January 1868, the conventions with Switzerland and Italy did not come into operation until 1 April 1868. The table of postages of the June issue [27] lists, among others, the convention rates, as follows:

Italy (direct closed mail via England)_____ *15 *l*
Switzerland (direct closed mail via England)_ *15 *l*
(*Optional prepayment.)

(*l* indicates a fine on unpaid or insufficiently paid letters.)

According to the previous terminology, "direct closed mail via England" is a contradiction. It now meant that the bags were closed in the United States and were conveyed in closed condition through England and the other intermediate countries until they reached their destination in Switzerland or Italy. In regard to mail for Belgium and the Netherlands, that, too, was sent in closed bags directly to the corresponding exchange office in Belgium or the Netherlands.

Articles Relating Only to United States-Belgian Mail

Exchange offices in the United States were established at New York and Boston; and in Belgium at Antwerp, Ostend (travelling office), and Ostend (local office). A table appended to the detailed regulations, however, provided that New York and Boston correspond only with the offices at Antwerp and Ostend (travelling office). The exchange of mails was to be effected by means of the steamship lines plying between Liverpool and New York, Bremen and New York by Southampton, Hamburg and New York by Southampton, and by Canadian packets. While the convention allowed either country to select its route for the dispatch of mail, these regulations limited the choice to specific lines, all of which conveyed mail via England.

While Article V set the single rate on prepaid letters from the United States at 15¢ and on prepaid letters from Belgium at 80 centimes, Article VI provided:

> Whenever there shall be established a direct line of steam communication between the ports of the United States and Belgium . . . it is agreed that the international single letter rate applicable to this route shall be reduced to 10 cents in the United States and 50 centimes in Belgium.

After the Ruger Brothers abandoned the run to Antwerp in 1866, only *City of Cork* and *Kangaroo* of the Inman line were plying between Antwerp and New York. The steamship lines listed in the annual reports of the postmaster general do not show service to Antwerp by the Inman line, nor do the tables of postages to foreign countries of the *U.S. Mail and Post Office Assistant* show a 10¢ direct rate to Belgium. It is not known, however, whether Belgium dispatched mail to the United States by this line.

Exchange Offices Established by the Other Conventions

Under the convention with the Netherlands, exchange offices were established at New York and Boston in the United States, and at Moerdyke (travelling office) in the Netherlands.

The convention with Switzerland established an exchange office at New York in the United States, and at Basle and at "Geneva (when the Swiss Confederation shall find it expedient)."

The United States-Italian convention of 8 November 1867 established an exchange office in the United States at New York and in Italy at (1) Susa—travelling office, (2) Camerlata—travelling office, and (3) Arona—travelling office. The United States-Italian convention of 8 July 1863, which did not become effective, had established these same offices for Italy, but

---

[27] On the tables for April and May the mail services are listed, but the figures for the rates, obviously through error, are omitted.

had been more explicit regarding the mails which were routed through them: [28]

> First, the travelling office from Turin to Susa, when transit is by way of France and England
>
> Second, the travelling office from Milan to Camerlata, or the travelling office from Arona to Magadino, when transit is by way of Germany and Switzerland.

Later Modifications in the Conventions

Great Britain

As had been agreed, the United States and British post offices considered a further reduction of the international rate during 1869. Additional articles to the convention of 7–24 November 1868 were signed at Washington on 3 December and at London on 14 December 1869.[29] These articles reduced the international rate to 3d. per half ounce in the United Kingdom, and to 6¢ per 15 grams in the United States. The fine for insufficiently paid and unpaid letters was set at 3d. in Great Britain and at 6¢ in the United States. Sea postage was to be computed at 6¢ per ounce or per 30 grams. Although sea postage was computed on the weight of mail, Postmaster General Creswell in his annual report for 1870 stated that the rate was divided, "2 cents being designated as sea postage, and 2 cents the inland postage of each country."

Although these articles mention only the international rate, the postage on transit letters was also affected. The United States now retained 2¢ inland postage as well as 2¢ sea postage on each single letter it dispatched in British mails. Thus, its share of the total postage on a transit letter sent under this convention was reduced from 10¢ to 4¢, resulting in a reduction of 6¢ per single rate in the postage of all such letters.

While the act of 14 June 1858 had required that the postmaster general pay the steamship lines the postage accruing on mails conveyed (paying American ships the sea and inland postages, and foreign ships the sea postage only), an act of 3 March 1865 [30] had allowed him to make contracts for amounts not exceeding these postages. As a result, he had contracted with some lines for less than the postage accruing on the mails they conveyed. When the above additional articles became effective on 1 January 1870, the postmaster general could pay the lines no more than 6¢ per an ounce or per 30 grams for the letters they conveyed. The Cunard, North German Lloyd, the Hamburg-American, and the Inman lines refused to transport the American mails for the reduced sea postage.[31] The Allan line appears to have continued to carry British mails, but from New York or Boston the dispatch of mails to Great Britain ceased. The requirement that each country make its own arrangements and pay for the dispatch of its mails rested upon the assumption that each country would provide about the same amount of service. The failure of the United States to render service angered the British. Questions were put to the British postmaster general in the House of Commons: [32]

> Mr. Bains said he would beg to ask the Postmaster General, If he has received any reply from the Postmaster General of the United States, in regard to the more speedy conveyance of the mails from America?
>
> The Marquess of Hartington replied that he had received an answer from the Postmaster General of the United States; but he was sorry to say it held out no hopes of an acceleration in the transmission of the mails from America as long as the packet companies refused to accept the remuneration which he was empowered by law to offer.

The stalemate was broken by the Liverpool and Great Western Steamship Company, Limited (called the Guion line), which signed a contract with the United States postmaster general on 23 February 1870 for a weekly service, sailing from New York on Wednesdays for Queenstown and Liverpool.[33] With this breaking of the ice, both the North German Lloyd and the Hamburg-American lines signed a contract with the postmaster general on 15 April 1870.[34] The North German Lloyd was to convey mails from New York on Saturdays for Southampton and Bremen, while the Hamburg-American line would sail on Tuesdays for the ports of Plymouth, Cherbourg, and Hamburg. Thus, the American packet service to England was partially, if inadequately, restored.

North German Union

On 7 April at Washington and on 23 April 1870 at Berlin, additional articles to the United States-North German Union convention of 21 October 1867 were signed.[35] The preamble explains that these articles

---

[28] 16 *Statutes at Large* 1005.
[29] Ibid. 869.
[30] 13 *Statutes at Large* 506.
[31] *Annual report of the Postmaster General for 1870*, p. 17.
[32] *Hansard's Parliamentary Debates*, vol. 201, p. 631.
[33] *Annual Report of the Postmaster General for 1870*, appendix, p. 147.
[34] Ibid., pp. 149–150.
[35] 16 *Statutes at Large*, p. 1003.

were concluded because the additional convention between the United States and Great Britain had reduced the closed-mail sea rate to 6¢ per ounce or per 30 grams, and subsequently the steamship lines running between New York and Bremen and Hamburg had agreed to reduce their compensation for direct conveyance of mails between those ports. The articles are summarized as follows:

I. Provided for reduced single-letter rates, as follows:
   A. In direct exchange via Bremen or Hamburg
      1. For letters from the North German Union
         a. When prepaid in Germany, 3 silbergroschen
         b. When paid in the United States, 14 cents
      2. For letters from the United States
         a. When prepaid in America, 7 cents
         b. When paid in Germany, 6 silbergroschen
I. B. In direct exchange in closed transit through England
      1. For letters from the North German Union
         a. When pepaid in Germany, 4 silbergroschen
         b. When paid in the United States, 20 cents
      2. For letters from the United States
         a. When prepaid in America, 10 cents
         b. When paid in Germany, 8 silbergroschen
II. Provided that insufficiently paid letters be charged with the postage of unpaid letters, after deduction of the amount prepaid.
IV. Provided that the amounts of foreign postage on letters in open transit be accounted for at full rates.
V. Provided that these additional articles be placed in operation on 1 July 1870.

The Franco-Prussian War played havoc with the German steamship service between New York and Europe. Although France did not declare war on Prussia until 19 July, the decision for war was made on 15 July 1870.[36] While France had a large navy, the German states had none worth mentioning. Danger of the German ships being captured while at sea led the North German Lloyd and the Hamburg-American lines to hold their ships in the neutral ports of Southampton and New York and to cease operations. The following notice appeared in the August 1870 issue of the *U.S. Mail and Post Office Assistant*:

Mails for Germany—Important Notice to Postmasters and the Public.
Post Office Department, Office of Foreign Mails.
July 23, 1870.

The direct line of German steamers heretofore plying between New York and Bremen and Hamburg, respectively, having suspended their trips to those ports, in consequence of the Franco-Prussian War, the reduced rates of postage chargeable under the existing Postal Convention with North Germany on letters and other correspondence for the North German Union and countries beyond, forwarded by the direct route are, for the present, inoperative.

All correspondence for North Germany will, consequently, until direct steamship service is resumed, be forwarded by closed mail via England, subject to the rates of international postage established for that route of transmission, viz.:

For letters, 10 cents per each ½ oz. or under, prepayment optional. . . .

Letters insufficiently paid at the above rates will be charged on delivery with the postage for unpaid letters, after deduction of the amount prepaid.

Although the above notice is dated 23 July 1870, the German lines stopped operating at an earlier date. On 28 September 1870, Postmaster General Creswell abrogated the contract with the North German Lloyd in order to make a two-year contract with the Inman line for a weekly service to Queenstown and Liverpool from New York on Saturdays, beginning on 1 October 1870. The order abrogating the contract with the North German Lloyd is illuminating:[37]

Whereas the North German Lloyd of Bremen . . . have withdrawn their steamships . . . and failed, since the 9th of July, 1870, to perform any of the weekly trips from New York to Southampton and Bremen.

The preceding indicates that the last sailing before the war by the North German Lloyd was on 9 July 1870. The next sailing by this line was scheduled for 16 July, and by that time war, although not yet declared, had become a certainty. Undoubtedly, the North German Lloyd management cabled their New York office to hold the ships in port. Only two trips, therefore, were made by the North German Lloyd after the 7¢ direct rate became effective on 1 July 1870, that is, on 2 July and 9 July 1870, before service was suspended. The Hamburg-American line, after 1 July 1870 had sailings scheduled on 5, 12, and 19 July, the first two of which were probably made, and possibly the last. No more than three trips, therefore, were made by this line upon which letters prepaid at the 7¢ direct rate could have been conveyed before the line suspended operations. In total, there were only five trips (or fewer) upon which letters prepaid with the 7¢ direct rate could have been conveyed before operations were suspended. This may account for the scarcity of covers prepaid with the 7¢ direct rate and used during July 1870.

In October 1870 the North German Lloyd decided it might be safe to send its ships from Bremen around the north of Scotland and thence to New York. The

---

[36] Langer, *World History,* p. 688.

[37] *Annual Report of the Postmaster General for 1870,* appendix, p. 152.

November 1870 issue of the *U.S. Mail and Post Office Assistant* carried the following notice:

> Resumption of Direct North German Union Mail Route, October 29, 1870.
>
> This department having been advised that the steamers of the North German Lloyd Company have resumed their regular departures from New York to Bremen, direct mails for Germany will hereafter be made up and dispatched by the steamers of that company sailing from New York on Saturdays direct.

Thus, the 7¢ direct rate was revived. Sailings around Scotland, however, were irregular, and after the wreck of *Union* near Rattray Head on 28 November 1870 they were virtually abandoned. Normal service was restored in February 1871.[38]

The Baltischer Lloyd (Baltic Lloyd) was founded in Stettin during 1870 with the intention of establishing a regular passenger and cargo service between Stettin and New York.[39] On 31 March at Washington and on 14 May 1871 at Berlin, an additional article to the United States-North German Union convention of 21 October 1867 was signed.[40] The preamble states:

> As a regular steamship line between a port of Germany and a port of the United States of America can be employed for the transportation of the German-American mails ...

There then followed:

Sole Article

The single rate on correspondence exchanged directly between the two administrations by means of such steamship line shall be as follows, viz.:—
1. For letters from Germany to the United States
   a. When prepaid in Germany, 2½ silbergroschen
   b. When paid in the United States, 12 cents
2. For letters from the United States to Germany
   a. when prepaid in the United States, 6 cents
   b. When paid in Germany, 5 silbergroschen

This additional article takes effect on the date of the dispatch of the first mail by such steamship line, and from that date forward has the same duration as the convention of the 21st October, 1867, and the additional convention of 7–23 April, 1870.

It should be noted that this article did not supersede, but was to operate concurrently with, the additional articles of 7–23 April 1870, which had established the 7¢ direct rate. The July issue of the *U.S. Mail and Post Office Assistant* contained the following announcement:

> Important arrangement, establishing a direct exchange of mails with Germany by the Baltic Lloyd mail steamships, via Stettin, of a reduced rate of letter postage. June 21, 1871.
>
> An additional article to the Postal Convention between the United States and the Empire of Germany has recently been concluded, *to take effect immediately,* which establishes a reduced international postage charge of six (6) cents per single rate on the direct correspondence exchanged with Germany, Austria, and Luxemburg by means of steamers of the Baltic Lloyd Line, plying between New York and Stettin ...
>
> The departure from New York of the steamers of the Baltic Lloyd Line will be so arranged as to perform at least a monthly mail service in each direction. The sailing days from New York, as far as reported, are as follows, viz.: July 12, August 10, August 31, September 28, October 19, and November 16, 1871. Further days of sailing from this side will from time to time be published for the information of the public.

The tables of postages to foreign countries published in the July and August issues of the *U.S. Mail and Post Office Assistant* (the author has not seen the September issue) show the following rates:

Austria, via North German Union direct ...	*7
do. do. closed mail, via England	*10
do. do. via Stettin, once a month ...	*6

(*Optional prepayment.)

Identical rates are listed for the German states. These tables indicate that the 7¢ and a 6¢ direct rate to Germany were in force at the same time.

In his annual report for 1871 Postmaster General Creswell said:

> An additional article to the postal convention between the United States and Germany was signed at Washington March 3, and at Berlin on May 14, 1871, reducing the postage on direct letter mails between the two countries, a copy of which is annexed. Arrangements have also been concluded with the German postal administration, and carried into operation on the 1st of October, 1871, further reducing the postage charge for prepaid letters between the United States and Germany transmitted by closed mail via England from 10 to 7 cents per single rate, and also the postage charges for prepaid letters by the direct routes *via* Bremen and Hamburg, respectively, from 7 to 6 cents per single rate.

Duly, the table of postages to foreign countries published in the October 1871 issue of the *U.S. Mail*

---

[38] N. R. P. Bonsor, *North Atlantic Seaway,* p. 169.
[39] Ibid., p. 275.
[40] 17 *Statutes-at-Large,* 859.

and Post Office Assistant shows rates for Austria as well as for the German states as follows:

Austria, via North German Union, direct			*6
do.	do.	closed mail via England	*7
do.	do.	via Stettin, once a month	*6

(*Optional prepayment.)

To summarize the situation just described, regarding the rates between the United States and the German states: On 1 July 1870, the single-letter rate for North German Union closed mail via England became 10¢. Also on the same date, the direct rate by North German Lloyd and Hamburg-American steamers became 7¢. Although the direct rate was inoperative during the Franco-Prussian War, no change was made in this rate until 1 October 1871. With the sailing on 12 July 1871 from New York of either *Franklin* or *Humboldt* of the Baltic Lloyd, the direct rate by steamers of that line became 6¢ per single rate.[41] Between 12 July and 1 October 1871 there were concurrently available a 7¢ and a 6¢ direct rate to Germany. From 1 October 1871 to 1 July 1875 the direct rate by any steamship line was 6¢, and the closed mail rate via England was 7¢.

Change in the United States-Italian Convention

On 16 January at Florence and on 8 February 1870 at Washington additional articles to the United States-Italian convention of 8 November 1867 were signed.[42] The single rate of postage was reduced to 10¢ in the United States and to 55 centesimi in Italy. Sea postage for closed mails conveyed across the Atlantic was to be paid to the United States at the rate of 6¢ per ounce or per 30 grams. Since this was the reduced rate included in the United States-British convention of 3–14 December 1869, it is thus indicated that direct closed mails for Italy were to be sent via England. These articles became effective on 15 February 1870.

Change in the United States-Swiss Convention

Additional articles to the United States-Swiss convention of 11 October 1867 were signed at Berne on 7 February and at Washington on 13 April 1870.[43] The single-letter rate of postage was reduced to 10¢ in the United States and to 50 centimes in Switzerland. Transatlantic sea postage for closed mails was set at 6¢ per ounce or per 30 grams. At the time the articles were signed, this sea rate applied only to mail via England, but after 1 July 1870 the same rate applied also to mail via the North German Union. Several types of markings on Swiss convention mail show service via England and Ostend, which indicates the mail was routed from England to Ostend, and thence through Germany to the Basle office. Some mail for Italy also took this route. The articles came into operation on 1 May 1870.

Changes in the United States-Belgian Convention

On 1 March 1870, additional articles to the convention of 21 August 1867 were signed at Washington.[44] These articles, which became effective on 15 March 1870, reduced the rate on prepaid letters from the United States to 10¢ and on prepaid letters from Belgium to 50 centimes. Transatlantic sea postage was reduced to 6¢ per ounce or per 30 grams, which the United States paid on all mail via Great Britain, Belgium repaying the United States for mail which it dispatched.

On 9 May 1873, a second group of additional articles to the convention of 21 August 1870 was signed at Washington.[45] These articles reduced the rate on direct mails, via England, to 40 centimes for prepaid letters from Belgium and to 8¢ on prepaid letters from the United States. Rates by direct steamship plying between the United States and Belgium of 6¢ in the United States and of 30 centimes in Belgium were also provided. Article III held that when the two administrations considered it advisable to exchange closed mails with foreign countries by direct packets plying between the two countries, the maritime rate was to be 3¢ (15 centimes) per 30 grams for letters. These articles became effective on 1 July 1873.

In 1872 the White Cross line began to ply between New York and Belgium.[46] The annual reports of the postmaster general listed the packet lines by which the United States mails were dispatched. None of these show that mail was carried by this line. On 19 January

---

[41] Bonsor, *North Atlantic Seaway*, p. 275. The first 2 ships of the fleet were *Franklin* and *Humboldt;* subsequently added: *Thorwaldsen, Ernst Moritz Arndt,* and *Washington.*

[42] 16 *Statutes at Large* 1029.

[43] *Ibid.* 1061.

[44] Ibid. 951.

[45] 18 *Statutes at Large* 795.

[46] Bonsor, *North Atlantic Seaway,* pp. 276–268.

1873, *Vaderland* of the Red Star line opened a service between Antwerp and Philadelphia.[47] While the annual report of the postmaster general for 1873 does not list this line among the mail carriers, the report for 1874 shows that the Red Star line made fourteen trips from Philadelphia to Belgium, and the value of the sea postage on the mails conveyed amounted to $17.74. In the report for 1875 the line is listed as also having made fourteen trips, but the value of the sea postage increased to $42.51. It is, therefore, not strange that this author has not seen a cover prepaid 6¢ in the United States, addressed to Belgium.

Changes in the United States-Netherlands Convention

Additional articles to the United States-Netherlands convention of 26 September 1867, similar to those made with Belgium, were signed at The Hague on 10 January and at Washington on 29 January 1870. They set a single rate of 10¢ on prepaid letters from the United States, and of 25 cents (Dutch) on letters from the Netherlands. A second group of additional articles was signed at The Hague on 19 June and at Washington on 14 September 1874.[48] The preamble stated:

> Whereas a regular line of direct steamers is soon to be established between the port of New York and the port of Rotterdam, which can be employed for the transportation of Netherlands-American mails, at a compensation for sea conveyance between the two frontiers not to exceed 5 cents (Dutch), or 2 cents (United States), for each single letter:
> Now, therefore, the undersigned . . . have agreed upon the following additional article. . . .

This article established a single-letter rate of 6¢ (U.S.) on letters from the United States and of 15 cents (Dutch) on letters from the Netherlands, when conveyed directly by steamers of the before-mentioned line.

The line referred to was the Netherlands-American Steam-Navigation Company, called the Holland America line.[49] The annual report of the postmaster general for 1874 does not list this line among the mail carriers, but the report for 1875 shows that it made four trips, and the value of the sea postage on mail conveyed amounted to $86.80.

The United States-Danish Convention

A United States-Danish postal convention was signed at Copenhagen on 7 November and at Washington on 1 December 1871.[50] In its letter-mail arrangements it was similar to that between the United States and the North German Union, hence only the points of difference will be discussed.

The preamble stated that the two post offices had agreed upon an exchange of mails by employing the steamers in regular service between their territories, as well as those running between Bremen or Hamburg and American ports.[51] Each office was to retain the postage it collected, and no accounts were to be kept for international correspondence. Closed mails to or from Sweden and Norway were provided for at a rate of 4 skilling rigsmont per 30 grams of letters.

The international rate for single letters of 15 grams was set at 12 skilling rigsmont in Denmark or at 7¢ in the United States. Insufficiently paid letters were subject to the deficient postage and a fine of 6 skilling in Denmark or of 4¢ in the United States. These fines also applied to unpaid letters.

The detailed regulations established exchange offices at New York and Chicago in the United States, and at Copenhagen and the travelling office between Korsör and Kiel in Denmark.[52] Letters fully paid to destination were to be marked PAID ALL in the United States and FRANKO in Denmark. Insufficiently paid letters were to be so marked in the United States and UTILSRAEKKELIG FRANKERET in Denmark. Letters dispatched by the direct line were to be marked DIRECT SERVICE, or SERVICE DIRECT, while those dispatched via Germany were to be so stamped as to indicate German transit.

The United States cent was equated to $1\frac{4}{5}$ skilling of Denmark, but on 1 January 1875 Denmark changed its unit of currency from the dollar, which had been equal to 96 skilling, to the crown, equal to 100 öre. Additional articles to the convention altered the Danish rates to conform with this currency change.[53] The international rate, which had been 12 skilling, now became 25 öre. The fine on insufficiently paid or unpaid letters was changed from 6 skilling to 12 öre, and the United States cent was now held to be worth $3\frac{3}{4}$ öre.

---

[47] Ibid., pp. 284–293.
[48] 18 *Statutes at Large* 831.
[49] Bonsor, *North Atlantic Seaway*, p. 294.
[50] 17 *Statutes at Large* 903.
[51] The American ports at that time were New York, Baltimore, and New Orleans.
[52] 17 *Statutes at Large* 908–911.
[53] 18 *Statutes at Large* 832.

The convention was to come into operation on a date to be agreed upon between the two office, and according to Postmaster General Creswell it became effective on 1 January 1872.[54]

The Convention Between the United States, Sweden, and Norway

On 15 March 1873, the United States signed a postal convention with the kingdoms of Sweden and Norway.[55] Although each had its own constitution and its own postal administration, Norway was united with Sweden under the same king, at that time, Oscar II. Arrangements for the exchange of mails were similar to those of the United States-North German Union convention of 21 October 1867. The rates of postage were as follows:

I. For a single letter of 15 grams:
  A. By closed mail via England, regardless of the route between England and Sweden or Norway
    1. For letters from Sweden for the United States
       a. When prepaid in Sweden, 36 öre
       b. When paid in the United States, 14 cents
    2. For letters from the United States for Sweden
       a. When prepaid in the United States, 9 cents
       b. When paid in Sweden, 56 öre
    3. For letters from Norway to the United States
       a. When prepaid in Norway, 12 skilling
       b. When paid in the United, States 15 cents
    4. For letters from the United States for Norway
       a. When prepaid in the United States, 10 cents
       b. When paid in Norway, 18 skilling
  B. By direct steamship between ports of the United States and Swedish or Norwegian ports
    1. For letters from Sweden for the United States
       a. When prepaid in Sweden, 24 öre
       b. When paid in the United States, 9 cents
    2. For letters from the United States for Sweden
       a. When prepaid in the United States, 6 cents
       b. When paid in Sweden, 36 öre
    3. For letters from Norway for the United States
       a. When prepaid in Norway, 7 skilling
       b. When paid in the United States, 9 cents
    4. For letters from the United States for Norway
       a. When prepaid in the United States, 6 cents
       b. When paid in Norway, 10 skilling
II. Insufficiently prepaid letters were to be charged with the postage of unpaid letters, after deducting the prepaid amount.

The detailed regulations required that letters prepaid to destination be marked PAID ALL in the United States and FRANKO in Sweden.[56] Insufficiently paid letters were to be so marked in the United States, and OFULLSTANDIG FRANKERAD in Sweden, and the amount of deficient postage was to be marked in black ink on the face. Letters dispatched by direct steamers were to be marked DIRECT SERVICE, or SERVICE DIRECT. Letters dispatched via England, or via Germany and Denmark, were to be stamped to indicate British, or German and Danish, transit. The convention was to come into operation on 1 July 1873.

The tables of postages to foreign countries published in the *U.S. Mail and Post Office Assistant* show that a 7¢ rate became available to Denmark for closed mail via Bremen or Hamburg on 1 January 1872. The rate, "via Stettin, once a month," however, was not reduced from 10¢ to 7¢ until some time between July and October 1872, and it remained at that amount until September 1874. The rate, via Stettin, to Norway was reduced from 10¢ to 6¢, prepayment compulsory, on 1 October 1871, and it remained at that level until some time between February and October 1872, when the tables discontinued the reporting of a via-Stettin rate to Norway. The convention rates to Norway of 10¢, via England, Bremen, or Hamburg, and of 6¢ by direct service (prepayment of both rates optional), were introduced in the table for July 1873, as were also the 9¢ via England, Bremen or Hamburg, and the 6¢ direct rates to Sweden. The via-Stettin, once-a-month rate to Sweden, however, continued to be reported at 10¢ until September 1874.

The reason for the introduction of a 6¢ rate, via Stettin, to Norway on 1 October 1871, and its discontinuance some time between February and October 1872 is not known. It is known, however, that a new direct line of steamships started to run between London, England, Bergen, Norway, and New York in 1871.[57] Its New York agents were evidently Funch, Edye and Company, who also handled the White Cross line to Belgium. The line, Norwegian owned, was officially known as the Norse American Line. The annual report of the Postmaster General for 1874 lists "Steamers of Funch, Edye & Co., for 5 trips from New York to Norway." This was for the fiscal year beginning 1 July 1873 and ending 30 June 1874. The value of the sea postage on all mail carried by the line during that year is reported at $13.01. The annual reports of the postmaster general for 1872 through 1875 disclose that the Baltic Lloyd did little

---

[54] *Annual Report of the Postmaster General for 1872*, p. 17.
[55] 18 *Statutes at Large* 762–767.
[56] Ibid. 767–770.
[57] Bonsor, *North Atlantic Seaway*, p. 271.

better. For the fiscal year ended 30 June 1872, the sea postage on all the mail it conveyed (letters, newspapers, etc.) amounted to $92.62; for the fiscal year ended 30 June 1873, $12.07; for 1874, nothing is reported, but for the fiscal year of 1875, the combined sea postage on letters sent and received amounted to $1.50.

According to Bonsor, the line abandoned its run to Norway in 1873, and ran between London, Havre, and New York until 1876, when its fleet was sold.[58]

The September 1874 edition of the *U.S. Mail and Post Office Assistant* contained the following announcement:

> *Mail for Sweden and Norway*
> The attention of postmasters and the public is called to the fact that there is at present no direct steamship communication between the United States and Sweden and Norway, and that correspondence mailed in the United States addressed to those countries can, therefore, only be forwarded in the closed mails by way of England and Germany.

Covers

Figure 96 illustrates a cover posted in New York, addressed to Berlin, and endorsed "p. Westphalia,"

---
[58] Ibid., p. 271.

a steamer of the Hamburg-American line which sailed from New York on Tuesday, 12 September 1871. The cover is prepaid 7¢ for direct service to Germany. While covers showing use of the 7¢ direct rate during July 1870 are rare, those showing use of this rate prior to 1 October 1871 are seldom seen. Many covers prepaid 7¢ and intended to be sent via England were sent by the direct route. Thus, covers showing a 7¢ prepayment and direct service markings after 1 October 1871 are 1¢ overpaid and are not scarce.

Figure 97 illustrates a cover posted in Washington, D.C., addressed to Contantinople. The schedule of foreign postages to be paid by the United States to the North German Union, appended to the regulations to the 21 October 1867 United States-North German Union convention, indicates the postage to be 2 silbergroschen. The convention makes no provision for these foreign postages to be expressed in United States currency. Two silbergroschen are equal to twenty-four pfennige, and at the agreed 5 pfennige to the United States cent, equal about 5¢. There were three parts to the total rate, that is, (1) the direct international rate, (2) the foreign postage, and (3) any other tax for exterior service. While this division is given for open-mail rates, the markings on covers indicate that it was also applied to closed mails. In this case, the rate was developed: 10¢ for the direct international

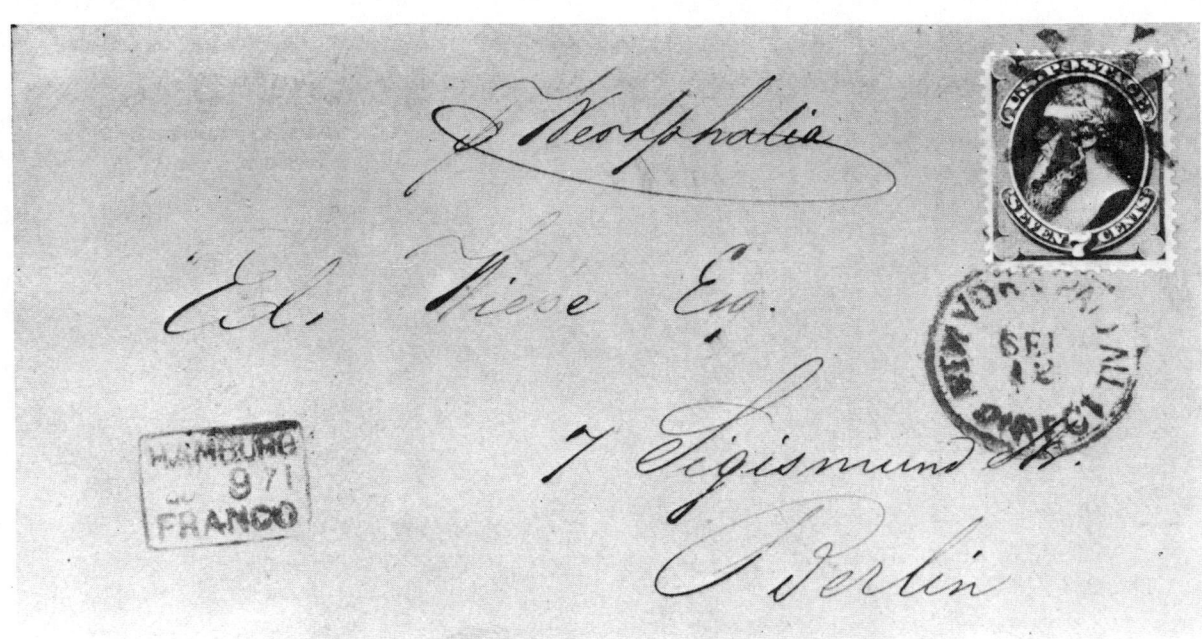

FIGURE 96.—COVER, from New York to Berlin, 1871. (*Melvin W. Schuh collection*)

FIGURE 97.—COVER, from Washington, D.C., to Constantinople, 1871.
(*Lester L. Downing collection*)

rate; 5¢ for foreign postage; and 5¢ for British transit, an exterior service. Thus, the cover is prepaid with 20¢ in stamps.

The cover was sent in closed mail to the office, Verviers–Cologne, and received the marking of that office, which also marked it in red crayon *f*2, and P.D. The 5 encircled on these covers is a mystery. On this cover, it could be a United States credit of 5¢. It has been noted, however, on covers at the 19¢ rate which were marked F1½. It has only been noted on covers that were sent via England, and covers by the direct route whose foreign postage was 2 silbergroschen do not show it. One is, therefore, led to suspect that it is a statement of the 5¢ charge for exterior British transit service. This marking and the Verviers–Cologne marking were not used after 1 July 1870.

Figure 98 illustrates a cover posted in Bishop Hill, Illinois, on 26 March 1868, addressed to Sweden. The cover is prepaid 16¢ for direct service by North German Union mail. The rate was divided: 10¢ international rate and 6¢ (2½ silbergroschen) foreign postage. Evidently there was no exterior service charge. The New York office simply marked it with a credit of 6¢. The Bremen office marked it with the characteristic boxed BREMEN/[date]/FRANCO marking, this time in purple. Also in purple is the boxed WEITERFR: 2½ SGR. marking, evidently applied at Bremen. This abbreviates *Weiterfranco* which literally means "paid beyond." There is a Swedish receiving mark on the reverse dated 16/4/1868.

Figure 99 illustrates a cover posted in Otsego, Wisconsin, on 10 August 1870, addressed to Norway. It is prepaid 15¢ for service by North German Union closed mail, via England. After 1 July 1870, the direct international rate was 7¢, the British transit 3¢, and the foreign postage 5¢ (2 silbergroschen). The New York office applied in red a NEW YORK/AUG/17/5 marking, indicating a credit of 5¢ for the foreign postage. A German office (perhaps Verviers–Cologne) marked it with WFRO 2 in red to indicate foreign postage of 2 silbergroschen. It was received in Christiania, Norway, on 5 September 1870.

Figure 100 illustrates another cover to Norway. It was posted in Woodstock (?) on 18 May 1873, addressed to Norway. It is prepaid 22¢ by a 10¢ and a 12¢ stamp of the 1870 issue (Nationals), affixed to a small mourning envelope. This was a double-rate letter, and the New York office marked lightly with a 2 in blue crayon at upper left. In May 1873 the North German Union closed-mail-via-England rate to Norway was 11¢, but the direct rate was 10¢. While this letter was prepaid to be sent via England, the New York office elected to send it by the direct route. By either route the foreign postage was the same: 1½

FIGURE 98.—COVER, from Bishop Hill, Ill., to Tyby, Söderhamn, Sweden, 1868.

FIGURE 99.—COVER, from Otsego, Wis., to Sogn, Norway, 1870.

FIGURE 100.—Cover, from Woodstock to Bergen [?], Norway, 1873.

silbergroschen (4¢) per single rate. Since this is a double-rate letter, the New York office marked it with a credit of 8¢. The 11¢ rate represented 6¢ direct international postage, 1¢ British transit, and 4¢ foreign postage, while the 10¢ rate comprised 6¢ direct international postage and 4¢ foreign. The Bremen office applied to the letter its boxed BREMEN/3/4 73/FRANCO marking in red and marked it in red crayon W*f* 3/ (2 x 1½ silbergroschen). It was received at Christiania on 7 April 1873. There are no markings on the reverse.

Figure 101 illustrates a cover addressed to Constantinople, Turkey. In 1774 the Treaty of Kainardji conceded to Austria a special service of overland messengers between Vienna and Pera.[59] Out of this grew a postal service administered by Austria through its many post offices established in Turkey. But Austria was not to hold a monopoly on this extraterritorial right. By the time Turkey signed the treaty of Berne in 1874, France, England, Russia, Germany, and Italy had also established post offices in Turkey.[60] Postmarks on covers indicate that as early as 1869 the North German Union had a post office in operation in Constantinople. This became a German post office after the formation of the German Empire in 1871. The Germans must have charged an internal postage in Constantinople equal to 1¢. This "tax for exterior service" was combined with the international rate, as were like charges on mail to other countries; it was accounted for by dividing the sum of all of these postages equally between the two offices. Thus, each country would retain an additional cent on mail to or from Constantinople. The United States, therefore, retained the direct international rate, plus 1¢ "exterior service" charge on direct North German Union letters to Constantinople, and also the British transit on closed mail, via England.

The cover illustrated in Figure 101 was posted in Cornwall-on-the-Hudson, New York, on 25 May 1872. It is prepaid with 12¢, which in May 1872 was the North German Union closed-mail rate, via England. The New York office marked it PAID ALL and credited Germany with 4¢ by marking the cover *4* in red crayon. The German office simply marked it W*fr*. meaning "paid beyond." On the reverse is a circular marking inscribed KAISEREICH DEUTSCHES POSTAMT which literally means "Imperial German Post Office." The rate was divided: 6¢ direct international rate, 1¢ British transit, and 1¢ for German postage in Constantinople, all of which was retained by the United States. To this 8¢ retention was added 4¢ foreign postage to arrive at the 12¢ rate.

Figure 102 illustrates a cover posted in Middleborough, Massachusetts, on 19 June (1874 or 1875), addressed to Constantinople and endorsed "via England." It is prepaid 11¢ by a 2¢, a 3¢, and a 6¢ stamp of the 1873 issue (Continentals). On 1 February 1873, the rate to Constantinople by North German Union

---

[59] One Born in Turkey. "The Turkish Situation," *American Review of Reviews* (Feb. 1902): p. 185.
[60] Ibid.

FIGURE 101.—Cover, from Cornwall-on-Hudson, N.Y., to Constantinople, Turkey, 1872.

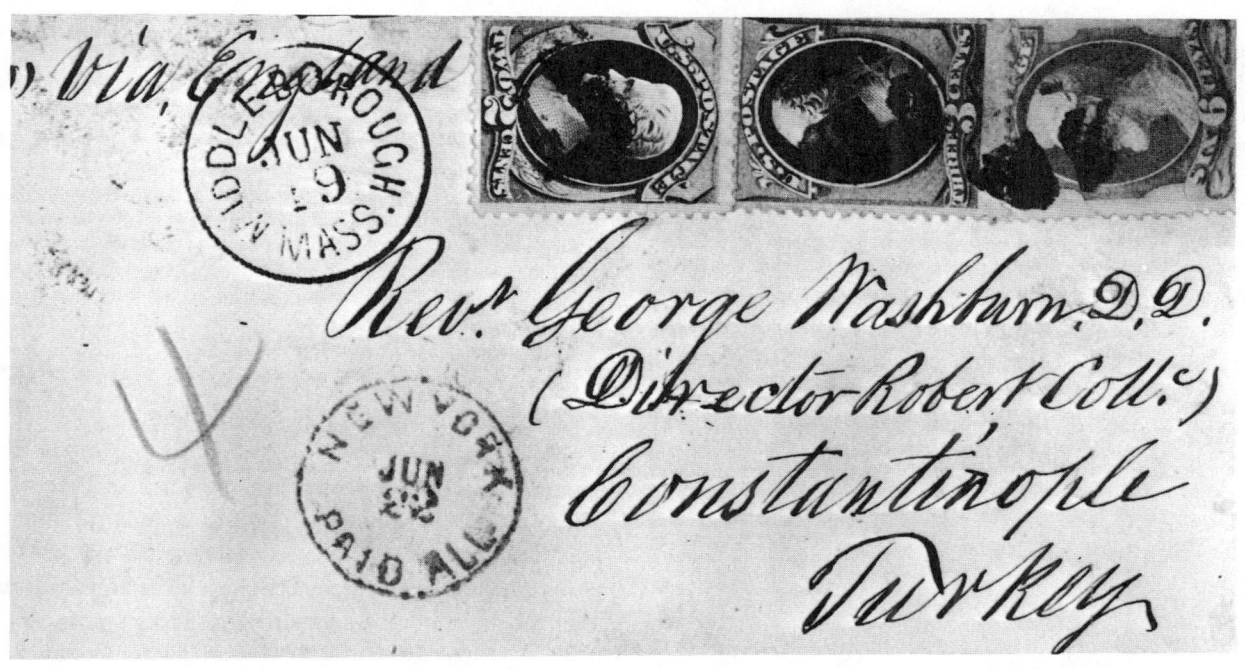

FIGURE 102.—Cover, from Middleborough, Mass., to Constantinople, Turkey, 1874 or 1875.
(*Photograph by Smithsonian*)

closed mail, via England, was reduced from 12¢ to 11¢, evidently by the abandonment of the exterior service charge for German postage in Constantinople. The 11¢ rate was divided: 6¢ for the direct international rate, 1¢ for British transit, and 4¢ for foreign postage. The New York office marked the cover PAID ALL and credited Germany with 4¢ foreign postage by marking it with a *4* in red crayon. The only other marking on the cover is that of the Imperial German Post Office on the reverse.

Chapter 9

Postal Relations with France, 1870–1876

Dissatisfaction with the United States-French postal convention of 2 March 1857 led the United States Post Office Department in December of 1866 to make it known to the French that a new and more liberal convention was necessary. On 4 February 1867, the government of the French emperor, Napoleon III, communicated to the United States Department of State that it, also, was of the belief that a new postal convention could be mutually advantageous, and requested that the United States Post Office Department send a special delegate to Paris. On 5 April 1867, the Honorable John A. Kasson was appointed a special commissioner of the Post Office Department and instructed to proceed to Paris and there negotiate and arrange the conditions of a more liberal postal convention.

After several months of fruitless effort Kasson became convinced that the French Post Office was unwilling to accept the liberal proposals of the United States, and he broke off negotiations. On 8 January 1868, the United States Post Office Department gave the French the required notice to terminate the convention of 2 March 1857 as of 1 February 1869. Later, at the request of the French Post Office, it was prolonged to 1 April 1869, and by mutual consent was further extended to 1 January 1870, at which time it finally expired.[1]

The Open Mail and Direct Rates

The December 1869 issue of the *U.S. Mail and Post Office Assistant* carried the following:

> Post Office Department, Office of Foreign Mails, November 30, 1869.
> On and after January 1, 1870, the exchange of mails between the United States and France will cease in consequence of the abrogation of the present convention between the two countries, to take effect on that date.
> The correspondence addressed to France or received from France on and after the 1st of January, sent by steamships or other vessels running direct between the two countries, will therefore be subject to the following rates of postage, to be prepaid by stamps at the office of mailing on matter set, and collected at the office of delivery on matter received:
> Letters, 10¢ per single rate of half an ounce or under. . . .
> Letters for France may also be sent from the United States in the ordinary open mail to England without prepayment of postage. But printed matter and samples cannot, under existing regulations, be so sent.
> Inasmuch as all direct postal relations between the Post Departments of the United States and France will cease on the 1st of January next, it will not be practicable to forward correspondence after that date to any foreign country or place 'by French Mail.' The rates of postage 'by French Mail,' as stated in the 'Table of Postages to Foreign Countries' will therefore be suspended after the 31st December proximo.
> By order of the Postmaster General
> Joseph H. Blackfan, SUPERINTENDENT OF FOREIGN MAILS.

The ordinary open-mail rate became 4¢ per half ounce on 1 January 1870 the effective date of the additional United States-British convention of 3–14 December 1869. The rate of 4¢ represented 2¢ inland and 2¢ sea postages, which were claimed by the United States on letters dispatched. Thus, when 4¢ were prepaid in the United States, the letter was paid only to England.[2] The London office forwarded such letters to France under the same articles and conditions of the

---

[1] *Annual Report of the Postmaster General for 1869.*

[2] For a discussion of the open-mail rate, see Millard H. Mack, "United States 4c Part Payment Rate to France, 1870–74," *The Collectors Club Philatelist* 38, 4 (July 1959): 159–164.

Anglo-French convention of 24 September 1856 as had been used to forward letters that arrived in England by American packet during the period 1 January to 1 April 1857. These covers bear a GB/4OC marking similar to O of Figure 18, an ANGL./AMB. CALAIS marking similar to N of Figure 18, and a due marking of 5 decimes or a multiple of 5 decimes, exactly as American packet covers had been marked during the first three months of 1857.

The 10¢ rate, referred to in the Post Office Department announcement, was based upon Section 8 of the act of 1 July 1864.[3] That section provided a rate of 10¢ for letters of one-half ounce or under when addressed to or received from foreign countries with whom the United States had no postal convention, and when conveyed by vessels regularly employed in the transportation of the mails. On letters posted in the United States, a prepayment of 10¢ paid the letter to the French frontier; on letters posted in France, postage from the French frontier of 10¢ was collected in the United States.

The direct service just described was performed by the French Ligne H between Havre and New York. Between 1 January 1870 and 3 January 1873 these vessels carried mail agents, and until 7 November 1874 they called at Brest.[4] The vessels of this line sailed from New York fortnightly on Saturdays. The Hamburg-American line, plying between New York and Hamburg with calls at Plymouth, England and Cherbourg, France, also conveyed direct service mail between New York and Cherbourg. Because of the Franco-Prussian War this service was suspended between July 1870 and February 1871. The vessels of this line sailed from New York weekly on Tuesdays.

By an imperial decree of 22 December 1869, effective on 1 January 1870,[5] letters arriving in France by the direct route were subject to a collection in France of 80 centimes (8 decimes) per 10 grams. On 1 July 1871, this collection was reduced to 50 centimes (5 decimes).[6]

On unpaid letters forwarded from the United States in the open mail, via England, the United States debited the British Post Office with 4¢ per half ounce. These covers bear a "currency" marking GB/2F, indicating that Great Britain forwarded such letters to France at the rate of 2 francs per 30 grams, bulk weight. Covers indicate that the French collected 8 decimes per single rate on these unpaid open-mail letters. It is presumed that this collection was for a letter of 7½ grams, since the Anglo-French additional convention,[7] which established the one-third ounce or 10 gram weight for a single rate, did not become effective between Great Britain and France until 1 July 1870. About the middle of 1871 the collection was increased to 12 decimes per single rate, evidently of 10 grams, on these unpaid open-mail letters.

Figure 103 presents a cover posted in New Orleans on 8 April 1870, addressed to Bordeaux. It is prepaid 4¢ by two pairs of the 1¢ stamp of the 1869 issue. The markings on this cover are typical of those used on open-mail letters to France, via England, at the prepaid 4¢ rate. Note the GB/4OC, the ANGL./AMB. CALAIS, and the 5 decimes French due marking.[8]

Figure 104 illustrates an unpaid letter to France sent in the open mail, via England. It was posted in New York, addressed to Bordeaux, and endorsed to the *Nevada*, a ship of the Guion line which sailed from New York on Wednesday, 5 October 1870. Note the NEW YORK/BR. TRANSIT and 4 markings applied in black by the New York office. The GB/2F and a London marking (on the reverse) were applied by the British, the ANGL./AMB. CALAIS and the 8 by the French.

Figure 105 illustrates a cover posted in San Francisco on 11 June 1872, addressed to La Rochelle, France. The debit of 4¢ is now included in the New York marking, and the collection in France has been increased from 8 to 12 decimes. In other respects the markings on this cover are the same as those on Figure 104.

Figure 106 illustrates a cover posted in Philadelphia on 20 June 1870, addressed to Paris, and endorsed *Per Steamer Cimbria—via Cherbourg, June 21*. *Cimbria* was a steamer of the Hamburg-American line which sailed from New York on Tuesday, 21 June and arrived in Cherbourg on 3 July 1870. This letter was prepaid 10¢ for direct service by a 10¢ National (grilled), and in this respect is unusual, since most covers showing a French due of 8 decimes were prepaid with a 10¢ stamp of the 1869 issue. The cover is also unusual because it shows the marking (in purple) of the Philadelphia office. The Cherbourg marking is in blue.

---

[3] John N. Luff, *Postage Stamps of the United States*, appendix, p. 395.
[4] Raymond Salles, *Laposte Maritime.*, vol. 4, p. 238.
[5] Ibid., p. 228.
[6] Ibid., p. 229.

[7] *British and Foreign State Papers*, vol. 59, p. 19.
[8] See Millard H. Mack, "Four Cent Part-Payment Rate to France," *Chronicle of the U.S. Classic Issues* 17, 2 (Feb. 1965): 72.

FIGURE 103.—COVER, from New Orleans to Bordeaux, France, 1870. (*Karl Jaeger collection*)

FIGURE 104.—COVER, from New York to Bordeaux, France, 1870. (*Photograph by Smithsonian*)

FIGURE 105.—COVER, from San Francisco to La Rochelle, France, 1872.
(*Photograph by Smithsonian*)

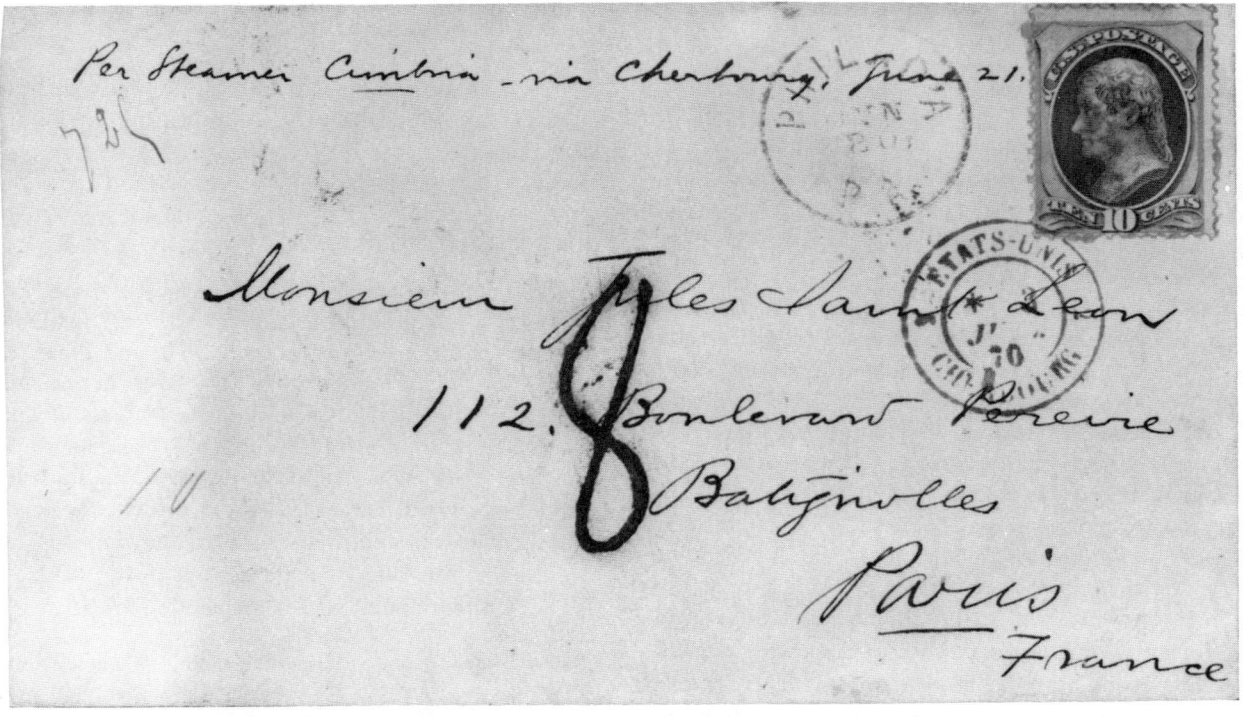

FIGURE 106.—COVER, from Philadelphia, Pa., to Paris, France, 1870.
(*Photograph by Smithsonian*)

FIGURE 107.—COVER, from New York to Angoulême, France, 1874. (*Photograph by Smithsonian*)

Figure 107 illustrates a cover posted in New York, addressed to France, and endorsed "per Str. 'Ville de Paris,'" a steamer of the French line. The Brest marking indicates that the letter entered France at that port, but the marking itself was applied at Paris.[9] Five decimes were collected in France.

When the United States-French convention expired on 31 December 1869, there was confusion among local postmasters and the public regarding the rates to France. Numerous covers indicate that many people continued to prepay their letters with the former convention rate of 15¢. It must be remembered that a new rate of 6¢, which paid a letter to destination in Great Britain, also became effective on 1 January 1870. Instructions to pay open-mail letters to England appear to have been frequently misunderstood, and letters were prepaid with 6¢ instead of 4¢, which paid the letter *through* England, rather than *to* England. Figure 108 illustrates one of the many covers showing this error. The cover bears a marking applied in red, NEW YORK/PAID TO ENGLAND, which appears on all covers seen which were prepaid with 6¢. Otherwise, the markings are the same as those appearing on Figure 103.

The Phantom Rate

The open-mail and direct rates were those announced by the postmaster general as being available on letters to France on 1 January 1870, and these remained the only rates reflected in the tables of postages to foreign countries published in the *U.S. Mail and Post Office Assistant* until the issue of November 1871. The New York exchange office, however, used a fully prepaid rate to France, via England, which was never published to local postmasters or to the public. The evolution of this rate is an interesting story.[10]

The United States-British convention of 18 June

---

[9] Raymond Salles, *La Poste Maritime,* vol. 4, p. 236.

[10] For a more extensive discussion of the "phantom" rate *see* George E. Hargest, "United States Mails to France in 1870—The 'Phantom' and Actual Prepaid Rates," *The Collectors Club Philatelist* 42, 6 Nov. 1963): 333–344. Reference to the "phantom" rate was first made in this article.

FIGURE 108.—COVER, from Richmond, Mass. to Point-Aven, Finistère, France, 1873.
(*Photograph by Smithsonian*)

1867, appended a table to the detailed regulations. The table showed the rates of postage to be accounted for by the United States to the British Post Office on letters conveyed in transit through England in ordinary mails between the United States and twenty-six listed countries.[11] The amount set beside the name of each country represented the existing rate between that country and Great Britain. In each case, the prepaid rate shown for the designated country in the tables of postages to foreign countries published in the *U.S. Mail and Post Office Assistant* was 10¢ higher than the rate reflected in the table appended to the detailed regulations. The twenty-six countries included in this table were largely British colonies traditionally served by British mail.

While Anthony Trollope represented Great Britain in the negotiation of the United States-British convention of 7–24 November 1868, the detailed regulations, signed at the same time, were negotiated by Joseph H. Blackfan for the United States and John Tilley for Great Britain.[12] Blackfan was superintendent of Foreign Mails, and Tilley was secretary of the General Post Office at London. Both of these gentlemen were intimately acquainted with the details of the foreign-mail services. Appended to these detailed regulations was a table similar to that appended to the detailed regulations for the 18 June 1867 convention. The list, however, was expanded to 155 countries and destinations, and included, as far as possible, the countries that were then being served by French mail. Since these detailed regulations were signed at Washington on 24 November 1868, about ten months after the United States had served notice to France of its intention to terminate the United States-French convention, there can be little doubt that the United States was preparing an alternate service to replace French mail.

The list included an entry for France and a separate entry for Algeria. It should be emphasized that Algeria was considered by the French a part of metropolitan France and all postal conventions after that of 3 April 1843 had joined France and Algeria as one contracting party, setting the same rate for each. Besides the names of both France and Algeria were entered the notation (*a*) 8. The 8 indicated that the United States was to credit Great Britain with 8¢, while the (*a*) denoted "Increase by an additional rate for every 7½ grams, or fraction thereof." This was the existing international

---

[11] 16 *Statutes-at-Large* 842.
[12] Ibid. 860–862.

rate between Great Britain and France and Algeria of 4d. per one-fourth ounce in Great Britain, or 40 centimes per 7½ grams in France and Algeria. It had been established for prepaid letters through additional articles to the Anglo-French treaty of 3 April 1843, and became effective on 1 January 1855.[13] Unpaid letters were at double this rate. The rate was unchanged by Article XIII of the Anglo-French convention of 24 September 1856, which superseded these articles.[14]

The United States-French convention expired on 31 December 1869, and on the following day, 1 January 1870, the additional United States-British convention of 3–14 December 1869, which reduced the United States share of the international rate from 10¢ to 4¢, became effective. Thus, on 1 January 1870, there was available by postal convention a fully prepaid rate to France and Algeria of 12¢ for a single letter of 7½ grams. On letters dispatched from the United States to France, via England, the rate to the British frontier under the United States-British convention was 4¢ per 15 grams, and this amount was to belong to the dispatching office. Great Britain was to receive a credit of 8¢ per 7½ grams from the United States to pay the then current international rate between Great Britain and France as prescribed by Article XIII of the Anglo-French convention of 24 September 1856. Although this rate was 4d. per one-fourth ounce in Great Britain, or 40 centimes per 7½ grams in France and Algeria, on prepaid letters, the weight stated by the dispatching office was accepted by the receiving office, except in case of manifest mistake. The combined prepaid rate, and its progression, was as follows:

TABLE 30.—*The Division and Progression of the "Phantom" Rate*

	Postage		
	U.S. (per 15 grams)	British (per 7½ grams)	Total Postage
Not over 7½ grams	4¢	8¢	12¢
Over 7½ but not over 15 grams	4	16	20
Over 15 but not over 22½ grams	8	24	32
Over 22½ but not over 30 grams	8	32	40, etc.

Although this rate represented the only possible fully prepaid rate to France and Algeria, United States Postmaster General J. A. J. Creswell failed to make it available to France; he did, however, announce it for Algeria. The "Table of Postages to Foreign Countries" included in the April 1870 issue of the *U.S. Mail and Post Office Assistant* gives the entries for France and for Algeria as follows:

	Not exceeding quarter ounce	Not exceeding half ounce
Algeria, via England	12¢	20¢
* * *		
France		10
do. open mail, via England		*4

*Indicates that in cases where it is prefixed, unless the letter is registered, prepayment is optional; in all other cases prepayment is required.

If the 12¢ rate was announced for Algeria, it would appear that it also should have been announced for France. On 1 January 1870, however, Postmaster General Creswell had a serious problem in regard to the mails sent to England. As has been pointed out in Chapter 8, all of the packet lines sailing from New York refused to carry the United States mails at the reduced rate of 6¢ per ounce or per 30 grams established by the additional United States-British convention of 3–14 December 1869. Until the Guion line signed a contract with the postmaster general on 23 February 1870, the United States mails were conveyed to England exclusively by the Allan line from Portland, Maine. Prior to 31 December 1869, mails had been dispatched to England on Tuesdays, Wednesdays, Thursdays, and Saturdays.[15] The postmaster general was now able to offer only a Saturday service. Faced with this inadequacy in the means of conveyance, he may not have wished to introduce a 12¢ fully prepaid rate to France, via England.

On the other hand, the ordinary British mail to Algeria was sent to the Mediterranean by the packet from Southampton. After the abrogation of the United States-French convention, this was the only route practical for its dispatch. The 12¢ rate was, therefore, announced for Algeria. The 4¢ open-mail rate should also have been available to Algeria, but it was not announced by the postmaster general.

There may, however, have been another reason for the postmaster general not announcing the 12¢ rate to France. On 21 September 1869, while the United States was still in negotiation with the French, and before the United States-French convention expired, France signed an additional postal convention with the

---

[13] *British and Foreign State Papers*, vol. 44, pp. 43–47.
[14] Ibid., vol. 46, p. 202.

[15] *Annual Report of the Postmaster General for 1870*, p. 17.

British which reduced the international rate between those two countries and abandoned the 7½ grams weight base.[16] This additional convention superseded Article XIII of the Anglo-French convention of 24 September 1856.

As has been pointed out, Article XIII was the convention provision upon which the United States and Great Britain had based the 8¢ credit included in the 12¢ rate. The additional convention set a rate of 3d. for every one-third ounce in Great Britain, or of 30 centimes for every 10 grams in France and Algeria. This change meant that the United States would credit Great Britain with only 6¢ instead of 8¢, and that the total rate would be reduced from 12¢ for a single letter of 7½ grams to 10¢ for a single letter of 10 grams.

Although this convention was signed on 21 September 1869, it was not to come into operation until the ratifications were exchanged. This could have required only a few days, and it may have been anticipated that the convention would become effective before the United States-French convention expired. Nine months were to elapse, however, before ratification was achieved. Postmaster General Creswell may have preferred to wait and place the 10¢ rate in force, rather than introduce the 12¢ rate for what was anticipated would be a short time. Whatever his motives may have been, the 12¢ rate was not announced to the public or to local postmasters as being available on letters to France.

While there was no announcement of a 12¢ rate to France, the evidence of covers indicates that at least by March 1870 (perhaps earlier) the New York exchange office began to forward some letters to France, via England, by crediting Great Britain with 8¢, provided they were prepaid with at least 12¢. Since the two published rates to France were less than 12¢, these letters were usually prepaid with the old convention rate of 15¢, or occasionally with double the 10¢ direct rate. These covers indicate that both Great Britain and France accepted them as fully prepaid to destination. The London office marked them PAID, while the French marked them PD, that is, paid to destination. The rarity of covers showing the 8¢ credit to Great Britain is such as to indicate that it was used sporadically rather than regularly.

There is no documentary evidence that explains this anomalous situation. There was no officially announced rate, but there was an 8¢ credit and a 4¢ postage to the British frontier established by postal conventions with Great Britain. The rate was available to and used by the New York exchange office, but unknown to local postmasters or to the person mailing the letter. Yet what was thought, in some cases, to be a partial payment turned out to be a prepayment to destination, but only at the caprice of the New York exchange office. The illusionary nature of this rate suggests the term "phantom" as being descriptive of it.

Figure 109 illustrates a cover posted in Eufaula, Alabama, on 18 May 1870, addressed to France. It is prepaid 15¢ which was the old convention rate, and it is suspected that the mailer did not know the rate had changed. The New York office forwarded it as fully prepaid to destination by crediting Great Britain with 8¢ (large 8 in red on face), and marked it NEW YORK/BR. TRANSIT on the reverse. The London office marked it PAID, while the French travelling office, Calais to Paris, used a double circle ANGL./AMB. CALAIS marking, and a PD ("paid to destination") marking applied in red. These markings are typical of phantom-rate covers.

Figure 110 presents a letter posted at Cape Elizabeth Depot, Maine, post office on 10 June 1870, addressed to Paris. The letter evidently weighed over half an ounce (14.18 grams) and required a prepayment of 20¢ for twice the 10¢ "direct" rate, and it was undoubtedly intended that it be sent by that route. At the New York exchange office (NEW YORK/BR. TRANSIT marking on reverse), however, the letter did not weigh over 15 grams, and it was sent fully prepaid to destination, via England. Great Britain was credited wtih 16¢ (2 x 8¢) by marking the cover on its face with a large 16 in red. Again, the London office marked it PAID, and the French office applied ANGL./AMB. CALAIS and PD markings.

Although it was undoubtedly anticipated that the ratification of the additional Anglo-French convention of 21 September 1869 would shortly be achieved, an obstacle was encountered. A British law required that any change in a secondary standard of length, weight, or capacity should be duly authenticated by comparison with the imperial standard;[17] that it should be made effective by an order in council which was to be laid before both Houses of Parliament and published in the London, Edinburgh, or Dublin Gazette.[18] The order

---

[16] *British and Foreign State Papers*, vol. 59, p. 19.

[17] *The Standards of Weights, Measures and Coinage Act,* 1866, sec. 6 (29 and 30 Vict. c82, sec. 6).

[18] Ibid., sec. 8.

FIGURE 109.—COVER, from Eufaula, Ala., to France, 1870. (*Lester L. Downing collection*)

FIGURE 110.—COVER, from Cape Elizabeth Depot, Me., to Paris, France, 1870.
(*Photograph by Smithsonian*)

in council appears to have taken some time to secure, but was finally issued on 4 June 1870: [19]

> Whereas the Lords of the Committee of the Privy Council for Trade have represented to her Majesty that, in order to carry out the terms of a Postal Convention with France, it is expedient that secondary standards of the weight of one-third of an ounce avoirdupois, and two-thirds of an ounce avoirdupois, should be legalized.

The preceding order in council was debated in the House of Commons on 13 June 1870,[20] and the ratifications of the convention were exchanged on 16 June 1870.[21] In answer to questions put to him in the House of Commons, the British postmaster general, Lord Hartington, said the additional Anglo-French postal convention would come into operation on 1 July 1870.[22]

Postmaster General Creswell, however, did not announce the 10¢ fully prepaid rate, via England, as being available to France in the July issue of the *U.S. Mail and Post Office Assistant*. There could have been several reasons for his not doing so. He may not have wished to introduce a rate based upon the peculiar weight base of one-third ounce at the local post offices (most of whom were not equipped to determine this weight), and of 10 grams at the exchange offices. He evidently preferred that mails, via England, be sent in the open mail, thus avoiding the unusual third-ounce weight base. He may also have wished to avoid the introduction of a 10¢ fully prepaid rate, via England, that would compete with a 10¢ direct rate, which paid a letter only to the French frontier, especially at a time when the packet service to England was inadequate. Whatever his reasons may have been, the 10¢ fully prepaid rate, via England, was not announced to local postmasters, or to the public, so they were not aware that such a rate existed.

The New York exchange office, however, continued to send some letters to France, via England, as fully prepaid to destination, provided the postage prepaid on them was of sufficient amount. In most cases, these letters were prepaid 10¢ and were intended to be sent by the direct route. The earliest cover showing a prepayment of 10¢ and a credit of 6¢ to England, reported by the late Stanley B. Ashbrook, was dated 28 June 1870.[23] Since any departing steamer would require at least a week to reach England, the New York office could have anticipated the effective date of the Anglo-French convention (1 July 1870) by a few days.

The November 1871 issue of the *U.S. Mail and Post Office Assistant* carried the following:

Office of Foreign Mails. October 28, 1871.

Inasmuch as correspondents in the United States are subjected to inconvenience because of their inability, since the abrogation of the Postal Convention with France, to fully prepay postage on letters for France and Algeria, the Postmaster-General has decided to so modify the existing regulations governing the collection of postage thereon as to permit the prepayment in full to destination of the postage on such letters for France and Algeria, as may hereafter be forwarded through the British mails.

Notice is therefore given that the following prepaid rates of postage are in full of all charges to destination on letters for France and Algeria, via England.

For letters not exceeding ⅓ oz. in weight, 10¢; exceeding ⅓, but not over ½ oz., 16¢; exceeding ½, but not over ⅔ oz., 20¢; exceeding ⅔, but not over one oz., 26¢; and so on, adding four cents for each ½ oz. for United States and ocean postage, and 6¢ for each ⅓ oz. for British postage.

This modification of existing regulations does not interfere with the mailing of letters for France and Algeria, either wholly unpaid, or partially prepaid, the United States inland and sea postage of 4¢ per single rate of ½ oz.

Although the United States-British convention stated rates in grams for the United States postage, local offices were not equipped to weigh in grams. The preceding rates, therefore, represent a translation of grams into ounces at the rate of 30 grams to the ounce. The exchange offices, of course, weighed letters in grams. This again caused a discrepancy in weight between the local offices (ounce held at 28.35 grams) and the exchange offices (rates based on grams at 30 grams to the ounce). See Table 31.

Beginning with the issue of November 1871, the tables of postages to foreign countries published in the *U.S. Mail and Post Office Assistant* showed the fully

TABLE 31.—*The Division and Progression of the Fully Prepaid Rate, via England*

Local Offices, ounces		Exchange Offices, grams		Postage Shares		Total Postage
Over	Not over	Over	Not over	U.S. (retained)	British (credit)	
—	⅓	—	10	4¢	6¢	10¢
⅓	½	10	15	4	12	16
½	⅔	15	20	8	12	20
⅔	1	20	30	8	18	26

---

[19] *British and Foreign State Papers*, vol. 65, p. 1213.
[20] Hansard's *Parliamentary Debates*, vol. 201, p. 1944.
[21] Hertslet, *Commercial Treaties*, vol. 13, p. 546.
[22] Hansard's *Parliamentary Debates*, 1944.
[23] Ashbrook, Stanley B., *Special Service*, 6th series, p. 568.

prepaid rates to France, via England, in a footnote designated as "CC." The 4¢ open-mail rate was also included in the footnote, while the 10¢ direct rate was included in the tables. The table of postages to foreign countries published in the *Postal Laws and Regulations*, stated to be "correct up to May 1, 1873," omitted the 4¢ open-mail rate, as did also the table included in the *Postal Guide*, 1 July 1873. The 4¢ open-mail rate, however, continued to be listed in the *CC* rates published in the *U.S. Mail and Post Office Assistant*, at least until the issue of March 1875.

Figure 111 illustrates a cover posted in New Orleans on 28 July 1870, addressed to Paris. It is prepaid 10¢ by a 10¢ stamp of the 1869 issue, which was undoubtedly intended to prepay the "direct" rate. The New York exchange office, however, forwarded it as fully prepaid to destination, via England. A large numeral 6 was applied in red to indicate a credit of 6¢ to Great Britain. On the reverse is a NEW YORK/BR. TRANSIT marking also applied at New York. London marked the letter PAID, while the French applied a double circle ANGL./AMB. CALAIS marking in black and a red PD. These markings are the same as those used during the phantom-rate period, and indicate that the service was the same. Only the rate had changed. Covers showing this rate during the period in which it was unannounced, that is, prior to 1 November 1871 are very scarce and of great historical interest. Characteristically, the credit to Great Britain was shown by the large numeral 6.

Figure 112 illustrates a cover posted in New Orleans on 12 September 1872, addressed to Rouen, France. It is prepaid 10¢ by a 7¢ and a 3¢ National. The New York exchange office had revived the markings that had been used on United States-French convention mail, and credited Great Britain with 6¢ by applying in red a marking that had formerly indicated British packet service through England on single-rate French-mail letters. These markings appear to have been revived about the time of the announcement of the rate by the Postmaster General. In other respects the remaining markings are similar to those that appear on Figure 110, except that the NEW YORK/BR. TRANSIT marking on the reverse is omitted.

Figure 113 illustrates a cover that passed through the Boston exchange office. There is no Boston postmark, but a Boston foreign mail killer was used to cancel the stamps.[24] The letter weighed over one-third but not over one-half ounce and required a prepayment of 16¢. The Boston office used no handstamps showing credits, but throughout the period marked credits in red crayon. Note the crayon *12* on this cover, which is in red.

Figure 114 illustrates a cover that passed through the New York exchange office on 16 May 1874, addressed to Paris. The letter weighed over one-half but not over two-thirds of an ounce and is prepaid with 20¢ in stamps. The credit of 12¢ is now included in a specially prepared handstamp that came into use some time after the middle of 1873.

[24] Maurice C. Blake and W. W. Davis, *Postal Markings of Boston, Massachusetts, to 1890*, Plate 59, no. 976, p. 195.

FIGURE 111.—COVER, from New Orleans, La., to Paris, France, 1870.
(*Robert de Wasserman collection*)

FIGURE 112.—COVER, from New Orleans, La., to Rouen, France, 1872. (*Photograph by Smithsonian*)

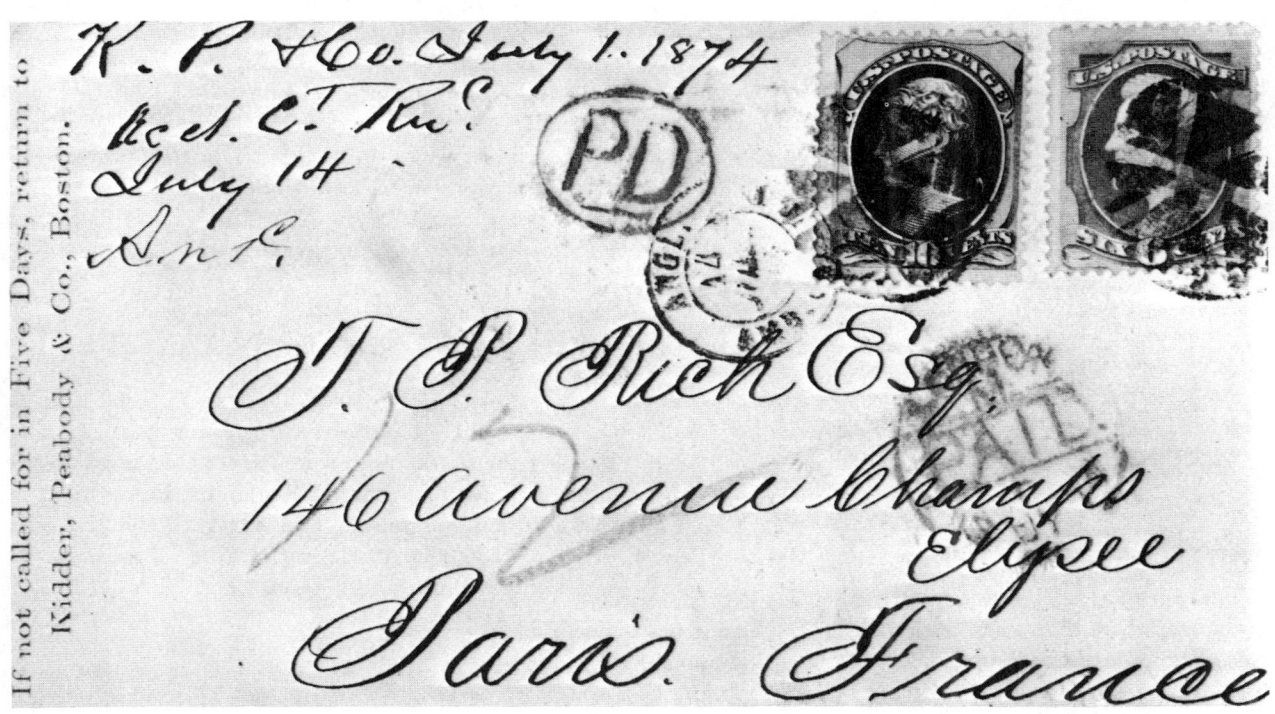

FIGURE 113.—COVER, from Boston [?] to Paris, France, 1874. (*Photograph by Smithsonian*)

FIGURE 114.—COVER, through New York to Paris, 1874. (*Melvin W. Schuh collection*)

Marginal-Weight Letters

Covers showing overpayments of postage in relation to the credits shown upon them are frequently seen. Some of these letters when weighed in ounces at the local offices required a prepayment of postage in excess of what was required when they were weighed in grams at the exchange offices. For example, a few covers have been seen that are prepaid with 16¢, but show an exchange office credit of only 6¢. Undoubtedly, these letters weighed over 9.45 grams (one-third of an ounce) at the local offices and required a 16¢ prepayment. At the exchange offices, however, these letters did not weigh over ten grams and required a credit of only 6¢. While some overpayments may be explained as marginal-weight letters, there are others which are prepaid with inexplicable amounts, and some of these may be fraudulent.

The Exchange Offices

The 4¢ open-mail rate was available at all of the exchange offices that made up British mails. Very few covers, however, bear an exchange office marking other than New York. One cover showing a Boston marking and one cover bearing a red PHIL'A/[DATE]/PA. have been seen. These two covers are the only ones showing exchange office markings other than New York recorded by the author. Certainly, covers showing markings of the Baltimore, Portland, Chicago, Detroit, or San Francisco offices should exist.

After 1 November 1871, the *CC* rates were also available at all of the exchange offices. Strange as it may seem, however, all covers seen by the author showing these rates bear New York or Boston markings. Only the markings of the New York and Philadelphia offices have been seen on covers by the direct route.

Rates from France to the United States

By imperial decree of 22 December 1869 and 31 January 1870,[25] a rate of 70 centimes per 10 grams was set for letters posted in France addressed to the United States and sent via England.[26] Prepayment of this rate was compulsory, and it became effective on 1 January 1870. Great Britain forwarded these letters to the United States under terms of the United States–

---

[25] Salles, *La Poste Maritime,* vol. 4, p. 282.
[26] It is doubted that this rate could have been for a letter of 10 grams until after the effective date (1 July 1870) of the Anglo-French convention of 21 Sept. 1869.

British convention of 7–24 November 1868, and credited the United States with 2¢ per half ounce.

About the middle of 1871 this rate was increased to 1 franc 20 centimes (12 decimes) for a letter of 10 grams. According to Smith,[27] M. Caillaux introduced in the National Assembly on 23 August 1871 a bill to increase French domestic postal rates, "solely as a fiscal measure." Since there is nothing to indicate that there was a change, at this time, in the amount of postage paid by France to Great Britain on letters dispatched from France through England, it is presumed that the increase in rate from 70 to 120 centimes was also a fiscal measure.[28] The *U.S. Postal Guide* for 1873 (rates as of 1 July) states:

> The postage on letters from France to the United States sent, via England, is 24 cents (1 franc, 20 centimes) per ⅓ ounce and letters so prepaid should be delivered in the United States free of charge, but letters sent by direct steamer are subject to postage of 10 cents per half ounce on delivery; no matter what amount of postage has been prepaid in France. Letters insufficiently prepaid for transmission, via England, are treated by the French Post Office as wholly unpaid and reach the United States with a claim for French and British postage, which must be collected on delivery.

Since there was no accounting between the post offices of the United States and France, all unpaid letters had to be sent via England. Letters insufficiently prepaid were sent as unpaid via England regardless of the route indicated by the mailer. Unpaid and insufficiently paid letters posted in France addressed to the United States bear "currency" markings which indicate they were forwarded by France to England charged at the rate of 2 francs per 30 grams, bulk weight of such letters. Great Britain evidently divided the bulk rate by 4 to arrive at a single rate of 50 centimes (10¢) per one-fourth ounce. To this rate was added the British postage of 4¢ per half ounce (2¢ British inland and 2¢ sea postage). Thus, on a single-rate letter, the British debited the United States with 14¢, while on a double-rate letter only the postage charged by France was double, and the British debit was 24¢. On these letters the United States postage was 2¢ per half ounce, and the total postage for a single rate was 16¢ and for a double rate, 26¢. Since collections in the United States were made in depreciated currency, the exchange office markings do not show the true rate. Support for this statement will be presented in Chapter 10 which deals with depreciated currency covers.

By an imperial decree of 22 December 1869, effective 1 January 1870, letters to be sent by direct steamer from France to the United States required a prepayment in France of 60 centimes per 10 grams. This paid the letter to the port of departure, and such letters were marked P.P.[29] A law of 21 April 1871, effective on 1 July 1871, and placed in force by a notification issued at Versailles on 25 May 1871, reduced the direct rate from 60 to 50 centimes.[30] On these direct letters, 10¢ per half ounce was collected on delivery in the United States.

Figure 115 illustrates a cover posted in Paris on 24 February 1870, addressed to New York, and endorsed VOIE ANGLAISE ("By English line"). It is prepaid 70 centimes, the fully prepaid rate, via England. The Paris office marked it PD ("paid to destination"). The London office marked it PAID on 25 February and credited the United States with 2¢. From the London office it was sent to Liverpool to be conveyed to New York by the R.M.S. *Samaria* of the Cunard line, which sailed from there on 26 February 1870. Unfortunately, the *Samaria* became disabled on 3 March and returned to Queenstown where it arrived on 1 April 1870.[31] Undoubtedly its mails were forwarded by the next steamer which was R.M.S. *Cuba,* which sailed from Liverpool on 2 April and arrived in New York on 13 April 1870. Usually these covers bear a NEW YORK/PAID ALL marking showing the date of arrival. On this cover there is no New York marking, and one wonders if it was omitted intentionally.

Figure 116 illustrates a cover posted in Paris on 9 February 1872, addressed to New York. It is prepaid 120 centimes to be sent fully prepaid to destination, via England. All British and French markings are similar to those appearing on Figure 115, except that New York marked it PAID ALL.

Figure 117 illustrates a cover posted in Paris on 19 September 1873, addressed to New York. It is prepaid 50 centimes to be sent by the direct route. The Paris office marked it in red P.P. (marking on left stamp). The New York office applied a circular N.Y. STEAMSHIP/10 marking in black, indicating that 10¢ were to be collected in United States notes on delivery.

---

[27] A. D. Smith, *Development of Rates of Postage*, p. 88.
[28] Salles makes no mention of the 120-centime rate.
[29] Salles, *La Poste Maritime,* vol. 4, p. 228.
[30] Ibid., p. 229.
[31] Taken from records of the Cunard line by Lester L. Downing.

FIGURE 115.—COVER, from Paris to New York, 1870. (*Photograph by Smithsonian*)

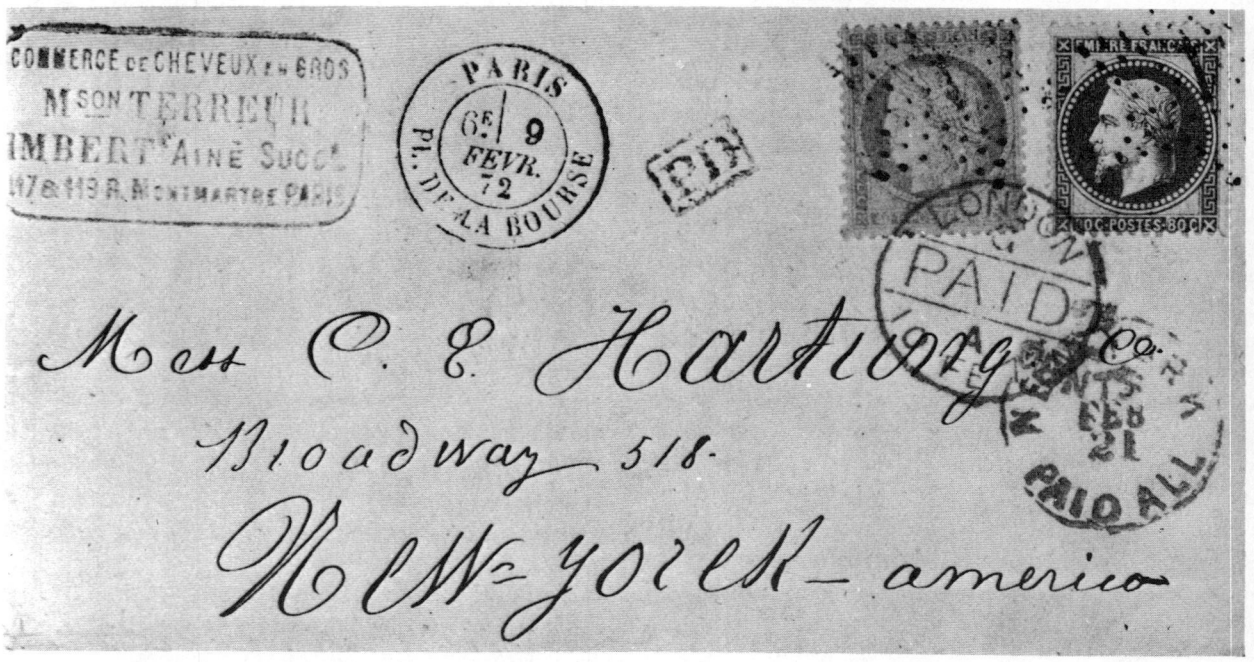

FIGURE 116.—COVER, from Paris to New York, 1872. (*Photograph by Smithsonian*)

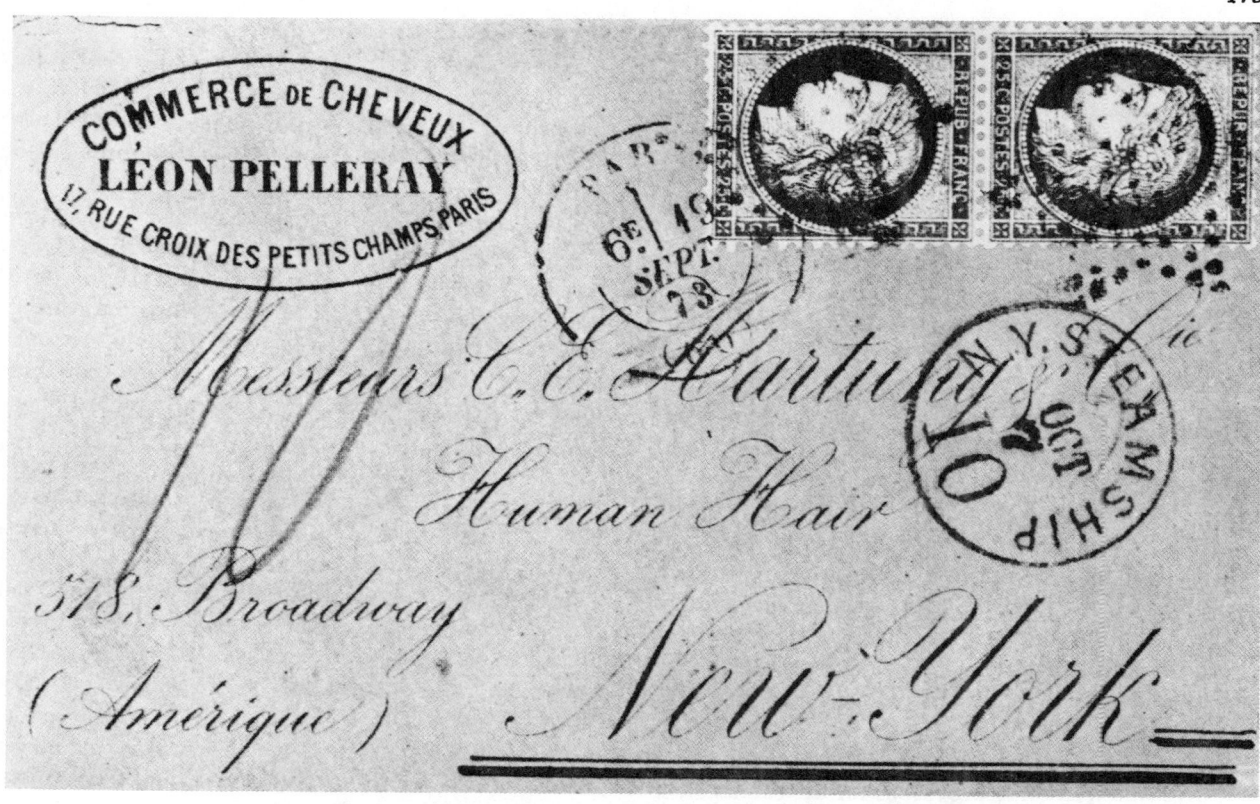

FIGURE 117.—COVER, from Paris to New York, 1873. (*Photograph by Smithsonian*)

The United States-French Convention of 28 April 1874

On 28 April 1874, the United States and France, after years of negotiation, signed a new postal convention at Washington.[32] The detailed regulations were signed at Washington on 9 June and at Paris on 24 June 1874,[33] and it was agreed that the convention come into operation on 1 August 1874.

Exchange offices were established in France at Paris, Le Havre, Cherbourg, Brest, the travelling office, Paris to Calais, and the travelling office, Lille to Calais. In the United States, offices were established at Boston and New York.

By Article 2 of the detailed regulations the exchange of mails was to be effected as follows:

> By way of French mail-packets—The offices of Paris, Le Havre, and Brest shall correspond with the office of New York.
> By way of packets of the Hamburg line—The offices of Paris and Le Havre shall make up mails for the office of New York, and the office of New York shall make up mails for the offices of Paris, Le Havre, and Cherbourg.
> By way of England—The offices of Paris and Le Havre and the travelling offices of Paris to Calais and Lille to Calais shall correspond with the offices of Boston and New York.

Thus, all mail passing through the Boston office was sent or received by way of England. A table appended to the detailed regulations states the origin and destination of the mails sent from or received at the offices of Boston or New York by the various routes.[34] This table discloses that the Boston office was to forward or receive letters posted in or addressed to the states of Massachusetts, Maine, Vermont, New Hampshire, and Rhode Island, only. Mail was to be dispatched by packets from Boston, but mail would be received by packets arriving at Boston. The New York office was to forward or receive letters posted in or addressed to any part of the United States. Letters, by any route, were exchanged in closed mails between the exchange office of origin and the exchange office of destination.

---

[32] 18 *Statutes at Large* 810.
[33] Ibid. 816.

[34] Ibid. 420.

Article III of the convention set the rates of postage. On letters posted in France or Algeria, addressed to the United States, the rate was set at 50 centimes per 10 grams or fraction of 10 grams. On letters posted in the United States, addressed to France or Algeria, the rate was 9¢ per 15 grams or fraction of 15 grams. Unpaid letters were to bear a fine of 25 centimes per letter in France, or of 5¢ per letter in the United States. Insufficiently paid letters were to be treated as unpaid, but the amount of postage prepaid by postage stamps was to be deducted.

Since each country was to retain the postage it collected, there was no accounting for international letters between the two post offices, and debit and credit markings were unnecessary. There is, therefore, no evidence of weight discrepancy between the local offices which rated letters per half ounce and the exchange offices which rated them per 15 grams. It was provided, however, that the United States exchange offices mark prepaid letters dispatched to France and Algeria PAID in red ink, while the French offices were to mark letters prepaid to United States destinations PD in red ink. Insufficiently prepaid letters were to be so marked by the dispatching offices.

There were elaborate provisions for the exchange of open mails which were to pass in transit through France or the United States to or from foreign countries. Similar provisions were made for closed mails. The conditions upon which these mails would be exchanged were set forth in tables appended to the detailed regulations.[35] The official *Postal Guide* for October 1874, makes no mention, either in its text or in its "Foreign Postage Table," of rates "by French Mail," or "via France," as shown in the detailed regulations. This is also true of the tables of postages to foreign countries published in various issues of the *U.S. Mail and Post Office Assistant*. It appears, therefore, that the postmaster general preferred not to make use of these transit provisions on mail dispatched from the United States.

Of the delegates from the twenty-one countries assembled at the Berne Postal Congress in 1874, only the delegate from France did not have the necessary powers to sign a treaty.[36] The Berne Postal Treaty was signed on 9 October 1874, and through a final protocol France was allowed to sign at a later date. On 3 May 1875, France's delegate, B. d'Harcourt, signed the treaty[37] on condition that France be allowed to place it in force on 1 January 1876, instead of 1 July 1875; that the rate would not be changed before the next congress; and that France be permitted to charge transit rates on the basis of the actual distance the mails were carried.[38]

Thus, the rates of the convention of 28 April 1874 were superseded on 1 January 1876 by the General Postal Union rates of 5¢ in the United States, or 40 centimes in France, per 15 grams. Since the convention of 28 April 1874 was in force for only seventeen months, covers showing its rates are scarce, and those showing the 9¢ rate from the United States are popular with collectors.

Figure 118 illustrates a cover posted in New York, addressed to Ain, France. The NEW YORK/PAID marking was introduced when the convention became effective. The date in this marking is 2 December 1874, a Wednesday, and according to the "Sailing of Mail Steamers" published in the October 1874 issue of the official *Postal Guide,* Wednesday sailings from New York were by steamers of the Cunard line. The double-circle ETATS-UNIS/[date]/V. ANGL. AMB. CAL. B marking which was applied in black by the travelling office, Calais to Paris, was introduced with the convention. This office also applied a P.D. marking in red.

Figure 119 illustrates a cover posted in New York, addressed to Ain, France, and forwarded to Paris. This letter weighed over half an ounce and was prepaid 18¢ by a pair of 3¢ and a pair of 6¢ stamps (Continentals). The New York office applied a foreign-mail killer (Milliken no. 16, Herst-Sampson no. 844) in black, and a NEW YORK/PAID marking bearing the date of 18 May (1875), a Tuesday. According to the "Sailing of Mail Steamers" included in the April 1875 issue of the official *Postal Guide,* Tuesday sailings, via England, were by steamers of the Guion line. The French markings are similar to those appearing on Figure 118, except that the P.D. marking was applied in black.

Figure 120 illustrates a cover posted in the New York "supplementary mail" on 21 October (1875). At dockside a mailbag was kept open after the regular mail had closed. Letters posted late to be sent in this supplementary mailbag required a prepayment of double postage for a single-rate letter. This letter is prepaid 18¢ (2 x 9¢) by a pair and a single of the 6¢ stamp (Continental). The New York office applied a foreign-mail killer (Milliken no. 50) in black, and a

---

[35] Ibid. 821–822.
[36] Arthur George Codding, Jr., *The Universal Postal Union,* pp. 27, 34.
[37] 19 *Statutes at Large* 587.
[38] Codding, *Universal Postal Union,* p. 34.

FIGURE 118.—COVER, from New York to Ain, France, 1874. (*Photograph by Smithsonian*)

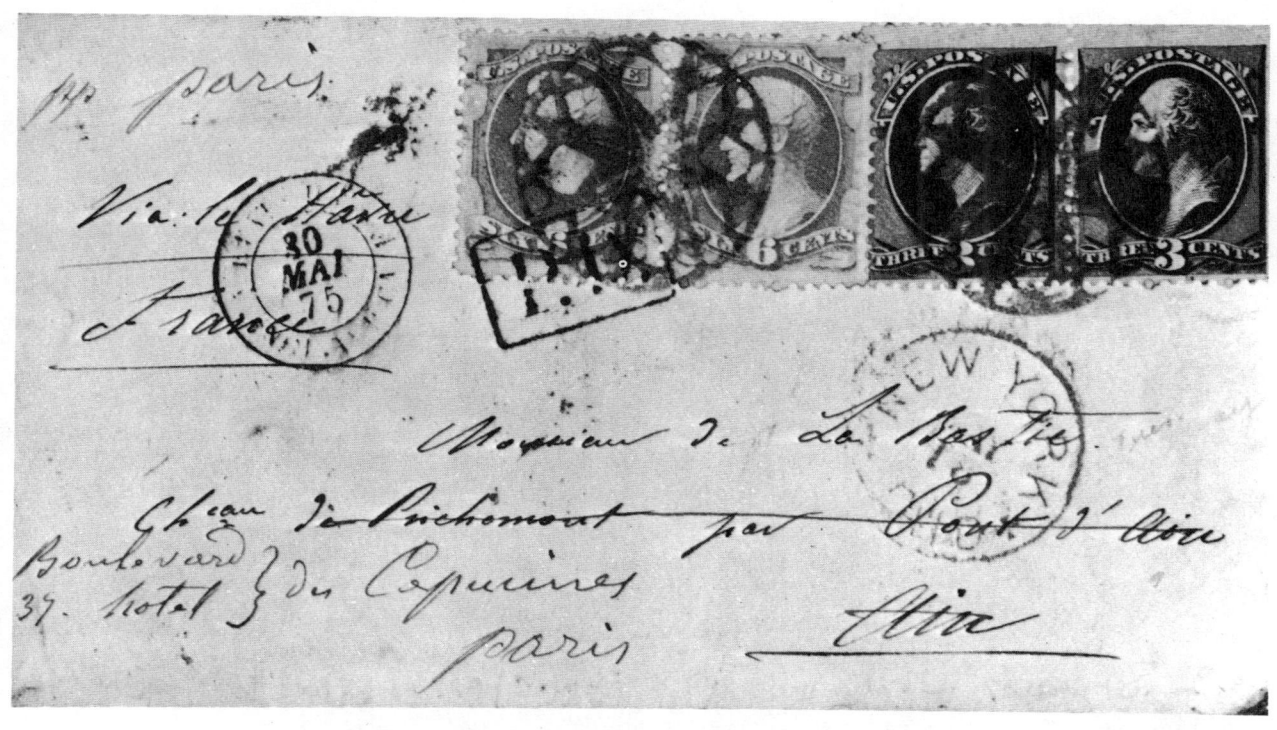

FIGURE 119.—COVER, from New York to Ain, France, forwarded to Paris, 1875.
(*Photograph by Smithsonian*)

FIGURE 120.—COVER, from New York to Richmond (Ain), France, 1875. (*Photograph by Smithsonian*)

FIGURE 121.—COVER, from Paris to New York, 1875. (*Photograph by Smithsonian*)

New York supplemtnary-mail marking in red (Scott's type *E*). On 21 October 1875 (see date in New York marking), *Klopstock* of the Hamburg-American line sailed from New York for Plymouth and Cherbourg. The Cherbourg receiving marking is unusual because it is applied in red.

Figure 121 illustrates a cover posted in Paris on 21 May 1875, addressed to New York. This letter did not weight over 10 grams and was prepaid 50 centimes in French stamps. It was marked PD and probably forwarded to New York by *Pereire* of the French line which sailed from Havre on 22 May 1875.[39] On the reverse is a circular NEW YORK/JUN/1/PAID ALL marking in red. Covers showing the convention rate of 50 centimes per 10 grams are not easy to find. Apparently, however, collectors have not realized this and these covers are not sought after as are their United States counterparts.

---

[39] Salles, *La Poste maritime,* vol. 4, p. 238.

Chapter 10

Depreciated Currency Covers

Brief Survey of United States Monetary History—1792–1862

On 2 April 1792, Congress enacted a mint act which adopted a decimal system of coinage and a bimetallic standard with silver and gold granted full legal tender at a ratio of 15 to 1, and established a United States mint. Some time after this act became effective, the market ratio between silver and gold became about 15½ to 1. On the market, 15½ ounces of silver could be purchased for 1 ounce of gold, but at the mint only 15 ounces of silver were required to buy 1 ounce of gold. Such a transaction would yield a profit of about one half ounce of silver. Under those conditions silver was brought to the mint for coinage, and gold was converted into bullion for the market. Silver overvalued at the mint was driving undervalued gold out of circulation.

Portions of this chapter appeared in the *Chronicle of the U.S. Classic Issues,* 20, 3, Whole No. 59 (Aug. 1968): 110–115; 20, 4, Whole No. 60 (Nov. 1968): 146–151.

In order to remedy this situation, laws were enacted in 1834 and in 1837 which established a new mint ratio of 15.988 to 1, usually expressed as 16 to 1. According to this new mint ratio, the standard silver dollar was to contain 371.25 grains of pure silver, or 412.5 grains of coin silver 0.9 fine, while the standard gold dollar was to contain 23.22 grains of pure gold, or 25.8 grains 0.9 fine.

This new coinage ratio undervalued silver at the mint, for the market ratio remained about 15½ to 1. At the mint, about 16 ounces of silver exchanged for 1 ounce of gold, but in the market only 15½ ounces of silver would buy 1 ounce of gold. Thus, overvalued gold was taken to the mint to exchange for undervalued silver, and silver, in consequence, gradually disappeared from circulation. This was the situation at the beginning of the Civil War.[1]

The "Greenbacks" and Fractional Paper Currency

On 30 December 1861, the banks in New York City suspended specie payments, and on 1 January 1862, the federal government also suspended payments in specie.[2] On 25 February 1862, the Legal Tender Act was passed by Congress which, among other things, authorized the issuance of $150 million in noninterest-bearing United States notes which were made legal tender for all debts, public and private; except customs duties and interest on public debt. The United States, therefore, adopted a de facto inconvertible paper standard for these notes, and through the operation of Gresham's law,[3] forced the gold coin out of circulation. During the first quarter of 1862 the average price of United States notes (greenbacks) in gold declined to 97.5.[4]

Until 1853 the silver content of a dollar's worth of

---

[1] See J. Laurence Laughlin, *Principles of Political Economy by John Stuart Mill,* pp. 344–364.
[2] Ibid.
[3] As stated by Sir Thomas Gresham (a merchant at the time of Elizabeth I), "Money of less value drives out money of more value." As usually stated, "Bad money drives good money out of circulation." Ibid., p. 313.
[4] Wesley C. Mitchell, *Gold, Prices, and Wages under the Greenback Standard,* p. 5.

subsidiary coins [5] of the United States was the same as that of a silver-dollar piece. Because of the discrepancy between the mint and market ratios of silver, these coins were disappearing from circulation. On 21 February 1853, a new coinage act was passed which reduced the silver content of a dollar's worth of subsidiary coins to 345.6 grains of pure silver, as compared with 371.25 grains in the silver-dollar piece. This represented a reduction of 6.91 percent, and made the silver content of a dollar's worth of subsidiary coins 93.09 percent of the silver-dollar piece.

While this reduction was barely sufficient to keep the subsidiary coins in circulation at that time, the suspension of specie payments and the introduction of United States notes, whose gold value soon fell below the gold value of the subsidiary coins, forced the latter out of circulation. By June 1862 a crisis developed because there was no small change available. Immediately a welter of fractional paper currency appeared, issued by private individuals and business firms which, perforce, temporarily served as money.[6] The Currency Act of 17 July 1862 sought to alleviate the stringency in small change by authorizing the use of postage stamps as currency. Stamps prepared for postage uses, however, were not adapted to the purposes of currency, and on 21 August the Treasury began the distribution of fractional postage currency notes which replaced the use of postage stamps as money.[7] On 3 March 1863, Congress further acted by authorizing the issuance of fractional United States notes of different design to replace the postage currency then in circulation.[8]

By the acts of 11 July 1862 and 17 January 1863, Congress authorized the further issuance of $300 million in United States notes. Thus, by the end of the first quarter of 1863 the issuance of a total of $450 million in greenbacks had been authorized, and their average price in gold for that quarter had fallen to 65.2.[9]

Depreciated Currency and the Post Office Department

As the inflation progressed, the Post Office Department realized that it was suffering a severe loss in revenue through the collection of postage on unpaid letters from foreign countries in depreciated paper, while international settlements with these same countries had to be made in specie. It also noted that foreign correspondents were taking advantage of the situation by sending more of their letters to the United States unpaid. Postmaster General Blair called the attention of Congress to the matter and asked that measures be taken to alleviate it.

On 17 February 1863, Mr. Collamer of the Senate Committee on the Post Office and Post Roads reported to Congress a joint resolution which authorized the Post Office Department to collect the postages due on unpaid-mail matter from foreign countries in coin. In presenting the measure he pointed to the great loss suffered in settling balances with foreign governments on unpaid-mail matter. He stated: "It gets to be a pretty severe operation when it [the Post Office Department] has to pay forty or fifty thousand dollars a year discount on the paper it receives, with which to get gold to pay back the balance of postage."[10] Mr. Trumbull recognized the gravity of the loss, but objected to the measure on the grounds of the great inconvenience it would cause the public. He felt it would be most onerous on the poor, for example, servants who were corresponding with relatives in Europe. "Where would they secure the coin," he asked, "when there was none in circulation?" Mr. Wilson moved that it lay on the table for the present. To this, Congress agreed.[11]

On 3 March 1863, a similar measure, which granted the postmaster general discretionary power in making collections on such mail matter, was introduced and approved:[12]

No. 35 A Resolution Authorizing the Collection in Coin of Postages Due on Unpaid Mail Matter from Foreign Countries:

Whereas, the failure to prepay foreign correspondence throws upon the Post Office Department of the United States large balances, which have to be paid in coin: Therefore,

---

[5] The silver subsidiary coins were, at this time, the half-dollar, the quarter-dollar, the dime, the half-dime, and the silver three-cent piece.

[6] These private fractional notes were popularly called "shinplasters."

[7] Neil Carothers, *Fractional Money*, p. 177.

[8] "A treasury official named Clark had his portrait engraved on one of the new fractional notes. This so incensed Congress that by a law of April 7, 1866, it was provided that portraits of living persons should not appear on any securities or currency of the United States." Ibid., note, p. 180.

[9] Mitchell, *Greenback Standards*, p. 5.

[10] U.S., Congress, *Congressional Globe*, 37th Cong., 3rd sess., p. 1017.

[11] Ibid., p. 1018.

[12] Ibid., *appendix*, p. 240.

Be it resolved by the Senate and House of Representatives of the United States in Congress assembled, That the Postmaster General be and is hereby authorized to take such measures as may seem advisable to him to collect postages on letters from abroad not prepaid, in order to avoid loss in payment of such balances.

On 1 April 1863, Postmaster General Blair issued an official circular which was distributed to all postmasters throughout the Loyal States. After some explanatory remarks he quoted the above joint resolution and issued the following order: [13]

In pursuance of the provisions of the resolution, you are hereby directed, *from and after the first of May next,* to collect in *gold or silver coin* all postages due on unpaid letters received from foreign countries in mails dispatched to this country from Great Britain and Ireland, France, Prussia, Hamburg, Bremen or Belgium and to hold the coin so collected subject to the special drafts or orders of the Department. Should however payment of such postage and of the premium on a corresponding amount of coin be tendered in United States notes, you are authorized to accept the same in lieu of coin. . . .

For the present this order will apply exclusively to the mails from the countries above mentioned. On outgoing letters the existing regulations remain unchanged.

The public was thus relieved of the absolute necessity of paying the postage due on unpaid letters from foreign countries in coin, if the equivalent (which included the premium on coin) was paid in United States notes.

The method to be used by the post offices in collecting the coin equivalent in United States notes must have caused some confusion, for editor Holbrook found it necessary to explain the procedure in the June issue of the *U.S. Mail and Post Office Assistant:* [14]

Collection in coin. It may be of service to some postmasters to explain the plan adopted in the New York Office in carrying out the recent ORDER to collect postage on unpaid foreign leters, in *coin or its equivalent.* [Italics added for emphasis throughout.]

Letter stamps are prepared with changeable figures, with which all such letters for this delivery are rated, *as soon as they arrive by steamer;* the premium on *silver* at that time being adopted as a basis. Thus on a letter from Great Britain 32 cts. would be stamped, if the *coin* then ruled at 33 per cent. No matter when the letter is called for, the rate stamped on the letter must be paid, unless the *gold or silver* is offered, when, of course, only 24 cts. can be demanded if the letter weighs a single rate only. This has been the practice up to the 1st inst., in the New York office respecting letters for delivery here, as before stated; but by order of the Department it was on the 1st inst., extended to all such foreign letters passing in transit through the other offices.

We mention this in order that distant postmasters may understand the new ruling, and collect accordingly. The arrangement will no doubt relieve them of some trouble. Similar instructions have been given to the postmasters of Philadelphia, Boston, Portland, Detroit, Chicago, and San Francisco, there being the regular United States Exchange offices for foreign mails.

If any coin had been offered to pay the postage due on unpaid letters from foreign countries, it would undoubtedly have been in the form of silver subsidiary coins. As has been previously pointed out, the silver content of these coins was 93.1 percent of that of the silver-dollar piece. On the other hand, in 1863 the market price of silver was higher than the mint price. This is reflected in columns 1 and 2 of Table 32. On the average during that year, only 15.37 ounces of silver would have bought one ounce of gold on the market, but 15.988 ounces were required to exchange for an ounce of gold at the mint. To state it another way, $1.039 in gold was required to buy $1.00 in silver (column 2). The price of silver in greenbacks (column 3) was, therefore, higher than the price of gold in greenbacks (column 4) in 1863. Column 5 of Table 32 presents the gold value of a dollar's worth of silver subsidiary coins. If, in 1863, the market and the mint ratios between silver and gold had been the same, the figure in column 5 for that year would have been 0.931, reflecting the lesser amount of silver in the subsidiary coins. The increase from 0.931 to 0.967 represents the higher market price of silver. This is clearly observed in the figures for 1873 when (column 1) the market ratio approached the mint ratio of 15.988, the market value of silver in gold (column 2) approached 100, and the gold value of silver subsidiary coins (column 5) approached 0.931.

Procedure Followed in Rating Letters

Although the preceding description of the procedure to be followed in rating these unpaid letters from abroad states that the *premium on silver at the time of the steamer's arrival* was to be used as the basis for rating, tests made on numerous covers indicate that this could not have been so. One is led to the conclusion that editor Holbrook did not fully explain what was meant by "premium on silver." More explicitly, he should have stated it as "premium on silver subsidiary coins." This is implied in his next sentence when

---

[13] *U.S. Mail and Post Office Assistant* 3, 8 (May 1863): 2.
[14] Ibid. 9, p. 2.

TABLE 32.—*Prices in Greenbacks of Gold, Silver, and Silver Subsidiary Coins**

Column 1 Market Ratio of Silver to Gold; Column 2 Market Value of Silver in Gold; Column 3 Price of Silver in Greenbacks; Column 4 Price of Gold in Greenbacks; Column 5 Gold Value of a Dollar's Worth of Silver Subsidiary Coins; Column 6 Price of Silver Subsidiary Coins in Greenbacks.

Year	Annual Averages					
	1	2	3	4	5	6
1863	15.37	103.9	150.9	145.2	0.967	140.2
1864	15.37	103.9	211.2	203.3	0.967	196.6
1865	15.44	103.5	162.8	157.3	0.963	151.5
1866	15.43	103.6	146.4	140.9	0.964	133.8
1867	15.57	102.7	141.9	138.2	0.956	132.1
1868	15.59	102.6	143.3	139.7	0.955	133.4
1869	15.60	102.5	136.3	133.0	0.954	126.9
1870	15.57	102.7	117.3	114.9	0.956	108.8
1871	15.57	102.7	114.7	111.7	0.955	106.6
1872	15.63	102.3	114.9	112.4	0.952	107.0
1873	15.92	100.4	114.3	113.8	0.938	106.7
1874	16.17	98.9	109.9	111.2	0.925	102.9
1875	16.59	96.4	110.8	114.9	0.888	103.5
1876	17.88	89.4	99.3	111.5	0.842	93.9
1877	17.22	92.8	97.3	104.8	0.869	91.1
1878	17.94	89.1	89.8	100.8	0.834	84.1

*Derived from table published in Hargest, George E., "Depreciated Currency Covers," *The Chronicle of the U.S. Classic Issues* (August 1968), vol. 20, no. 3, p. 113.
Source: Columns 1 and 5: Carothers, Neil, 1930, appendix F, p. 323; Column 4: Mitchell, Wesley C., 1908, p. 4; Column 2: 15.988 divided by the figures in Column 1; Column 3: figures in Column 4 multiplied by figures in Column 2; Column 6: figures in Column 4 multiplied by figures in Column 5.

he speaks of the *coin* (not the silver) *ruling at 33 percent*. While many examples could be cited, several will suffice to illustrate how these covers were rated.

Marking *A* of Figure 122 appears on a cover posted in London on 10 June 1867, addressed to Boston.[15] This marking indicates that 24¢ were to be collected in coin, or 31¢ in United States notes (greenbacks). On 13 June (the date of the steamer's arrival as indicated in the postmark) the lowest and highest prices of gold in greenbacks were, respectively, 137 and 137¼.[16] If the premium on gold had been used as the basis for calculation, the lowest possible amount to be collected would have been 33¢ (24 × 137 = 32.88), or 2¢ higher than the amount shown in the postmark. Since the price of silver in greenbacks (column 3) was higher than the price of gold (column 4), the amount to be collected would have been higher than 32.88, if the premium on silver had been used as the basis for calculation.

It is evident that neither the premium on gold nor the premium on silver was used as the basis for calculating the amount due in United States notes on these covers. The price of silver subsidiary coins in greenbacks, however, not only reflects the lesser amount of silver they contain, but also the higher market price of silver (column 6). It appears that the premium on gold was reduced by applying the percentages shown in column 5 in order to secure the premium on silver subsidiary coins. Thus, 137 (premium 37) was multiplied by 24 and the product multiplied by 0.956 (column 5 figure for 1867), the final product of which is 31.43, or 31¢, which agrees with the amount shown in the postmark. It must be borne in mind that the figures in column 5 are annual averages and at any particular time could be more or less than the amount shown. Although declining gradually until 1873, this series shows great stability, and its application to daily figures appears justified. Undoubtedly, the exchange

---

[15] Courtesy of Lester L. Downing.
[16] Mitchell, *Greenback Standards*, pp. 291–338, presents the *daily* lowest and highest premium on gold and price of greenbacks in gold for the period 1862 through 1878.

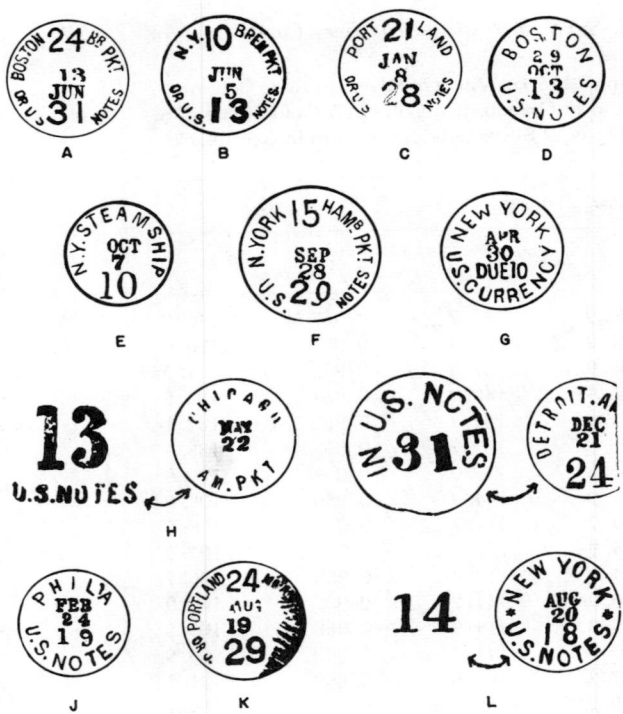

FIGURE 122.—MARKINGS on unpaid letters during depreciated currency period.

offices were furnished the price of silver subsidiary coins in greenbacks on a daily basis, but such a series has not been found in the government records to which reference has been made.

Applying the same procedure to marking *B* of Figure 122, a similar situation arises. The letter showing this marking was posted in Bremen on 20 May 1865, addressed to Philadelphia. The postmark indicates that 10¢ were to be collected in coin, or 13¢ in United States notes. On 5 June 1865 (the date in the postmark), the lowest and highest prices of gold in greenbacks were $135\frac{7}{8}$ and $136\frac{1}{2}$, respectively. The product of $10 \times 135\frac{7}{8}$ is 13.59, or 14¢, which is 1¢ higher than the 13 in the postmark. When, however, 13.59 is multiplied by 0.963 (column 5 figure for 1865) the product is 13.08, or 13¢, which agrees with the amount shown in the postmark.

Marking *C* of Figure 122 appears on a cover posted in Minorca, Spain, on 21 December 1867, addressed to Pottsville, Pennsylvania.[17] The postmark indicates that the British open-mail rate of 21¢ by American packet was to be collected in coin, or 28¢ in United States notes. On 8 January 1868 (the date in the postmark), the lowest and highest prices of gold in greenbacks were $136\frac{1}{8}$ and $137\frac{3}{4}$, respectively. The product of $136\frac{1}{8} \times 21$ is 28.58, or 29¢, which is one cent higher than the amount in the postmark. When, however, 28.58 is multiplied by 0.955 (the 1868 figure in column 5) the product is 27.29, less than the indicated collection. In this case, however, the highest, or higher, price for the day was used. The product of $21 \times 137\frac{3}{4} \times 0.955$ is 27.69, or 28¢, which agrees with the amount in the postmark.

Marking *F* of Figure 122 appears on a cover posted in Germany on 5 September 1867, addressed to Alabama. On 28 September 1867, the lowest and highest prices of gold in greenbacks were 143 and $143\frac{5}{8}$, respectively. The product of 15×143 is 21.45, or 21¢, which is 1¢ more than the 20¢ shown in the postmark. The product of 21.45×0.956 is 20.51, which would also round to 21¢. Since 0.956 is an annual average, at any particular time this figure could be more or less than 0.956. It appears that on 28 September 1867, it was less. If it were only 0.955, the 20¢ indicated for collection would have been validated.

A number of new postal conventions between the United States and European countries became effective during 1868. Each of these conventions prescribed a fine on unpaid letters which was to be assessed and retained by the country collecting the postage. In the United States this fine was always payable in United States notes, that is, it was not assessable in coin. As a result, dual-rate postmarks applied to letters from these countries disappeared during 1868. They were replaced by new postmarks which showed the amount to be collected in United States notes only.

Marking *D* of Figure 122 appears on a cover posted in Liverpool on 15 October 1870, addressed to Boston.[18] On 29 October 1870 (the date in the postmark), the lowest and highest prices of gold in greenbacks were, respectively, $111\frac{1}{4}$ and $111\frac{5}{8}$. The collection on this cover was evidently computed at the highest price for the day. The rate after 1 January 1870, was 6¢ per half ounce and, hence, $6 \times 111\frac{5}{8}$ is 6.7, or 7¢. To this 7¢ was added the unpaid letter fine of 6¢ (which was always payable in notes) to produce a rate of 13¢, which is the amount indicated for collection in the postmark.

As explained in Chapter 9 (page 165), section 8 of the Act of 1 July 1864 provided a 10¢ rate per half ounce on letters addressed to or received from foreign countries when conveyed in vessels regularly employed

---

[17] Cover lent through courtesy of Melvin W. Schuh.

[18] Cover lent through courtesy of Lester L. Downing.

in the transportation of the mails. This act particularly pertained to those countries with whom the United States had no postal convention.[19] When the United States-French convention expired on 31 December 1869, this 10¢ rate was immediately applied to mail between the United States and France, when conveyed by steamers plying directly between the ports of the two countries. The 10¢ rate under this act was always collectible in United States notes. Marking E of Figure 122 illustrates one of several N.Y. STEAMSHIP markings that appear on these covers. Evidently, there was some confusion about this rate being collected in coin. Marking G of Figure 122 settled the matter by indicating that the rate was to be collected in currency.

Change in the Basis of Rating

The Coinage Act of 21 February 1873 removed from the list of legal coins the silver dollar-piece, which had not been in circulation since long before 1853. This was, in fact, the demonetization of silver. At about the same time this act was passed, several European countries also demonetized silver, and large deposits were discovered in the United States. This increased production of silver coupled with its loss of utility as money, forced the price to decline rapidly. The sharp decrease in the market price of silver after 1873 is observed in columns 2 and 3 of Table 20. It appears that about this time the exchange offices began to use the premium on gold instead of the premium on silver subsidiary coins as the basis for determining the amount due in United States notes on unpaid letters from foreign countries. In 1874 the Post Office Department authorized the publication of a *United States Official Postal Guide,* which was "revised and published quarterly, by authority of the Post Office Department." In the first issue, which is dated October 1874, the following appeared:

> The Postmaster General is by law authorized to collect unpaid postages due on correspondence from foreign countries, in gold or its equivalent in currency, in order to secure the Department from loss on balances due foreign offices. Under this law, unpaid postages on correspondence from Great Britain and Ireland, Belgium, the Netherlands, Germany, Switzerland, Sweden and Norway, are calculated at gold rates.

---

[19] John N. Luff, *Postage Stamps of the United States,* appendix, p. 395.

Earliest Depreciated Currency Covers

While the Post Office order issued by Postmaster General Blair required depreciated currency rating on and after 1 May 1863, the description by editor Holbrook of the procedure to be used by the exchange offices indicates that it came into force during May only at the New York office. It was to become effective at the other offices on 1 June 1863. Since no steamer arrived at New York or Boston on 1 May 1863, the earliest possible rating at the New York office for mail by British packet would have been for the arrival in Boston of R.M.S. *Europa* on 2 May, the mail being rated at New York on 3 May 1863. The first rating at New York for American packet mail would have been on 4 May for the arrival on that date of *Etna* of the Inman line.

The earliest possible rating at the Boston office would have been on 4 June for the arrival in New York on 3 June of R.M.S. *Persia* of the Cunard line. *Edinburgh* of the Inman line also arrived in New York on 3 June, and the earliest rating at the Boston office for American packet mail would also have been on 4 June 1863. It is assumed that the depreciated currency ratings were actually placed in force at the New York office on 1 May and at the other offices on 1 June 1863.

Figure 123 presents the earliest depreciated currency cover rated by the Boston office seen by the author. It was posted in Paris on 25 May 1863 and arrived in New York on 7 June 1863 by either *Hammonia* of the Hamburg-American line, or by *America* of the North German Lloyd, both of which arrived on that date. As a French-mail letter by American packet through England, it bears a French debit of 6¢. Boston evidently did not yet have dual-rate markings showing collections in coin and in notes. This cover was, therefore, marked for a collection of 20¢ in United States notes, instead of the convention rate of 15¢ which was collectible in coin. Since 7 June was a Sunday, it was rated according to the quotations of 8 June 1863. On that date both the lowest and highest price of gold in greenbacks was 143. The product of $15 \times 143 \times 0.967$ is 20.74¢, which may indicate that the gold value of silver subsidiary coins (column 5) on that date was slightly less than its annual average of 0.967.

Although there was nothing stated in the Legal Tender Act of 1862 regarding the redemption in specie of the greenbacks, it was always tacitly assumed that they would at some time be redeemed. Their value, therefore, rested upon the public confidence in their

FIGURE 123.—COVER, from Paris to Boston, 1863.

ultimate redemption. That they did not become worthless, as so many other inconvertible currencies had become, attests to the faith of the public that the Union cause would eventually prevail. Every act of the Civil War, military, political, and financial, affected their value. Collectors may like to collect these covers to demonstrate the effect specific events had upon the premium.

The height of the inflation occurred on 11 July 1864, when the price of gold in greenbacks reached 285. The immediate cause of this rise in premium was General Jubal Early's raid into Maryland and his attack on Washington on 9 July 1864. Since no steamer arrived in New York or Boston on 11 July, there are no covers that reflect the highest point of the inflation. *Etna* arrived in New York on the following day when the prices of gold in greenbacks ranged from 271 to 282, and *Australasian* of the Cunard line arrived in New York on 13 July, but by that time the prices ranged from 268¾ to 273. Throughout most of August the highest daily prices hovered around 255. Covers during this period of high premium are scarce and interesting.

Figure 124 illustrates a cover posted in Newcastle-on-Tyne, England, on 28 July 1864, addressed to Providence, Rhode Island. It is prepaid 1s., but weighing over a single rate of half an ounce was marked INSUFFICIENTLY PREPAID, and the prepayment was not recognized. Considered as an unpaid letter, it was given a double-rate debit of 6¢ for American packet service to the United States. It is endorsed to *City of London* of the Inman line which arrived in New York on 8 August 1864. The New York office marked it for a collection in coin of 48¢, and with U.S. NOTES/120. On 8 August 1864, the price of gold in greenbacks ranged from 256¾ to 259½. *City of London* must have arrived when the highest price prevailed, for 259½ × 48 × 0.967 is 120.44, or $1.20.

Figure 125 illustrates another highly rated cover. It was posted in Hamburg on 7 August 1864, addressed to New Bedford, Massachusetts. It arrived in New York on 22 August, onboard *Etna* of the Inman line, in the Prussian closed mail, and was rated for a collection of 30¢ in coin or 75¢ in United States notes. On 22 August 1864, the price of gold in greenbacks ranged from 256⅞ to 257.5. The product of 256⅞ × 30 × 0.967 is 74.52, or 75¢.

Figure 126 illustrates a cover showing the rare triple rate from England. It was prepaid two rates by two 1s. stamps, but was found to weigh over one ounce

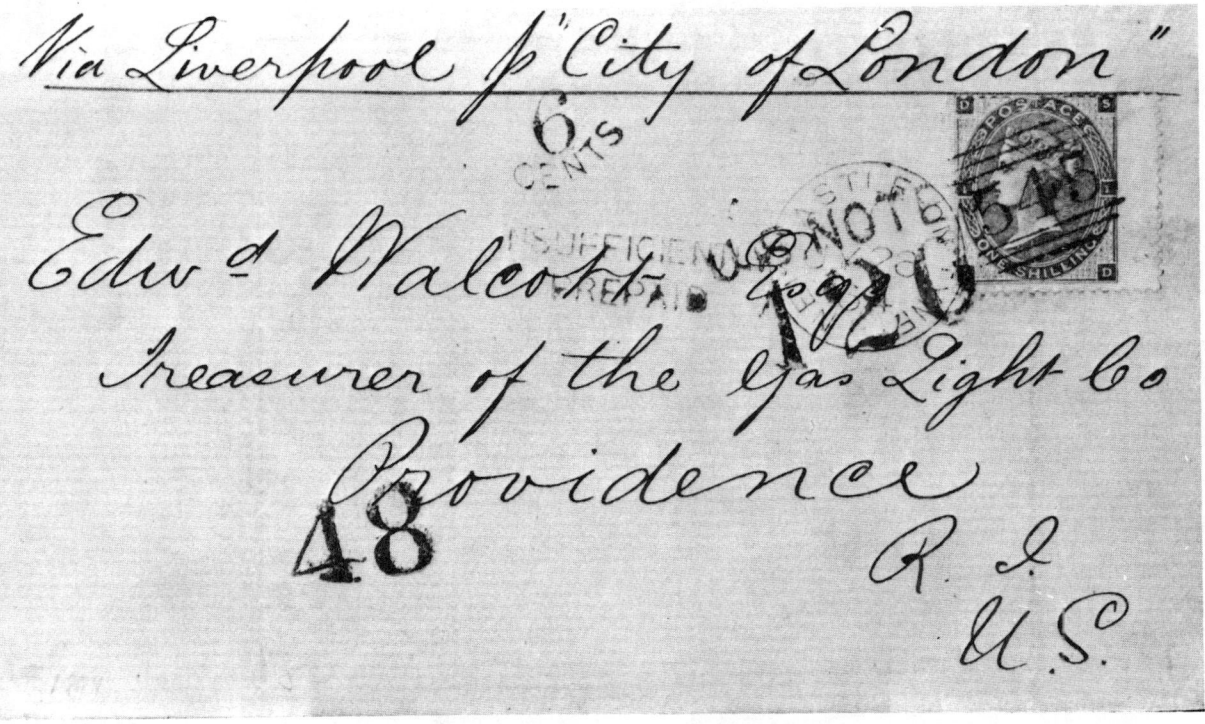

FIGURE 124.—COVER, from Newcastle-on-Tyne, England, to Providence, R.I., 1864.

FIGURE 125.—COVER, from Hamburg to New Bedford, Mass., 1864.

Figure 126.—Cover, from Dundee, Scotland, to Andover, Massachusetts, 1866. (*Melvin W. Schuh collection*)

which required three rates. The letter was marked *over 1 oz.* and INSUFFICIENTLY PREPAID, and was also marked by the British office: *57/3*. This was a debit for British packet service of 57¢ (3×19), the *3* indicating the number of rates. The Boston office marked it *72/.91*, that is, 3×24, or 72¢ if paid in coin, 91¢ if paid in notes. Since the price of gold in greenbacks on 21 June 1866 ranged from 148½ to 151¼, the lowest possible collection on this letter (148½ × 72 × 0.964) should have been 103.07, or $1.03. One can only conclude that the clerk made an error in computing the amount to be collected in United States notes.

Although the Specie Resumption Act was passed on 14 January 1875, to become effective on 1 January 1879, there was no permanent reduction of the premium until April 1876, due largely to the fact that it was not taken seriously by the public at the time of its passage. After April 1876 the premium gradually declined until the price of gold in greenbacks reached 100 on 17 December 1878. "The reason for this decline—at least after March, 1877, when John Sherman became secretary of the treasury—is obviously found in the effective preparations to execute the resumption act of 1875, and the fortunate turn of foreign trade which facilitated Sherman's operations." [20] With the resumption of specie payments, depreciated currency markings finally expired.

The Exchange Offices

The markings designated as *H* in Figure 122 are on a cover belonging to Mr. William C. Coles, Jr., who has an extensive collection of depreciated currency covers. This letter was posted in England and arrived at the Chicago exchange office on 22 May 1871. On that date, the price of gold in greenbacks ranged from 111.625 to 112. The international rate between the United States and England was 6¢. Thus, 6¢ × 1.12 × 0.955 (Table 20, column 5 figure for 1871) amounts to 6.4, shown as 7¢, and to this was added an unpaid letter fine of 6¢, the sum of which is 13¢. Evidently, the Chicago office did not have dual-rate markings, but showed the 13¢ to be collected in notes by use of a handstamp separately applied.

Mr. Coles also reports the cover upon which the

---

[20] Mitchell, *Greenback Standard*, p. 14.

markings designated as *I* in Figure 122 appear. This letter was posted in London on 3 December, and arrived at the Detroit office on 21 December 1867. On that date the lowest and highest prices of gold in greenbacks were 133¼ and 133⅝, respectively. Thus, 24¢ x 1.33¼ x 0.956 is equal to 30.6, or 31¢. Like the Chicago office, the Detroit office did not use a marking showing dual rates, but applied the amount to be collected in United States notes separately by use of a handstamp designed for that purpose.

Marking *J* of Figure 122 appears on a cover posted in Bremen on 2 February 1868, addressed to Philadelphia, and endorsed "Str. Hansa," a vessel of the North German Lloyd. By the "Regulations" for the execution of the United States-North German Union convention of 21 October 1867 (effective 1 January 1868), Philadelphia became an exchange office for North German Union mail. Philadelphia had not previously been an exchange office for any of the German mails. The direct international rate between the North German Union and the United States was 10¢ per half ounce. This letter arrived at the Philadelphia office on 24 February 1868, and on that date the price of gold in greenbacks ranged from 142¼ to 144. Thus, 10 x 1.42¼ x 0.955 is equal to 13.6, or 14¢. To this 14¢ was added an unpaid letter fine of 5¢, which resulted in a collection of 19¢ in United States notes, indicated in the postmark. This cover is also in the collection of Mr. Coles.

Marking *K* of Figure 122, also in the collection of Mr. Coles, illustrates a dual-rate marking of the Portland office. This is of a different type from that illustrated as marking *C*.

Since the greenbacks never circulated on the Pacific coast, it is unlikely that any markings showing depreciated currency ratings from the San Francisco office will be found. Cut off as it was by the mountains, with its own supply of metals and a mint at San Francisco, the Pacific coast circulated coin during the entire period, 1863 through 1878.

Unpaid Letters From France, 1870–1874

Markings designated as *L* in Figure 122 appear on a cover posted in Bordeaux, France, on 6 August 1873, addressed to New York, and sent as an unpaid letter. The rate represented on this cover was in effect from 1 January 1870 until 1 August 1874. These unpaid letters bear *currency* markings of various types applied in France to indicate that the letters were forwarded to England charged at the rate of 2 francs per 30 grams, bulk weight, of such mail. London markings appear on the reverse of these letters, and on the face all are marked 14 for a single rate. Until the daily prices of gold in greenbacks became available, it was thought that the 14 on these covers was applied by the United States and represented the amount to be collected in coin, while the amount to be collected in United States notes was shown in the exchange office marking.[21] It is now known that the 14 represents a British debit to the United States, and the true rate on these letters was 16, and not 14¢.

The New York marking on the cover from which marking *L* is taken bears the date of 20 August (1873), and on that date the price of gold in greenbacks ranged from 115⅜ to 115½. Thus, 16 × 1.15⅜ amounts to 18.46, or 18¢. The application of these gold prices to 14¢ does not produce the indicated collection of 18¢. On this cover, it is also evident that the amount due was calculated at gold rates. This same situation has been noted on a number of unpaid letters from France during this period.

Reconstruction of the British debit of 14¢ indicates that the British divided the 2 francs per 30 grams rate by 4 to arrive at a single rate per one-fourth ounce of 50 centimes, or 10¢.[22] To this 10¢ were added 2¢ sea and 2¢ British postage per one-half ounce, for a total British share of 14¢. The United States collected the 14¢ British postage plus 2¢ United States inland postage, for a total of 16¢ in coin. On letters weighing over one-fourth but not over one-half ounce, only the French postage of 10¢ was doubled, and these letters show a British debit of 24¢, and a collection in the United States of 26¢ in coin. The 2 francs per 30 grams rate under the Anglo-French convention was for unpaid letters, and was twice the rate of prepaid letters. Since the unpaid letter was already penalized, the United States did not collect an unpaid-letter fine.

---

[21] George E. Hargest, "Unpaid and Part-Paid Rates Between United States and France, 1870–74," *Postal History Journal* 7, 1 June 1963: 10.

[22] Anglo-French postal convention of 24 Sept. 1856, Art. 14, clause 3, *British and Foreign State Papers*, vol. 46, p. 203.

Bibliography

Books

ALBION, ROBERT GREENHALGH. *Square Riggers on Schedule.* Princeton: Princeton University Press, 1938.

———. *The Rise of New York Port.* New York: Charles Scribner's Sons, 1939.

ASHBROOK, STANLEY B. *The United States One Cent Stamp of 1851–1857.* Vol. 2. New York: H. L. Lindquist, 1938.

BLAKE, MAURICE C., and DAVIS, WILBUR W. *Postal Markings of Boston, Massachusetts, to 1890.* Portland, Maine: Severn-Wylie-Jewett Co., 1949.

BONSOR, N. R. P. *North Atlantic Seaway.* Prescot: T. Stephenson & Sons, 1955.

BOURSELET, V.; MARÊCHAL, G. FRANÇOIS, L.; and GILBERT, G. *Les Paquebots français et leurs cachets, 1780–1935.* Published by the authors, undated.

BOWEN, FRANK C. *A Century of Atlantic Travel: 1830–1930.* Boston: Little, Brown & Co., 1930.

BROOKMAN, LESTER G. *The United States Stamps of the 19th Century.* Vols. 1–3. New York: H. L. Lindquist, 1966.

BRUNEL, GEORGES. *Le Timbre-Poste français.* Paris: Librairie chez Delagrave, 1896.

CAROTHERS, NEIL. *Fractional Money.* New York: John Wiley & Sons, 1930.

CHASE, CARROLL. *The 3¢ Stamp of the United States, 1851–1857 Issue.* Reprint. Springfield, Mass.: Tatham Stamp and Coin Co., 1842.

CODDING, GEORGE A., Jr. *The Universal Postal Union.* New York: New York University Press, 1964.

DOE, F. *Les Estampilles postales françaises.* Amiens: Yvert & Tellier, 1900.

GIBBS, C. R. VERNON. *Passenger Liners of the Western Ocean.* 2nd ed. London: Staples Press, 1957.

KULL, IRVING, and KULL, NELL M. *An Encyclopedia of American History.* Popular Library ed., New York: 1952.

HERST, HERMAN, JR., and SAMPSON, E. N., eds. *Fancy Cancellations on Nineteenth Century United States Postage Stamps.* Published by the authors, Shrub Oak, N.Y.: 1963.

LANGER, WILLIAM L., ed., *An Encyclopedia of World History.* Rev. ed. Boston: Houghton Mifflin Co. 1948.

LAUGHLIN, J. LAURENCE. *Principles of Political Economy by John Stuart Mill,* as abridged and annotated. New York: D. Appleton & Co., 1887.

LUFF, JOHN N. *The Postage Stamps of the United States.* New York: SCOTT STAMP AND COIN Co., 1902.

MAGINNIS, ARTHUR J. *The Atlantic Ferry, Its Ships, Men and Working.* New York: Macmillan Co., 1893.

MARVIN, WINTHROP L. *The American Merchant Marine: Its History and Romance from 1620 to 1902.* New York: Charles Scribner's Sons, 1910.

MAURY, ARTHUR, *Catalogue descriptif de toutes les marques postales de la France.* Paris: Arthur Maury, circa 1900.

MITCHELL, WESLEY C. *Gold, Prices, and Wages under the Greenback Standard.* Berkeley: The University Press, University of California Publications in Economics, 1908.

MORRISON, SAMUEL ELIOT. *The Maritime History of Massachusetts, 1783–1860.* Boston: Houghton Mifflin Co., 1921.

MYERS, GUSTAVUS. *History of Great American Fortunes.* New York: Random House, Modern Library Ed., 1936.

NEINKEN, MORTIMER L. *The United States Ten Cent Stamps of 1855–1859.* New York: The Collectors Club, 1960.

PIEFKE, CHRISTIAN. *Geschichte der bremischen Landespost.* Bremer Schlüssel Verlag Hans Kasten: 1947. (Translated by C. J. Starnes.)

RAINEY, THOMAS. *Ocean Steam Navigation and the Ocean Post.* New York: D. Appleton & Co., 1858.

ROBERTSON, ALAN W. *The Maritime Postal History of London.* London: Robson Lowe, 1960.

ROBINSON, HOWARD. *Carrying the British Mails Overseas.* New York: New York University Press, 1964.

ROUSSELIN, RAYMOND. *L'Acheminement des correspondances entre Le Havre et les pays d'outre-mer.* Le Havre: Imprimerie Rolland, 1957.

SALLES, RAYMOND. *La Poste Maritime Française Historique et Catalogue.* Edited by the author. Vol. 3, Les Paquebots de l'Atlantique Sud. Vol. 4, Les Paquebots de l'Atlantique Nord. Paris: 1961.

SIMPSON, TRACY W. *United States Postal Markings and Related Mail Services, 1851 to 1861.* Berkeley, California: American Philatelic Society, U.S. 1851–60 Unit No. 11, 1959.

SMITH, A. D. *The Development of Rates of Postage.* London: George Allen & Unwin, 1917.

STAFF, FRANK. *The Transatlantic Mail.* London: Adlard Coles, 1956.

TAYLOR, GEORGE R. *The Transportation Revolution.* New York: Holt, Rinehart & Winston, 1951.

Periodicals

American Philatelist, American Philatelic Society.
American Review of Reviews (particularly February 1902).
Balasse Magazine, Willy Balasse, Brussels.

Chronicle of the U.S. Classic Issues, U.S. Philatelic Classics Society, Unit 11 of American Philatelic Society (Referred to in the text as the *Chronicle*).
The Collectors Club Philatelist, The Collectors Club, New York.
The Philatelist, Robson Lowe, London.
The Postal History Journal, Postal History Society of the Americas.
Postal History Society Bulletin, Postal History Society, Great Britain.
Postscript, Society of Postal Historians, Great Britain.
Spécialités, M. Jamet, Paris (particularly June 1955).
The Stamp Lover, National Philatelic Society, Great Britain.
S.P.A. Journal, Society of Philatelic Americans.
Steamboat Bill, Steamship Historical Society of America.

Newspapers

The New York Tribune (daily).
The New York Recorder (weekly), 1853.
Shipping and Commercial List and New York Prices Current, every Wednesday and Saturday, 1840–1868.
Stamps, weekly magazine of philately.
U.S. Mail and Post Office Assistant, semiofficial. Privately published, but information furnished by the Post Office Department. Distributed monthly to subscribing postmasters.
Weekly New York Times.

Government Sources

United States

Annual Reports of the Postmaster General. Published as *House Documents,* as *Senate Documents,* separately published, and published in abridged editions; variously paginated. Appendices, *Reports of the Auditor of the Treasury for the Post Office Department,* not included in abridged editions.
Congress, Executive Documents and Reports, House and Senate. 30th to 43rd Congress.
Congressional Globe. 36th to 38th Congress.
Department of State, *Treaties and Other International Acts of the United States of America.* Edited by Hunter Miller. Washington, D.C.: (Government Printing Office, 1937).
Postal Laws and Regulations. 1847–1859 and 1866–1875.
Official Postal Guides. Quarterly, October 1874 and April 1875.
Statutes at Large.

British

British and Foreign State Papers.
Hansard's Parliamentary Debates.
Hertslet, Edward, ed. *Commercial Treaties.*

Semiofficial

Information furnished by Post Office Department

American Almanac. Privately published (1830–1857).
Postal Directories. Various publishers in different years.
Postal Guides. Various publishers in different years.

Private Publications

ASHBROOK, STANLEY B. *Special Service,* Series 1–7. Distributed to subscribers.
PERRY, ELLIOTT. *Pat Paragraphs,* Nos. 1–58. Distributed to subscribers.

Appendix

Postal Rates to Foreign Countries, 1848-1875

The postal rates to foreign destinations are given in two tables: Table *A* covers the period from 1848 to 1 January 1868, Table *B*, 1868 to 1 July 1875. When available, the date of introduction or change in rate is given by month and year, otherwise only the year is given. While in many cases the day of the month of introduction or change in rate is known, only the month and year are given.

These tables should be traced from left to right. The mail service and route are first noted, next the date the rate was introduced, followed by dates of and changes in rates. The last column gives the date the rate was discontinued. If the rate was continued beyond 1 January 1868, in Table *A*, or beyond 1 July 1875, in Table *B*, "Continue" is written in the last column; if, on either table, there are more changes than there are columns, "Next line" is written in the last column, and subsequent changes should be traced on the following line.

Abbreviations and notations

Table A

Br./Am. Pkt.	By British or American packet
B.O.M.	British open mail
Brem./Hamb.	Bremen or Hamburg service
Br. M.	British mail
Fr. M.	French mail
Hapag	Hamburg-American Line
H. & de H.	Hérout et de Handel
P.C.M.	Prussian closed mail
St. T.	St. Thomas
d	Paid to destination
f	Paid to frontier
(c)	Except Lombardy and Venice
(d)	Except Lombardy, Modena, Parma, Tuscany, and Papal States
(e)	Except Yucatan, Matamoros, and Pacific coast
(f)	Matamoros and Pacific coast
(g)	Except Aspinwall, Panama, Bogatá, and Buenaventura
(h)	U.S. postage to San Francisco
(i)	Gulf coast, San Juan del Norte
(j)	Except Cuba
(a) 24	U.S. rates of 1845—24¢ in the port; 29¢ under 300 miles, 34¢ over 300 miles
5/21	5¢ by British packet; 21¢ by American packet
28/30u	28¢ when prepaid; 30¢ when unpaid, and all rates presented in like manner show prepaid and unpaid rates
*	Prepayment optional
†	Rate according to distance

Table B

a	When the rate was prefixed by the letter *a* the United States postage was by the half ounce, while the foreign postage, until 1 July 1870, was by the quarter ounce; after 1 July 1870, the foreign postage was by the one-third ounce.
Am. Pkt. v. N.O.	American packet via New Orleans
C.M. v. E.	Closed mail via England
N.G.U.	North German Union
(r)	Special prepaid rates for registered letters

NOTE. All other abbreviations are as given for Table A, or are self-evident.

Designation of Special Rates

AA Following are the rates of letter postage to Spain, Gibraltar, and the Canary and Balearic Isles *via* BELGIUM:

On letters for Spain (except Gibraltar) and her possessions, including the Canary and Balearic Isles, when not over one-third ounce, 16¢; over one-third but not over one-half ounce, 22¢; over one-half, but not over two-thirds ounce, 32¢; over two-thirds, but not over one ounce, 38¢, and the same charge and progression for each succeeding ounce or fraction thereof: *prepayment optional.*

On letters for Gibraltar, of one-third ounce or under, 18¢; over one-third but not over one-half ounce, 26¢; over one-half but not over two-thirds ounce, 36¢; over two-thirds but not over one ounce, 44¢, and the like charges for each additional ounce, or specified part thereof: *prepayment optional.*

To Spain and the Canary Islands, via Marseilles, the rates are as follows: For not over one-third oz., 16¢; over one-third but not over one-half oz., 28¢; over one-half but not over two-thirds oz., 32¢; over two-thirds but not over one oz., 44¢.

BB Following are the rates used by the New York exchange office on letters sent via England when prepaid with sufficient postage, and when the exchange office elected to use this route (the "phantom" rate): 7½ grams or under, 12¢; over 7½ but not over 15 grams, 20¢; over 15 but not over 22½ grams, 32¢; over 22½ but not over 30 grams, 40¢.

CC Open mail to England, 4¢ per one-half oz., prepayment optional. Via England: For one-third oz. and under, 10¢; over one-third but not over one-half oz., 16¢; over one-half but not over two-thirds oz., 20¢; over two-thirds but not over one oz., 26¢; prepayment compulsory.

List *A*—Adrianople, Antivari, Beyrout, Burgas, Caifia, Cavallo, Candia, Canea, Constantinople, Czernarroda, Dardanelles, Durazzo, Gallipoli, Jaffa, Janina, Jerusalem, Ineboli, Kustendji, Lagos, Larnica, Mitilene, Phillippopolis, Prevesa, Rhodes, Rustchuck, Salonica, Samsaun, Seres, Santi Quaranti, Sinope, Smyrna, Sophia, Sulina, Tenedos, Trebizond, Tchesme, Tulcha, Valona, Varna, Valo, and Widdin.

Sources
Table A

1848   Bremen rates as set forth in *Senate Executive Document* 25, 30th Congress, 2nd session, serial 531, pp. 18–19.

1849   *American Almanac* for 1850. Rates as of 1849.

1850   *Broadside of the Post Office of the City of New York.* William V. Brady, Postmaster. 13 February 1851; rates as of 1850.

1851   *Post Office Department Instructions to Postmasters.* 14 June 1851; rates as of 1 July 1851.

1852   *Postal Laws & Regulations,* 1852. Rates as of 3 April 1852.

1854   *Postal Directory & Postal Guide,* 1 April 1854.

1855   *List of Post Offices in the United States,* also Principal Regulations of the Post Office Department. Table of postages to foreign countries as of 1 July 1855.

Table of postages to foreign countries, *American Almanac* for 1856. Rates as of October 1855.

1856   *Post Office Directory* for 1856. Rates as of 1 July 1856.
       American Almanac for 1857. Rates as of October 1856.

1857   *Postal Laws & Regulations,* 1857. Rates as of 1 September 1857.

1858   *Postal Laws & Regulations* for 1858. Rates as of 1 September 1858.

1859   *Postal Laws & Regulations,* 1859. No date indicated for rates.

U.S. Mail and Post Office Assistant, tables of postages to foreign countries. Published monthly—All issues from October 1860 through December 1867.

The above information is supplemented by the effective dates of the various postal conventions to which reference has been made.

Table B

While it has been possible to see tables of postages to foreign countries for every month from October 1860 through December 1867, the same is not true for the period from January 1868 through December 1875. Why the later issues of the *U.S. Mail and Post Office Assistant* are so difficult to find is somewhat of a mystery. It is true that after 1872 they were printed on a cheap newsprint which has not been able to withstand the passage of time. Many of the original copies of the later issues seen are brown with age and break up when handled. Disintegration may be one of the causes for their scarcity. There must, however, be other reasons which can only be surmised.

Of the eighty-four months between January 1868

and December 1875, tables of postages for fifty-seven months have been seen. They are as follows:

1868 All months
1869 January, February, March, April, May, June, August, September, and December.
1870 April, May, June, July, August, September, October, November, and December.
1871 April, May, June, July, August, October, November, and December.
1872 January and October.
1873 January, February, May, and July.
1874 January, May, June, September, October, and November.
1875 January, February, April, July, August, October, and December.

Supplementing the above information are the effective dates as set forth by the various postal conventions to which reference has been made. Additional information regarding effective dates of rates is also occasionally supplied in the annual reports of the postmaster general. As will be noted, however, there is a nine-month period during 1872 in which rate information is not available. The dates given for Table *B*, therefore, should be interpreted as occurring on the date given, or *at least by* the stated date.

TABLE A.—*Postal Rates to Foreign Countries, 1848–1868*

Destination	Service	Route	Introduction			Change in Rate			Change in Rate			Date Discontinued
			Date	Rate ¼ oz.	Rate ½ oz.	Date	Rate ¼ oz.	Rate ½ oz.	Date	Rate ¼ oz.	Rate ½ oz.	
Acapulco	U.S.		7/51	—	20†	9/62	—	10		—	—	Continue
Aden	Br. M.	v. Southampton	1849	—	45	1/57	—	33		—	—	1/68
	Fr. M.	v. Marseilles	1849	65	75	1/57	39	45		—	—	1/68
Adrianople	Fr. M.		4/57	30	60		—	—		—	—	Continue
Africa, West Coast	Fr. M.		4/57	30*	60*		—	—		—	—	1/68
	Br. M.		1857	—	45	1859	—	—		—	—	1/68
Alexandretta	B.O.M.	Br./Am. Pkt.	1855	—	5/21		—	—	3/67	—	35	1/68
	P.C.M.		1855	—	40	5/63	—	38		—	—	1/68
	Fr. M.		4/57	30*	60*		—	—		—	—	Continue
Alexandria	Bremen	Direct	3/48	—	(see Table 3)		—	—	8/53	—	30	1859
	Brem./Hamb.	Direct	1859	—	30*		—	—		—	—	1/68
	B.O.M.	Br./Am. Pkt.	1849	—	5/21		—	—		—	—	1/68
	Fr. M.		4/57	30*	60*		—	—		—	—	Continue
	P.C.M.		1854	—	38*	5/63	—	36/38u	3/67	—	35*	1/68
Algeria	(see France)											
Altona	Bremen	Direct	3/48	—	(see Table 3)		—	—	8/53	—	22*	7/57
	Brem./Hamb.	Direct	7/57	—	22*	2/67	—	18*		—	—	1/68
	B.O.M	Br./Am. Pkt.	1855	—	5/21		—	—		—	—	4/57
	P.C.M.		10/52	—	33*	5/63	—	31/33u	3/67	—	28/30u	1/68
	Fr. M.		4/57	27*	54*		—	—		—	—	1/68
Antivari	B.O. M.	Br./Am. Pkt.	1855	—	5/21		—	—		—	—	1/68
	P.C.M.		1855	—	40	10/61	—	None	3/67	—	35*	1/68
	Fr. M.		1857	30*	60*		—	—		—	—	1/68
Arabia	Br. M.	v. Southampton	1/57	—	33		—	—		—	—	1/68
		v. Marseilles	1/57	39	45		—	—		—	—	1/68
Argentina	Br. M.	v. England	1854	—	45	1859	—	33	1/61	—	45	1/68
	Fr. M.	v. Bordeaux	1860	30	60		—	—		—	—	8/67
Aspinwall	U.S.	Am. Pkt.	8/67	18	25	(from N.Y. once a month)				—	—	Continue
	U.S.	Am. Pkt., direct	9/57	—	10/20†	8/64	—	10		—	—	Continue
Australia	Br. M.	v. Southampton	1849	—	53	1852	—	None	1/57	—	33	1/68
		v. Marseilles	1849	73	83	7/54	65	75	7/55	43	53	Next line
		v. Plymouth	6/52	—	45	1/57	39	45		—	—	1/68
		Private ship	1849	—	37	7/55	—	33		—	—	1/57
	Private ship from N.Y.		1854	—	5	(from U.K.)				—	—	1/57
	Fr. M.		4/57	30	60	5/62	30*	60*	(ex South Australia)			8/66
						9/57	—	—	(from N.Y. & Boston)			Continue

TABLE A.—*Postal Rates to Foreign Countries, 1848–1868*—Continued

Destination	Service	Route	Introduction			Change in Rate			Change in Rate			Date Discontinued
			Date	Rate ¼ oz.	Rate ½ oz.	Date	Rate ¼ oz.	Rate ½ oz.	Date	Rate ¼ oz.	Rate ½ oz.	
Australia—Continued	Br. M.	v. Panama	8/66	—	22		—	—		—	—	Continue
	Brem./Hamb.	v. Marseilles & Suez	7/57	50	1.02	2/67	—	37*		—	—	1/68
Austria	Fr. M.	v. Trieste	7/57	—	55		—	—		—	—	1/68
			4/57	27*	54*	1859	21*	42*		—	—	1/68
	(all other rates same as German States)											
Azores	Br. M.	v. Southampton	1849	—	63		—	—		—	—	1860
		v. Lisbon	1860	29	37		—	—		—	—	1/68
	Fr. M.		9/66	27*	54*		—	—		—	—	Continue
Baden	Bremen	Direct	3/48	(Table 3)		8/53	—	None	1855	—	22*	7/57
	Brem./Hamb.	Direct	7/57	—	22*	1860	—	15*		—	—	1/68
	B.O.M.	Br./Am. Pkt.	1849	—	5/21		—	—		—	—	4/57
	P.C.M.		10/52	—	30*	5/63	—	28/30u		—	—	1/68
	Fr. M.		4/57	21*	42*		—	—		—	—	1/68
Bahamas	B.O.M.	Br./Am. Pkt.	1849	—	5/21		—	—		—	—	7/51
Bankok	Am. Pkt. from N.Y. (see Siam)		7/51	—	10/20†	1859	—	5		—	—	Continue
Batavia	Br. M.	v. Southampton	1/57	39	33	12/61	—	45		—	—	1/68
		v. Marseilles	1/57	—	45	9/61	—	45	12/61	51	57	Next
	B.O.M.	Br./Am.Pkt.	1849	30	5/21	7/63	—	53		—	—	1/68
	Fr. Mail		4/57	—	60		—	—		—	—	4/57
Bavaria	(see German states)											Continue
Belgium	B.O.M.	Br./Am. Pkt.	1849	—	5/21		—	—		—	—	1/68
	Belgium C.M.	v. England	1/60	—	27*		—	—		—	—	1/68
	Fr. M.		4/57	21*	42*		—	—		—	—	1/68
Belgrade	Brem./Hamb.	Direct	2/67	—	18*		—	—		—	—	1/68
	B.O.M.	Br./Am. Pkt.	1857	—	5/21		—	—		—	—	1/68
	Fr.M.		1859	21*	42*		—	—		—	—	1/68
Beyrout	B.O.M.	Br./Am. Pkt.	1849	—	5/21		—	—		—	—	4/57
	P.C.M.		1852	—	40*	5/63	—	38/40u	3/67	—	35*	1/68
	Fr. M.		4/57	30*	60*		—	—		—	—	1/68
B.N.A. Provinces	Br. Pkt.	v. Halifax	1849	—5/10†	10	at least by 1856				—	5	7/67
	U.S.	to the line	1849	—	10	(U.C. & N.B.)						4/51
		to the line	1849	—	5	(L.C.)						4/51
	U.S.–Canada	(by treaty)	4/51	—10/15†		7/64	—10*		(Canada & New Brunswick)			7/67

Place	Service	Route	Start								End
Bogata, New Granada	Br. M.	v. Aspinwall	9/57	—	18	—	—	—	—	—	Continue
Bolivia	Br. M.		7/51	—	50	—	—	48	9/57	—	34	Continue
Borneo	Br. M.	v. Southampton	1849	—	53	—	33	9/61	—	45	1/68
	Br. M.	v. Marseilles	1849	73	83	39	45	9/61	—	45	Next line
				—	—	51	57	7/63	—	53	1/68
Bourbon	Fr. M.		4/57	30	60	—	33			—	Continue
	Br. Mail	v. Southampton	1849	—	53	—	33			—	1857
		v. Marseilles	1849	73	83	39	45			—	
Bourghas	Fr. M.		4/57	30*	60*	—	—			—	
	B.O.M.	Br./Am. Pkt.	1855	—	5/21	—	—			—	10/61
	P.C.M.		1855	—	40	(see Turkey in Europe)				—	10/61
	Fr. M.		1859	30*	60*	" "				—	1/68
Brazil	Br. M.	v. England	1849	—	87	—	45	1854	—	—	Continue
	U.S.	Am. Pkt., direct	1855	—	34/44†	1857	None			—	10	Continue
	Fr. M.	v. Bordeaux	1860	33*	66*	—	—	12/65	—	10*	1/68
Bremen	Bremen	Direct	3/48	(see Table 3)						—	1/68
	Hamburg	Hapag	7/57	—	15*	—	—	8/53	—	—	1/68
Brunswick	(all other rates same as German states)										
	(see German States)										
Buenaventura	Br. M.	v. Aspinwall	9/57	—	18	—	—	—	—	—	1/68
Buenos Ayres	Br. M.	v. Falmouth	1849	—	83	1854	45	1859	—	33	Next line
				—	—	1/61	45			—	1/68
	Fr. M.	v. Bordeaux	1860	30	60	—	—			—	8/67
	U.S.	Am. Pkt.	8/67	18	25	(from N.Y. once a month)				—	Continue
Caiffa	(same rates as Alexandretta, except no Fr. M.)										
Canada	U.S.-Canada		7/64	—	10*	(see B.N.A. Provinces)				—	Continue
Canary Islands	Br. M.	v. England	1849	—	65	1859	33	45	—	33	1/68
Candia	(same rates as Beyrout, except no Fr. M.; B.O.M. introduced in 1854)										
Canea	(same rates as Beyrout, except Fr. M. introduced in 1859; B.O.M. in 1854)										
Cape of Good Hope	Br. M.	v. Southampton	1854	45	45	1/57	33	5/63	—	45	1/68
		v. Marseilles	1/65	—	53	—	—	—	—	—	1/68
	B.O.M.	Br./Am. Pkt.	1859	—	5/21	—	—	1859			5/63
Carthagena	U.S. & Br. Pkts.		1855	—	34/44†	1857	34	—			1859
	Br. M.	v. Aspinwall	1859	—	18	—	—	—			Continue
Central America:											
East Coast	U.S.	v. Panama	7/51	—	35/45†	(see also separate countries)					1854
Pacific Slope	U.S.	v. Panama	1849	—	30	1859	20	5/65	—	10	Continue
Ceylon	Br. M.	v. Southampton	1849	—	45	1859	33			—	1/68
		v. Marseilles	1849	65	75	1859	45			—	1/68
	B.O.M.	Br./Am. Pkt.	1857	—	5/21	10/20†	—			—	Continue
Chagres	Fr. M.		4/57	30	60	—	(See Panama)			—	7/63
	U.S.		1849	—	20	1851	48			—	1857
Chili	U.S.	v. Panama	1851	—	50	1854	—			—	Continue
	Br. N.		1857	—	34	—	—			—	

TABLE A.—*Postal Rates to Foreign Countries, 1848–1868*—Continued

Destination	Service	Route	Introduction			Change in Rate			Change in Rate			Date Discontinued
			Date	Rate ¼ oz.	Rate ½ oz.	Date	Rate ¼ oz.	Rate ½ oz.	Date	Rate ¼ oz.	Rate ½ oz.	
China (except Hong Kong)	Br. M.	v. Southampton	1849	—	45	1855	—	33	9/61	—	45	1/68
		v. Marseilles	1849	65	75	1855	43	53	1/57	39	45	Next line
	P.C.M.	v Trieste	9/61	—	45	12/61	51	57	7/63	—	53	1/68
	Fr. M.		1853	—	63		—	—		—	—	4/57
	Private ship from San Fran.		4/57	30	60		—	—		—	—	Continue
	U.S.	v. San Fran.	1854	—	6	4/55	—	10	7/63	—	3	6/67
	Brem./Hamb.	v. Marseilles	7/67	—	10		—	—		—	—	Continue
		v. Trieste	7/57	40	72	2/67	—	37		—	—	1/68
Constantinople	Bremen	Direct	7/57	—	55		—	—		—	—	1/68
	Brem./Hamb.	Direct	3/48	(see Table 3)					8/53	—	33*	7/57
	B.O.M.	Br./Am. Pkt.	7/57	—	32*		—	—		—	—	1/68
	P.C.M.		1854	—	5/21		—	—		—	—	1/68
	Fr. M.		1852	—	40*	5/63	38/40u	3/67		—	35*	1/68
Corfu	Bremen	Direct	4/57	30*	60*	(see Ionian Islands)						
	Brem./Hamb.	Direct	8/53	—	30	"				—	—	7/57
	P.C.M.		7/57	—	30	"				—	—	1859
	Fr. M.		1857	—	30	"				—	—	1859
Corsica	(see France)		4/57	27	54					—	—	1859
Cuba	U.S.	Direct	1849	—	12½	7/51	—	10/20†	8/64	—	10	Continue
Curacoa	B.O.M.	Br./Am. Pkt.	1849	—	5/21		—	—		—	—	7/51
Dardanelles	Br. M.	v. England	1859	—	33	1863	—	45		—	—	1/68
	(same rates as Beyrout)											
Denmark	Bremen	Direct	3/48	(see Table 3)		1859	—	—	8/53	—	27*	7/57
	Brem./Hamb.	Direct	7/57	—	27*	1859	—	20*	2/67	—	18*	1/68
	B.O.M.	Br./Am. Pkt.	1849	—	5/21		—	—		—	—	4/57
	P.C.M.		1852	—	37*	1855	—	35*	5/63	—	33/35u	Next line
	Fr. M.		4/57	27*	—	10/65	—	31/33u		—	—	1/68
Durazzo	(same rates as Alexandretta)				54*							1/68
East Indies	Br. M.	v. Southampton	1849	—	45	1856	—	None	1859	—	33	1860
		v. Marseilles	1849	65	75	1856	—	None	1859	39	45	1860
	B.O.M.	Br./Am. Pkt.	1856	—	5/21		—	—		—	—	1/68
(British)	P.C.M.	v. Trieste	1852	—	38	5/63	—	36	3/67	—	35	1/68
(others)		v. Trieste	1852	—	70	5/63	—	68	3/67	—	59	1/68
		v. Marseilles & Suez	1857	40	72	2/67	—	37		—	—	1/68
	Brem./Hamb.	v. Trieste	1857	—	64	2/67	—	55		—	—	1/68

Country	Mail	Route	Date								End
Ecuador	Fr. M.		4/57	30	60						1/68
	U.S.	v. Panama	7/51	—	50			48		—	1857
Egypt (except Alexandria)	Br. M.	v. Southampton	1857	—	34		1854	33	(except Cairo & Suez)	—	Continue
	Br. M.	v. Marseilles	1849	61	57	39	1/57	45	9/63	45	1/68
		v. Fr. Pkt.	1849	57	71		1/57	38		—	1/68
	P.C.M.	v. Trieste	1849	—	71		1855	35	5/63	36	4/57
			1852		30		3/67				Next line
	Fr. M.		4/57	30	60						1/68
	Brem./Hamb.		7/57	—	30*						1/68
Falkland Islands	Br. M.	v. England	1857	—	33						1/68
France	French	H.deH.	1847	—	5/10†						2/48
	B.O.M.	Br./Am. Pkt.	1849	—	5/21		1/53	21/21	2/53	5/21	4/57
	U.S.	Direct to Havre	1850	(a)	24		7/51	20			4/57
	Fr. M.		4/57	15*	30*						Continue
Frankfort-on-Main	Bremen	Direct	3/48	(see Table III)	22*			15*	8/53	22*	7/57
	Brem./Hamb.	Direct	7/57	—	5/21		1860				1/68
	B.O.M.	Br./Am. Pkt.	1849	—	30*			28/30u		—	1855
	P.C.M.		1857	21*	42*		5/62				1/68
Galatz	(same rates at Beyrout, except B.O.M. introduced in 1854)										1/68
Gallipoli	(same rates as Beyrout)										
German States	Bremen	Direct	3/48	(see Table III)	15*			—	8/53	15*	7/57
	Brem./Hamb.	Direct	7/57	—	30*		9/61	28/30u			1/68
	P.C.M.		10/52	—	5/21						1/68
	B.O.M.	Br./Am. Pkt.	1849	—	42*						4/57
	Fr. M.		4/57	21*	33		5/63	45	1/67	29	1/68
	Br. M.	v. England	1860	—	—		3/67	18			Next line
Guadaloupe											1/68
Guatemala	U.S.		9/62	—	10		1859	None	1860		Continue
Gibraltar	B.O.M.	Br./Am. Pkt.	1852	—	5/21					5/21	1/68
	Br. M.	v. London	1859	39	33				1860		1860
		v. France	1859	21*	45						1860
	Fr. M.		4/57	—	42*						1/68
	Brem./Hamb.	Direct	2/67	—	25*						1/68
Great Britain	(to or from Pacific Coast)		2/49	—	24*		(except to or from Pacific Coast)				1/68
	B.O.M.	Br./Am. Pkt.	1849	—	59*		7/51	29*		24*	1/68
Greece	Bremen	Direct	1849	—	5/21				7/63	—	1/68
	Brem./Hamb.	Direct	3/48	(see Table 3)	35*			—	8/53	33*	7/57
	Br. M.	v. Southampton	7/57	—	57						1/68
	P.C.M.		1852	—	42*		5/63	40/42u	2/67	None	4/57
			1852		60*		3/67	38*		—	Next line
	Fr. M.		4/57	30*							1/68
											Continue

TABLE A.—*Postal Rates to Foreign Countries, 1848–1868*—Continued

Destination	Service	Route	Introduction			Change in Rate			Change in Rate			Date Discontinued
			Date	¼ oz.	½ oz.	Date	¼ oz.	½ oz.	Date	¼ oz.	½ oz.	
Hamburg	Bremen	Direct to Brem.	3/48	(see Table 3)					8/53	—	15*	1/68
	Hamburg	Direct to Hamb.	7/57	—	10*					—	—	1/68
Hanover	(All other rates same as German States)											
	(rates of German States, except P.C.M. is same as Frankfort-on-Main)											
Hayti	Br. M.	v. England	1859	—	33	5/63	—	45	1/67	—	29	8/67
	(see West Indies)											
Heligoland	Br. M.	v. London	1849	—	33	1859	—	33	(Private ship from London)			1/68
Holstein	P.C.M.		1857	—	35*	5/63	—	33/35u	10/65	—	31/33u	2/67
	Fr. M.		4/57	27*	54*	(see Schleswig-Holstein)				—	—	2/67
	Brem./Hamb.	Direct	7/57	—	25*					—	—	2/67
Honduras	U.S. & Br. Pkts.		1855	—	34/44†	1857	—	34		—	—	1/68
Hong Kong	B.O.M.	Br./Am. Pkt.	1849	5/21		1859	—	None	1860	—	5/21	9/61
	Br. M.	v. Southampton	1859	—	33	1860	—	None	9/61	—	45	1/68
		v. Marseilles	1849	65	75	1855	—	None	1859	39	45	Next line
			1860	—	None	9/61	—	45	12/61	51	57	Next line
			7/63	—	53							1/68
	P.C.M.	v. Trieste	1852	—	38	5/63	—	36	3/67	—	35	1/68
	Brem./Hamb.	Direct	7/57	—	30					—	—	1/68
	Fr. M.		4/57	30	60					—	—	1/68
	Am Pkt. from San Fran.		7/67	—	10							Continue
Ibraila	B.O.M.	Br./Am. Pkt.	1854	—	5/21	(see Turkey)						4/57
	P.C.M.		1852	—	40*	1859	30*	60*	(see Turkey)			10/61
	Fr. M.		4/57	30	60	1854	—	None	1857	—	73	10/61
Indian Archipelago	Br. M.	v. Marseilles	1849	73	83	1859	39	45				Next line
												1/68
Ineboli	Fr. M.		4/57	30	60	10/61	30*	60*		—	—	Continue
	Fr. M.		4/57	30	60					—	—	1/68
Ionian Islands	(all other rates same as those of Antivari)											
	B.O.M.	Br./Am. Pkt.	1849	—	5/21	1855	—	38	5/63	—	36/38u	4/57
	P.C.M.		1852	—	37*	3/67	30*	38*		—	—	Next line
						1858	30*	60*		—	—	1/68
	Fr. M.		4/57	27	54	4/65	35	49		—	—	1/68
	Br. M.	v. England	1860	—	45					—	—	1/68
Italy: Eastern towns	Bremen	Direct	3/48	(see Table 3)					8/53	—	(c)33	7/57
	B.O.M.	Br./Am. Pkt.	1854	—	5/21					—	—	1857
	P.C.M.		1852	—	(d)30*					—	—	1857

205

Place	Route										
Jaffa	(same rates as Antivari)										
Janina	Fr.M.	4/57	30*	60*	—	—	—	—	—	—	1/68
Japan	Br. M. v. Southampton	1859	—	33	—	—	45	—	—	51	—	1/68
	v. Marseilles	1859	39	45	—	—	45	12/61	—	51	57	Next line
	Fr. M.	1860	30	60	—	—	53	—	—	—	—	1/68
	Am. Pkt. from San Fran.	7/67	—	10	8/65	(optional prepayment to Yokohama only)						Continue
Jerusalem	P.C.M.	3/67	—	59	—	—	—	—	—	—	—	1/68
	B.O.M. Br./Am. Pkt.	1859	—	5/21	—	—	—	—	—	—	—	3/61
	Br. M. v. England	3/61	—	33	—	—	—	—	—	—	—	1/68
Karikal	Fr. M.	1860	30*	60*	—	—	—	—	—	—	—	Continue
Kerassund	Fr. M.	4/57	30*	60*	—	—	—	—	—	—	—	Continue
	Fr. M.	4/57	30*	60*	—	—	—	—	—	—	—	Continue
Labuan	Br. M. v. Southampton	1849	—	53	1856	—	41	—	—	—	33	Next line
	v. Marseilles	1849	73	83	9/61	61	45	1857	—	39	45	1/68
			—	—	1856	—	71	1857	—	—	—	Next line
Larnica	Fr. M.	4/57	30	60	9/61	—	45	7/63	—	—	53	1/68
	Fr. M.	1859	30*	60*	7/63	—	53	—	—	—	—	1/68
Latakia	(Same rates as Alexandretta)										
Lauenburg	B.O.M. Br./Am. Pkt.	1855	—	5/21	—	—	—	—	—	—	—	4/57
	P.C.M.	1855	—	33*	5/63	—	31/33u	—	—	—	—	1/68
	Brem./Hamb. Direct	7/57	—	25*	—	—	—	—	—	—	—	2/67
	Bremen N.G. Lloyd	2/67	—	15*	10/67	—	15*	—	—	—	—	1/68
	Hamburg Hapag	2/67	—	18*	—	—	—	—	—	—	—	1/68
	Fr. M.	4/57	27*	54*	—	—	—	—	—	—	—	1/68
Liberia	Br. M. v. England	1859	—	33	—	—	—	—	—	—	—	1/68
Lombardy	B.O.M. Br./Am. Pkt.	1854	—	5/21	—	—	33*	1860	—	—	42*	4/57
	P.C.M.	1852	—	30*	1855	—	40/42u	—	—	—	—	Next line
	Brem./Hamb. Direct	7/57	—	15*	5/63	21*	24*	—	—	—	—	1/68
	Fr. M.	4/57	27*	54*	1859	—	42*	—	—	—	—	1/68
Lubec	(see German States)										
Lucca	Br. M. v. France	1849	—	31	—	—	—	—	—	—	—	1854
	B.O.M. Br./Am. Pkt.	1859	—	5/21	—	21*	42*	—	—	—	—	1867
	Fr. M.	1860	27*	54*	1/62	—	28/30u	—	—	—	—	1/68
	P.C.M.	1857	—	30*	9/61	—	—	—	—	—	—	1/68
Luxemburg	Fr. M.	4/57	21*	42*	—	—	—	—	—	—	—	1/68
	Brem./Hamb. Direct	7/57	—	22*	—	—	—	—	—	—	—	1860
	Bremen N.G. Lloyd	1860	—	15*	—	—	15*	—	—	—	—	1/68
	Hamburg Hapag	1860	—	22*	2/67	—	15*	—	—	—	—	1/68
Madeira, Island of	Br. M.	1849	—	65	1860	29	37	—	—	—	—	1/68
	Fr. M. v. Southampton	9/66	27*	54*	—	—	—	—	—	—	—	Continue

TABLE A.—*Postal Rates to Foreign Countries, 1848–1868*—Continued

Destination	Service	Route	Introduction			Change in Rate			Change in Rate			Date Discontinued
			Date	¼ oz.	½ oz.	Date	¼ oz.	½ oz.	Date	¼ oz.	½ oz.	
Mahé	Fr. M.		4/57	30*	60*		—	—		—	—	Continue
Majorca	Br. M.	v. England	1859	—	33		—	—		—	—	1/68
Malta	B.O.M.	Br./Am. Pkt.	1849	—	5/21	1859	—	None	1860	—	5/21	1859
	Bremen	Direct	8/53	—	30		—	—		—	—	1860
	Br. M.	v. Southampton	1859	39	33		—	—		—	—	1860
		v. Marseilles	1859	—	45		—	—		—	—	Continue
	Fr. M.		4/57	30*	60*		—	—		—	—	7/51
Martinique	B.O.M.	Br./Am. Pkt.	1849	—	5/21	(see West Indies)						
Mauritius	Br. M.	v. England	1859	—	33	5/63	—	45	1/67	—	29	1/68
	Br. M.	v. Southampton	1849	—	45	1857	—	33		—	—	1/68
		v. Marseilles	1849	65	75	1857	39	45		—	—	1/68
	Fr. M.		4/57	30	60		—	—		—	—	Continue
Mecklenburg-Schwerin	P.C.M.		1852	—	30*	5/62	—	28/30u		—	—	1/68
Mecklen**b**urg-Strelitz	P.C.M.		1852	—	30*	9/61	—	28/30u		—	—	1/68
		(rates by all other services same as German States)										
Messina	B.O.M.	Br./Am. Pkt.	1855	—	5/21		—	—		—	—	4/57
	P.C.M.		1855	—	40	5/63	—	38		—	—	1/63
	Brem./Hamb.	Direct	7/57	—	33	1859	—	22*	2/67	—	24*	1/68
	Fr. M.		4/57	30*	60*	1/62	21*	42*		—	—	1/68
	Br. M.		1859	—	33		—	—		—	—	1/68
	Fr. M.		1860	21	42		—	—		—	—	1/68
Mexico	U.S.		7/51	—	35/45†	1854	—	10/20†	5/63	—	(e)10	12/65
	U.S. & Br. Pkt.		5/63	—	(f)34		—	—		—	—	2/66
	U.S.	Direct from N.Y.	12/65	—	10		—	—		—	—	Continue
Minorca	(Same rates as Majorca)											
Mitylene	(same rates as Alexandretta)											
Modena	Br. M.	v. France	1849	—	31		—	—		—	—	1852
	B.O.M.	Br./Am. Pkt.	1852	—	5/21		—	—		—	—	4/57
	P.C.M.		1852	—	33*	1860	—	42*	5/63	—	40/42u	1/68
	Brem./Hamb.	Direct	7/57	25*	33*	2/67	—	24*		—	—	1/68
	Fr. M.		4/57	27*	54*	1/62	21*	42*		—	—	1/68
Moldavia	B.O.M.	Br./Am. Pkt.	1849	—	5/21		—	—		—	—	4/57
	P.C.M.		1852	—	30	5/63	—	28		—	—	1/68
	Brem./Hamb.		7/57	—	30	12/61	—	32*		—	—	1/68
	Fr. M.	Direct	1859	30*	60*		—	—		—	—	1/68

Moluccas	Br. M.	v. Southampton	1849	—	53	1856	—	41	—	33	Next line
						9/61	—	45	—	—	1/68
		v. Marseilles	1849	73	83	1856	61	71	39	45	Next line
Montevideo	Fr. M.	v. Falmouth	9/61	30	45	12/61	51	57	—	53	1/68
	Br. M.	v. Bordeaux	4/57	30	60	7/63	—	53	—	60	1/68
	Fr. M.	Am. Pkt.	1854	30	45	1860	—	33	—	45	1/68
	U.S.	Br./Am. Pkt.	1860	18	60	(from N.Y. once a month)				—	8/67
Naples	B.O.M.	Direct	8/67	—	25					—	Continue
	P.C.M.	Direct from N.Y.	1849	—	5/21				1/57		4/57
	Fr. M.		1852	—	30	5/63	—	28	1/57	—	1/68
	Brem./Hamb.	Direct	4/57	30*	60*	1/62	21*	42*	7/63	—	1/68
Nassau, New Providence	U.S.	Direct from N.Y.	7/57	—	22	2/67	—	24*	5/65	—	1/68
Nassau, G.A.P.U.			1860	—	5				1/61	—	Continue
	(same rates as Frankfort-on-Main)										
Netherlands	B.O.M.	Br./Am. Pkt.	1849	—	5/21	—	—	—	—	—	7/66
	Bremen	Direct	8/53	—	25*	—	—	—	—	—	7/57
	Brem./Hamb.	Direct	7/57	—	25*	1859	—	None	2/67	18*	1/68
	Belgium C.M.	v. England	7/66	—	27*					—	1/68
	Fr. M.	v. Belgium	4/57	21*	42*					—	1/68
New Brunswick	Am. Pkt.		10/66	—	17*					—	1/68
	(see B.N.A. Provinces and Canada)										
Newfoundland	Land route through New Brunswick		5/63	—	10	7/67	—	10/15†	(see B.N.A. Provinces for prior rates)		
New Granada	Cunard Pkt.	v. Boston & Halifax	4/65	—	5	—	—	—	—	—	1/68
	Br. M.	v. Southampton	1849	—	45	—	—	—	—	—	7/51
	U.S. & Br. Pkts.		1859	—	50	1854	—	20	—	(g)34	1859
New South Wales	Br. M.	v. Aspinwall	1849	—	18	(except Aspinwall & Panama)				—	Continue
	Br. M.	v. Southampton	1849	43	53	1854	39	45	1855	33	1/68
		v. Marseilles	1855	—	53	1/57	—	None	1855	—	1/68
		Private ship	1849	—	37	(from U.K.)				—	1854
		v. Plymouth	1854	—	45					—	1855
		Private ship(h)	1854	30	6	4/55	—	10	7/63	3	7/67
New Zealand	Fr. M.	v. Southampton	4/57	—	60	5/63	30*	60*		—	Continue
	Br. M.	v. Marseilles	1849	73	53	1855	—	33		—	1/68
		v. Private ship	1849	—	83	1/57	39	45		—	1/68
	Fr. M.		4/57	30	37	(from U.K.)				—	1859
	Br. M.	v. Panama	8/66	—	60	5/63	30*	60*		—	Continue
Nicaragua	U.S.	Gulf coast	1854	—	22	1857	—	34	2/61	(i)34	Continue
		v. Panama	2/61	—	34/44†	3/64	—	10	(Pacific Slope)		1/68
Norway	B.O.M.	Br./Am. Pkt.	1849	(see Table 3)	20					—	Continue
	Bremen	Direct	3/48	—	5/21				8/53	37*	4/57
	Brem./Hamb.	Direct	7/57	—	38*	2/67	—	25*		—	7/57
	P.C.M.	Direct	1852	—	48*	1855	—	46*	5/63	44/46u	1/68
			6/65	—	42/46u	10/65	—	40/44u	11/65	38/42u	Next line
	Fr. M.		4/57	33*	66*					—	1/68

TABLE A.—*Postal Rates to Foreign Countries, 1848–1868*—Continued

Destination	Service	Route	Introduction			Change in Rate			Change in Rate			Date Discontinued
			Date	Rate ¼ oz.	½ oz.	Date	Rate ¼ oz.	½ oz.	Date	Rate ¼ oz.	½ oz.	
Nova Scotia	(see B.N.A. Provinces and Canada)											
	Cunard Pkt. v. Boston & Halifax		1851	—	5							1/68
Oldenburg	Bremen	Direct	3/48	(see table 3)					8/53	—	13*	7/57
	Brem./Hamb.	Direct	7/57	—	12*	1859	—	13*				2/67
	Bremen	N.G. Lloyd	2/67	—	13*							1/68
	Hamburg	Hapag	2/67	—	15*							1/68
	P.C.M.		1852	—	30*	9/61	—	28/30u				4/57
	B.O.M.		1849	—	5/21							1/68
	Fr. M.	Br./Am. Pkt.	4/57	21*	42*							
Panama	U.S.		1849	—	30	7/51	—	20				1852
	U.S.		1852	—	10/20†	8/64	—	10				Continue
Paraguay	Br. M.	v. England	1860	—	33	1/61	—	45				1/68
	U.S.	Am. Pkt.	8/67	18	25	(once a month from N.Y.)						Continue
Parma	(same rates as Modena)											
Penang	B.O.M.	Br./Am. Pkt	1857	—	5/21							1859
	Br. M.	v. Southampton	1859	—	33	9/61	—	45				1/68
		v. Marseilles	1859	39	45	9/61	—	45	12/61	51	57	Next line
						11/63	—	53				1/68
	Fr. M.		4/47	30	60							Continue
Peru	U.S.		7/51	—	50	1854	—	32	1857	—	22	10/67
	Br. M.	v. Panama	10/67	—	34							Continue
Philippines	Br. M.	v. Southampton	1849	—	45	1856	—	41	1/57	—	33	Next line
						9/61	—	45				1/68
		v. Marseilles	1849	65	75	1856	61	71	1/57	39	45	Next line
					45	12/61	51	57	7/63	—	53	1/68
	Fr. M.		9/61	30	60							Continue
Placentia	P.C.M.		1852	—	30	5/63	—	28				1/68
	Fr. M.		4/57	27*	54*							1/68
Poland	(all other rates same as Modena)											
	B.O.M.	Br./Am. Pkt.	1849	—	5/21							1/68
	P.C.M.		1852	—	37*	5/63	—	35/37u				1/68
	Bremen	Direct	8/53	—	29*	8/67	—	20				7/57
	Brem./Hamb.	Direct	7/57	—	29*							1/68
Pondicherry	Fr. M.		4/57	30*	60*							Continue
	Fr. M.		4/57	30*	60*							Continue

209

Portugal	Br. M.	v. Southampton	1849	—	63	1860	—	—	—	1860
		v. France	1/57	37	43	2/67	29	37	33	1/68
	Brem./Hamb.	Direct	7/57	30	42	9/66	—	25	45	1/68
	Fr. M.	v. Behobia	4/57	21	42		27*	54*	—	Continue
		v. Bordeaux	1860	30	60		—	—	—	9/66
Prevesa	(same rates as Alexandretta)									
Prince Edward's Island	(see B.N.A. Provinces and Canada)									
Prussia	(see German States)									
Rhodes	(same rates as Dardanelles)									
Romagna	P.C.M.		1860	—	42*	5/63	40/42u	—	—	1/68
Roman States	Bremen	Direct	3/48	(see Table 3)						1852
	B.O.M.	Br./Am. Pkt.	1849	—	5/21					4/57
	P.C.M.		1852	—	35*	1860	—	46	44	1/68
	Brem./Hamb.	Direct	7/57	—	28*	2/67	—	24	—	1/68
	Fr. M.		4/57	27*	54*		—	—	—	Continue
Russia	B.O.M.	Br./Am. Pkt:	1849	—	5/21		—	—	—	4/57
	Bremen	Direct	3/48	(see Table 3)					29*	7/57
	Brem./Hamb.	Direct	7/57	—	29*	2/67	20*	—	8/53	1/68
	P.C.M.		1852	—	37*	5/63	35/37u	—	—	1/68
	Fr. M.		4/57	30*	60*		—	—	—	1/68
Rustchuck	Fr. M.		1859	30*	60*		—	—	—	4/57
Salonica	B.O.M.	Br./Am. Pkt:	1849	—	5/21	5/63	—	38/40u	35*	1/68
	P.C.M.		1852	—	40*	1859	—	60*	—	1/68
	Fr. M.		4/57	30	60		30*	3/67	—	
Samsoun	(same rates as Salonica)									
Sandwich Islands	U.S.—private ship from San Francisco		1854	—	6	4/55	—	10	3	Next line
						6/67		10		Continue
Sardinia	Br. M.	v. France	1849	41	51					1852
	B.O.M.	Br./Am. Pkt.	1852	—	5/21					4/57
	P.C.M.		1852	—	30	1855	—	38*	42*	Next line
						5/63		40/42u		1/68
	Fr. M.		4/57	21*	42*					Continue
	Brem./Hamb.	Direct	7/57	—	30*	3/61	—	23*	24*	1/68
Saxe-Altenburg	Bremen	Direct	3/48	(see Table 3)				8/53	15*	7/57
	Brem./Hamb.	Direct	7/57	—	15*					1/68
	P.C.M.		1852	—	30*	5/62	—	28/30u	—	1/68
	Fr. M.		4/57	21*	42*					1/68
Saxe-Meiningen, Weimar, and Coburg-Gotha	(Same rates as Frankfort-on-Main)									
Saxony	(see German States)									
Schleswig	Bremen	Direct	3/48	(see Table 3)		(see Schleswig-Holstein)		8/53	27*	7/57
	Brem./Hamb.	Direct	7/57	—	25*					2/67
	P.C.M.		1857	—	35*	5/63	—	33/35u	31/33u	2/67
	Fr. M.		1859	27*	54*		—	—	—	2/67

TABLE A.—*Postal Rates to Foreign Countries, 1848–1868—Continued*

Destination	Service	Route	Introduction			Change in Rate			Change in Rate			Date Discontinued
			Date	¼ oz. Rate	½ oz. Rate	Date	¼ oz. Rate	½ oz. Rate	Date	¼ oz. Rate	½ oz. Rate	
Schleswig-Holstein	Brem./Hamb.	Direct	2/67	—	18*	10/67	—	15*		—	—	1/68
	P.C.M.		2/67	—	30*	3/67	—	28/30u		—	—	1/68
Scio	Fr. M.		2/67	27*	54*		—	—		—	—	1/68
Scutari	Fr. M.		1859	30*	60*		—	—		—	—	1/68
	B.O.M.	Br./Am. Pkt.	1849	—	5/21		—	—		—	—	1/68
	P.C.M.		1852	—	f30	5/63	—	f28	3/67	—	d35	1/68
Seres	Fr. M.		4/57	30	60		—	—		—	—	Continue
Servia (Serbia)	Fr. M.		4/57	30*	60*		—	—		—	—	4/57
	B.O.M.	Br./Am. Pkt.	1853	—	5/21		—	—		—	—	1/68
	P.C.M.		1852	—	f30	5/63	—	f28	3/67	—	35	1/68
Siam	Fr. M.	v. Austria	4/57	27*	54*	1858	21	42		—	—	Continue
	Br. M.	v. Southampton	1858	33	45	9/61	—	45		—	—	1/68
		v. Marseilles	2/61	39	45	9/61	51	45	12/61	51	57	Next line
Sicilies, Two	Br. M.	v. Southampton	1849	51	71	1/65	—	53		—	—	1/68
	B.O.M.	Br./Am. Pkt.	1852	—	5/21	(and Fr. Pkt. from Marseilles)						1852
	P.C.M.		1852	—	f30	1860	—	49	5/63	—	47	1/68
Sinope	Brem./Hamb.	Direct	7/57	22	22	2/67	21*	24*		—	—	1/68
	Fr. M.		4/57	30	60	1/62	—	42*	(see Italy)			Continue
	B.O.M.	Br./Am. Pkt.	1856	—	5/21	5/63	—	f30	3/67	—	35*	1/68
Sophia	P.C.M.		1856	40	40	1859	30*	60*		—	—	1/68
	Fr. M.	v. Austria	4/57	30	60		—	—		—	—	Continue
Spain	Fr. M.	v. Austria	1859	30*	60*		—	—		—	—	Continue
	Br. M.	v. Southampton	1849	—	73		—	—		—	—	1859
		v. France	1849	41	51	1/57	37	43		—	—	1859
	B.O.M.	Br./Am. Pkt.	1859	—	5/21		—	—		—	—	1/68
St. Helena	Fr. M.	v. Behobia	4/57	21	42		—	—		—	—	Continue
Sulina	Brem./Hamb.	Direct	7/57	30	42	2/67	—	25*		—	—	1/68
	Br. M.	v. England	1/57	33	33	5/63	—	45		—	—	1/68
	Fr. M.	v. Austria	4/57	30	60	1859	30*	60*		—	—	1/68
Sumatra	Br. M.	v. Southampton	1849	—	53	1856	41	41	1/57	—	33	Next line
						9/61	—	45				1/68
		v. Marseilles	1849	73	83	1856	61	71	1/57	39	45	Next line
			9/61	—	45	12/61	51	57	9/63	—	53	1/68
St. Helena	Fr. M.		4/57	30	60		—	—		—	—	Continue
Sweden	Bremen	Direct	3/48	(see Table 3)					8/53	—	33	7/57
	Brem./Hamb.	Direct	7/57	33*	33*	2/67	—	21*		—	—	1/68

210

	B.O.M.		1849		5/21		40/42u	6/65	36/40u	4/57
	Fr. M.	Br./Am. Pkt.		33*	66*		34/38u			1/68
	P.C.M.		1852		42*	5/63				Next line 1/68
Smyrna	(same rates as Dardanelles)					11/65				
Switzerland	Bremen	Direct	3/48	(see Table 3)				8/53	25*	7/57
	Brem./Hamb.	Direct	7/57	—	27*	1860	19*	—	—	1/68
	B.O.M.	Br./Am. Pkt.	1849	21*	5/21	—	—	—	—	4/57
	Fr. M.		4/57	—	42*	—	—	—	—	Continue
	P.C.M.		1852	—	35*	5/63	33/35u	—	—	1/68
Syria	Br. M.	v. Southampton by Fr. Pkt.	1849	51	57	1/57	45	(from Marseilles)	—	1/57
		v. Marseilles	1849	61	71	—	—	—	—	1/68
		Br./Am. Pkt.	1852	—	71	—	—	—	—	1/57
	B.O.M.		1/57	—	5/21	33	—	—	—	1/68
	Fr. M.		4/57	30	60	—	—	—	—	1/68
Tangiers	Fr. M.		4/57	30*	60*	—	—	—	—	1/68
Tchesme (Cesme)	B.O.M.	Br./Am. Pkt.	1853	—	5/21	—	—	—	—	1/68
	P.C.M.		1853	—	40*	5/63	38/40u	3/67	35*	1/68
Tenedos	B.O.M.	Br./Am. Pkt.	1853	—	5/21	—	—	—	—	1/68
	P.C.M.		1853	—	40	5/63	38	3/67	—	1/68
	Fr. M.		1859	30*	60*	—	—	—	35*	1/68
Trebizond	B.O.M.	Br./Am. Pkt.	1853	—	5/21	—	—	—	—	1/68
	P.C.M.		1853	—	40*	5/63	38/40u	3/67	35*	1/68
	Fr. M.		4/57	30*	60*	—	—	—	—	1/68
Tulcha	(same rates as Trebizond)									
Tunis	Br. M.	v. Southampton	1849	51	71	1/57	45	(Fr. Pkt. from Marseilles)	—	1/68
	Fr. M.		4/57	30*	60*	—	—	—	—	Continue
Turkey—except places mentioned	P.C.M.		1853	—	30	5/63	28	3/67	35	1/68
	B.O.M.	Br./Am. Pkt.	1849	—	5/21	—	—	—	—	1/68
	Brem./Hamb.		7/57	—	32*	—	—	—	—	1/68
	Fr. M.		4/57	21*	42*	—	—	—	—	Continue
Turks Is.	U.S.	v. Austria	1855	—	34/44†	1857	34	1859	10	Continue
Tripoli, Syria	Fr. M.		4/57	30*	60*	—	—	—	—	5/63
	P.C.M.		3/67	—	35	—	—	—	—	1/68
Tuscany	(same rates as Modena, except no Br.M. rate in 1849; Brem./Hamb. mail 28¢ instead of 25¢ until 2/67.)									
Uruguay	U.S.		1855	—	34/44†	—	—	—	—	1857
	Fr. M.	v. Bordeaux	1860	30	60	—	—	—	—	8/67
	U.S.	Am. Pkt.	8/67	18	25	(once a month from N.Y.)	—	—	—	Continue
	Br. M.	v. England	1860	—	33	1/61	45	—	—	1/68
Valona	(same rates as Alexandretta)									
Van Diemen's Land	Br. M.	v. Southampton	1049	—	53	1854	None	1857	33	1/68
		v. Marseilles	1849	73	83	1854	None	1857	45	1/68
	Br. M.	v. Plymouth	1954	—	45	—	—	39	—	1857
		v. England	1855	—	33	—	—	—	—	1857
	Fr. M.		4/57	30	60	—	—	—	—	Continue

211

212

TABLE A.—*Postal Rates to Foreign Countries, 1848–1868*—Continued

Destination	Service	Route	Introduction			Change in Rate			Change in Rate			Date Discontinued
			Date	¼ oz. Rate	½ oz. Rate	Date	¼ oz. Rate	½ oz. Rate	Date	¼ oz. Rate	½ oz. Rate	
Varna	(same rates as Salonica)											
Venetian States	B.O.M.	Br./Am. Pkt.	1849	—	5/21							1/68
	P.C.M.		1852	—	30*	5/63	—	28/30				1/68
	Brem./Hamb.		7/57	—	15*	2/67	—	24*				1/68
	Fr. M.		4/57	27	54	1860	27*	54*				1/68
Venezuela	Br. M.	v. Southampton	1849	—	45	1851	—	None	1854	—	45	12/67
		v. Aspinwall	12/67	—	18							1/68
	U.S.		1/67	—	10	(Am. or Venezuelan Pkt.)						Continue
Victoria	Br. M.	v. Plymouth	1854	—	45							1/57
		v. Southampton	1/57	—	33							1/68
		v. Marseilles	1/57	39	45							1/68
		v. private ship	1849	—	37	(from U.K.)						1/57
Volo	(same rates as Jaffa)											
Wallachia	Fr. M.		4/57	30	60	6/62	30*	60*				Continue
	B.O.M.	Br./Am. Pkt.	1849	—	5/21							1860
	Bremen	Direct	8/53	—	30							7/57
	Brem./Hamb.	Direct	7/57	—	30							1/68
	P.C.M.		1852	—	f30	5/63	—	f28				1/68
West Indies:												
British	B.O.M.	Br./Am. Pkt.	1849	—	5/21							1851
	U.S.	Am. Pkt.	1851	—	10/20†	8/64	—	10				8/67
Not British	Br. M.	v. England	1849	—	55							1851
	U.S.	Am. & Br. Pkts.	1851	—	35/45†	1854	—	†34/44	1857	—	(j) 34	1/67
	Br. M.	v. Havana	1/67	—	(j)18							Continue
Danish	U.S.-Am. Pkt.	v. St. T.	1854	—	34/44†	1859	—	34				1/68
		v. Kingston	1854	—	18/28†	1859	—	18				1/68
Brit./Danish	U.S.	Am. Pkt.	8/67	—	10	(22nd of month from N.Y.)						Continue
Wurtemberg	Bremen	Direct	3/48	(see Table 3)					8/53	—	22*	7/57
	Brem./Hamb.	Direct	7/57	—	15*							1/68
	B.O.M.	Br./Am. Pkt.	1849	—	5/21							4/57
	P.C.M.		1852	—	30*	10/61	—	28/30u				1/68
	Fr. M.		4/57	21*	42*							1/68
Yanaon	Fr. M.		4/57	30*	60*							Continue

TABLE B.—*Postal Rates to Foreign Countries, 1868–1875*

Destination	Service	Route	Introduction			Change in Rate			Change in Rate			
			Date	Rate ¼ oz.	Rate ½ oz.	Date	Rate ¼ oz.	Rate ½ oz.	Date	Rate ¼ oz.	Rate ½ oz.	Date Discontinued
Acapulco	U.S.		9/62	—	10	—	—	—	—	—	—	7/75
Accra	Br. M.		7/75	—	d15*	—	—	—	—	—	—	Continue
Aden	Fr. M.		4/57	30	60	—	—	—	—	—	—	1/70
	Br. M.	v. Marseilles	5/68	—	36	1/70	—	30	—	—	d21*	4/71
		v. Southampton	5/68	—	28	1/70	—	22	7/75	—	—	Continue
		v. Brindisi	4/71	—	28	7/75	—	d27	—	—	—	Continue
	N.G.U., direct	v. Trieste	4/71	—	27*	10/71	—	26*	—	—	—	7/75
		v. Brindisi	4/71	—	21	10/71	—	20	—	—	—	7/75
	C.M. v. E.	v. Trieste	4/71	—	30*	10/71	—	27*	—	—	—	7/75
		v. Brindisi	4/71	—	24	10/71	—	21	—	—	—	7/75
	U.S.	v. San Fran.	11/68	—	10	—	—	—	—	—	—	7/75
Adrianople (see Turkey)	German M.	All routes	7/75	—	d17*	—	—	—	—	—	—	Continue
Africa, West Coast	Br. M.	v. E.	1/68	—	22	5/68	(see separate countries)					
	Br. M.	Br. possessions	7/75	—	d15*	—	—	—	—	—	—	Continue
		Foreign	7/75	—	f15	—	—	—	—	—	—	Continue
Alexandretta	Fr. M.		4/57	30*	60*	—	—	—	—	—	—	1/70
	N.G.U.	Direct	1–4/70	—	15	7/70	—	12	10/71	—	11	7/75
		C.M. v. E.	1–4/70	—	20	7/70	—	15	10/71	—	12	7/75
Alexandria	Fr. M.		4/57	30*	60*	—	—	—	—	—	—	1/70
	Br. M.	v. Southampton	1/68	—	22	1/70	—	16	—	—	—	7/75
		v. Marseilles	1/68	—	a22	11/68	a22	34	1/70	a16	28	4/71
		v. Brindisi	4/71	—	28	1/72	—	20	—	—	—	7/75
	N.G.U.	Direct	1/68	—	15*	7/70	—	12*	10/71	—	11*	7/75
		C.M. v. E.	1/68	—	20*	7/70	—	15*	10/71	—	12*	7/75
	Direct	v. Brindisi (r)	4/71	—	15*	10/71	—	14*	2/73	—	12*	7/75
	C.M. v. E.	v. Brindisi (r)	4/71	—	18*	10/71	—	15*	2/73	—	13*	7/75
	Italian	Open M. (r)	4/71	—	14*	—	—	—	—	—	—	7/75
Algeria	Fr. M.	v. E.	4/57	15*	30*	—	—	—	—	—	—	1/70
	Br. M.		1–4/70	—	BB	1–4/71	—	10	11/71	—	CC	8/74
Altona (see German States)												
Anam (Cochin China)	N.G.U.	Direct	7/68	—	27	7/70	—	24	10/71	—	23	7/75
		C.M. v. E.		—	—		—	—	10/71	—	24	7/75
Antivaeri (see Turkey)												
Argentina	U.S.	Am. Pkt.	8/67	18	25	1–4/70	—	18	(from N.Y.)	—	—	9/74
	Br. M.	v. Southampton	4/71	—	28	7/75	—	f27	—	—	—	Continue
	U.S.	Am. Pkt.	7/75	—	f23	(v. Brazil)	—	—	—	—	—	Continue

TABLE B.—*Postal Rates to Foreign Countries, 1868–1875*—Continued

Destination	Service	Route	Introduction			Change in Rate			Change in Rate			Date Discontinued
			Date	Rate ¼ oz.	Rate ½ oz.	Date	Rate ¼ oz.	Rate ½ oz.	Date	Rate ¼ oz.	Rate ½ oz.	
Aspinwall	U.S.	Direct	8/64	—	10	7/75	—	f5		—	—	Continue
Australia	Br. M.	v. Southampton	1/68	—	22	1/70	—	16	7/75	—	d15	Continue
	Fr. M.	v. Marseilles	4/57	30*	60*	1/70	—	24		—	—	1/70
	Br. M.	v. Brindisi	1/68	—	30	7/75	—	d21		—	—	4/71
	N.G.U., direct	v. Brindisi (r)	4/71	—	22	10/71	—	23	11/71	—	20	7/75
	C.M. v. E.	v. Brindisi (r)	4/71	—	27	10/71	—	24	11/71	—	21	7/75
	Br. M.	v. Panama	8/66	—	22	(Br. colonies)						3/69
	U.S.	v. San Fran.	5–6/70	—	10	(10th of each month)			7/75	—	f5	Continue
		C.M. v. E.	7/68	—	32	7/70	—	27	10/71	—	24	7/75
Austria	(see German States)											
Azores	Fr. M.	v. Southampton	9/66	27*	54*	1/70	—	16		—	—	1/70
	Br. M.	v. E. & France	2/69	—	22	1/70	a16	28		—	—	7/75
			2/69	a22	34							4/71
	N.G.U.	Direct	5/73	—	11		—	—		—	—	7/75
		C.M. v. E.	5/73	—	12		—	—		—	—	7/75
Baden	(see German States)											
Bahamas	Direct from N.Y.		1859	—	f5	3/68	—	f3		—	—	Continue
Bakeu	N.G.U.	Direct	1/68	—	13*	7/70	—	10*	10/71	—	9*	7/75
		C.M. v. E.	1/68	—	18*	7/70	—	13*	10/71	—	10*	7/75
Balearic Isl		v. Belgium	10/70	—	AA (see Spain)		—	—		—	—	7/75
Batavia	(see Java)											
Bavaria	(see German States)											
Belize, Br. Honduras	U.S.	Am. Pkt. v. N.O.	1/68	—	10	10/69	—	12		—	—	1872
	Br. Pkt.	v. Kingston	1872	—	18	7/75	—	f13 (v. St. T.)		—	—	Continue
Berlat	(same rates as Baku)											
Bermuda	Br. M.	v. Halifax	12/67	—	10		—	—		—	—	12/71
	U.S.	Direct	12/71	—	f10	7/75	—	f5		—	—	Continue
Beyrout	(see Turkey)											
Bogota	Br. M.	v. Aspinwall	9/57	—	18	7/75	—	f13		—	—	Continue
	U.S.	Direct	7/75	—	f5		—	—		—	—	Continue
Bolivia	Br. M.	v. Panama	9/57	—	34	1/70	—	22	7/75	—	f17	Continue
Borneo	Fr. M.	v. Southampton	4/57	30	60	1/70	—	—		—	—	1/70
	Br. M.	v. Brindisi	1869	—	34	1/70	—	28	7/75	—	f27	Continue
Botutchany	(same rates as Baku)		7/75	—	f33		—	—		—	—	Continue

Country	Mail	Route	Date								End
Bourbon	Fr. M.		4/57	30*	60*	—	—	—	—	—	1/70
	Br. M.	v. E.	1/70	—	24	—	—	—	—	—	7/75
Belgium	U.S.-Belgian treaty—any route		1/68	—	15*	—	—	—	10*	—	7/73
		Direct	7/73	—	6*	—	3/70	—	—	—	7/75
		C.M. v. E.	7/73	—	8*	—	—	—	—	—	7/75
Belgrade	Fr. M.		1859	21*	42*	—	—	—	—	—	1/70
	N.G.U.	Direct	1/68	—	15	—	7/70	9	10/71	8	7/75
		C.M. v. E.	1/68	—	20	—	7/70	12	10/71	9	7/75
Brazil	Br. M.	v. E.	1/68	—	34	—	1/70	28	7/75	f27	Continue
	Fr. M.	v. Bordeaux	1860	33*	66*	—	—	—	—	9	1/70
	U.S.	Am. Pkt., direct	12/65	—	10	—	10/70	d15	—	—	Continue
Bremen	(see German States)										
Brunswick	(see German States)										
Buenaventura	Br. M.	v. Aspinwall	9/57	—	18	—	(see New Granada and Colombia)	—	—	—	5/73
Buenos Ayres	Br. M.	v. E.	1/68	—	34	—	1/70	28	1/70	—	7/75
	U.S.	Am. Pkt., direct	8/67	18	25	—	1/70	18	(see Argentina)	—	9/74
Caiffa	(see Turkey)										
Canada	U.S.		7/64	—	10*	—	4/68	6/10u	2/75	3	Continue
Canary Islands	Br. M.	v. England	6/68	—	a22	a22	1/69	34	1/70	28	10/70
		v. Belgium	10/70	(see Spain)							7/75
		v. Marseilles	10/70	—	AA	—	—	—	—	—	7/75
C. of Good Hope	Br. M.	v. England	1/68	—	34	—	1/70	28	7/75	d27*	Continue
	Private ship	from England	7/75	—	d11*	—	—	—	—	—	Continue
Cape Verde Islands	Fr. M.	v. Bordeaux	1860	30	60	—	—	—	—	—	1/70
Carthagena	Br. M.	v. E.	1/70	—	16	—	7/75	d11*	12/75	f15*	Continue
	Br. M.	v. Aspinwall	1859	—	18	—	(See New Granada)				7/75
Central America	Pacific Slope	v. Panama	5/65	—	10	—	(See Seprate Countries)				7/75
Ceylon	Br. M.	v. Southampton	1/68	—	22	—	7/75	d21*	—	—	Continue
		v. Marseilles	1/68	—	30	—	—	—	—	—	4/71
		v. Brindisi	4/71	—	28	—	7/75	d27*	—	—	Continue
Chili	Fr. M.	v. Brindisi	4/57	30	60	—	10/71	23	11/71	20	1/70
	N.G.U., direct	v. Brindisi	4/71	—	24	—	10/71	24	11/71	21	7/75
	C.M. v. E.	v. Panama	4/71	—	27	—	1/70	f22	7/75	f17	7/75
China	Br. M.	v. San Fran.	1857	30	f34	—					continue
	Fr. M.	v. Southampton	4/57	30	60	—	(see Hong Kong and Shanghai)				1/70
	Am. Pkt.	v. Marseilles	7/67	—	10	—	1/70	28	7/75	d27*	7/75
	Br. M.	v. Brindisi	1/68	—	34	—	1/70	36	(except Hong Kong)		Continue
		Direct	1/68	—	42	—	7/75	d33*	—	—	4/71
	N.G.U.		4/71	—	34	—	7/70	24	10/71	23	Continue
	N.G.U.	Direct	7/68	—	27	—	7/70	27	10/71	24	7/75
		C.M. v. E.	4/71	—	24	—	10/71	23	2/73	20*	7/75
		v. Brindisi	4/71	—	27	—	10/71	24	2/73	21*	7/75

216

TABLE B.—*Postal Rates to Foreign Countries, 1868–1875*—Continued

Destination	Service	Route	Introduction			Change in Rate			Change in Rate			Date Discontinued
			Date	Rate ¼ oz.	Rate ½ oz.	Date	Rate ¼ oz.	Rate ½ oz.	Date	Rate ¼ oz.	Rate ½ oz.	
Constantinople	Fr. M.	v. E.	4/57	30*	60*							1/70
	Br. M.	v. Marseilles	1/68	—	a22	9/68	a22	34	1/70	a16	28	4/71
		Direct	4/71	—	20							7/75
	N.G.U.	Direct	1/68	—	15*	7/70	—	12*	10/71	—	11*	Next line
						2/73	—	10*				7/75
		C.M. v. E.	1/68	—	20*	7/70	—	15*	10/71	—	12*	Next line
						2/73	—	11*				7/75
Costa Rica	U.S.	Direct	6/63	—	10	7/74	—	f5				Continue
Cuba	U.S.	Direct	8/64	—	10	7/75	—	f5				Continue
Curacoa	Br. M.	v. St. T.	1/68	—	18	7/75	—	f13				Continue
Czernarroda	N.G.U.	Direct	1/68	—	15*	7/70	—	12*	10/71	—	11*	7/75
		C.M. v. E.	1/68	—	20*	7/70	—	15*	10/71	—	12*	7/75
Dardanelles	(see Turkey)											
Denmark	N.G.U.	Direct	1/68	—	13/14u	6/68	—	13/16u	7/70	—	10*	Next line
						10/71	—	9*				7/75
	N.G.U.	C.M. v. E.	1/68	—	18/19u	6/68	—	18/21u	7/70	—	13*	Next line
						10/71	—	10*				7/75
		v. Stettin	7/71	—	10	1872	—	7*				9/74
		C.M. v. B/H	1/72	—	7	4/73	—	7*				7/75
Durazzo	(see Turkey)											
East Indies	Br. M.	v. Southampton	1/68	—	22	3/68	—	28	1/70	—	22	Next line
						7/75	—	d21*				Continue
		v. Marseilles	1/68	—	30	3/68	—	36	1/70	—	30	4/71
		v. Brindisi	4/71	—	28	7/75	—	d27*				Continue
	N.G.U.	Direct	1/68	—	27	7/70	—	24	10/71	—	23	7/75
		C.M. v. E.	1/68	—	32	7/70	—	27	10/71	—	24	7/75
	N.G.U., direct	v. Brindisi	4/71	—	24	10/71	—	23	11/71	—	20	Next line
						1872	—	20*				7/75
		v. Trieste	4/71	—	27*	10/71	—	26*				7/75
	C.M. v. E.	v. Brindisi	4/71	—	27	10/71	—	24	11/71	—	21	Next line
						1872	—	21*				7/75
		v. Trieste	4/71	—	30*	10/71	—	27*				7/75
Ecuador	U.S.	v. San Fran.	11/68	—	10	(see Straits Settlements)						
	Br. M.	v. Panama	1857	—	34	7/70	—	22	6/72	—	d20	Continue
		v. Colon	1/72	—	22	7/75	—	f17	—	—	—	Continue

Country	Service	Route									
Egypt:											
	Br. M.	v. Southampton	1/68	—	22	1/70	16	—	1874	20	7/75
		v. Marseilles	1/68	—	a22	9/68	34	a16	1/70	28	4/71
		v. Brindisi	4/71	—	20	1874	24*	—	—	—	7/75
	N.G.U.	Direct	1/68	—	15*	—	—	—	—	—	1/69
Lower (except Alexandria)		C.M. v. E.	1/68	—	20*	—	—	—	—	—	—
		Direct	1/69	—	20*	7/70	17*	—	10/71	16*	7/75
		C.M. v. E.	1/69	—	25*	7/70	20*	—	10/71	17*	7/75
Middle	N.G.U.	Direct	1/69	—	20*	7/70	17*	—	10/71	16*	7/75
		C.M. v. E.	1/69	—	25*	7/70	20*	—	10/71	17*	7/75
Upper	N.G.U.	Direct	1/69	—	20	7/70	17	—	10/71	16	7/75
		C.M. v. E.	1/69	—	25	7/70	20	—	10/71	17	7/75
All	N.G.U., direct	v. Brindisi (r)	4/71	—	15	10/71	14	—	—	—	2/73
		C.M. v. E.	4/71	—	18	10/71	15	—	—	—	2/73
	Italian	Open M. (r)	4/71	—	14*	(see Alexandria)					7/75
England	U.S.-Br.		1/68	—	12*	1/70	6*	—	—	d15*	Continue
Falkland Islands	Br. M.	v. E.	16/8	—	22	7/70	16	—	7/75	9*	7/75
Fakshan	N.G.U.	Direct	1/68	—	13*	7/70	10*	—	10/71	—	7/75
		C.M. v. E.	1/68	—	18*	7/70	13*	—	10/71	10*	7/75
France	Fr. M.		4/57	15*	30*	—	—	—	—	—	1/70
	B.O.M.	(paid to England)	1/70	—	4*	—	—	—	—	—	7/75
	Br. M.	v. E.	1–3/70	—	BB	6/70	CC	—	—	—	8/74
	U.S.	Direct	1/70	—	f10		—				
	U.S.-Fr.		8/74	—	9*		—				1/76
Frankfort-on-Main	(see German States)										
Galatz	(same rates as Bakeu)										
Gallipoli	(see Turkey)										
Gambia	Br. M.	v. England	1/68	—	22	1/70	16	—	7/75	d15*	Continue
German States	N.G.U.	Direct	1/68	—	10*	7/70	7*	—	10/71	6*	7/75
		C.M. v. E.	1/68	—	15*	7/70	10*	—	10 71	7*	7/75
		v. Stettin	7/71	—	6*	(Baltic Lloyd, once a month)					7/75
Gibraltar	Br. M.	v. E.	1/68	—	22	1/70	16	—	7/75	d8*	Continue
	Fr. M.		4/57	21*	42*	(see Spain)					1/70
	Br. M.	v. Belgium	10/70	—	AA	1/70	16	—	7/75	d15*	7/75
Gold Coast	Br. M.	v. E.	1/68	—	22	1/70	16	—	7/75	d15*	Continue
	Fr. M.		4/57	30*	60*	6/68	—	—	—	—	1/70
Greece	Br. M.	v. E.	1/70	—	20*	10/71	18*	—	7/70	15*	7/75
	N.G.U.	Direct	1/68	—	19*	6/68	14*	—	—	—	Next line
			—	—	—	10/71	23*	—	7/70	18*	7/75
		C.M. v. E.	1/68	—	24*	6/68	15*	—	—	—	Next line
			—	—	—	10/71	—	—	—	—	7/75
Guadaloupe	Italian	Direct	4/71	—	16*	7/75	f13	—	—	—	7/75
Guatemala	Br. M.	v. St. T.	1/68	—	18		—			—	Continue
Hamburg	U.S.	Open M	1/67	—	f10		—			—	Continue
Hanover	(see German States)										

218

TABLE B.—*Postal Rates to Foreign Countries, 1868–1875*—Continued

Destination	Service	Route	Introduction				Change in Rate				Change in Rate			Date Discontinued
				Rate				Rate				Rate		
			Date	¼ oz.	½ oz.		Date	¼ oz.	½ oz.		Date	¼ oz.	½ oz.	
Honduras, Br.	(see Belize)													
Hong Kong	Br. M.	v. Southampton	1/68	—	34		1/70	—	28			—	—	7/75
		v. Marseilles	1/68	—	42		1/70	—	36			—	—	4/71
		v. Brindisi	4/71	—	34							—	—	7/75
	N.G.U., direct	v. Brindisi	4/71	—	20		2/73	—	20*			—	—	7/75
	C.M. v. E.	v. Brindisi	4/71	—	21		2/73	—	21*			—	—	7/75
	U.S. Pkt. from San Fran.		7/67	—	d10		(also to Canton, Swatow, Amoy, and Foochow)								Continue
Hungary	(see Austria)													
Ibraila	(same rates as Bakeu)													
India	(see East Indies)													
Indian Archipelago	Fr. M.		4/57	30	60			—	—			—	—	1/70
Ineboli	(see Turkey)													
Ionian Islands	Fr. M.	v. E.	4/57	30*	60*		(see Greece)					—	—	1/70
	Br. M.		1/70	—	20			—	—			—	—	1874
Italy	N.G.U.	Direct	1/68	—	14*		7/70	—	11*		10/71	—	10*	7/75
		C.M. v. E.	1/68	—	19*		7/70	—	14*		10/71	—	11*	7/75
	Direct C.M. Italian	v. E.	4/68	—	15*		1/70	—	10*			—	—	7/75
		Direct	2/70	—	10*									7/75
Jaffa	(see Turkey)													
Jamaica	(see West Indies)													
Janina	(see Turkey)													
Japan	Fr. M.	v. Yokohama	1860	—	60			—	—			—	—	1/70
		to Yokohama	8/65	30*	60*			—	—			—	—	1/70
	Br. M.	v. Southampton	1/68	—	34		1/70	—	28		7/75	—	d27*	Continue
		v. Marseilles	1/68	—	42		1/70	—	36			—	—	4/71
	Br. M.	v. Brindisi	4/71	—	34		7/75	—	d33*			—	—	Continue
	N.G.U.	Direct	7/68	—	27		7/70	—	24		10/71	—	23	7/75
		C.M. v. E.	7/68	—	32		7/70	—	27		10/71	—	24	7/75
	Direct	v. Brindisi	4/71	—	24		10/71	—	23		2/73	—	20*	7/75
	C.M. v. E.	v. Brindisi	4/71	—	27		10/71	—	24		2/73	—	21*	7/75
	Am. Pkt. from San Fran.		7/67	—	10		7/75	—	d15			—	—	Continue
Java	Fr. M.	v. Southampton	4/57	30	60		1/70	—	28			—	—	1/70
	Br. M.	v. Marseilles	1/68	—	34		1/70	—	36		7/75	—	d27*	Continue
			1/68	—	42									4/71
		v. Brindisi	4/71	—	34		7/75	—	d33*			—	—	Continue
Jassy	(Same rates as Bakeu)													

Place	Mail	Via											
Jerusalem	Fr. M.		1860	30*	60*						—	—	1/70
	N.G.U.	Direct	1/68	—	15*			—	12*	10/71	—	11*	7/75
Karikal	Fr. M.		1/68	30*	20*		7/70	—	15*	10/71	—	12*	7/75
	Br. M.	v. E.	4/57	60*	60*		7/70	—	—	—	—	—	1/70
Kerassund	Fr. M.		1/70	—	22		—	—	—	—	—	—	7/75
	N.G.U.	Direct	4/57	30*	60*		—	—	12	10/71	—	11	Next line
					15		7/70	—	11*		—		7/75
N.G.U.		C.M. v. E.	1/70	—	20		7/70	—	15	10/71	—	12	Next line
					—		1872	—	12*		—		7/75
Kustendji	(see Turkey)						1872						
Labaun	Br. M.	v. Southampton	1/68	—	34		1/70	—	28	7/75	—	d27*	Continue
		v. Marseilles	1/68	—	42		1/70	—	36		—		4/71
		v. Brindisi	4/71	—	34		7/75	—	d33*		—		7/75
	N.G.U, direct	v. Brindisi	2/73	—	17		—	—	—		—		7/75
	C. M. v. E.	v. Brindisi	2/73	—	18		—	—	—		—		4/71
Lagos	Br. M.	v. E.	1/68	—	22		1/70	—	16		—		Continue
		v. Brindisi	4/71	—	16		7/75	—	d15*		—		4/71
	N.G.U.	Direct	1/68	—	15*		7/70	—	12*		—		4/71
		C.M. v. E.	1/68	—	20*		7/70	—	15*		—		
Larnica	(see Turkey)												
Latakia	(see Turkey)												
Lauenburg	(See German States)												
Liberia	Br. M.	v. E.	1/68	—	22		1/70	—	16	7/75	—	d15*	Continue
Lombardy	(see Italy)												
Lubec	(see German States)												
Luxemburg	(see German States)												
Madeira	Fr. M.	v. E.	4/57	30*	60*		—	—	—		—	—	1/70
	Br. M.	v. E.	1/70	—	16		—	—	—		—	—	7/75
	N.G.U.	Direct	5/73	—	11*		(see Portugal)	—	—		—	—	7/75
		C.M. v. E.	5/73	—	12*		(see Portugal)	—	—		—	—	1/70
Mahé	Fr. M.		4/57	30*	60*		(see Mauritius)	—	16		—	—	1/70
Majorca	Fr. M.		4/57	21	42		(see Spain)	—	—		—	—	7/75
Malta	Fr. M.		4/57	30*	60*		—	—	—		—	—	7/75
	Br. M.	v. Southampton	1/68	—	22		1/70	—	16		—	20	7/75
		v. Messina	1/68	22	44		1/70	16	28	4/71	—	—	7/75
	N.G.U, direct	v. Brindisi	4/71	—	15*		10/71	—	14*		—	—	Continue
	C.M. v. E.	v. Brindisi	4/71	—	18*		10/71	—	15*		—	—	1/70
Martinique	Br. M.	v. St. T.	1/68	—	18		7/75	—	f13		—	d23*	Continue
Mauritius	Fr. M.		4/57	30	60		—	—	—		—	—	1/70
	Br. M.	v. Marseilles	1/68	—	30		1/70	—	24	7/75	—	—	7/70
Mecklenburg	(see German States)												
Messina	Fr. M.	Direct	1/62	21*	42*		(see Italy)	—	10*		—	—	7/70
	N.G.U.	C.M. v. E.	1/68	—	14*		(see Italy)	—	—		—	—	7/70
		C.M. v. E.	1/68	—	19*		(see Italy)	—	—		—	—	
	Italian, direct		4/68	—	15*		1/70	—	—	(see Italy)	—	—	4/71

219

TABLE B.—*Postal Rates to Foreign Countries, 1868–1875*—Continued

Destination	Service	Route	Introduction			Change in Rate			Change in Rate			Date Discontinued
			Date	¼ oz. Rate	½ oz. Rate	Date	¼ oz. Rate	½ oz. Rate	Date	¼ oz. Rate	½ oz. Rate	
Mexico	From N.Y.	Direct by sea	12/65	—	f10		—	—		—	—	Continue
		by land	1862	—	£3		—	—		—	—	Continue
Minorca	Fr. M.		1860	21	42	(see Spain)						1/70
Mitylene	(same rates as Kerassund)											
Modena	(same rates as Messina)											
Moldavia	Fr. M.	Direct	1859	30*	60*		—	—		—	—	1/70
	N.G.U.	C.M. v. E.	1/68	—	13*	7/70	—	10*	10/71	—	9*	7/75
			1/68	—	18*	7/70	—	13*	10/71	—	10*	7/75
Moluccas	Fr. M.	v. Southampton	5/65	—	60		—	—		—	—	1/70
	Br. M.	v. Marseilles	1/68	—	34	1/70	—	28	(see Straits Settlements)			7/75
		v. Brindisi	1/68	—	42	1/70	—	36				4/71
			4/71	—	34	(see Straits Settlements)						7/75
Montevideo	Am. Pkt. from N.Y.		8/67	18	25	1/70	—	18	(see Uruguay)			7/75
	Br. M.	v. E.	1/68	—	34	1/70	—	28	(see Uruguay)			7/75
Naples	(same rates as Messina)											
Natal	Br. M.	v. E.	1/68	—	34	1/70	—	28	7/75	—	d27*	Continue
	Private ship from U.K.		7/75	—	d11*		—	—		—	—	Continue
Netherlands	(Treaty)	v. E.	1/68	—	15*	2/70	—	10*		—	—	7/75
		Direct	10/74	—	6*		—	—		—	—	7/75
New Brunswick	(see Canada)											
Newfoundland	Land route through N. B		7/67	—	10/15†	10/71	—	10	12/72	—	d6	Continue
	Br. M.	v. Aspinwall	1859	—	18	7/75	—	f13	(except Aspinwall & Panama)			Continue
New Granada												
New South Wales	U.S.	Direct	1/75	—	f10	7/75	—	f5		—	—	Continue
	Br. M.	v. Southampton	1/68	—	22	1/70	—	16	7/75	—	d15	Continue
		v. Marseilles	1/68	—	30	1/70	—	24		—	—	4/71
		v. Brindisi	4/71	—	22	7/75	—	d21		—	—	Continue
	Fr. M.	v. San Fran.	5/63	30*	60*		—	—		—	—	1/70
New Zealand	U.S., direct		5–6/70	—	10	11/74	—	d12		—	—	Continue
	Fr. M.	v. Panama	5/63	30*	60*		—	—		—	—	1/70
	Br. M.	v. Southampton	8/66	—	22	7/75	—	d15		—	—	Continue
		v. Marseilles	1/70	—	16	7/75	—	—		—	—	4/71
		v. Brindisi	1/70	—	24	7/75	—	d21		—	—	Continue
		v. San Fran.	4/71	—	22	7/75	—	d12		—	—	Continue
Nicaragua	U.S., direct (Pacific Slope)	v. Panama	5–6/70	—	10	12/70	—	—		—	—	1/70
		Direct	3/64	—	10		—	—		—	—	1/70
			1/70	—	10	7/75	—	f5		—	—	Continue

Norway	N.G.U.	Direct	1/68	—	20/23u	5/68	16/18u	1/70	—	15/18u	Next line
			7/70	—	12*	10/71	11*	2/73	—	10*	Next line
			7/75	—	6*	—	—	—	—	—	9/74
		C.M. v. E.	1/68	—	25/28u	5/68	21/23u	1/70	—	20/23u	Next line
			7/70	—	15*	10/71	12*	2/73	—	11*	Next line
			7/73	—	10*	—	—	—	—	—	9/74
	v. E., Bremen or Hamburg		7/71	—	10	10/71	6	—	—	—	1872
	U.S.		9/74	—	10*	4/68	6/10u	2/75	—	3	7/75
Nova Scotia	(see German states)		8/64	—	10*	—	—	—	—	—	Continue
Oldenburg											
Panama	U.S.	Direct	8/64	—	10	7/75	f5	—	—	—	Continue
Paraguay	Am. Pkt. from N.Y.		8/67	18	25	1/70	18	—	—	—	7/75
	U.S. Pkt.	v. Brazil	7/75	—	f23	—	—	—	—	—	Continue
Parma	(same rates as Messina)										
Penang	Fr. M.	v. Southampton	4/57	30	60	1/70	—	(see Straits Settlements)	—	—	1/70
	Br. M.	v. Marseilles	1/68	—	34	1/70	28			—	7/75
		v. Brindisi	1/68	—	42	—	36			—	4/71
		v. Brindisi	4/71	—	34	(see Straits Settlements)				—	7/75
	N.G.U., direct	v. Brindisi	4/71	—	21*	10/71	20*	(see Straits Settlements)	—	—	7/75
		v. Trieste	4/71	—	27*	—	—			—	10/71
	C.M. v. E.	v. Brindisi	4/71	—	24*	10/71	21*	(see Straits Settlements)	—	—	7/75
		v. Trieste	4/71	—	30*	—	—			—	10/71
Peru	Br. M.	v. Panama	10/67	—	34	1/70	22	—	—	—	7/75
		v. Colon	7/75	—	f17	—	—	—	—	—	Continue
Philippines	Fr. M.	v. Southampton	4/57	30	60	1/70	—	—	—	—	1/70
	Br. M.	v. Marseilles	1/68	—	34	1/70	28	—	—	—	Continue
		v. Brindisi	1/68	—	42	1/70	36	7/75	—	f27	4/71
		v. Brindisi	4/71	—	34	7/75	f33	—	—	—	Continue
	N.G.U.	Direct	1872	—	17	—	—	—	—	—	7/75
	U.S.	C.M. v. E	1872	—	18	—	—	—	—	—	7/75
		v. San Fran.	1872	—	10	—	—	—	—	—	7/75
Poland: Prussian or Austrian	Fr. M.	Direct	4/57	30*	60*	7/70	7*	10/71	—	6*	1/70
	N.G.U.	C.M. v. E.	1/68	—	10*	7/70	10*	10/71	—	7*	7/75
Russian	N.G.U.	Direct	1/68	—	15*	7/70	12*	10/71	—	11*	7/75
		C.M. v. E.	1/68	—	20/23u	7/70	15*	10/71	—	12*	7/75
Pondicherry	Fr. M.	v. Southampton	4/57	30*	60*	—	—	—	—	—	1/70
	Br. M.	v. San Fran.	1869	—	28	1/70	22	(see India)	—	—	7/75
	U.S.		1/70	—	10	(see India)	—		—	—	7/75
Port Said	Fr. M.	v. Southampton	7/67	30*	60*	(see Egypt)	—	—	—	—	1/70
	Br. M.	v. Marseilles	1/68	—	22	(see Egypt)	a22	—	—	—	2/69
		v. E.	2/69	—	42	(see Egypt)	—	—	—	—	12/69

TABLE B.—*Postal Rates to Foreign Countries, 1868–1875*—Continued

Destination	Service	Route	Introduction			Change in Rate			Change in Rate			Date Discontinued
			Date	¼ oz.	½ oz.	Date	¼ oz.	½ oz.	Date	¼ oz.	½ oz.	
Port Said—Continued	N.G.U.	Direct	1/68	—	15*	1/70	—	20*	7/70	—	17*	Next line
						10/71	—	16*				7/75
		C.M. v. E.	1/68	—	20*	1/70	—	25*	7/70	—	20*	Next line
						10/71	—	17*				7/75
Porto Rico	Br. M.	v. San Juan	1/67	—18	—							Continue
		v. St. T.	7/75	—	d13*							12/75
		Direct	7/75	—	d5							1/70
Portugal	Fr. M.	v. E.	9/66	27*	54*				1/70	a16	28	4/71
	Br. M.	v. E.	7/68	—	a24	11/68	—	a22				7/75
		v. Southampton	4/71	—	16	5/73	—	16*				7/75
	N.G.U.	Direct	5/73	—	11							7/75
		C.M. v. E.	5/73	—	12							
Prevesa	(same rates as Jerusalem)											
Prince Edwards Is.	(see Canada)											
Prussia	(see German states)											
Queensland	Br. M.	v. Southampton	1/68	—	22	1/70	—	16	(see Australia)			7/75
		v. Marseilles	1/68	—	30	1/70	—	24				4/71
		v. Brindisi	4/71	—	22	(see Australia)						7/75
	U.S.	v. San Fran.	5–6/70	—	f10	(see Australia)						7/75
	Br. M.	v. Panama	8/66	—	22							3/69
Rhodes	(same rates as Jerusalem)											
Roman States	Fr. M.	Direct	4/57	27*	54*	5/69	—	d14*	7/70	—	d11*	1/70
	N.G.U.		1/68	—	f14	10/71	—	d10*	(see Italy)			7/75
		C.M. v. E.	1/68	—	f19	5/69	—	d19*	7/70	—	d14*	Next line
						10/71	—	d11*	(see Italy)			7/75
	Italian, direct		10/70	—	10*	(see Italy)						7/75
Russia	N.G.U.	C.M. v. E.	1/68	—	15/18u	7/70	—	12*	10/71	—	11*	Next line
		Direct	1/68	—	—	1874	—	10*				7/75
		C.M. v. E.	1/68	—	20/23u	7/70	—	15*	10/71	—	12*	Next line
						1874	—	11*				7/75
Salvadore	Brem./Hamb.	Direct	1873	—	10							1874
	U.S.	v. Panama	10/70	—	f10	1/72	—	f10	v. (Colon)			Continue
Sandwich Islands	Direct	v. San Fran.	6/67	—	10	7/70	—	6				Continue
Sardinia	Fr. M.		4/57	21*	42*							1/70

Saxe-Altenburg	N.G.U.	Direct	1/68	—	14*	7/70	11*	(see Italy)	—	7/75
Saxe-Coburg	Italian	C.M. v. E.	1/68	—	19*	7/70	14*	(see Italy)	—	7/75
Saxe-Gotha	(see German States)	C.M. v. E.	4/68	—	15*	2/70	10*	(see Italy)	—	7/75
Saxony	(see German States)									
Schleswig-Holstein	(see German States)									
Scio	(same rates as Kerassund)									
Scutari	(same rates as Kerassund)									
Seres	(see Turkey)									
Servia (Serbia)	Fr. M.	v. Austria	1858	21	42	(except Belgrade)	12	7/70	9	1/70
	N.G.U.	Direct	1/68	—	15	12/69	8	—	—	Next line
					—	10/71	—	—	—	7/75
		C.M. v. E.	1/68	—	20	12/69	17	7/70	12	Next line
					—	10/71	9	—	—	7/75
Shanghai	(see China)									
Sierra Leone	Br. M.	v. England	1/68	—	22	1/70	16	7/75	d15*	Continue
Singapore	Fr. M.	v. Southampton	4/57	30	60	—	—	—	—	1/70
	Br. M.	v. Southampton	1/68	—	34	1/70	28	(see Straits Settlements)	—	7/75
		v. Marseilles	1/68	—	42	1/70	36	—	—	4/71
		v. Brindisi	4/71	—	34	(see Straits Settlements)	—	—	—	7/75
	N.G.U., direct	v. Brindisi	4/71	—	21*	10/71	20*	—	—	7/75
		v. Trieste	4/71	—	27*	10/71	26*	—	—	11/71
	C.M. v. E.	v. Brindisi	4/71	—	24	10/71	21	1872	21*	7/75
		v. Trieste	4/71	—	30*	10/71	27*	—	—	11/71
	U.S.	v. San Fran.	11/68	—	10	—	—	—	—	7/75
Sinope	(see Turkey)									
Smyrna	(same rates as Jerusalem)									
Sophia	(see Turkey)									
Spain	Fr. M.	v. Behobia	4/57	f21	42	—	42	—	—	1/70
	Br. M.	v. E.	7/68	—	a22	1/69	a22	1/70	28	4/71
	B. O. M.	Paid to E.	1/69	—	10	1/70	4*	a16	—	7/75
	U.S.	Direct	1/68	—	f10	—	—	—	—	1/69
	Direct	v. New Orleans	11/71	—	f10	—	—	—	—	7/75
	Br. M.	v. Belgium	10/70	—	AA	—	—	—	—	7/75
		v. Marseilles	10/70	—	AA	7/75	d12*	—	—	1/76
	Brem./Hamb.	Direct	1872	—	11	—	—	—	—	7/75
		C.M. v. E.	1872	—	12	—	—	—	—	7/75
St. Helena	Br. M.	v. E.	1/68	—	34	1/70	28	7/75	d27*	Continue
Straits Settlements	Br. M.	v. Southampton	7/75	—	d27*	—	—	—	—	Continue
		v. Brindisi	7/75	—	d33*	—	—	—	—	Continue

TABLE B.—*Postal Rates to Foreign Countries, 1868–1875*—Continued

Destination	Service	Route	Introduction			Change in Rate			Change in Rate			Date Discontinued
			Date	¼ oz.	½ oz.	Date	¼ oz.	½ oz.	Date	¼ oz.	½ oz.	
Sumatra	Br. M.	v. Southampton	1/68	—	34	1/70	—	28	(see Straits Settlements)			7/75
		v. Marseilles	1/68	—	42	1/70	—	36				4/71
		v. Brindisi	4/71	—	34	(see Straits Settlements)						7/75
	Fr. M.		4/57	30	60							1/70
Sweden	N.G.U.	Direct	1/68	—	16/18u	1/70	—	14/16u	7/70	—	11*	Next line
						10/71	—	10*				9/74
		C.M. v. E.	1/68	—	21/23u	1/70	—	19/21u	7/70	—	14*	Next line
						10/71	—	11*				9/74
	Swedish-U.S.	v. Stettin	7/71	—	10	(once a month)						9/74
		Direct	7/73	—	6*							9/74
	Swedish	C.M. v. E.	7/73	—	9*							9/74
		C.M. v. E. or Germany	9/74	—	9*							7/75
Switzerland	N.G.U.	Direct	1/68	—	15*							5/68
		C.M. v. E.	1/68	—	20*							5/68
	Fr. M.		4/57	21*	42*							1/70
	U.S.-Swiss	D. C.M. v. E.	4/68	—	15*	5/70	—	10*				7/75
		v. Brem./Hamb.	1872	—	8							7/75
Syria	Fr. M.		4/57	30	60	(see Turkey)						1/70
Tangiers	Fr. M.		4/57	30*	60*							1/70
	Br. M.	v. E.	1/70	—	16	7/75	—	f15				Continue

Tunis	Fr. M.		1/68		60		—	—	—	1/70
	Br. M.	v. E.	1/70	30	28	10/71	28	—	—	12/71
	N.G.U., direct	v. Brindisi (r)	4/71	a16	14*		—	—	—	7/75
	C.M. v. E.	v. Brindisi (r)	4/71	—	15*		—	—	—	7/75
	Italian	Open M.	4/71	—	14*	7/75	d7*	—	—	Continue
Turkey: to places not mentioned	Fr. M.	v. Austria	4/57	21*	42*		—	—	—	1/70
List A	N.G.U.	Direct	1/68	—	15*	7/70	12*	10/71	11*	7/75
		C.M. v. E	1/68	—	20*	7/70	15*	10/71	12*	7/75
to places not listed		Direct	1/68	—	15	7/70	12	10/71	11	7/75
		C.M. v. E.	1/68	—	20	7/70	15	10/71	12	7/75
Turks Is.	U.S.	Direct	1859	—	10		—	—	—	7/73
	Br. M.	v. St. T.	7/73	—	18	7/75	f13	—	—	Continue
Tuscany	(see Italy)									
Uruguay	U.S.	Am. Pkt.	8/67	18	25	1/70	18	(from N.Y.)	—	7/75
		v. Brazil	7/75	—	f23		—		—	Continue
Van Dieman's Land	[Tasmania]	(see Australia)								
Venezuela	U.S.	Am./Venez. Pkt.	1/67	—	f10		—	—	—	Continue
	Br. M.	v. St. T.	9/74	—	f18	7/75	f13	—	—	Continue
Victoria	(see Australia)									
Wallachia	N.G.U.	Direct	1/68	—	13*	7/70	10*	10/71	9*	7/75
		C.M. v. E.	1/68	—	18*	7/70	13*	10/71	10*	7/75
West Indies:										
British	U.S. (r)	Am. Pkt.	8/67	—	f10	7/75	f5	—	—	Continue
Not British	Br. M. (r)	v. St. T.	1/68	—	10		—	—	—	1872
British	Br. M.	v. St. T.	1/68	—	18	7/75	f13	—	—	Continue
	Br. M.	v. St. T. or Havana	1872	—	18	7/75	f13	—	—	Continue
Wurtemberg	(see German States)									
	Fr. M.		4/57	30*	60*		—	—	—	1/70
Yanaon	U.S.	Direct	1/70	—	10	(see India)	—	—	—	7/75

225

Index

Aachen, 9, 87, 141. *See also* Exchange offices
Accounting, international, 3
Acknowledgment of receipt, 28
Adelaide, British Post Office at, 142
Aden, British Post Office at, 142
Admiralty, British, 1
Agency, U.S. Postal, at Bremen, 12, 13, 14, 119
Agents, forwarding, 2, 9, 11
Agents, mail, 78, 165
Ain, France, 180
Aix-la-Chapelle. *See* Aachen
Algeria, 169, 170
Allentown, Pa., 123
Anglo-Belgian mail. *See* Mail services
Anglo-Bremen mail. *See* Mail services
Anglo-Prussian mail. *See* Mail services
Alexandria, Egypt, Austrian Post Office at, 142
American Almanac, 35
American packets, 4, 5, 25, 29, 38, 39, 43, 44, 45, 47, 48, 50, 63, 65, 85, 93, 100, 102, 103, 110, 111, 115, 116, 120, 123, 125, 128, 130, 134, 135, 146, 153, 188, 189, 190
Amsterdam, Netherlands, 105
Antwerp, Belgium, 4, 102, 104, 105, 106, 157. *See also* Exchange offices
Articles in the accounts, 40, 41
Article LII of Anglo-French (1843) convention, 37, 40, 41, 44, 45
Article XII of U.S.-British (1848) treaty, 27, 38, 41, 42, 43, 44
Article XVII, articles of execution, U.S.-British (1848) treaty, 36
Ashbrook, Stanley B., 92, 101, 173
Ashbrook's Special Service, 92, 101, 102, 104
Atlantic's Return—Schottische, 125
Auckland, British Post Office at, 142
Auditor of the Treasury for the Post Office Department, reports of, 20, 131, 134, 135
Au dos, 78
Augusta, Ga., 131
Australia, 141
Austria, 4, 140, 155; Post Office of, 142; Post Office in Turkey, 162

Baden, 21, 110, 141, 142
Bahia, Brazil, 108
Baltimore, Md., 4, 9, 11, 20, 52, 78, 90, 116. *See also* Exchange offices

Baker, J. David, 93
Bancroft, George: Canadian mails, 37; decision for treaty, 26; exclusion of France, 41; memo to Maberly, 42, 43, 47, negotiations with British, 23, 24, 25; optional prepayment, 37, 38; packet rate, 37; progression, 34; treaty of reciprocity, 42; uniform rates, 26
Bartsch, Dr., Director of Bremen Posts, 20, 116, 130
Basle, Switzerland, 95. *See also* Exchange offices
Bates, Barnabus, 2
Bath, Me., 138
Bavaria, 140
Belgian closed mail. *See* Mail services
Berlin, Prussia, 17, 94, 113, 159
Berne Postal Congress, 180
Bishop Hill, Ill., 160
Blackfan, Joseph H., 164, 169
Blair, Montgomery, 138, 147, 185, 186, 189
Blake, Maurice C., 36
Bombay, India, British Post Office at, 142
Bordeaux, France, 50, 58, 66, 67, 69, 79, 108, 165
Boston, Mass., 36, 46, 79, 82, 126, 127, 137, 187, 188; steamship arrivals in, 5, 6, 9, 11, 18, 30, 31, 68, 127, 189; steamship sailings from 5, 16, 30, 31, 46, 48, 55, 67, 68, 90, 106, 135, 138, 143. *See also* Exchange offices
Bremen, Free Hansiatic City of, 4, 11, 12, 13, 14, 17, 20, 121, 125, 140, 142, 153, 154, 155, 187, 193. *See also* Exchange offices
Bremen closed mail. *See* Mail services
Bremen-Hamburg mail. *See* Mail services
Bremen mail. *See* Mail services
Bremen packets, 110, 111, 112, 113, 120, 121, 123
Bremerhaven, 6, 12, 13, 14, 18, 19, 85, 119, 130
Brest, France, 4, 78, 165. *See also* Exchange office
Brigade, 66, 78
Brisbane, British Post Office at, 142
Bristol, England, 4
British Columbia, 76
British East India Company, 112
British mail. *See* Mail services
British open mail. *See* Mail services
British packets, 1, 5, 38, 39, 43, 45, 46, 47, 48, 50, 63, 85, 93, 100, 102, 103, 127, 138, 139, 189, 192
British Post Office, 38, 87, 99, 100, 127, 144
Brown, Aaron V., 116, 119; contract with Vanderbilt, 115; single trip contracts, 118; "Miscellaneous" line, 118
Brunswick, 13, 140, 143
Buchanan, James, 26, 41, 43
Burritt, Elihu, 2

Caillaux, M., 117
Caird & Co., 119
Calcutta, British Post Office at, 142
California, 26, 28, 76, 137
Campbell, James, 89, 105, 111; arrangement with Hamburg, 119; Collins line subsidy, 113; credit for sea postage, 39; French scale, 70; New York port, 114; "retaliatory" order, 46; sailing irregularities, 19; sea postage, 47; transit rates, 42
Canada, provisional government of, 134
Canadian mail packets, 134, 135, 137, 152. *See also* Steamship lines.
Canadian mails, 23, 24, 37, 42, 43
Canadian Post Office Department, 134
Cape Elizabeth Depot, Me., 171
Carpenter, Samuel, 46
Charleston, S.C., 31, 100, 101
Charlottesville, Va., 50
Cherbourg, France, 54, 153, 165. *See also* Exchange offices
Chicago, Ill., 134, 135. *See also* Exchange offices
Christiania, Norway, 160, 162
Civil War, 77, 119, 125, 136, 184, 190
Clanricarde, Lord, 27, 37, 38; decision for treaty, 26; desired postal convention, 24; offer to France, 43, 44; proposals, 25; protection of Cunard line, 23
Clarendon, Lord, 39, 62
Clermont, N.Y., 123
Closed mail: defined, 8
Coal, British: for steam packets, 1, 17; consumption of, 17
Coinage: Mint and market ratios, 184; silver subsidiary, 185, 186
Coles, William C., Jr., 192, 193
Collamer, Jacob, 19, 35, 185
Collins, E. K.: packets as cruisers, 4; lobbied for subsidy, 113, 114, 115
Cologne, Prussia, 9, 141. *See also* Exchange offices
Colonial rate, 24, 150
Columbia: Me., 90; S.C., 113
Commission of Bremen agent, 14, 119
Commissions of postmasters, 39
Compulsory prepayment, 11, 38, 76, 82, 88, 127, 140, 143, 155, 156, 176
Congress, U.S., 1, 2, 12, 14, 24, 34, 46, 113–115 *passim*, 183–185 *passim*
Congress of Vienna, 13
Constantinople, 141, 159, 162
Consuls, U.S.: as forwarding agents, 2
Convention, commercial: U.S.-Great Britain (1815), 24, 25
Conventions, postal, 2, 24; Anglo-Belgian (1844), 99; (1849), 102; (1857), 103; Anglo-Bremen (1841), 6, 7, 8, 19; Anglo-French (1843), 40, 41, 43, 62, 170; (1856), 44, 63, 64, 65, 70, 165, 170; (1869), 169, 171; Anglo-Prussian (1846), 8, 9, 85; (1852), 86, 93, 95, 140; (1859), 140; (1862), 141, 142; common provisions of, 148, 149; Berne, treaty of, 162, 180; Bremen-Hanover, 12; German-Austrian (1850), 15, 85, 86; Kainardji, treaty of, 162; U.S.-Belgium (1859), 105, 106; (1863), 148; (1867), 148, 151, 152; (1870), 156; (1873), 156; U.S. Bremen (1847), 12, 13, 14, 15, 16, 112; (1853), 110, 111, 112, 120, 144; U.S.-Denmark (1871), 157, 158; U.S.-France (1857), 56, 66, 70–78, 93, 94, 136, 138, 164, 167, 169, 170, 189; (1874), 179, 180; U.S.-Great Britain (1848), 9, 19, 24–28, 36, 38, 99, 100, 133–136, 140, 142; (1867), 149, 169; (1868), 149 169, 177; (1869), 153, 167, 170; U.S.-Hamburg (1857), 119, 144; U.S.-Italy (1863), 148, 152, 153; (1867), 148, 151; (1870), 156; U.S.-Netherlands (1867), 148, 151, 152; (1870), 157; (1874), 157; U.S.-North German Union (1867), 148, 150, 151, 193; (1870), 153, 154; (1871), 155; U.S.-Prussia (1852), 20, 82, 85, 86, 93, 106, 138; U.S.-Sweden and Norway (1873), 158; U.S.-Switzerland (1867), 149, 151; (1870), 156; Wickliffe Agreement, 24
Corn laws, 1
Cornwall-on-the-Hudson, N.Y., 162
Corridor countries, 100
Covers (by Mail services): Anglo-Bremen mail, 9; Anglo-Prussian closed mail, 9–11; Belgian closed mail, 106–108; Bremen mail, direct, 17, 21, 22, 112, 113; Bremen closed mail, 20, 21; Bremen-Hamburg mail: Bremen service, 121, 123; Hamburg service, 121, 123; U.S. service, 121, 123, 125. British closed mail from France: American packet, 52; British packet, 50, 52; three months' period, 69. British open mail: to Bavaria, 96; to Belgium, 100, 101, 102, 104; from Belgium, 104; to France, 46, 48, 50, 52, 66, 67, 165, 167; to Germany, 94, 95; to Switzerland, 95, 96, 97, 98. New York-Havre line, direct, 58, 59, 60, 62; Direct service to France (1870–74), 165, 167, 177. British mail—international: partial payment recognized, 36; Philadelphia exchange office, 133, 134; Portland exchange office, 138; triple rate, 144, 145. British mail, via Southampton, 127. Depreciated currency: Bremen-Hamburg mail, 188; British mail—international, 187, 188, 190, 192; British open mail, 188; Boston exchange office, 189; Chicago exchange office, 192; Detroit exchange office, 193; Philadelphia exchange office, 193; Portland exchange office, 193; Prussian closed mail, 190; Unpaid letter from France, 193. French mail—international: American packet, direct, 79; American packet, via England, 78; British packet, 78; Baltimore exchange office, 136; Chicago exchange office, 139, Direct service, rerated, 132; (1874), 180, 183. French mail-transit: to Belgium, 108; to Norway, 82, 84; to Rome, 79, 82; to Sicily, 82; to Switzerland, 79, 138, North German Union mail—international, 159. North German Union mail—transit: to Constantinople, 159, 160, 162, 163; to Norway, 160, 162; to Sweden, 160. Ocean line service to France, via Southampton, 57, 58. Prepaid to France, via England (1870–74): "phantom rate," 171; "CC" rates, 174. Prepaid from France, via England, 177. Prussian closed mail: international, 90, 92, 93, 143; Bremen service intended, 116, 129, 130, 131. Prussian closed mail—transit: to Finland, 139; to Norway, 93; to Switzerland, 131, 143, 144. United States-Great Britain: "restored" rates, 31, 33; "retaliatory" rates, 29, 31; 1845 rates, 5, 6. U.S. to France (1846), 48.
Cowes, England, 55
Creswell, John A. J., 73, 153, 154, 155, 158; "phantom rate" to France, 170, 171; prepaid rate to France, 173
Crimean War, 112, 128
Cuxhaven, 6, 19, 42, 85

Daniels, Bruce G., 46
Davis, Congressman from Mississippi, 114
Davis, John C. B., 43, 44, 56
Decrees of France, 45, 57, 96, 165, 176, 177
Denmark, 4. *See also* Conventions, postal
Deep River, Conn., 102
Delivery fee, 21, 88, 92
Depreciated currency: exchange office procedure, 186; unpaid letters, collections on, 185, 186. *See also* Greenbacks
De Sartiges, Count, 47
De Wasserman, Dr. Robert, 66, 103, 106
Direct closed mail, via England, 152. *See also* Mail services
Direct mail: defined, 8, 9
Double sea postage, 23, 25, 29, 31, 39, 45, 50
Dover, England, 9. *See also* Exchange offices
Downing, Lester L., 58
Dresden, Saxony, 20
Duckwitz, Arnold, 4, 12, 13, 109, 110, 116
Düsseldorf, Prussia, 9

Early, General Jubal, 190
Edinburgh, Scoltand, 5
Emigrant trade, 125, 126
Endicott, William and Company, 128
Eufaula, Ala., 171
Everett, Edward, 42
Exchange office accounting, 28; Belgian closed mail, 107; French mail–international rate, 74; French mail to countries beyond France, 75; Prussian closed mail, 87; U.S.-Bremen (1853), 111; U.S.-British (1848)—international rate, 28
Exchange offices: Under the Conventions: Anglo-Belgian (1844), 99; (1857), 103; Anglo-Bremen (1841), 6; Anglo-Prussian (1846), 9; (1862), 141; U.S.-Belgium (1859), 105; (1867), 152; U.S.-Bremen (1847), 13, 14 (1853), 110; U.S.-Denmark (1871), 157; U.S.-France (1857), 71, 73, 136, 137; (1874), 179; U.S.-Great Britain (1848), 29, 133–136; U.S.-Italy (1863), 153; (1867), 152, 153; U.S.-Netherlands (1867), 152; U.S.-North German Union (1867), 150; U.S.-Prussia (1852), 87, 138; U.S.-Switzerland (1867), 152. Functions of, 28, 29; procedures, 186, 187; relations between, 137. Individual offices: Aachen, 9, 87, 88, 89, 90, 92, 93, 95, 129, 138, 144; Antwerp 99, 100, 103, 105, 152; Arona travelling office, 152, 153; Baltimore, 136, 176; Basle, 152; Boston, 29, 36, 38, 39, 44, 50, 52, 71, 79, 84, 87, 97, 105, 135, 137, 150, 152, 174, 176, 179, 186, 189, 192; Boulogne, 48; Bremen, 150; Bremen City Post Office, 9, 12, 13, 110, 111, 112, 113, 121; Brest, 179; Brussels-Quievrain travelling office, 103; Calais, 44, 48; Calais-Paris travelling office, 50, 52, 66, 67, 71, 78, 79, 84, 171, 179; Camerlata travelling office, 152, 153; Cherbourg, 179; Chicago, 134, 135, 137, 138, 150, 157, 176, 186, 192; Cologne, 9, 93, 94; Copenhagen, 157; Cork, 135; Detroit, 97, 134, 135, 137, 138, 176, 186, 193; Dover, 9, 99, 100, 103, 104; Dublin, 135; Emmerich, 9; Galway, 135; Geneva, 152; Glasgow, 135; Ghent-Mouscron travelling office, 103; Hamburg, 9, 150; Hamburg City Post Office, 121; Hull, 9, 99, 103; Korsor and Kiel travelling office, 157; Le Havre, 71, 77, 78, 108, 132, 179; Lille-Calais travelling office, 179; Liverpool, 29, 36, 90, 100, 133, 135; Liverpool Packet letter office, 146; London, 9, 48, 66, 67, 93–100 *passim*, 102, 103, 104, 105, 133, 135, 146, 164, 171, 177; Londonderry, 135; Moerdyke travelling office 152; New York, 29, 38, 44, 52, 66, 71, 77, 78, 79, 82, 87, 90, 93, 95, 97, 102, 105, 107, 110, 112, 116, 119, 121, 123, 131, 132, 135, 137, 143, 144, 146, 150, 152, 157, 160, 162, 163, 167, 171, 173, 174, 176, 179, 189; Ostend—local office, 99, 100, 102, 103, 105, 152; Ostend travelling office, 103, 105, 152; Paris, 44, 78, 79, 137, 139, 177; Philadelphia, 71, 74, 77, 79, 107, 133, 137, 146 150, 165, 176, 186, 193; Portland, 134, 135, 137, 138, 176, 186, 193; San Francisco, 71, 76, 77, 136, 137, 176, 186, 193; Southhampton, 29, 57, 99, 104, 132, 133; Susa travelling office, 152, 153; Verviers-Cologne travelling office, 141, 150

Far East, places in, 143
Fond du Lac, Wis., 138
Foreign currencies: Austria, 88, 89; Baden, 21, 22, 88, 110; Bavaria, 88, 92, 96; Belgium, 74, 75, 100, 102, 103, 149, 152, 156; Brazil, 108; Bremen, 6, 9, 11, 13, 20, 21, 22, 121; Denmark, 157; France, 40, 43, 45, 48, 50, 52, 56, 57, 58, 62, 65, 67, 69, 71, 72, 73, 74, 76, 139, 165, 176, 177, 180, 183; Germany, northern, 21, 88, 131; Germany, southern, 88, 94, 110, 144; Great Britain, 5, 6, 8, 9, 11, 31, 40, 43, 86, 94, 99, 100, 101, 102, 149; Hamburg, 121; Hanover, 13, 123; Italy, 149, 152, 156; Netherlands, 149, 152, 157; North German Union, 149, 150, 151, 154, 155, 159, 160, 162; Prussia, 9, 11, 13, 21, 86, 88, 90, 92, 94, 95, 131, 140, 144; Rome, 76; Russia, 140; Sardinia, 76; Saxony, 21; Switzerland, 76, 96, 98, 144, 149, 152, 156; Thuringia, 92; Wurttemberg, 88, 110
Foreign trade, 1, 192
Fox and Livingston, 4, 55
Fractional postage currency notes, 185
Franco-Prussian War, 154, 156, 165
Frankfort-on-the-Main, 4, 13
French mail. *See* Mail services
French packets, 71, 72, 75, 179
French Post Office in Turkey, 162
Funch, Edye and Company, 158

Galway, Ireland, 126. *See also* Exchange offices
Gand, Belgium, 100
Garonne, France, 66
Geelong, British Post Office at, 142
General Postal Union, 180
Geneva, Switzerland, 144. *See also* Exchange offices
Georgetown, D.C., 58
German-Austrian Postal Union, 85–89 *passim*, 92, 120, 131, 141, 144
German mail packets, 141
Germany, Post Office in Turkey, 162
Gevekoht, C. Th., 4, 12, 14
Glasgow, Scotland, 135. *See also* Exchange offices
Graebe, Charles, 13
Greenbacks, 184, 185; issuance authorized, 184; height of inflation, 190; prices of, 186, 187; redemption, 189

Halifax, Nova Scotia, 1, 54, 55, 126
Hall, Nathan K., 46, 85

Halle, Prussia, 129
Hamburg, Free Hansiatic City of, 4, 6, 9, 12, 13, 112, 140, 142, 153, 159,165, 190. *See also* Exchange offices
Hamburg packets, 119, 121, 123
Hanover, 4, 12, 13, 123
Hart, Creighton C., 5, 102, 104
Hartington, Marquess of, 153, 173
Havre, France. *See* Le Havre
Hesse-Darmstadt, 4
Hesse, Grand Duchy of, 123
Hesse-Nassau, 4
Hobart Town, British Post Office at, 142
Hobbie, Major Selah R., 12, 13, 23, 24, 25, 37
Holbrook, James, 186, 189
Holt, Joseph, 106, 134
Holyhead, England, 135
Hong Kong, British Post Office at, 39, 142
House of Commons, 153, 173
Hubbard, Samuel D., 39, 42, 45
Hubbard, Walter, 58, 66
Hull, England, 9. *See also* Exchange offices

Illinois, 137
India, 141
Indiana, 137
Indian Mutiny, 112, 116
Ingersoll, J. R., 39, 62
Instructions to postmasters, 15
Insufficiently paid letters, 103, 139, 149, 151, 153, 154, 157, 158, 177, 190
Ionian Islands, 141
Iowa, 137
Irish nationalists, 126
Italy, 4; Post Office in Turkey, 162. *See also* Conventions, postal

Johnson, Cave, 3, 4, 13, 14, 23, 27, 33, 35, 42

Kanalle Depot, Ill., 139
Kansas territory, 137
Kasson, John A., 148, 150, 164
Kentucky, 137
King George's Sound, British Post Office at, 142
Kingstown, Ireland, 135

La Rochelle, France, 78
Late-mailing fee, 29
Launceston, British Post Office at, 142
Lawrence, Abbott, 43, 44, 56, 85, 86
Leavitt, Joshua, 2
Legislation: Great Britain: Standards act (1866), 171n; order in council, 173. U.S.: Coinage acts, 184, 185, 189; Currency act, 185; issuance of notes, 185; Legal Tender act, 184, 189; metric system, 148; Mint act, 184; Specie Resumption act, 192.
Legislation, postal: France: Decrees of, 45, 57, 96, 165, 176, 177; Law of 1871, 177. U.S.: Acts of (1825), 3, 24, 26; (1845), 2, 3, 4, 5; (1848), 25, 100; (1849), 35; (1851), 15, 36; (1852), 19; (1858), 115, 153; (1864), 165, 188; (1865), 153. Joint resolutions of Congress: (1844), 2, 3, 13, 36, 37; (1863), 153. Resolution of the House, 12; Resolution of the Senate, 12.
Le Havre, 4, 12, 52, 54, 77, 78, 116, 117, 129, 131, 132, 165. *See also* Exchange offices
Lehmkuhl, Karl, 109
Letter-bills, 28, 36, 40, 97
Letters, duplicate copies of, 2
Lever, John Orr, 126
Lisbon, Portugal, 4, 108
Liverpool, England, 4, 5, 15, 50, 67, 78, 79, 97, 100, 127, 133, 134, 136, 138, 146, 153, 154, 177, 188. *See also* Exchange offices
Livingston, Mortimer, 55
Lobbying, 4, 113
London, England, 6, 9, 12, 19, 31, 65, 135, 158, 159, 187, 193. *See also* Exchange offices
Louisville, Ky., 121
Lubeck, 140
Luxembourg, 140, 155
Lyons, France, 59

Maberly, William L.: protection of Cunard line, 23; credit for sea postage, 39; memo to Bancroft, 42, 47; closed mail to France, 45; provisional Anglo-French agreement, 46
Madras, British Post Office at, 142
Mail agents, 78, 113, 165
Mail, closed: defined, 8
Mail, direct: defined, 8, 9
Mail, open: defined, 8
Mail services: Anglo-Belgian, 99–104; Anglo-Bremen, 6; Anglo-Prussian closed mail, 9, 93–95; Baltic Lloyd, via Stettin, 155, 158; Belgian closed mail, 105, 120; Bremen closed mail, 19, 20, 42, 85, 130; Bremen-Hamburg mail, 94, 106, 119–125, 131; Bremen mail, 12–19 *passim,* 109, 110, 120; British closed mail from France, 44, 45; British open mail, 37, 38; British open mail to Belgium, 99–104 *passim;* British open mail to France, 41–52 *passim,* 62–65 *passim;* British open mail to France (1870–74), 164, 165; British open mail to Germany, 85, 93–95 *passim;* British open mail to Spain, 188; British mail, 38, 39, 97, 116, 135; British mail to France (1870–74), 167–174 *passim;* British mail, via Southampton, 170; Direct to France, via Havre line, 55; Direct to France (1870–74), 165; French mail, 70–84 *passim,* 97, 106, 108, 120, 127, 131, 137, 138, 139, 169; North German Union, closed mail, via England, 151, 160; North German Union, direct mail, 151, 159; Ocean line to France, via Southampton, 56–58; Prussian closed mail, 20, 82, 85–93 *passim,* 95, 106, 109, 112, 116, 117, 120, 129, 130, 131, 138, 139, 140, 142, 143, 190; U.S.-Bremen (1841), 6; U.S.-Prussia (1846), 9
Mainz, Germany, 94
Mann, Colonel A. Dudley, 4
Marcy, W. L., 39, 46
Marginal weight letters, 176
Maurin, M., 43, 56
Mecklenburg-Schwerin, 141
Mecklenburg-Strelitz, 140
Melbourne, British Post Office at, 142

Metric system: use authorized, 148
Michigan, 137
Middleborough, Mass., 162
Mills, Edward, 4, 55
Minnesota, 137
Minorca, Spain, 188
Mishicott (Wisconsin ?), 96
Missouri, 137
Mons, Belgium, 104
Moville, Ireland, 135
Munck, Johann, 128
Munich, Bavaria, 92
Myers, Gustavus, 114

Napoleon III, Louis, 45, 148, 164
Nantasket Roads, 18
Nantes, France, 52
Nationalism, 1, 3, 4, 115
Navy: Department of, 114, 118; United States, 136
Nebraska territory, 137
Netherlands, 12. See also Conventions, postal
New Bedford, Mass., 190
Newcastle-on-Tyne, England, 190
New Orleans, 48, 50, 52, 58, 66, 67, 78, 79, 82, 95, 131, 165, 174
Newport, R.I., 54
New York, N.Y., 17, 19, 20, 21, 46, 56, 59, 69, 92, 94, 104, 105, 108, 113, 114, 116, 119, 120, 125, 126, 134, 143, 153, 154, 155, 156, 158, 159, 165, 177, 180; steamship arrivals in, 18, 20, 54, 55, 59, 62, 66, 68, 79, 93, 95, 105, 111, 112, 117, 120, 121, 130, 134, 135, 177, 189, 190; steamship sailings from, 11, 15, 17, 21, 46, 48, 50, 54, 55, 57, 58, 66, 68, 77, 78, 79, 82, 89, 90, 96, 100, 101, 112, 113, 116, 117, 120, 121, 123, 130, 132, 137, 153, 155, 156, 159, 165. See also Exchange offices
New York Recorder, 46
New York Times (Weekly), 46
New York Tribune (Daily), 36, 45, 46
News by telegraph, 126
North German Confederation (Union), formation of, 150
North German Postal District, 150
North German Union mail. See Mail services
Norway, 4, 82, 93, 141, 142, 143, 160. See also Conventions, postal
Novelty Works, 5
Nuremburg, Bavaria, 96

Ohio, 137
Oldenburg, 4, 12, 110, 140
Open mail, 8
Optional prepayment, 3, 11, 13, 14, 36–38 *passim*, 76, 82, 87, 88, 93, 105, 110, 127, 140, 143, 155, 156, 176
Oregon, 28, 76, 137
Ostend, Belgium, 141. See also Exchange offices
Otsago, Wis., 160
Ottawa, Ill., 139
Oxford, Ohio, 112

Palermo, Sicily, 82
Palmerston, Lord, 23, 24, 25, 26, 85, 86

Paris: conference, 147; France, 12, 46, 48, 50, 78, 138, 139, 164, 165, 171, 174, 177, 183, 189. See also Exchange offices
Partial payments, recognition of, 36, 76, 87, 92, 97, 105, 110, 123, 139, 151, 192
Penang, British Post Office at, 142
Pernambuco, Brazil, 108
Philadelphia, Pa., 9, 46, 60, 96, 106, 133, 135, 137, 144, 157, 165, 187, 193. See also Exchange offices
Plymouth, England, 153, 165, 183
Point de Galle, British Post Office at, 142
Polk, James K., 3, 25, 42
Portland, Me., 97, 132, 134, 136. See also Exchange offices
Port Louis, British Post Office at, 142
Postage: as protective tariff, 24; basis of taxation, 24, 42; function of, 24
Postage stamps: Belgium: 1863 issue, 20c, 40c, 104. France: 1849 issue, 1f, 50; 1853 issue, 5c, 52; 20c, 62; 40c, 52, 62, 69; 80c, 52. Great Britain: 1841 issue, 1d., 29; 2d., 5; 1847 issue, 1s., 6, 29, 31, 36. Thurn and Taxis-southern district: 1852 issue, 1k, 9k, 94. United States: Boston penny post, 48; New York postmaster's, 48; "Nesbitt" stamped envelope, 58, 91; 1847 issue, 5¢, 11, 48, 100, 101; 10¢, 5, 21, 101; 1851 issue, 1¢, 50, 60; 1¢, type II, 52, 66; 1¢, type IV, 60, 102; 3¢, orange brown, 59, 96, 112; 3¢, red, 50, 58, 60, 66, 94; 5¢, 52, 67; 10¢, type II, 66, 90, 102; 10¢, type III, 60, 90, 123; 12¢, 58, 59, 60; 1857 issue, 1¢, type V, 79; 3¢, type II, 79, 82, 108, 131; 5¢, type I, red brown, 78; 5¢, type II, brown, 132; 10¢, type II, 82, 123; 10¢, type III, 82; 10¢, type V, 79, 82, 121, 132; 12¢, 79, 108, 123, 131, 138; 30¢, 78; 1861 issue, 1¢, 93, 138; 3¢, 79, 106; 5¢, brown yellow, 123; 10¢, type I, 123; 10¢, type II, 138; 12¢, 79; 15¢, 125; 24¢, red lilac, 106; 24¢ lilac, 146; 30¢, 144; 90¢, 93; 1869 issue, 1¢, 165; 10¢, 174; 1870 issue, grilled, 10¢, 165; ungrilled, 3¢, 174; 7¢, 174; 10¢, 160; 12¢, 160; 1873 issue, 2¢, 162; 3¢, 162, 180; 6¢, 162, 180
Postal Guide: (1873), 174, 177; (1874), 180, 189
Postal Laws and Regulations: (1857), 93; (1873), 174
Postal markings: accounting markings, 28; "America/uber Bremen," 17, 21, 114, 123; Anglo-Bremen (1841) 6, 8, 9; Anglo-French (1843) 41, 44, 45, 50; (1856) 63, 69, 165; Anglo-Prussian (1846) 9–11; Anglo-Prussian closed mail, 94; Belgian boxed rate marking, 101, 102; Belgian closed mail, 107; Boston "PAID" grid, 79, 82; Bremen-Hamburg mail, 114, 120, 123, 125; Bremen mail (1847) 14, 19, 21; (1853) 112, 113; British open mail to Belgium, 101, 102, 103, 104; British open mail to France: "Colonies/&c ART 13," 41, 44, 45, 50, 65, 96; provisional agreement, 44; decree (1851) 45, 51, 52; three months' period, 63, 65–67, 69, 95, 165; (1870–74) 165, 167. British open mail to Germany and Switzerland, 94–97; British mail to Tunis, 127; British treaty mail (1848) 29, 30, 134, 138, 146, 190, 191; currency, tray or partitioned marks, 63, 95, 165, 177, 193; depreciated currency markings, 187–189, 193; direct service from France, 177; direct service to France, 55, 58, 59, 60, 62, 165, 167. Exchange offices, 29, 76, 77: Baltimore office, 136; Boston office, 138, 176; Bremen City Post Office, 9, 121; Chicago office, 135, 139, 140, 192; Detroit office, 135, 138, 139, 193; Hamburg City Post Office, 112, 121; Liverpool office, 5, 11, 31; London office, 6, 9, 11, 31;

Postal Markings—Continued
  Philadelphia office, 134, 165, 176, 193; Portland office, 135, 138, 193; San Francisco office, 136, 193. French mail: (1857) 71, 76, 79, 82, 84, 108, 132, 138, 139, 189; (1874) 180, 183; by Allan line, 138, 139; American packet through England, 76, 78, 79; British packet, 76, 78; direct service, 76, 79; Exchange offices; 76, 77; to Belgium, 108; to Norway, 82, 83; to Rome, 79, 82; to Sicily, 82; to Switzerland, 79, 138, 139; unpaid letter, 79. Havre maritime office, 59, 62; Imperial German Post Office in Constantinople, 162, 163; New York American packet, 57, 59, 60, 62, 66, 128, 129; New York foreign mail, 180; New York "PAID ALL," 14, 162, 163, 177, 183; New York square grid, 48, 101; New York "supplementary mail," 180, 183; N.Y. Steamship, 189. North German Union mail: 151, 159, 160, 162, 163; to Norway, 160, 162, to Turkey, 162, 163. Ocean line service to France, 57, 58; "phantom rate" to France, 171; prepaid to France, via England, 174; Prussian closed mail, 88, 89, 90, 92, 93, 94, 116, 130, 131, 140, 144, 190. Restatements of rate, 77, 92; U.S.-Denmark, 157; U.S. and Great Britain (1845) 5, 6; U.S.-Sweden and Norway, 158; U.S.-Switzerland, 156; Unpaid letter from France (1870-74), 177, 193

Poste Restante, 78, 113
Post Office announcements, 33, 141, 165
Post Office Department, U.S., 2, 18, 19, 24, 34, 39, 42, 45, 46, 47, 59, 73, 93, 113, 116, 118, 136, 142, 150, 164, 165, 185, 189
Post Office Orders: Belgian, 103; Great Britain, 1, 23, 26, 100, 136; U.S., 29, 35, 45, 46, 186, 189
Pottsville, Pa., 188
Princeton, N.J., 31
Progression of rates, 8, 9, 33, 36, 87, 99, 101-105 *passim*, 144, 146, 170, 173, 190
Providence, R.I., 190
Provisional agreement, Anglo-French, 44, 45, 46, 50, 52, 57, 96
Prussia, 4, 12, 13, 85, 116, 140. *See also* Conventions, postal
Prussian closed mail. *See* Mail services

Quebec, Canada, 132, 134
Queenstown, Ireland, 97, 127, 128, 130, 135, 146, 153, 154, 177

Railroads: Antwerp and Belgium, Netherlands and Germany, 105; Baltimore and Ohio, 136; Hanover and countries beyond, 4, 12; Midland and Great Western, 126; Grand Trunk, 134
Randall, Alexander W., 148
Rates of postage: Bremen closed mail, 19, 42; Bremen-Hamburg mail, 82, 120-123, 125, 131; Bremen mail, 13-16, 19, 110, 111, 112, 113; British closed mail from France, 44, 45, 50; British open mail to Belgium, 100, 101, 103, 104. British open mail to France: American packet, 42, 45, 46, 48, 50, 52; Anglo-French (1843), 40, 41, 48, 50; British packet, 42, 45, 46, 48, 50, 52; French circulaire 44, 57, 67; decree (1851), 45, 52, 56; provisional agreement, 44, 45, 52, 56; "retaliatory" order, 45, 46; sea postage, 45, 46, 47; three months' period, 65, 66, 67, 69, 71, 72, 82, 165; from Germany, 94, 95; to Germany, 94, 96; to Switzerland, 95, 96, 97, 98. British mail: credit for sea postage, 39, 102, 103, 104; via Southampton to Tunis, 127. British transit rate: to Bremen, 19, 42; to France, 43, 44, 47, 48, 56, 58, 62, 65, 66, 70; to Prussia, 85, 86. Colonial rate, 24, 150. Rates by Convention: Anglo-Belgian (1844) 99; (1849) 102; (1857) 103; Anglo-Bremen (1841) 6; Anglo-French (1843) 40, 41 (1855) 62, 63 (1856) 63-65 (1869) 169, 171; Anglo-Prussian (1846) 9 (1852) 86, 93, 94, 95, 96 (1859) 140; German-Austrian (1850) 15, 85, 86; U.S.-Belgian (1859) 105, 106, 107 (1867) 151, 152 (1870) 156 (1873) 156; U.S. Bremen (1847) 13-16, 19 (1853) 110, 112, 120, 125, 129; U.S.-Denmark, 157; U.S.-French (1857) 71-73, 75, 82, 97, 131, 138, 139 (1874) 180, 183; U.S.-Great Britain (1848) 26-28, 33, 38, 133, 138, 144-146, 190 (1867-68) 149, 150, 169, 170 (1859) 153; U.S.-Hamburg (1857) 119, 144; U.S.-Italy (1867) 151 (1870) 156; U.S.-Netherlands (1867) 151 (1870) 157 (1874) 157; U.S.-North German Union (1867) 150, 151, 159 (1870) 154, 156 (1871) 155, 156; U.S.-Prussia (1852) 86-90, 92, 93, 129, 130, 139, 140, 143, 144, 190; U.S.-Sweden and Norway (1873) 158; U.S.-Switzerland (1867) 151 (1870) 156. Delivery fee, 21, 88, 92. Depreciated currency: calculation of rates, 186, 187, 188; highest ratings, 190, 192; unpaid letters from France, 193. Direct service, U.S.-France, 55, 56, 58, 59, 60, 62, 164, 165, 177, 189. Double sea postage, 23-35 *passim*, 28, 29, 31, 39, 45, 50. Fines or postage on unpaid letters, 63, 149, 152-155 *passim*, 157, 188, 193; French inland, 40, 43, 48, 50, 70, 177; French mail: international, 71, 72, 73, 75, 82, 97, 131, 138, 139; to Belguim, 108; to countries beyond France, 75; to Switzerland, 79, 138, 139; to Tunis. General Postal Union, 180; German-Austrian Postal Union, 86, 121; German Post Office in Constantinople, 162; Insufficiently paid letters, 103, 139, 149, 151, 153, 154, 157, 158, 177, 190; Marginal weight letters, 176; North German Union mail: international, 150, 151, 154, 155, 156, 159; to Constantinople, 159, 160, 162, 163; to Norway, 160; to Sweden, 160; open mail to France (1870-74), 164, 165, 167; Partial payments, recognition of, 36, 76, 87, 92, 97, 105, 110, 123, 139, 151, 192; "phantom" rate to France, 167-173; prepaid from France (1870-74), 176, 177; prepaid to France (1870-74), 170, 173, 174; Prussian closed mail: international, 86, 87, 88, 90, 92, 93, 129, 130, 139, 140, 141, 142, 190; to Finland, 139, 140; to Rome, 82, 143; to Switzerland, 131, 144. Private ship: British, 8, 24, 29, 99; French, 56, 57; U.S., 5, 11. Progressions: Belgian, 9, 99, 101-105 *passim*; Bremen-Hamburg, 144; British, 8, 9, 33, 34, 35, 36, 101, 103, 144-146, 190; French, 170-173; Prussian, 9, 87. "restored" rates, 29, 31, 100; "retaliatory" rates, 25, 29, 31, 100, 101; Sole rates, 11, 41, 43, 100; split rates, 38; Triple rate, 36, 144, 146, 190, 192; U.S. (1851), 15, 56; U.S. and Great Britain (1845), 5, 8, 56, 58; U.S. and Prussia (1846), 9; Unpaid letters to France, 165, 177, 193
Ratisbon, Bavaria, 13
Reform, postal, 1, 2
Returned letters, 78, 79
Richmond, Va., 78
Rio de Janeiro, Brazil, 107
Rivalry between Bremen and Hamburg, 116

River du Loup. *See* Riviere du Loup
Riviere du Loup, 97, 135, 136, 139
Rochester, N.Y., 94
Rome, Roman States, 79, 143
Rouen, France, 174
Routes: Anglo-Prussian closed mail, 141; Bremen closed mail, 19, 20, 141; U.S.-Prussian closed mail, 141
Ruger Brothers, 125
Rush, Richard, 42
Russell, Lord John, 26
Russia, 4, 141, 142; Post Office in Turkey, 162
Russian Poland, 141, 142

Sailing packets, 1, 4, 55
Saint Vincent, Cape Verde Islands, 108
Salles, Raymond, 58, 78
Salt water, used in boilers, 17
San Antonio, Texas, 104
San Francisco, 76, 93, 121, 165. *See also* Exchange offices
Sandwich Island, 76
Saxony, 4, 140
Schenectady, N.Y., 21
Schleiden, R., 109
Seward, William H., 147
Sharon Springs, N.Y., 60
Sherman, John, 192
Shipping and Commercial List and New York Prices Current, 18, 54, 125, 128, 132, 138
Ship postage, 5, 6, 8, 9, 11, 23, 56, 57
Simpson, Tracy W., 66, 106
Singapore, British Post Office at, 142
Smith, A. D., 177
Smithsonian collection, 46, 57, 62, 132
Sole rates, 11, 41, 43, 100
Southampton, England, 4, 17, 18, 23, 38, 39, 55, 56, 78, 102, 116, 117, 119, 120, 125, 131, 153. *See also* Exchange offices
Southern Germany, 94
Specie payments suspended, 184
State Department, 25, 39, 164
Staunton, Va., 123
Steamship companies. *See* Steamship lines.
Steamship contracts: compensation of lines, 115, 120; conditions for making, 3. Contracts between: Collins line and U.S., 114, 118; Cunard line and U.S., 132; Galway line and Great Britain, 126, 127; Guion line and U.S., 153; Hamburg-American line and U.S., 120, 153; Havre line and U.S., 114, 115, 118; Inman line and U.S., 154; Mills, Edward, and U.S., 4; New York and Bremen Steamship Company and U.S., 125; North American Lloyd and U.S., 125; North German Lloyd and U.S., 120, 153; Ocean line and U.S., 114; Vanderbilt, Cornelius, and U.S., 115, 118. Fines for non-performance, 18, 117, 119; tenders under Act of 1845, 4. *See also* Steamship subsidies
Steamship lines: Allan line *also* Canadian line (Montreal Ocean Steam Ship Company), 97, 132, 134–138 *passim,* 153; Baltic Lloyd (Baltischer Lloyd), 155, 156, 158, 159; Baltimore and Liverpool Steamship Company, 136; City of Dublin Steam Packet Company, 135; Collins line, 19, 20, 28, 55, 66, 85, 95, 113, 116, 118, 128, 133; Compagnie Transatlantique Belge, 105; Cunard line, 1, 4, 5, 6, 11, 15, 19, 20, 23, 30, 39, 66, 68, 85, 90, 100, 118, 128, 132, 133, 135, 138, 153, 180; European and American Steam Shipping Company, 116; European and Australian line, 132; French line *also* Ligne H (Compagnie Général Transatlantique), 77, 78, 165, 179; Fritze, W. A. and Company, 109, 111, 112, 113, 120, 126; Galway line (Atlantic Steam Navigation Company), 112, 125, 126, 127, 132; Glasgow & New York Steam Ship Co., 118; Guion line (Liverpool and Great Western Steamship Company), 153, 165, 170, 180; Hamburg-American line *also* Hapag (Hamburg Amerikanische Paketfahrt Aktien Gesellschaft), 116, 119, 120, 123, 131, 153, 154, 156, 165; Herout et de Handel (Transatlantic General Steam Packet Company), 54, 55; Holland-American line (Netherlands-American Steam Navigation Company), 157; Inman line *also* Dales line, 78, 82, 118, 132, 133, 135, 152, 153, 154; Messageries Impérials, 108; "Miscellaneous" line, 118, 132; New York and Bremen Steamship Company, 125; New York-Havre line *also* Havre line (New York and Havre Steam Navigation Company), 4, 19, 20, 55, 58, 59, 77, 85, 102, 114, 115, 129, 137; Norse American line, 158, 159; North American Lloyd, 125, 152; North Atlantic Steamship Company, 77, 131, 132; North German Lloyd, 78, 119, 120, 123, 130, 153–156 *passim;* Ocean line *also* Bremen line (Ocean Steam Navigation Company), 3–5 *passim,* 15, 18, 19, 20, 30, 39, 55–58 *passim,* 99, 100, 109, 112, 125, 129, 130, 137; Pacific Mail Steamship Company, 114; Red Star line, 157; U.S. Mail Steamship Company, 114; Vanderbilt European line, 77, 115, 116, 117, 125, 131; White Cross line, 156, 158. Lack of regularity, 118; refused to carry U.S. mail, 153; winter voyages avoided, 18, 19, 55, 112, 118
Steamships: *Acadia,* 5, 6, 30; *Adriatic* (Collins line), 127; *Adriatic* (North Atlantic SS Company), 131; *Adriatic* (Galway line), 127, 131; *Africa,* 46, 50, 66, 68, 82, 90, 128, 132; *Allegany,* 136; *America* (Cunard line), 11, 30, 31, 48, 50, 68; *America* (North German Lloyd), 189; *Anglia,* 127; *Arabia,* 46, 68, 78, 90, 92; *Arago,* 60, 77, 102; *Arctic,* 20, 48, 65, 128; *Argo,* 116; *Ariel,* 116, 117, 121; *Asia,* 46, 52, 68, 90, 95, 128; *Atlantic* (Collins line), 52, 65, 66, 67, 89, 94, 127, 128, 133; *Atlantic* (North American SS Company), 131, 132; *Atlantic* (North American Lloyd), 125; *Australasian,* 132, 190; *Baltic* (Collins line), 65, 66, 96, 118, 128, 133; *Baltic* (North American Lloyd), 125; *Bavaria,* 120; *Belgique,* 105; *Bohemian,* 139; *Borussia,* 117, 119, 120; *Bremen,* 78, 120, 121, 123, 130; *Britannia,* 1, 9, 15, 25, 30, 31; *Caledonia,* 11, 25, 30, 48; *Cambria,* 30; *Canada,* 21, 30, 31, 46, 50, 68, 128; *Carroll,* 136; *Cimbria,* 165; *City of Baltimore,* 107, 118; *City of Cork,* 152; *City of London,* 146, 190; *City of Paris,* 146; *City of New York,* 97; *City of Washington,* 78, 79, 118, 133, 134, 144; *Columbia* (Collins line), 133; *Columbia* (Galway line), 127; *Connaught,* 126; *Constitution,* 105; *Cuba,* 177; *Edinburgh* (Glasgow & New York Steam Ship Company), 118; *Edinburgh* (Inman line), 132; *Edinburgh* (North American Lloyd), 125; *Ericsson* (Collins line), 65, 66, 93, 95, 133; *Ernst Moritz Arndt,* 156n; *Etna,* 132, 189, 190; *Europa,* 30, 31, 46, 67, 68, 106, 143, 189; *Franklin* (Baltic Lloyd),

Steamships—Continued
156; *Franklin* (Havre line), 55, 58, 60, 62; *Fulton,* 62, 77, 82, 104, 108; *Glasgow,* 82, 105; *Germania,* 109, 110, 111, 112, 113, 120; *Great Britain,* 5; *Great Western,* 5; *Guiding Star,* 77; *Hammonia,* 116, 119, 189; *Hansa* (Fritze Co.) 109–112 *passim,* 120; *Hansa* (North German Lloyd), 78, 193; *Hermann,* 5, 15, 17, 18, 30, 31, 58, 109, 111, 112, 129; *Hibernia,* (Cunard line), 5, 30, 55, 100, 127; *Hibernia* (Galway line), 127; *Hudson,* 120, 130; *Humboldt* (Baltic Lloyd), 156; *Humboldt* (Havre line), 55, 59, 60; *Hungarian,* 132; *Illinois,* 117, 131; *Indian,* 132; *Indiana,* 116; *Indian Empire,* 112, 126; *Jason,* 116; *Kangaroo,* 116, 117, 118; *Klopstock,* 183; *Lebanon,* 132; *Leopold I,* 105; *Massachusetts,* 5; *Melita,* 132; *Mirrimack,* 125; *Mississippi* (Havre line), 77; *Mississippi* (North American Lloyd), 125; *Missouri,* 54, 55; *Navarre,* 108; *Nevada,* 165; *New York* (Glasgow & New York SS Co.), 118, *New York* (Herout et de Handel), 54; *New York* (North German Lloyd), 120, 130, 131; *Niagara,* 30, 31, 46, 68, 69, 101, 128; *North Briton,* 138; *Northern Light,* 117; *North Star,* 115, 116, 121; *Norwegian,* 138; *Ocean Queen,* 117; *Olympus,* 132; *Pacific,* 60, 65, 128; *Pereire,* 183; *Persia,* 67, 68, 79, 189; *Philadelphie,* 54, 55; *President,* 128; *Prince Albert,* 126; *Queen of the South,* 116; *Sarah Sands,* 5; *Samaria,* 177; *Saxonia,* 117; *Shawmut, U.S.S.,* 107; *Somerset,* 136; *Teutonia,* 121; *Thorwaldson,* 156n, *Union* (Herout et de Handel), 54; *Union* (North German Lloyd), 155; *Vaderland,* 157; *Vanderbilt,* 79, 116, 117, 118, 119, 131; *Vesuvius, H.B.M.S.,* 132; *Vigo,* 118; *Ville de Paris,* 167; *Washington* (Baltic Lloyd), 156n; *Washington* (Ocean line), 5, 12, 15, 17, 18, 21, 23, 25, 30, 58, 66, 109, 111, 112, 123, 129; *Weser,* 120, 130; *Western Metropolis,* 125; *Westphalia,* 159; *Worcester,* 136

Steamship sailings: American packet, via England (1 Jan.–1 April 1857), 66; Collins line, 1851, 128; Cunard line "retaliatory" to France, 46; Cunard line, Dec. 1856-Apr. 1857, 68; Cunard and Ocean lines—triple rate, 36; Cunard and Ocean lines—restored rates, 31; Cunard and Ocean lines—retaliatory rates, 30; W. A. Fritze and Company, 112; Galway line, mail sailing of, 127; Havre line to July 1851, 59; Herout et de Handel, 54, 55; irregularities in, 18, 19, 116, 117, 127, 129, 130; Miscellaneous line, 118; North American Lloyd, 125; North Atlantic Steamship Company, 132; North German Lloyd, 1860, 130

Steamship subsidies: Abandoned, 115; Allan line, 134; American mail packets, 2–5 *passim;* Collins line, 112, 113, 114; Cunard line, 1, 113, 149; Herout et de Handel, 54; lines to California, 114; method of paying, 18, 55; New York-Havre line, 55, 78; no longer necessary, 114; Ocean line, 4, 109

Steerage passengers, 116
Stettin, Prussia, 155
Stibbe, Dr. Jacques, 99n
Stonington, Mass., 18
Subsidiary coins, 185–187 *passim*
Supplementary mail, New York, 180
Sweden, 4, 141, 142, 143, 160
Switzerland, 4, 94, 97, 131, 138

Sydney, British Post Office at, 142
Syke, Prussia, 121

Taunton, Mass., 129
Thayer, M., 43, 44, 52
Thuringian states, 4, 125
Thurn and Taxis posts, 12, 13, 110, 123, 141, 150
Tilley, John, 169
Toombs, Robert A., 114, 115
Toppan, Carpenter, Casilear and Company, 46
Toppan-Carpenter correspondence, 46, 60
Toppan, Charles, 46
Treasury Warrants (British), 29, 100, 144
Treaties, postal. *See* Conventions, postal
Trieste, Austria, 142
Triple rate, 36, 144, 146, 190, 192
Trollope, Anthony, 149, 169
Tunis, Africa, 127
Turkish towns and territory, 141, 142, 143
Tyler, John, 3

Underwood, Senator, 51
U.S. Mail and Post Office Assistant, 73, 88, 125, 136, 140, 142, 144, 151, 152, 154, 156, 158, 159, 164, 167, 170, 173, 174, 180
U.S. Official Postal Guide (1874), 189
U.S. postal agency at Bremen, 12, 13, 14, 119
Unpaid letters, fines or postage on, 63, 149, 152–155 *passim,* 157, 158, 188, 193

Vancouver Island, 76
Vanderbilt, Cornelius, 114, 115, 116, 117
Van Vlissingen yards, 105
Verviers, Belgium, 141
Vessels of war, mail packets as, 3, 4
Victoria Bridge, Montreal, 134
Virginia City, Nevada Territory, 143
Von Falke, Privy Councilor, 12
Von Gerolt, Freiherr, 4

Warsaw, Ill., 90
Washington, D.C., 1, 36, 159, 190
Washington territory, 76, 137
Webster, Daniel, 1, 56, 85
Weimar, Thuringia, 91
Wellington, British Post Office at, 142
Weser river, 12, 13
West, Captain James, 128
Westervelt and McKay, 5, 55
Wiborg, Finland, 139
Wickliffe agreement, 24, 25
Wickliffe, Charles A., 3
Wilmington, Del., 5
Winter voyages, 18, 19, 20, 55, 112, 118
Wisconsin, 137, 139
Wood, Sir Charles, 24, 26, 27, 28, 38, 41, 43
Wurttemberg, 110, 140